HIGH COURT CASE SUMMARIES

CRIMINAL PROCEDURE

Keyed to Kamisar, LaFave, Israel, and King's Casebook on Criminal Procedure, 11th Edition

THOMSON
WEST™

Mat #40424078

610 Opperman Drive
P.O. Box 64526
St. Paul, MN 55164–0526
1–800–328–9352

Printed in the United States of America

ISBN 0–314-16625–4

TEXT IS PRINTED ON 10% POST
CONSUMER RECYCLED PAPER

Table of Contents

*

Alphabetical Table of Cases

CHAPTER FOUR

The Right to Counsel, "By Far the Most Pervasive" Right of the Accused; Equality and the Adversary System

Betts v. Brady

Instant Facts: A robber challenged a state procedure, which only appointed counsel for capital crimes, as denying due process.

Black Letter Rule: Federal courts must appoint counsel for all federal crimes, but state courts need not appoint attorneys for all indigent criminal defendants.

Gideon v. Wainwright

Instant Facts: Indigent represented himself in a burglary trial, after requesting assistance of counsel, and was convicted.

Black Letter Rule: The Sixth Amendment's right to counsel, through the Fourteenth Amendment, requires states to appoint counsel for indigents in felony cases.

Ross v. Moffitt

Instant Facts: An indigent convicted forger challenged a state policy of not providing appointed counsel for discretionary appeals to the state supreme court or certiorari petitions to the federal Supreme Court.

Black Letter Rule: States need not appoint counsel for indigent convicts' discretionary appeals.

Betts v. Brady

(*Criminal Defendant*) v. (*State Official*)

316 U.S. 455, 62 S.Ct. 1252, 86 L.Ed. 1595 (1942)

PREVIOUSLY, COURTS DID NOT HAVE TO APPOINT COUNSEL FOR ALL CRIMINAL DEFENDANTS

■ **INSTANT FACTS** A robber challenged a state procedure, which only appointed counsel for capital crimes, as denying due process.

■ **BLACK LETTER RULE** Federal courts must appoint counsel for all federal crimes, but state courts need not appoint attorneys for all indigent criminal defendants.

■ PROCEDURAL BASIS

In criminal prosecution for robbery, appeal from conviction.

■ FACTS

Betts (D), an indigent, was indicted for robbery in Maryland. Under Maryland law, counsel is appointed only for rape and murder charges [presumably because both were capital crimes in 1942]. Betts' (D) request for counsel was denied, so he represented himself. He pled not guilty, elected trial without jury, and called witnesses who testified he was elsewhere at the time. However, Betts (D) was convicted and sentenced to 8 years' imprisonment. Betts (D) appeals, contending Maryland's refusal to appoint counsel was a denial of *Fourteenth Amendment* due process.

■ ISSUE

Must state courts appoint counsel for all indigent criminal defendants?

■ DECISION AND RATIONALE

(Roberts) No. Federal courts must appoint counsel for all federal crimes, but state courts need not appoint attorneys for all indigent criminal defendants. The *Fourteenth Amendment* due process clause does not specifically incorporate the *Sixth Amendment*'s right to counsel, so due process is a less rigid concept than that required by the *Sixth Amendment*, though denial of any provision of the Bill of Rights may, in some circumstances, be deemed to violate *Fourteenth Amendment* due process. Asserted denials of due process are tested by considering the totality of facts in each case. Previously, we held that indigent criminal defendants must be appointed attorneys if the state's law requires such appointment. *Powell v. Alabama* [redneck state cannot deny black capital defendants a lawyer in blatant violation of its own law]. Moreover, we construed the *Sixth Amendment* to require appointment of counsel in all *federal* cases where the defendant is unable to procure an attorney, and has not waived that right intentionally and competently. *Johnson v. Zerbst.* This holding does not necessarily suggest that *states* must also appoint attorneys under similar circumstances to avoid violating *Fourteenth Amendment* due process, and we are unwilling to imply such obligations on the states. In most states, it was the citizens' considered judgement that appointed counsel is not a fundamental right essential to a fair trial, and we are reluctant to disturb this policy decision. State courts' practice should not be straight-jacketed by such a construction of the *Fourteenth Amendment*, which makes no distinction between criminal charges of differing magnitude or courts of varying jurisdiction. Here, we find Maryland's expedited trial procedure was reasonable, and find Betts (D) was competent to defend himself, since he previously served time for larceny. [By that reasoning, if you're hit by a car, you're presumed an automotive engineer.] Affirmed.

■ DISSENT

(Black) Here, Betts (D) should have been assigned counsel, since he was uneducated and incompetent to represent himself. Had this been a federal court, counsel would be required. I believe the right to counsel is "fundamental," because defendants should not be subjected to increased danger of conviction merely because they are too poor to afford counsel.

Analysis:

This case is no longer good law, and is presented for its historic value. It was decided on the then-popular doctrine that the Bill of Rights is not directly binding on states, and that states had great discretion in providing procedures which met "due process" standards. This case, and Maryland's procedure, suggests that counsel was deemed necessary at least in capital cases, and possibly other (unspecified) serious offenses. This suggestion was later affirmed expressly by the Supreme Court. Modern case law holds that all courts, state and federal, must appoint counsel for indigent defendants charged with felonies and misdemeanors punishable by over 6 months' imprisonment.

■ CASE VOCABULARY

DUE PROCESS: Under the Constitution's *Fourteenth Amendment*, the government may not "deprive any person of life, liberty, or property, without *due process of law.*" A due process claim contends that a convict's arrest or trial was procedurally flawed, usually because it violated other provisions in the Bill of Rights.

INDICTED: Charged with a crime.

INDIGENT: Poor. Here, "indigent" means too poor to hire an attorney.

Gideon v. Wainwright

(*Burglar*) v. (*State*)
372 U.S. 335, 83 S.Ct. 792 (1963)

SIXTH AMENDMENT RIGHT TO COUNSEL REQUIRES STATES TO APPOINT COUNSEL FOR INDIGENTS IN FELONY CASES

■ **INSTANT FACTS** Indigent represented himself in a burglary trial, after requesting assistance of counsel, and was convicted.

■ **BLACK LETTER RULE** The Sixth Amendment's right to counsel, through the Fourteenth Amendment, requires states to appoint counsel for indigents in felony cases.

■ PROCEDURAL BASIS

Certification to the U.S. Supreme Court after habeas corpus proceeding to Florida Supreme Court.

■ FACTS

Gideon (D) was charged with breaking and entering a poolroom with the intent to commit a misdemeanor. In Florida, this was a felony. He could not afford a lawyer so he asked the court to appoint one for him. The court denied this request. Gideon (D) represented himself at his trial and was convicted.

■ ISSUE

Does the Sixth Amendment's right to counsel require the States to appoint counsel to indigents in felony cases?

■ DECISION AND RATIONALE

(Black, J.) Yes. The right to counsel is a fundamental right. It is obvious that any person hauled into court who is too poor to hire a lawyer cannot be assured a fair trial unless counsel is provided for him. In criminal cases, lawyers are necessities, not luxuries. Thus, we overrule *Betts v. Brady* [right to counsel based on case-by-case Analysis:]. Judgment reversed and remanded.

■ CONCURRENCE

(Clark) The right to counsel should attach in both capital and non-capital criminal prosecutions, since the *Fourteenth Amendment* requires due process for the deprival of "liberty" just as for deprival of "life."

■ CONCURRENCE

(Harlan) I agree *Betts* should be overruled, but consider it entitled to a more respectful burial, since it required counsel in many circumstances.

Analysis:

On retrial with appointed counsel, Gideon (D) was acquitted. His case became something of a cause celebre, spawning the book and movie *Gideon's Trumpet.* *Gideon* obviously overrules the ill-conceived

Betts *and follows* Powell, *extending its obligation to provide counsel to non-capital crimes as well.* Gideon *suggests that states must appoint counsel for indigent defendants in* all *criminal prosecutions, which is the law today. However, practitioners often contend that, while* Gideon *guarantees the right to counsel in the abstract, it does not guarantee an adequate level of legal representation, and that in practice public defenders can devote only minimal time and expense for individual defendants' cases.*

Ross v. Moffitt

(Convicted Forgers) v. *(North Carolina State Official)*
417 U.S. 600, 94 S.Ct. 2437, 41 L.Ed.2d 341 (1974)

STATES NEED NOT APPOINT COUNSEL FOR DISCRETIONARY APPEALS

■ **INSTANT FACTS** An indigent convicted forger challenged a state policy of not providing appointed counsel for discretionary appeals to the state supreme court or certiorari petitions to the federal Supreme Court.

■ **BLACK LETTER RULE** States need not appoint counsel for indigent convicts' discretionary appeals.

■ PROCEDURAL BASIS

In criminal prosecution for forgery, consolidated appeal from habeas grant of appointed counsel, on writ of certiorari.

■ FACTS

Two forgers, including Ross (P), were convicted of forgery in North Carolina (D) and wished to make discretionary appeals, either to the federal Supreme Court (on writ of certiorari) or North Carolina's (D) supreme court (on discretionary review). Under North Carolina (D) law, counsel is to be appointed for appeals (as of right) to the state intermediate court of appeals, but not (discretionary) appeals to the Supreme Court or state supreme court. Ross (P) appealed on a federal writ of habeas corpus, contending the denial of counsel violated constitutional due process and equal protection. On appeal, the Fourth Circuit held both discretionary state court review and federal Supreme Court certiorari required appointed counsel, under *Douglas.* North Carolina (D) appeals.

■ ISSUE

Must states appoint counsel when indigent convicts wish to make a discretionary appeal to the state supreme court or petition the federal Supreme Court for certiorari?

■ DECISION AND RATIONALE

(Rehnquist) No. States need not appoint counsel for indigent convicts' discretionary appeals. *Griffin* stands for the proposition that States cannot arbitrarily curtail indigents' appeal rights while leaving open avenues of appeal for affluent persons. *Douglas* went further, holding States must not only waive transcripts and appeals fees for indigents, but also provide counsel on their first appeal as of right. These cases' exact rationale was never explicitly stated, but is derived partly from the *Fourteenth Amendment*'s *Equal Protection Clause* and partly from its *Due Process Clause.* "Due process" emphasizes fairness between the State and individuals dealing with it, regardless of how other individuals in the same situation are treated. "Equal protection" emphasizes States' disparate treatment of classes of individuals whose situations are arguably indistinguishable. We believe the *Due Process Clause* does not require North Carolina (D) to provide counsel for discretionary appeals to the State Supreme Court. Unlike the criminal prosecution, the criminal appeal is initiated by the defendant, and the constitution does not require States to allow any appeal at all. The fact that a State allows appeals does not obligate it to provide counsel to indigents at every stage; unfairness results only if indigents are singled out by the State and denied meaningful appeals because of their poverty. Under the *Equal Protection Clause*, indigents must have adequate opportunity to present their claims fairly in an adversarial system, and States cannot adopt procedures which leave indigents cut off from any meaningful appeal. But the *Fourteenth Amendment* does not require states to equalize economic conditions absolutely. Here, we believe the *Equal Protection Clause* does not require North Carolina (D) to provide free counsel for discretionary appeals. In this case, we find Ross (D) already received the benefit of counsel for appeal purposes, since his appointed trial lawyer examined his trial record and prepared an appellate brief, and he likely has a transcript and opinion, which together with Ross' (D) *pro se* submissions provide the North Carolina Supreme Court with adequate basis to decide whether to grant review. This is especially true because the North Carolina Supreme Court grants certiorari based not on each case's merits, but on whether the appeal's subject has sufficient public interest. Counsel is not constitutionally required even if it would help defendants on appeal. There is a significant difference between the source of the right to seek discretionary review in the state supreme court and the right to seek certiorari in the federal Supreme Court; the former is conferred by state statute, while the latter is granted by Congressional statute, independent of the State's consent. The suggestion that States are responsible for providing counsel for petitioning the federal Supreme Court because it initiated the prosecution is unsupported by reason or authority. This Court has consistently denied appointed counsel to petitioners seeking to file jurisdictional statements or certiorari petitions. We do not mean this opinion to discourage States which made the legislative choice to provide counsel; we only hold that the *Fourteenth Amendment* leaves this choice to the State. Reversed.

■ DISSENT

(Douglas) The court below found no distinction between the need for counsel on appeals to the state supreme court or appellate court, and we defer to its judgement. Also, unrepresented indigent defendants are at a substantial disadvantage compared to represented ones in seeking discretionary review, which may require sophisticated arguments beyond alleging error. Further, certiorari petitions are highly technical, and require a lawyer to prepare correctly. Counsel should be appointed to provide a fair opportunity on both types of appeals.

Analysis:

Where *Douglas* explicitly reserved the question of whether states allowing discretionary appeal must appoint counsel for indigent appellants, *Ross* resolves the question with a resounding "no." The reasoning is that states are not obligated to provide an appeal and thus are not obligated to provide appellate counsel, and that states are not responsible for petitions to the federal Supreme Court. Accordingly, most state statutes provide counsel on the first appeal as of right, but not for later discretionary appeals, to limit the public's cost of legal representation. From a policy standpoint, the practice of denying appointed counsel on secondary appeal is much less troubling than such denial on the first appeal, since discretionary appeal only happens after the defendant has had 2 chances to prove his innocence at trial, and continued appeals are increasingly likely to be unfounded and wasteful.

■ CASE VOCABULARY

CERTIORARI: "Be informed." Discretionary permission by a state supreme court, or the federal Supreme Court, to hear an appeal for a certain case. In both federal and state courts, certiorari is discretionary rather than of right.

DISCRETIONARY APPEAL: An appeal which the appellate court may choose not to grant. The opposite of an appeal "as of right." Typically, states allow convicts one appeal as of right (with appointed counsel); any further appeals are discretionary (and without appointed counsel).

HABEAS CORPUS [WRIT]: "You must have the body." Petition allowing *state* convicts to challenge their imprisonment in *federal* court as unlawful, usually on constitutional grounds.

PRO SE: "For oneself." Lawsuit or legal paper prepared by a party representing himself, without a lawyer.

CHAPTER FIVE

The Role of Counsel

Faretta v. California

Instant Facts: After first accepting a criminal defendant's waiver of the assistance of counsel, a state judge reversed his ruling, appointed the public defender to the case, and ordered that the defense be conducted only through the public defender's office.

Black Letter Rule: The Sixth Amendment guarantees that a defendant in a state criminal trial has an independent constitutional right of self-representation and that he may proceed to defend himself without counsel when he voluntarily and intelligently elects to do so.

Iowa v. Tovar

Instant Facts: Tovar (D) was convicted of felony driving under the influence of alcohol after pleading guilty on a first offense without the assistance of counsel.

Black Letter Rule: The Sixth Amendment is satisfied when the trial court informs the accused of the nature of the charges against him, his right to be counseled regarding his plea, and the range of allowable punishments attendant upon the entry of a guilty plea.

Caplin Drysdale, Chartered v. United States

Instant Facts: Pursuant to a statute authorizing forfeiture of assets, the federal government froze the defendant's assets and rendered him unable to pay for the attorney he had retained to defend him in the criminal proceedings.

Black Letter Rule: The forfeiture statute does not impermissibly burden a defendant's Sixth Amendment right to retain counsel of his choice.

Strickland v. Washington

Instant Facts: Washington (D) was sentenced to death after pleading guilty to capital offenses, and thereafter sought reversal of his conviction based upon ineffectiveness of counsel.

Black Letter Rule: In order to reverse a conviction based upon ineffectiveness of counsel, the defendant must show that (1) counsel's performance was deficient, requiring a showing that counsel made errors so serious that counsel was not functioning as the "counsel" guaranteed defendant by the Sixth Amendment, and (2) the deficient performance prejudiced the defense, by showing that counsel's errors were so serious as to deprive defendant of a fair trial, a trial whose result is reliable.

Mickens v. Taylor

Instant Facts: Mickens (P) alleged ineffective assistance of counsel because his attorney briefly represented the victim of Mickens' (P) crime.

Black Letter Rule: When counsel represents successive defendants with a potential conflict of interest, a defendant must demonstrate that a conflict existed that affected the outcome of his case.

Wheat v. United States

Instant Facts: Wheat's (D) motion to substitute in the counsel of his choice was denied, in spite of waiver, because of potential for conflict of interest.

Black Letter Rule: The court is allowed substantial latitude in refusing waivers of conflicts of interest with respect to a criminal defendant's chosen counsel both in cases where there is an actual conflict and in those where a serious potential for conflict exists.

Faretta v. California

(*Convicted Thief*) v. (*State*)

422 U.S. 806, 95 S.Ct. 2525 (1975)

THE SIXTH AMENDMENT GRANTS CRIMINAL TRIAL DEFENDANTS A CONSTITUTIONAL RIGHT TO REPRESENT THEMSELVES

■ **INSTANT FACTS** After first accepting a criminal defendant's waiver of the assistance of counsel, a state judge reversed his ruling, appointed the public defender to the case, and ordered that the defense be conducted only through the public defender's office.

■ **BLACK LETTER RULE** The Sixth Amendment guarantees that a defendant in a state criminal trial has an independent constitutional right of self-representation and that he may proceed to defend himself without counsel when he voluntarily and intelligently elects to do so.

■ PROCEDURAL BASIS

Appeal to the United State Supreme Court, challenging the California Court of Appeal's decision to affirm the defendant's conviction.

■ FACTS

Anthony Faretta (D) was charged with grand theft auto. After the trial judge appointed the public defender to represent Faretta (D), but well before trial, Faretta (D) requested permission to represent himself. The trial judge's questioning revealed that Faretta (D) feared the public defender's office was too busy. The judge warned Faretta (D) that he was making a mistake, but nevertheless, accepted his waiver of the assistance of counsel. Prior to trial, the judge *sua sponte* held a hearing where he questioned Faretta (D) on several points of law. Unsatisfied with Faretta's (D) responses, the judge reversed his ruling and again appointed the public defender's office to the case. The judge held that Faretta (D) had no constitutional right to conduct his own defense, and ordered that the entire defense be conducted through the public defender's office.

■ ISSUE

Does a defendant in a state criminal trial have a constitutional right to proceed without counsel when he voluntarily and intelligently elects to do so?

■ DECISION AND RATIONALE

(Stewart, J.) Yes. There is a universal conviction, on the part of our people and our courts, that forcing a lawyer upon an unwilling defendant contravenes the basic right to represent oneself. The right of self-representation finds support in the structure of the Sixth Amendment and in the English and colonial jurisprudence from which the Amendment emerged. The Sixth Amendment rights are granted to the *accused* himself. This structure implies a guaranteed right to self-representation. This right is given to the accused because he is the one who suffers the consequences of a failed defense. The language and the spirit of the Sixth Amendment contemplate that counsel is to aid a willing defendant, not an organ of the State imposed upon him. Although the value of state-appointed counsel was not unappreciated by the Founders, the notion of compulsory counsel was utterly foreign to them.

Personal liberties are just that, personal. The fact that the assistance of counsel will, more often that not, be advantageous to a defendant does not matter. Forcing a lawyer upon a defendant leads him to believe the law contrives against him. Because the assistance of counsel carries with it many advantages, an accused who wishes to represent himself must "knowingly and intelligently" forego those benefits. The accused need not possess the skills of an attorney, but should be made aware of the dangers and disadvantages of self-representation. Here, Faretta (D) clearly and unequivocally declared his desire to proceed *pro se.* Faretta (D) was literate, competent, understanding, and voluntarily exercised his free will. Furthermore, the judge warned Faretta (D) of the mistake he was making. Faretta's (D) lack of legal knowledge was not relevant to an assessment of his knowing exercise of the right to defend himself. In forcing Faretta (D) to accept a state-appointed public defender, the California courts deprived him of his constitutional right to represent himself. Vacated and remanded.

■ DISSENT

(Burger, C.J.) There is simply no constitutional basis for the Court's holding. The Court's assertion that the right to self-representation is "implied" in by the Sixth Amendment is contradicted by the Amendment's language and its interpretation. The fact that the Sixth Amendment grants rights to the accused himself does not lead to the conclusion that the right to counsel may be dispensed with at the whim of the accused. A widespread exercise of this right will congest courts and diminish the quality of justice.

■ DISSENT

(Blackmun) I cannot agree that the Constitution requires the States to subordinate the solemn business of conducting a criminal prosecution to the whimsical—albeit voluntary—caprice of every accused who wishes to use his trial as a vehicle for personal or political self-gratification. In addition, there are numerous procedural problems that, I suspect, will occur in the future because of this decision. These procedural problems will far outweigh whatever tactical advantage the defendant may feel he has gained by electing to represent himself. If there is any truth to the old proverb that "one who is his own lawyer has a fool for a client," the Court by its opinion today now bestows a *constitutional* right on one to make a fool of himself.

Analysis:

This case provides a perfect example of non-textual constitutional interpretation. The Court determines that the Sixth Amendment grants a defendant the right to represent himself at trial. The Court bases its holding on the "structure" of the Sixth Amendment rather than its explicit language. The opinion notes that the Sixth Amendment grants the right to the "accused." The implication being that the accused can exercise these rights himself as he deems necessary to aid in his defense. However, the Court's decision lies more in notions of free choice. The Court notes that the Framer's were unaware of compulsory representation, and that their main concern in drafting the Constitution was the free will of individuals. In the Court's opinion, the free choice of men, however foolish, should be respected. After establishing the right to self-representation, the Court determines whether it was deprived in this case. The Court holds that a decision to proceed *pro se* must be "knowing and intelligent." By this the Court meant that the defendant must be warned of the pitfalls of such a decision, but he need not have the skills of a lawyer. Since the trial court had warned Faretta (D) of the mistake he was making, and because Faretta was literate and competent, the court's failure to allow him to proceed without counsel amounted to a denial of his Sixth Amendment right. The Court reverses the conviction, but leaves open the question of whether reversal is always required for a violation of this right. The Court subsequently answers this question in the affirmative.

■ CASE VOCABULARY

PRO SE: On one's own behalf; without counsel.

SUA SPONTE: On the court's own initiative.

Iowa v. Tovar

(*Prosecuting Authority*) v. (*Drunk Driver*)
541 U.S. 77, 124 S.Ct. 1379, 158 L.Ed.2d 209 (2004)

THE COURT NEED NOT TELL THE DEFENDANT EVERYTHING BEFORE ACCEPTING A GUILTY PLEA

■ **INSTANT FACTS** Tovar (D) was convicted of felony driving under the influence of alcohol after pleading guilty on a first offense without the assistance of counsel.

■ **BLACK LETTER RULE** The Sixth Amendment is satisfied when the trial court informs the accused of the nature of the charges against him, his right to be counseled regarding his plea, and the range of allowable punishments attendant upon the entry of a guilty plea.

■ PROCEDURAL BASIS

Certiorari to review a decision of the Iowa Supreme Court reversing the defendant's conviction.

■ FACTS

Tovar (D) was arrested for driving under the influence of alcohol. During his initial court appearance, Tovar (D) waived his right to counsel while receiving a copy of the complaint and being informed of the charges against him. At his arraignment, the court explained Tovar's (D) right to a fair trial with the assistance of counsel and advised him of the possible punishment a guilty plea carried. Tovar (D) waived his right to a trial and pleaded guilty. At sentencing, which coincided with his arraignment on a subsequent charge of driving with a suspended license, the court again accepted Tovar's (D) guilty plea after advising him of his rights and the consequences of a guilty plea. Tovar (D) again pleaded guilty and was sentenced to a small jail term and a fine.

Two years later, Tovar (D) was again charged with driving under the influence of alcohol. With the representation of counsel, Tovar (D) pleaded guilty. And then two years later again, Tovar (D) was charged with his third driving under the influence of alcohol offense, a felony under state law. Through counsel, Tovar (D) filed a motion to exclude the use of his first conviction because, he argued, the court's failure to explain the possible future consequences of his plea rendered his waiver of counsel involuntary. The motion was denied and Tovar (D) was convicted. After the Iowa Court of Appeals affirmed, the Iowa Supreme Court reversed the conviction, holding that a trial court must advise a pro se defendant of the dangers of self-representation to enable him to make a knowing and intelligent waiver of his right to counsel.

■ ISSUE

Before accepting a guilty plea, must a trial court advise the defendant that waiving the assistance of counsel entails the risk that a viable defense will be overlooked and admonish the defendant that waiver of the right to counsel will result in a lost opportunity for advice on the wisdom of his plea?

■ DECISION AND RATIONALE

(Ginsburg, J.) No. While the Sixth Amendment requires that all defendants be afforded the right of counsel, a defendant may forego that right through a knowing, voluntary, and intelligent waiver of counsel. Before a pro se defendant may be permitted to waive the right to counsel, he must be specifically advised of the danger of self-representation. At a criminal trial, the type of warning required by the Sixth Amendment is rigorous because of the importance of the defendant's liberty interests and constitutional rights. At earlier stages, however, the dangers are "less substantial and more obvious to an accused than they are at trial."

Here, Tovar (D) has not demonstrated that additional warnings would have led him to consult with counsel before entering his plea. Based on the trial court's warnings, Tovar (D) fully understood the nature of the charges against him, his potential punishment, and what further assistance counsel would have provided to cause him to plead not guilty. Accordingly, there is nothing to suggest that Tovar's (D) waiver of counsel was not knowing, intelligent, and voluntary. This Sixth Amendment requires no more. Reversed.

Analysis:

The Court's suggestion that a defendant's Sixth Amendment rights are less significant at the plea stage than at trial is curious. When a waiver of counsel at the plea stage accompanies a guilty plea, the defendant's right to a trial is likewise waived. Thus, a waiver of counsel at the plea stage affects the very Sixth Amendment rights at trial the Court deems substantial and important.

■ CASE VOCABULARY

PRO SE: One who represents oneself in a court proceeding without the assistance of a lawyer.

RIGHT TO COUNSEL: A criminal defendant's constitutional rights, guaranteed by the Sixth Amendment, to representation by a court-appointed lawyer if the defendant cannot afford to hire one.

SIXTH AMENDMENT: The constitutional amendment, ratified with the Bill of Rights of 1791, guaranteeing in criminal cases the right to a speedy and public trial by jury, the right to be informed of the nature of the accusation, the right to confront witnesses, the right to counsel, and the right to compulsory process for obtaining favorable witnesses.

WAIVER: The voluntary relinquishment or abandonment—express or implied—of a legal right or advantage.

Caplin & Drysdale, Chartered v. United States

(*Law Firm*) v. (*Government*)

491 U.S. 617, 109 S.Ct. 2646 (1989)

FORFEITURE STATUTES THAT RENDER A DEFENDANT UNABLE TO PAY FOR COUNSEL DO NOT IMPERMISSIBLY BURDEN A DEFENDANT'S SIXTH AMENDMENT RIGHT TO RETAIN COUNSEL OF CHOICE

■ **INSTANT FACTS** Pursuant to a statute authorizing forfeiture of assets, the federal government froze the defendant's assets and rendered him unable to pay for the attorney he had retained to defend him in the criminal proceedings.

■ **BLACK LETTER RULE** The forfeiture statute does not impermissibly burden a defendant's Sixth Amendment right to retain counsel of his choice.

■ PROCEDURAL BASIS

Appeal to the United States Supreme Court, challenging the Court of Appeals' decision to reverse the District Court's order granting counsel a share of the forfeited assets.

■ FACTS

Christopher Reckmeyer was charged with running a drug scheme alleged to be a continuing criminal enterprise (CCE) in violation of 21 U.S.C. § 848. That statute authorized the forfeiture of assets obtained as a result of drug-law violations. Accordingly, the District Court restrained Reckmeyer from transferring any of the potentially forfeitable assets. Prior to the order, Reckmeyer had obtained Caplin & Drysdale (P) to represent him in the ongoing grand jury investigation. Reckmeyer moved to have the order modified so that he could pay his legal fees; but before a hearing was held, Reckmeyer pled guilty and forfeited all of his assets. Caplin & Drysdale (P) alleged that the statute created an exemption from forfeiture for attorney's fees, and if not, the failure of the statute to do so rendered it unconstitutional. Caplin & Drysdale (P) contended that the forfeiture statute infringes on a criminal defendant's Sixth Amendment right to counsel of choice, and upsets the "balance of power" between the Government (D) and the accused in a manner inconsistent with the Due Process Clause. The District Court granted Caplin & Drysdale's (P) claim for a share of the forfeited assets.

■ ISSUE

Consistent with the Fifth and Sixth Amendments, may the government forfeit a criminal defendant's illegally obtained assets, thereby rendering him unable to pay for his counsel of choice?

■ DECISION AND RATIONALE

(White, J.) Yes. The Sixth Amendment guarantees defendants in criminal cases the right to adequate representation, but those who lack the means to hire a lawyer have no complaint so long as they are adequately represented by appointed attorneys. The Sixth Amendment also grants defendants the right to be represented by an attorney they can afford to hire. Nothing in the statute at issue prevents a defendant from hiring an attorney of choice or disqualifies any attorney from serving as defendant's counsel. Yet, Caplin & Drysdale (P) urges that the statute violates the Sixth Amendment because of the forfeiture, at the instance of the government, of assets that defendants intend to use to pay their attorneys. The burden the statute imposes upon defendants is limited. The statute permits defendants to obtain counsel of choice by using nonforfeitable assets. Defendants may also find attorneys willing to represent them, hoping that their fees will be paid in the event of an acquittal. Even if a defendant is completely deprived of a choice of counsel, the Sixth Amendment places no limit on such forfeiture. A defendant has no Sixth Amendment right to spend another person's money for services rendered by an attorney, even if those funds are the only way that that defendant will be able to retain the attorney of his choice. A robbery suspect, for example, may not use funds stolen from a bank to pay for an attorney. Caplin & Drysdale (P) also argues that the government has a modest interest in forfeitable assets used to pay an attorney, because the principle ends of forfeiture have been achieved—dispossessing the drug dealer of the proceeds of his wrong doing. This argument misses the mark for three reasons. First, the Government (D) has a pecuniary interest in forfeiture, as those assets help fund law enforcement. Second, rightful owners are permitted to make claims for forfeited assets. Finally, one intent of the statute is to prevent organized crime and drug enterprises from using ill-gotten gains to retain private counsel. It is our view that there is a strong governmental interest in recovering all forfeitable assets, an interest that outweighs any Sixth Amendment interest in permitting criminals to use forfeitable assets to pay for their defense. We therefore reject Caplin & Drysdale's (P) claim of a Sixth Amendment right of criminal defendants to use assets that are the Government's (D). We also reject Caplin & Drysdale's (P) claim that the statute is invalid under the Due Process clause. We are unsure whether this contention adds anything to the Sixth Amendment claim since the Due Process Clause's guarantee of a fair trial is defined through several provisions of the Sixth Amendment. Even if there are additional protections, we find the claim unavailing.

■ DISSENT

(Blackmun, J.) The court moves too rapidly from the observation that a defendant may not insist on representation he cannot afford to the conclusion that the Government (D) is free to deem the defendant indigent by declaring his assets "tainted." The Court's holding implies that the Sixth Amendment right to counsel of choice may be outweighed by the legal fiction created by forfeiture. This demonstrates the Court's unawareness of the function of independent lawyers as guardians of freedom. When the Government (D) insists upon choosing counsel for the defendant, the defendant's confidence in the system is undermined. The right to choose counsel assures some equality between the Government (D) and those it prosecutes. The right to counsel of choice also serves the broader interest in maintaining a healthy and independent defense bar, one unfettered by government standardization. The Court's contention that the statute does not prevent a defendant from hiring an attorney of choice with other funds is untenable. If the Government (D) restrains the defendant's assets, private counsel will be unwilling take on the defense. It is also unlikely that many attorneys are willing to violate ethical norms, or create conflicts of interest, by taking on the defense in hopes of an acquittal. Most troubling is the fact that the statute places the Government (D) in the position to exercise power over any attorney who represents a defendant in a criminal forfeiture case. The Government (D) could easily use this weapon over talented or aggressive attorneys.

Analysis:

This opinion upholds the validity of forfeiture statutes that render a defendant unable to afford an attorney. The difficulty presented by this issue can be summarized as follows: On the one hand it seems perfectly logical to deny a criminal defendant access to ill-gotten gains in order to fund his defense; yet it seems unfair to allow the government to render a defendant—who has not been found guilty—indigent, and deprive him of his constitutional right to choose his attorney. The Court bases its decision, partially, on the fact that an indigent defendant has no right to choose an attorney, but the question presented is whether the government can render a defendant indigent, thereby depriving him of his right. In any event, the court concludes that the government can, reasoning that a robbery suspect cannot use stolen funds to pay for an attorney. The problem with this analogy is that stolen bank money is easier to trace than money obtained from an illegal enterprise. It is more difficult to determine what is and what is not forfeitable in this case. The Court finally holds that the government's interest in collecting forfeitable assets outweighs any Sixth Amendment right a defendant has to use such assets for his defense. The dissent points out that this legal fiction—the government's "ownership'' of forfeitable assets—should not outweigh the institutional interest permitting defendants to hire an attorney of choice, because such choices allow for the maintenance of an independent bar.

Strickland v. Washington

(*Not Stated*) v. (*Convicted Criminal*)

466 U.S. 668, 104 S.Ct. 2052, 80 L.Ed.2d 674 (1984)

SUPREME COURT SETS FORTH TEST FOR DETERMINING INEFFECTIVENESS OF COUNSEL CLAIMS

■ **INSTANT FACTS** Washington (D) was sentenced to death after pleading guilty to capital offenses, and thereafter sought reversal of his conviction based upon ineffectiveness of counsel.

■ **BLACK LETTER RULE** In order to reverse a conviction based upon ineffectiveness of counsel, the defendant must show that (1) counsel's performance was deficient, requiring a showing that counsel made errors so serious that counsel was not functioning as the "counsel" guaranteed defendant by the Sixth Amendment, and (2) the deficient performance prejudiced the defense, by showing that counsel's errors were so serious as to deprive defendant of a fair trial, a trial whose result is reliable.

■ PROCEDURAL BASIS

Review by Supreme Court of court of appeals' reversal of district court's denial of petition for writ of habeas corpus in criminal action alleging ineffective assistance of counsel.

■ FACTS

Washington (D) pled guilty to three capital murder charges—torture, kidnapping and attempted murders—all occurring over a 10-day period. In the plea colloquy, Washington (D) told the trial judge that that he had no significant prior criminal record, that at the time of his crime spree he was under extreme stress caused by his inability to support his family, but that he accepted responsibility for the crimes. The trial judge said that he had a great deal of respect for people who were willing to step forward and admit their responsibility but that he was making no statement at all about his likely sentencing hearing. Against his counsel's advice, Washington (D) waived his right to an advisory jury at his capital sentencing hearing and chose to be sentenced by the judge without a jury recommendation. In preparing for the sentencing hearing, Washington's (D) attorney spoke to the wife and mother of Washington (D), but did not seek out other character witnesses. The attorney did not request a psychiatric exam, since there were no indications of psychological problems. The attorney, for various reasons, did not present and did not look further for evidence concerning Washington's (D) emotional state and character. The attorney also did not request a pre-sentence report. The attorney's strategy was based upon the judge's remarks at the plea colloquy as well as his reputation as a sentencing judge who thought it important for a convicted defendant to own up to his crime. [Unfortunately, for the defense, this strategy failed.] The judge found numerous aggravating circumstances and no mitigating circumstances, and sentenced Washington (D) to death. The convictions and sentences were upheld by the State Supreme Court. Washington (D) sought federal habeas corpus relief on the ground that counsel had rendered ineffective assistance at the sentencing proceedings in several respects. The district court found errors in judgment by trial counsel but concluded that there was no prejudice to Washington's (D) sentence from such error. The court of appeals reversed and remanded. The Supreme Court took the matter up on review.

■ ISSUE

Can a defendant be deprived of the right to effective counsel where his counsel fails to render adequate legal assistance?

■ DECISION AND RATIONALE

(O'Connor) Yes. A defendant can be deprived of the right to effective counsel where his counsel fails to render adequate legal assistance. In giving meaning to the requirement of effective counsel, the benchmark for judging any claim of ineffectiveness must be whether counsel's conduct so undermined the proper function of the adversarial process that the trial cannot be relied on as having produced a just result. This same principle applies to capital sentencing hearings as well. In order to reverse a conviction on ineffectiveness of counsel, the defendant must show that (1) counsel's performance was deficient and (2) the deficient performance prejudiced the defense. The proper standard now used for attorney performance is that of reasonably effective assistance based upon an objective standard of reasonableness. Guidelines that are more specific are not appropriate. Representation of a criminal defendant entails certain basic duties, such as the duty to assist the defendant, the duty of loyalty, a duty to avoid conflicts of interest, the duty to advocate for the defendant's cause, the duty to consult with the defendant on important decisions and keep him informed concerning the case, and the duty to bring to bear such skill and knowledge as will render the trial a reliable adversarial testing process. These basic duties neither exhaustively define the obligations of counsel nor form a checklist for judicial evaluation of attorney performance. The prevailing norms of practice as reflected in American Bar Association standards and the like are guides for determining what is reasonable, but they are only guides. No detailed rules for counsel's conduct can properly take account of the variety of circumstances faced by defense counsel. A fair assessment of attorney performance requires that every effort be made to eliminate the distorting effects of hindsight, to reconstruct the circumstances of counsel's challenged conduct, and to evaluate the conduct from counsel's perspective at the time. A court must therefore indulge a strong presumption that counsel's conduct falls within the wide range of reasonable professional assistance. Thus, a court deciding an actual ineffectiveness claim must judge the reasonableness of counsel's challenged conduct on the facts of the particular case, viewed as of the time of counsel's conduct. A convicted defendant making a claim of ineffective assistance must identify the acts or omissions of counsel that are alleged not to have been the result of reasonable professional judgment. The court must then determine whether, in light of all the circumstances, the identified acts or omissions were outside the wide range of professionally competent assistance. Any deficiencies in counsel's performance must be prejudicial to the defense in order to constitute ineffective assistance under the Constitution. The defendant must also affirmatively prove prejudice. It is not enough for the defendant to show that the errors had some conceivable effect on the outcome of the proceedings. The defendant must show that there is a reasonable probability that, but for counsel's unprofessional errors the result of the proceeding would have been different. [Doesn't this call for some speculation?] A reasonable probability is a probability sufficient to undermine confidence in the outcome. Finally, there is no reason for a court deciding an ineffective assistance claim to approach the inquiry in the same order or even to address both components of the inquiry if the defendant makes an insufficient showing on one. Thus, the court need not determine whether counsel's performance was deficient before examining the prejudice suffered by the defendant as a result of the alleged deficiencies. Applying these standards to the facts of this case, it is clear that the conduct of Washington's (D) counsel cannot be found unreasonable. Even if we assumed that the conduct was unreasonable, Washington (D) suffered insufficient prejudice to warrant setting aside his death sentence. Counsel made a strategic choice to argue for the extreme emotional distress mitigation circumstances and to rely as fully as possible on Washington's (D) acceptance of responsibilities for his crimes. This strategy was well within the range of professionally reasonable judgments, and not seeking more character or psychological evidence was likewise reasonable. With respect to prejudice, the evidence that Washington (D) contends his counsel should have offered at the sentencing hearing would barely have altered the sentencing profile presented to the judge. There is no reasonable probability that the omitted evidence would have changed the conclusion and the sentence imposed. We therefore conclude that the District Court properly declined to issue a writ of habeas corpus.

■ CONCURRENCE AND DISSENT

(Brennan) I concur with the standards set forth in the opinion, but dissent from its judgment on the ground that the death penalty is in all circumstances forbidden cruel and unusual punishment.

■ DISSENT

(Marshall) I object to the "reasonableness" performance standard adopted by the Court because it will either have no grip at all or will yield excessive variation in the manner in which the Sixth Amendment is interpreted and applied by different courts. To tell lawyers and the courts that the counsel must behave in an objectively "reasonably" manner is to tell them almost nothing. I also object to the prejudice standard for two reasons. First, it is often very difficult to tell whether a convicted defendant would have fared better if not for the ineffective representation. It is senseless to impose on a defendant whose lawyer has been shown to be incompetent the burden of demonstrating prejudice. Second, I would hold that a showing that the performance of a defendant's lawyer departed from constitutionally prescribed standards requires a new trial regardless of whether the defendant suffered demonstrable prejudice thereby. The facts of this case show that counsel made virtually no investigation of the possibility of obtaining testimony from Washington's (D) relatives, friends, or former employers pertaining to his character or background. Had counsel done do, he would have found several persons willing to testify that Washington (D) was a responsible, nonviolent man, devoted to his family, and active in the affairs of his church. If counsel had investigated, he might well have decided to present some such mitigating evidence. If he had done so, there is a significant chance that Washington (D) would have been given a life sentence.

Analysis:

This landmark case clarified the standards used in determining whether a defendant's Sixth Amendment guarantee of effective counsel had been violated. The decision developed a two-part test to establish ineffective assistance of counsel. First, the errors must be so serious that the counsel was not functioning as "counsel" guaranteed by the Sixth Amendment Second, there must be a showing of prejudice to the defendant because of the deficient performance. The court rejected the idea developed from previous decisions that in order to determine the reasonableness of counsel's performance, there must be certain guidelines applied. Instead, the court held that such specific guidelines are not appropriate and that the reasonableness determination should be guided by prevailing professional norms and consideration of all the circumstances. Finally, the court held with respect to the prejudice prong of the test, that there must be a showing of a reasonable probability that, but for the errors, the results would have been different.

■ CASE VOCABULARY

ADVISORY JURY: A jury that hears a case for which there is no right to a jury trial, and the judge may accept or reject the verdict.

EN BANC: Where all members of the appellate court for a particular district or circuit hear a case on review, rather than just the limited quorum members initially assigned to hear the case.

Mickens v. Taylor

(*Convicted Murderer*) v. (*Warden*)

535 U.S. 162, 122 S.Ct. 1237, 152 L.Ed.2d 291 (2002)

A COURT NEED NOT INQUIRE INTO A POTENTIAL CONFLICT OF INTEREST UNLESS IT KNEW OR SHOULD HAVE KNOWN ABOUT IT

■ **INSTANT FACTS** Mickens (P) alleged ineffective assistance of counsel because his attorney briefly represented the victim of Mickens' (P) crime.

■ **BLACK LETTER RULE** When counsel represents successive defendants with a potential conflict of interest, a defendant must demonstrate that a conflict existed that affected the outcome of his case.

■ PROCEDURAL BASIS

Certiorari to review a decision of the Fourth Circuit Court of Appeals affirming the denial of a petition for habeas corpus.

■ FACTS

Mickens (P) was convicted of the murder of Hall and was sentenced to death. After trial, Mickens's (P) counsel in a federal habeas corpus action learned that the judge had earlier appointed Mickens's (P) trial counsel to represent Hall in relation to earlier charges. The attorney did not disclose to the court, co-counsel, or Mickens (P) that he had previously represented Hall. The trial court denied the petition for habeas corpus relief and the Fourth Circuit Court of Appeals affirmed. The court held that Mickens (P) had not demonstrated that he suffered any adverse effect from his attorney's conflict of interest.

■ ISSUE

Was Mickens (P) denied the effective assistance of counsel?

■ DECISION AND RATIONALE

(Scalia, J.) No. Generally, a Sixth Amendment violation requires a showing of "a reasonable probability that, but for counsel's unprofessional errors, the result of the proceeding would have been different." When a defendant is denied counsel entirely or at a critical stage of the proceeding, such an effect may be presumed because of the high probability that the verdict is unreliable. Likewise, when counsel actively represents conflicting interests, a presumption may arise that the assistance of counsel was ineffective. When defense counsel is compelled to represent codefendants over his objection, reversal of a conviction is required unless the court determined no actual conflict exists. However, when counsel fails to object to his representation of multiple defendants, automatic reversal is not appropriate, and the defendant must show that a conflict of interest affected the outcome of the case. Under such circumstances, the court need not inquire into a potential conflict unless it knew or should have known that a conflict affecting the adequacy of representation exists.

Here, counsel did not object to his representation of Mickens (P) and the court's failure to make a conflict inquiry does not lessen Mickens' (P) burden to demonstrate a conflict affected the outcome of his trial. Because Mickens (P) has made no such showing, his conviction must stand. Affirmed.

■ **CONCURRENCE**

(Kennedy, J.) Mickens's (P) attorney worked under the belief that he owed no further duty to Hall, and counsel's trial strategies were not affected by any confidential information obtained while representing Hall. Even if the judge should have known of a conflict, the conflict did not influence the choices the attorney made during the trial or affect its outcome.

■ **DISSENT**

(Stevens, J.) Counsel's failure to disclose his prior representation of Hall resulted in an indefensible conflict of interest. Upon conviction of his client, counsel must offer evidence in the best light to the defendant to reduce the impact of the crime in the eyes of the jury. Yet, his continuing ethical duty to Hall required him to protect the reputation and confidences of his former client. Moreover, when the court appoints counsel, it must do so in a manner that preserves the defendant's constitutional right to the assistance of counsel. Without an inquiry into potential conflicts of interest, the court places the defendant in an attorney-client relationship in which the attorney cannot possibly serve his client's undivided interests. His conviction should be set aside to maintain public confidence in the legal system and ensure that Mickens (P) receives his constitutional right to the effective assistance of counsel.

■ **DISSENT**

(Souter, J.) It should be immaterial whether Mickens's (P) counsel objected to his appointment, for the court was aware of a potential conflict of interest and failed to inquire about it. When the judge knows of a potential conflict, his or her duty to investigate the nature of the conflict to ensure the effective assistance of counsel does not depend on whether counsel insists the judge act. The judge is under a constitutional duty to uphold the Sixth Amendment. The defendant should not be held to a burden of proving actual prejudice from such a violation when the judge blatantly breaches his or her constitutional duty.

■ **DISSENT**

(Breyer, J.) Because of the egregious conflict at issue, Court precedent addressing the issue of the duty to inquire does not govern. This is a capital murder case in which the defendant's lawyer represented the murder victim only days before his appointment. The victim's character in such cases is often a key piece of evidence to exonerate or mitigate criminal liability. When defense counsel has divided loyalties, the risk of actual prejudice is easily surmised. Likewise, the conflict was not merely overlooked by the court, but actually created by it. This is not a situation in which a court was required to consider the potential for conflict upon meeting defense counsel for the first time, but rather knew of the conflict before it arose. In such unique situations, prejudice is so likely to occur that it should be presumed as a matter of law.

Analysis:

It is difficult to imagine the kind of prejudice that would justify overturning a conviction under the standard enunciated by the Court. Cases that discuss the adequacy of representation afford counsel a wide range of discretion on how to proceed and find adequate representation in most cases in which a particular course of action or inaction could have some tactical justification. Even if a conflict of interest leads an attorney to make consistently bad, but justifiable, tactical decisions, a defendant may have a difficult time proving actual prejudice.

■ **CASE VOCABULARY**

CONFLICT OF INTEREST: A real or seeming incompatibility between the interests of two of a lawyer's clients, such that the lawyer is disqualified from representing both clients if the dual representation adversely affects either client or if the clients do not consent. *See* Model Rules of Professional Conduct 1.7(a).

HABEAS CORPUS: A writ employed to bring a person before a court, most frequently to ensure that the party's imprisonment or detention is not illegal.

INEFFECTIVE ASSISTANCE OF COUNSEL: Representation in which the defendant is deprived of a fair trial because the lawyer handles the case unreasonably, usually either by performing incompetently or by not devoting full effort to the defendant, especially because of a conflict of interest. In determining whether a criminal defendant received ineffective assistance of counsel, courts generally consider several factors: (1) whether the lawyer had previously handled criminal cases; (2) whether strategic trial tactics were involved in the allegedly incompetent action; (3) whether, and to what extent, the defendant was prejudiced as a result of the lawyer's alleged ineffectiveness; and (4) whether the ineffectiveness was due to matters beyond the lawyer's control.

Wheat v. United States

(Drug Conspirator) v. *(Government)*
486 U.S. 153, 108 S.Ct. 1692, 100 L.Ed.2d 140 (1988)

COURT REJECTS CRIMINAL DEFENDANT'S CHOSEN COUNSEL ON GROUND OF A POTENTIAL CONFLICT

■ **INSTANT FACTS** Wheat's (D) motion to substitute in the counsel of his choice was denied, in spite of waiver, because of potential for conflict of interest.

■ **BLACK LETTER RULE** The court is allowed substantial latitude in refusing waivers of conflicts of interest with respect to a criminal defendant's chosen counsel both in cases where there is an actual conflict and in those where a serious potential for conflict exists.

■ PROCEDURAL BASIS

Review by Supreme Court following jury trial conviction for criminal conspiracy.

■ FACTS

Wheat (D) was charged with participating in a far-flung drug conspiracy with numerous codefendants, including Gomez-Barajas and Bravo. These two codefendants were represented by attorney Iredale. Gomez-Barajas was tried and acquitted. To avoid a second trial on other charges, he plead guilty to certain offenses stemming from the conspiracy. At the commencement of Wheat's (D) trial, the district court had not yet accepted Gomez-Barajas' plea, and he was free to withdraw it and proceed to trial. Bravo pled guilty. Wheat (D) moved for the substitution of Iredale as his counsel shortly before his trial was to commence. The Government (P) objected on the ground that Iredale's representation of the two other codefendants created a serious conflict of interest for two reasons. One, if the plea and sentencing arrangement were rejected by the court, Wheat (D) would likely be called as a witness for the prosecution of Gomez-Barajas's trial. This would pose a conflict of interest for Iredale, who would be prevented from cross-examining Wheat (D) and thereby from effectively representing Gomez-Barajas. Second, if Bravo was called as a witness for the prosecution against Wheat (D), ethical proscriptions would prevent Iredale from cross-examining Bravo in any meaningful way, and thus Iredale would be unable to provide Wheat (D) with effective assistance of counsel. [The Government's (P) third reason may have been its fear that Iredale would obtain an acquittal for Wheat (D).] Wheat (D) asserted his right to have counsel of his own choosing and his willingness to waive the right to conflict-free counsel. He also argued that the Government's (P) circumstances giving rise to a conflict were highly speculative, and it was manufacturing implausible conflicts. The district court denied Wheat's (D) request to substitute Iredale as his counsel, and the matter went to trial with his original counsel. Wheat (D) was convicted and the court of appeals affirmed. Wheat (D) petitioned the Supreme Court for review.

■ ISSUE

Is a criminal defendant's right under the Sixth Amendment to his chosen attorney qualified by the fact that the attorney has represented other defendants charged in the same criminal conspiracy?

■ DECISION AND RATIONALE

(Rehnquist) Yes. There are certain limitations on the Sixth Amendment's right to choose one's own counsel. One who is not a member of the bar may not represent clients in court, a defendant may not insist on representation by an attorney he cannot afford, nor may a defendant insist on the counsel of an attorney who has a previous or ongoing relationship with an opposing party, even when the opposing party is the Government. The Federal Rules of Criminal Procedures provide: "[T]he court shall promptly inquire with respect to such joint representation and shall personally advise each defendant of his right to the effective assistance of counsel, including separate representation. Unless it appears that there is good cause to believe no conflict of interest is likely to arise, the court shall take such measures as may be appropriate to protect each defendant's right to counsel." It has been suggested that the court may order that the defendants be separately represented in subsequent proceedings in the case. The trial courts face the prospect of being "whip-sawed" by assertions of error no matter which way they rule in multiple representation cases. If multiple representation is allowed and the advocacy of counsel is thereafter impaired, the defendant may claim that he did not receive effective assistance. On the other hand, if multiple representation is refused, the defendant may claim denial of the right to have counsel of his own choosing. [Just like the old saying, "Your damned if you do and damned if you don't."] Nor does a waiver necessarily solve the problem. Thus, where a court justifiably finds an actual conflict of interest, it may decline a proffer of waiver, and insist that the defendants be separately represented. We hold that the district court must be allowed substantial latitude in refusing waivers of conflicts of interest both in cases where there is an actual conflict and in those where a potential for conflict exists. In this case, the motion for substitution of counsel was made so close to the time of trial, we do not think the court exceeded the broad latitude that must be accorded it in making this decision. Thus, the court was within its discretion and did not violate Wheat's (D) Sixth Amendment rights. The district court must recognize a presumption in favor of Wheat's (D) counsel of choice, but that presumption may be overcome not only by a demonstration of actual conflict but by a showing of a serious potential for conflict.

■ DISSENT

(Marshall) I disagree with the Court's suggestion that the trial court's decision as to whether a potential conflict justifies rejection of a defendant's chosen counsel is entitled to some kind of special deference on appeal. The Court appears to limit appellate review to determining whether an abuse of discretion has occurred. A trial court that rejects a criminal defendant's chosen counsel on the ground of a potential conflict should make findings on the record to facilitate review, and an appellate court should scrutinize closely the basis for the decision. I believe that a reversal is in order. The only possible conflict this Court can divine from Iredale's representation of both Wheat (D) and Gomez-Barajas rests on the premise that the trial court would reject the negotiated plea agreement and that Gomez-Barajas then would decide to go to trial. This argument rests on speculation of the most dubious kind. The Court offers no reason to think that the trial court would have rejected Gomez-Barajas's plea agreement; neither did the Government (P) posit any such reason in its argument or brief before this Court. Similarly, Iredale's prior representation of Bravo was not a cause for concern. Bravo could not have testified about Wheat's (D) involved in the criminal scheme because he did not know and could not identify Wheat (D). The notion that Iredale's prior representation of Bravo might well have caused a conflict of interest at Wheat's trial is nothing short of ludicrous.

■ DISSENT

(Stevens) The court's Analysis: of this case is seriously flawed. The Court exaggerates the significance of the potential conflict. Moreover, the Court gives inadequate weight to the informed and voluntary character of the waiver of conflict-free representation.

Analysis:

In *Cuyler v. Sullivan,* the court held that the mere possibility of a conflict of interest does not deprive a defendant of his right to counsel. In this case, however, the mere possibility of conflict of interest may cause the court to refuse a defendant's waiver of a conflict of interest with respect to his chosen counsel where a serious potential for conflict exists. The facts of this case caused the court to uphold the overriding of the presumption favoring a defendant's choice of counsel. It concluded that the trial court should be allowed "substantial latitude in refusing waivers." Recall that Wheat (D) argued that the Government (P) was manufacturing implausible conflicts. The two dissenting opinions disputed the potential conflict. Justice Marshall called the majority's argument concerning the potential conflict "speculation of the most dubious kind" and "nothing short of ludicrous." Justice Stevens said that the Court "exaggerates the significance of the potential conflict." If the members of the Supreme Court cannot agree on whether the facts of this particular case constitute a series potential for conflict, it illustrates the problems faced by trial courts in making such determinations, without the benefit of hindsight. The Court refused to establish a set rule and instead held that each case must be evaluated under its own circumstances by the trial court to determine if a serious potential for conflict exits, keeping in mind the presumption favoring the right to have one's counsel of choice.

■ CASE VOCABULARY

WAIVER OF CONFLICT OF INTEREST: The voluntary relinquishment of conflict-free representation by counsel.

CHAPTER SIX

Arrest, Search and Seizure

Wolf v. Colorado

Instant Facts: Not Stated.

Black Letter Rule: The Fourth Amendment's prohibition of unreasonable searches and seizures does apply to the states, but does not require state courts to exclude evidence obtained in violation of the Fourth Amendment as it does in federal courts.

Mapp v. Ohio

Instant Facts: Mapp's (D) home was forcibly searched without a search warrant. Mapp (D) seeks to have the evidence seized therein suppressed under the Fourth Amendment's exclusionary rule.

Black Letter Rule: The exclusionary rule requiring evidence gathered in violation of the Fourth Amendment to be excluded from criminal proceedings applies equally to both the state and federal governments.

United States v. Leon

Instant Facts: Police conducted a search using a warrant they believed in good-faith to be based on sufficient probable cause, but which was later found to be lacking in that regard.

Black Letter Rule: So long as the police have a good-faith belief that a warrant has been properly issued by a magistrate and based on sufficient probable cause, evidence obtained pursuant to the warrant is admissible.

Katz v. United States

Instant Facts: FBI agents (P) bugged a public telephone booth and recorded Katz's (D) end of telephone conversations in that booth.

Black Letter Rule: Government investigative activity that intrudes upon a justifiable expectation of privacy constitutes a search within the meaning of the Fourth Amendment.

Kyllo v. United States

Instant Facts: Without a warrant, federal agents (P) used a thermal imaging device to determine whether Kyllo's (D) home was emitting enough relative heat to indicate a marijuana grow.

Black Letter Rule: The Government (P) conducts a search when it uses sense-enhancing technology that is not in general public use to obtain information about the interior of a home that it could not otherwise obtain without physical intrusion into the home.

Andresen v. Maryland

Instant Facts: Police seized papers pertaining to a fraudulent land sale from Andresen's (D) law office. Andresen (D) challenges the seizure as a Fifth Amendment violation.

Black Letter Rule: The Fifth Amendment does not prohibit government seizure of preexisting documents and other tangible items tending to inculpate the owner of those documents and items.

Spinelli v. United States

Instant Facts: Based on a sparsely corroborated tip from an informant the FBI obtained a search warrant that led to the discovery of evidence tending to indicate that Spinelli (D) was running an illegal bookmaking operation.

Black Letter Rule: To give rise to probable cause an informant's tip must either contain (1) a sufficient statement of the underlying circumstances from which the informant gained his knowledge, or (2) information supporting the applying officer's belief that the informant is reliable and credible.

Illinois v. Gates

Instant Facts: Based on a corroborated informant's tip regarding Gates' (D) travel plans police obtained a search warrant and discovered about 350 pounds of marijuana in Gates' (D) automobile, which the trial court excluded as fruits of an illegal search.

Black Letter Rule: A search warrant based on an informant's tip may be properly issued if, given the totality of the circumstances set forth in the warrant application, including the veracity and basis of knowledge of the informant and any corroboration of the informant's information, there is a fair probability that contraband or evidence will be found in the place to be searched.

Maryland v. Pringle

Instant Facts: Pringle (D) was arrested after cocaine was found in the rear seat of a vehicle in which Pringle (D) was riding, albeit in the front.

Black Letter Rule: Probable cause generally requires a reasonably particularized ground for belief of a defendant's guilt.

United States v. Watson

Instant Facts: A federal postal inspector, acting on a tip from a reliable informant, arrested Watson (D) without a warrant even though the inspector had time to secure a warrant. Watson (D) challenges the warrantless arrest on constitutional grounds.

Black Letter Rule: An officer with probable cause to make a felony arrest is not required, under the Fourth Amendment, to obtain an arrest warrant.

United States v. Robinson

Instant Facts: During a pat-down incident to Robinson's (D) arrest for driving while his license was revoked, the officer (P) removed a crumpled cigarette pack from Robinson's (D) pocket, opened it, and found heroin.

Black Letter Rule: Any lawful custodial arrest justifies a full search of the arrestee's person.

Chimel v. California

Instant Facts: Based on Chimel's (D) arrest, officers (P) searched his entire home for evidence without a search warrant.

Black Letter Rule: A warrantless search incident to arrest may extend only to the person of the arrestee and the area within his immediate control.

Payton v. New York

Instant Facts: This involves companion cases in which police entered homes to make an arrest without arrest warrants, found evidence of crimes therein and used that evidence to convict the defendants. Both challenge the admission of such evidence on Fourth Amendment grounds.

Black Letter Rule: Absent exigent circumstances, police are required to have an arrest warrant before entering a suspects home to make an arrest, otherwise any evidence seized therein is inadmissible against the suspect.

California v. Carney

Instant Facts: Police with probable cause to believe Carney (D) was dealing drugs searched his motor home without a warrant and discovered illegal narcotics therein.

Black Letter Rule: Any vehicle that is readily mobile and subject to the pervasive laws regulating motor vehicles may be searched, without first obtaining a search warrant, so long as there is probable cause supporting the search.

California v. Acevedo

Instant Facts: Officers who had probable cause to search a bag in the trunk of Acevedo's (D) car for drugs stopped the car, opened the trunk and the bag, and found marijuana.

Black Letter Rule: Police may search a closed container in an automobile without a warrant if they have probable cause to search the container.

Thornton v. United States

Instant Facts: A police officer searched Thornton's (D) vehicle although he was arrested for drug possession outside his vehicle.

Black Letter Rule: A police officer may search a vehicle incident to lawful arrest once probable cause exists to arrest a recent occupant of the vehicle who had access to the interior of the vehicle.

Colorado v. Bertine

Instant Facts: Bertine (D) was pulled over and arrested for driving under the influence of alcohol. Before the tow truck arrived to take Bertine's (D) van, an officer inventoried the van's contents and discovered narcotics.

Black Letter Rule: An inventory of a motor vehicle and the containers therein pursuant to established police department administrative policy does not violate the Fourth Amendment's prohibition of unreasonable searches and seizures.

Terry v. Ohio

Instant Facts: A police officer observed Terry (D) and two other men casing out a store as if planning to rob it. When confronted the men acted suspiciously so the officer frisked them and discovered Terry (D) and another were armed.

Black Letter Rule: Where an officer observes conduct that, in light of experience and all other circumstances, would lead to an objectively reasonable belief that a suspect is armed and dangerous, the officer may conduct a frisk limited in scope to searching for weapons.

Schneckloth v. Bustamonte

Instant Facts: Bustamonte (D) was a passenger in a car owned by his brother that was stopped by the police for an equipment violation. Bustamonte (D) gave the police permission to search the car and now seeks to have the evidence excluded.

Black Letter Rule: For a consent search to be valid the State need only prove consent was voluntarily given and not the result of duress or coercion, either express or implied; the consent giver need not know his right to refuse consent, although such knowledge is one factor in determining if the consent was voluntary.

Illinois v. Rodriguez

Instant Facts: Rodriguez's (D) former girlfriend used her key to Rodriguez's (D) apartment to let police in to arrest him. While inside the police discovered evidence of narcotics trafficking. Rodriguez (D) challenges the entry as a Fourth Amendment violation.

Black Letter Rule: A warrantless entry based on consent of a third party is reasonable, and thus valid under the Fourth Amendment, so long as it was objectively reasonable for law enforcement to believe the third party had authority to give consent.

Wolf v. Colorado

(*Not Stated*) v. (*People*)
338 U.S. 25, 69 S.Ct. 1359 (1949)

ALTHOUGH THE FOURTH AMENDMENT DOES APPLY TO THE STATES, IT DOES NOT REQUIRE THE EXCLUSION OF EVIDENCE OBTAINED IN VIOLATION OF THE AMENDMENT

■ **INSTANT FACTS** Not Stated.

■ **BLACK LETTER RULE** The Fourth Amendment's prohibition of unreasonable searches and seizures does apply to the states, but does not require state courts to exclude evidence obtained in violation of the Fourth Amendment as it does in federal courts.

■ PROCEDURAL BASIS

Certification to the U.S. Supreme Court from the highest state appellate court.

■ FACTS

Not stated.

■ ISSUE

Does the federal exclusionary rule barring the use of evidence obtained in violation of the Fourth Amendment apply to the states as well?

■ DECISION AND RATIONALE

(Frankfurter, J.) No. The security of one's privacy against arbitrary police intrusion as guaranteed by the Fourth Amendment is implicit in the concept of ordered liberty and as such enforceable against the States through the Due Process Clause. Accordingly, we have no hesitation in saying that were a state affirmatively to sanction such police incursion into privacy it would run counter to the guaranty of the Fourth Amendment. The way in which such sanctions should work, however, is a problem that should be left up to the individual states to solve in whatever way they decide. In *Weeks v. United States*, we held that in a federal prosecution the Fourth Amendment barred the use of evidence secured through an illegal search and seizure. This ruling was not based on any explicit constitutional provision or any congressional policy in the enforcement of the Constitution. It was a matter of judicial implication. The ruling has subsequently been stoutly applied and we adhere to it today. The immediate question we must answer though, is whether this exclusionary rule should be extended to the states. In considering this question, we realize it is an issue as to which men with complete devotion to the protection of the right of privacy might give different answers. Indeed, most of the English-speaking world does not regard as vital such a rule. Furthermore, the contrariety of views of the States is particularly impressive in view of the careful reconsideration, which they have given the problem in the light of the Weeks decision. [Justice Frankfurter continued by summarizing state case law on the issue. Most states had rejected *Weeks*, but 16 adopted it.] Those jurisdictions that have rejected *Weeks* have provided other means of protection. Indeed, the exclusion of evidence serves to protect only those upon whose premises something incriminating has been found. We cannot, therefore, regard it as a departure from basic standards to relegate such persons to the remedies of private action and such protection as the internal discipline of the police, under the eyes of an alert public opinion, may afford. It is not for this

Court to condemn a state's reliance upon other methods that, if consistently enforced, would be equally effective. What's more, there are reasons for excluding evidence unreasonably obtained by the federal police that are less compelling in the case of police under State or local authority. Public opinion of a community can far more effectively be exerted against oppressive conduct on the part of the police directly responsible to the community itself than can local opinion, sporadically aroused, be brought to bear upon remote authority pervasively exerted throughout the country. We therefore hold that in a State court prosecution for a State crime, the Fourteenth Amendment does not forbid the admission of evidence obtained by an unreasonable search and seizure.

■ CONCURRENCE

(Black, J.) The federal exclusionary rule is not a Fourth Amendment requirement, but a judicially created rule which Congress might negate.

■ DISSENT

(Murphy, J.) Of course I agree with the Court that the Fourteenth Amendment prohibits activities that are proscribed by the search and seizure clause of the Fourth Amendment. But it is difficult for me to understand how the Court can go this far yet refuse to take the step that would give meaning to the pronouncement it utters. The two alternatives—criminal prosecution of police and civil actions in trespass against violators—are illusory if deterrence of unreasonable searches and seizures is the goal to be achieved. The only true remedy is exclusion. Only by exclusion can we impress upon prosecutors that a violation of the Constitution will do them no good. Only when this point is driven home can we expect them to instruct the police in the importance of observing constitutional demands.

■ DISSENT

(Douglas, J.) Without an exclusionary rule, the Fourth Amendment would have no effective sanction.

Analysis:

Justice Murphy's dissent correctly depicts the Court's opinion as creating an illusory right when it comes to state violations of the Fourth Amendment. Justice Frankfurter should be commended for his staunch adherence to the ideals of federalism, but in doing so it should also be recognized that his proposed alternatives to application of the exclusionary rule to the states are hollow. The general law abiding public not only doesn't hear much about illegal police searches, if it did most would not care so long as it didn't happen to them. It's a variant of the "Not in My Backyard" approach to nuclear waste disposal. Public opinion, therefore, is not likely to develop to the critical point for effecting change. The proposal of civil trespass suits is equally illusory. The people who would ostensibly be most likely to file a civil suit are those law-abiding people who were erroneously searched by the police. Because of the police error and the fact they are law abiding, these people will be more likely to accept an apology and restitution to make up for any property damage that occurred and just be glad its all over. True criminals will not likely have the resources to hire legal counsel, but even if they do, a judge and jury will not likely be too sympathetic. Moving on, Justice Frankfurter's assertion that the exclusion of evidence illegally obtained serves only to protect those upon whose premises something incriminating has been found is flatly wrong. The correct theory is that by excluding such evidence, the police will be less apt to commit violations of the Fourth Amendment with regard to all citizens, not just those in possession of contraband.

■ CASE VOCABULARY

INCORPORATION: Means by which provisions of the Bill of Rights are applied to the states through the 14th Amendment's Due Process Clause which has been held to encompass those provisions.

Mapp v. Ohio

(*Homeowner*) v. (*State Government*)
367 U.S. 643, 81 S.Ct. 1684 (1961)

THE EXCLUSIONARY RULE IS APPLIED TO PROSECUTIONS IN STATE COURTS

■ INSTANT FACTS Mapp's (D) home was forcibly searched without a search warrant. Mapp (D) seeks to have the evidence seized therein suppressed under the Fourth Amendment's exclusionary rule.

■ BLACK LETTER RULE The exclusionary rule requiring evidence gathered in violation of the Fourth Amendment to be excluded from criminal proceedings applies equally to both the state and federal governments.

■ PROCEDURAL BASIS

Certification to the U.S. Supreme Court after the State's highest appellate court affirmed the conviction and refused to apply the exclusionary rule.

■ FACTS

On May 23, 1957, three police officers arrived at Mapp's (D) residence armed with information that "a person [was] hiding out in the home who was wanted for questioning in connection with a recent bombing, and that there was a large amount of policy paraphernalia being hidden in the home." Upon their arrival, the officers knocked and demanded entrance, but Mapp (D) refused to admit them without a warrant. Three hours later, when some additional officers arrived on the scene, Mapp (D) refused to answer the door and the officers then forced their way into the residence. The officers conducted a widespread search and found obscene materials. No search warrant was ever produced, nor was this failure explained in any way. Mapp (D) was convicted on the strength of the evidence seized. The Ohio Supreme Court, after acknowledging that no warrant was ever produced, affirmed the conviction.

■ ISSUE

Should the federal rule requiring the exclusion of evidence gathered in violation of the Fourth Amendment be applied to evidence used in state court proceedings as well?

■ DECISION AND RATIONALE

(Clark, J.) Yes. In 1949, prior to the Wolf case, almost two-thirds of the States were opposed to the use of the exclusionary rule. Now more than half of those states have wholly or partly adopted or adhered to the *Weeks* rule requiring exclusion of evidence seized in violation of the Fourth Amendment. The highest court of California has gone so far as to state that it was "compelled to reach that conclusion [adopting the exclusionary rule] because other remedies have completely failed to secure compliance with the constitutional provisions. This view is buttressed by the experiences of other states. Thus the rationale supporting the failure of the *Wolf* court to extend the exclusionary rule to the states can no longer be deemed controlling. We therefore hold that all evidence obtained by searches and seizures in violation of the Constitution is, by that same authority, inadmissible in state court. Since the Fourth Amendment's right of privacy has been declared enforceable against the States through the Due Process Clause of the Fourteenth, it is enforceable against them by the same sanction of exclusion as is used against the Federal Government. Were it otherwise the Fourth Amendment would be reduced to a mere "form of words." Our holding is not only the logical dictate of prior cases, but it also makes very good sense. Presently, a federal prosecutor may make no use of evidence illegally seized, but a State's attorney across the street may, although he is supposedly operating under the enforceable prohibitions of the same Amendment. There are those who say, as did Justice Cardozo, that under our constitutional exclusionary doctrine "the criminal is to go free because the constable has blundered." This will no doubt be the case in some cases. But there must be another consideration, the imperative of judicial integrity." The criminal goes free, if he must, but it is the law that sets him free. Nothing can destroy a government more quickly than its failure to observe its own laws. Nor can it lightly be assumed that, as a practical matter, adoption of the exclusionary rule fetters law enforcement. Only last year the Court expressly considered that contention and found that pragmatic evidence of a sort to the contrary was not wanting. Once we have recognized that the right to privacy embodied in the Fourth Amendment is enforceable against the States, and that the right to be secure against rude invasions of privacy by state officers is, therefore, constitutional in origin, we can no longer permit that right to remain an empty promise. Our decision today gives to the individual no more than that which the Constitution guarantees him, to the police officer no less than that to which honest law enforcement is entitled, and, to the courts, that judicial integrity so necessary in the true administration of justice.

■ DISSENT

(Harlan, J.) I would not impose upon the States this federal exclusionary remedy. The reasons given by the majority for suddenly turning its back on *Wolf* seem to me notably unconvincing. Our concern here should not be with the desirability of the *Wolf* rule, but only with the question whether the States are Constitutionally free to follow it or not as they may themselves determine. The preservation of a proper balance between state and federal responsibility in the administration of criminal justice demands patience on the part of those who might like to see things move faster among the States in this respect. Problems of criminal law enforcement vary widely from state to state. The States should be allowed to use what works best for them. I do not believe that the Fourteenth Amendment empowers this Court to mould state remedies effectuating the right to freedom from "arbitrary intrusion by the police" to suit its own notions of how things should be done. The majority also maintains that its ruling is supported by the established doctrine that the admission into evidence of a coerced confession renders a state conviction invalid. This is so, they say, because the doctrine is ample precedent that the manner in which evidence is obtained, and not just its relevance, is constitutionally significant to the fairness of a trial. I believe this analogy to be false. The "coerced confession" rule is not a rule that any illegally obtained statements may not be used in evidence. I would suppose that a statement obtained during an illegal detention is as much unlawfully seized evidence, illegally obtained, but we have consistently refused to reverse state court convictions resting on the use of such statements. What is crucial in the decision to exclude coerced statements is that the trial defense of an accused should not be rendered an empty formality by illegally coerced statements, for then a "prisoner" has been made an instrument of his own conviction. This is a procedural right and its violation occurs at the time the illegally obtained statement is admitted at trial. The rationale behind this right is to safeguard the giving of testimony whether by an accused or any other witness. This is different than the rationale behind the rule the Court extends today—the deterrence of unlawful police practices. In sum, I think the coerced confession analogy works strongly against what the Court does today.

Analysis:

One of the points Justice Harlan tries to make in his dissent is that the Court's decision violates one of the fundamental tenets of federalism: the ability of the states to act as laboratories for experimentation in the application of different ideas and processes. He is right in implying that this is an important quality of our federalist system. He is wrong, however, in his assertion that the Court's decision denies this value of federalism. As with any form of experimentation, when one alternative is found to have failed and there are better alternatives available, there should be no hesitation in adopting the viable alternative. The alternatives outlined in *Wolf*—civil trespass suits and criminal prosecution of police—have turned out to be no alternatives at all. The Court gave these alternatives a chance to work in *Wolf*. Federalism was given a chance. It failed and now the working alternative is given uniform application. *Mapp* is no more than judicial recognition of the State's failure to properly enforce the Fourth Amendment through means other than an exclusionary rule.

■ CASE VOCABULARY

EXCLUSIONARY RULE: The general rule in criminal procedure that evidence obtained in violation of the Fourth Amendment may not be used against the individual whose rights were violated in obtaining the evidence.

United States v. Leon

(People) v. *(Drug Conspirator)*
468 U.S. 897, 104 S.Ct. 3405 (1984)

EVIDENCE OBTAINED BY AN OFFICER IN GOOD-FAITH BUT MISTAKEN BELIEF THAT A WARRANT IS BASED ON SUFFICIENT PROBABLE CAUSE WILL NOT BE EXCLUDED

■ **INSTANT FACTS** Police conducted a search using a warrant they believed in good-faith to be based on sufficient probable cause, but which was later found to be lacking in that regard.

■ **BLACK LETTER RULE** So long as the police have a good-faith belief that a warrant has been properly issued by a magistrate and based on sufficient probable cause, evidence obtained pursuant to the warrant is admissible.

■ PROCEDURAL BASIS

Certification to the U.S. Supreme Court after the defendant's suppression motion was granted by the District Court and affirmed by the Circuit Court of Appeals.

■ FACTS

Based on information from an informant and other investigation, a police officer obtained a facially valid search warrant. The search pursuant to the warrant turned up large quantities of drugs and other evidence that the Government proffered against several alleged coconspirators, including Leon (D). Leon (D), along with the other defendants, filed suppression motions. The District Court granted the motions in part because it concluded the warrant affidavit was insufficient to establish probable cause. In response to the Government's request, the court made clear that the officer had acted in good-faith reliance on the validity of the warrant, but declined to hold the Fourth Amendment exclusionary rule inapplicable to evidence seized in such a situation where there is good-faith reliance.

■ ISSUE

Does the exclusionary rule apply to evidence seized by police who have acted in reasonable, good-faith reliance on the facial validity of a search warrant?

■ DECISION AND RATIONALE

(White, J.) No. The question presented her is whether the Fourth Amendment exclusionary rule should be modified so as not to bar the admission of evidence seized in reasonable, good-faith reliance on a search warrant that is subsequently held to be defective. We have concluded that it should and, accordingly, reverse the judgment of the Court of Appeals. The Fourth Amendment has never been construed to proscribe the introduction of illegally seized evidence in all proceedings or against all persons. Thus, the use of fruits of a past unlawful search or seizure works no new Fourth Amendment wrong. The rule thus operates as a judicially created remedy designed to safeguard Fourth Amendment rights generally through its deterrent effect, rather than a personal constitutional right of the party aggrieved. The question before us can only be resolved by weighing the costs and benefits of preventing the use in the prosecution's case-in-chief of inherently trustworthy tangible evidence obtained in reliance on a facially valid search warrant that is later found to be defective. The substantial costs of the exclusionary rule for the vindication of Fourth Amendment rights have long been a source of concern. Particularly when law enforcement officers have acted in objective good-faith, the magnitude of the benefit conferred on defendants offends basic concepts of the criminal justice system. As yet we have not recognized any form of good-faith exception to the rule. But the balancing approach that has evolved during our years of experience with the rule provides strong support for the modification presently urged upon us. We have expressed a strong preference for warrants and declared that "in a doubtful or marginal case a search under a warrant may be sustainable where without one it would fail." Moreover, we recognize that reasonable minds may differ on whether an affidavit has established probable cause or not. We have thus concluded that the preference for warrants is most appropriately effectuated by allowing the magistrate's determination great deference. First, the exclusionary rule is designed to deter police misconduct rather than to punish the errors of judges. Second, there is no evidence that judges and magistrates are inclined to ignore or subvert the Fourth Amendment or that lawlessness among these actors requires application of the extreme sanction of exclusion. Third, and most important, we discern no basis for believing that exclusion of evidence seized pursuant to a warrant will have a significant deterrent effect on the issuing judge or magistrate simply because they are not part of the law enforcement team. They are neutral judicial officers with no stake in the outcome of particular prosecutions. If exclusion of evidence obtained pursuant to a subsequently invalidated warrant is to have any deterrent effect, therefore, it must alter the behavior of the police. We have frequently questioned whether the exclusionary rule can really have any deterrent effect when the offending officers acted with an objectively reasonable belief that their conduct did not violate the Fourth Amendment. But even assuming that it does deter some police misconduct and provide incentive for the profession as a whole to conduct itself in accord with the Fourth Amendment, it cannot be expected, and should not be applied, to deter objectively reasonable law enforcement activity. This is especially true when the officer has obtained a warrant and acted within its scope. In most such cases, there is no police illegality and thus nothing to deter. Also, ordinarily, an officer cannot be expected to question the magistrate's probable cause determination or his judgment that the form of the warrant is technically sufficient. Penalizing the officer for the magistrate's error, rather than his own, cannot logically contribute to the deterrence of Fourth Amendment violations. We must point out, however, that suppression will remain an appropriate remedy where the issuing magistrate has been misled by the affiant, has wholly abandoned his judicial role, acts as a "rubber stamp," or there are other discrepancies with the process. When the principles we have enumerated today are applied to the facts of this case, it is apparent the judgment from below must be reversed. The officer's warrant application was clearly supported by much more than a "bare bones" affidavit. When such is the case, an officer's reliance on the magistrate's determination of probable cause will be objectively reasonable, and application of the extreme sanction of exclusion is inappropriate. Reversed.

■ CONCURRENCE

(Blackmun, J.) I write separately to underscore what I regard as the unavoidably provisional nature of today's decision. If it should emerge from experience that, contrary to our expectations, the good-faith exception to the exclusionary rule results in a material change in police compliance with the Fourth Amendment, we shall have to reconsider what we have undertaken here.

■ DISSENT

(Brennan, J.) The majority supports its decision by referring to the exclusionary rule as a "judicially created remedy designed to safeguard Fourth Amendment rights generally through its deterrent effect, rather than a personal constitutional right." This view relegates the judiciary to the periphery. It appears plausible because the Fourth Amendment makes no express provision for the exclusionary rule. A short answer to this claim, however, is that many of the Constitution's most vital imperatives are stated in general terms and the task of giving them meaning falls to the judiciary. A more direct answer is that the Amendment, like other provisions of the Bill of Rights, restrains the power of the government as a whole. The judiciary is responsible, no less than the executive, for ensuring that constitutional rights are respected. The admission of illegally seized evidence implicates the same constitutional concerns as the initial seizure of that evidence. So that by admitting such evidence, the judiciary becomes a part of what is in fact a single governmental action prohibited by the terms of the Amendment. Because the evidence-gathering role of the police is directly linked to the evidence-admitting function of the courts, a person's Fourth Amendment rights may be undermined as completely by one as the other. Because of the high "cost" of excluding evidence and the effect the

Amendment has in forcing law enforcement to follow certain procedures, some criminals will go free. But not, as Justice Cardozo has said, "because the constable has blundered," but rather because compliance makes it more difficult to catch criminals. Understood in this way, the Amendment directly contemplates that some reliable evidence will be lost; therefore, it is not the exclusionary rule, but the Amendment itself that has imposed this cost. Even if I were to accept the Court's general approach to the exclusionary rule, I could not agree with today's result. The deterrence rationale has proven to be a very powerful tool for limiting the scope of the rule. The key to the Court's conclusion is that the deterrent effect operates only on police who, when deciding to go forward with a search, know it will violate the Amendment. Such logic captures only one small element of the deterrent purpose of the rule. The Court overlooks the fact that the deterrence rationale is not designed to "punish" the police for failing to obey the commands of the Fourth Amendment. Instead, the chief deterrent function of the rule is to promote institutional compliance on the part of law enforcement agencies generally. So even when an officer in one case has acted with a reasonable good-faith belief the application of the rule can still have a considerable long-term deterrent effect. If evidence is consistently excluded in such situations, police departments will surely instruct their officers to pay greater attention when applying for and executing warrants. A chief consequence f this decision will be to convey the message to magistrates that their warrant issuing decisions are now insulated from subsequent judicial review. And the police will now know that so long as the issuance of a warrant is not "entirely unreasonable," their conduct pursuant to that warrant will be protected from further judicial review. This is especially true under the relaxed standards for warrant probable cause announced last term in *Illinois v. Gates.* The full impact of today's decision will only be known when the Court attempts to extend this rule to situations where police have conducted a warrantless search solely on the basis of their own judgment on probable cause and exigent circumstances. I will not be surprised if my colleagues once again decide that we simply cannot afford to protect Fourth Amendment rights.

■ DISSENT

(Stevens, J.) [Omitted.]

Analysis:

The *Leon* decision represents one fork in a two fork road the Court decided to travel down when it first announced the exclusionary rule. The rule has long been held to be a way of deterring police misconduct by neutralizing the fruits of that misconduct. However, the Court did not include judicial misconduct in the rationale behind the rule. Judges and magistrates suffer from the same character flaws and weaknesses as police officers do. They want their cities and towns to be free from crime too. As is the case with police officers, judges sometimes let their personal feelings enter into the equation when conducting their official duties, like determining probable cause in a warrant application. The Court's decision ignores this by suggesting that the exclusionary rule is not needed to deter judicial misconduct. Why? Because "Judges and magistrates are not adjuncts to the law enforcement team; as neutral judicial officers, they have no stake in the outcome of particular criminal prosecutions, and, therefore, imposition of the exclusionary sanction is not necessary to inform judicial officers of their errors. This assertion is correct under the Court's ruling in *Illinois v. Gates* [search warrant based on informant's tip is proper if the totality of the circumstances in the application indicates a fair probability that evidence will be found], because judicial decisions on probable cause will rarely be scrutinized.

■ CASE VOCABULARY

PROFFER: To submit something, especially evidence, to the court. Evidence is generally proffered to the court for acceptance into the record.

Katz v. United States

(*Gambler*) v. (*Federal Government*)
389 U.S. 347, 88 S.Ct. 507 (1967)

LANDMARK CASE ESTABLISHES THE "REASONABLE EXPECTATION OF PRIVACY" TEST FOR FOURTH AMENDMENT SEARCHES AND SEIZURES

■ **INSTANT FACTS** FBI agents (P) bugged a public telephone booth and recorded Katz's (D) end of telephone conversations in that booth.

■ **BLACK LETTER RULE** Government Investigative activity that intrudes upon a justifiable expectation of privacy constitutes a search within the meaning of the Fourth Amendment.

■ PROCEDURAL BASIS

Certiorari granted after conviction affirmed by Court of Appeals.

■ FACTS

FBI agents (P) attached an electronic listening device to the outside of a public telephone booth that Katz (D) used to place what he assumed to be private calls. Over Katz's (D) objection, the trial court permitted the Government (P) to introduce evidence of Katz's (D) end of the telephone conversations, and Katz (D) was convicted of transmitting wagering information by telephone.

■ ISSUE

Does government investigative activity constitute a search within the meaning of the Fourth Amendment where it intrudes upon a justifiable expectation of privacy?

■ DECISION AND RATIONALE

(Stewart) Yes. We decline to adopt Katz's (D) formulation of the issues, specifically, whether a public telephone booth is a constitutionally protected area, and whether physical penetration of a constitutionally protected area is necessary for government conduct to constitute a search within the Fourth Amendment. The Fourth Amendment is not simply a general "right to privacy." The Amendment does provide some, though not absolute, protection for individual privacy against certain kinds of government intrusion, but it also provides other protections that have nothing to do with privacy. Moreover, the phrase "constitutionally protected area" sometimes deflects attention from the true problem. The Fourth Amendment protects people, not places. What a person knowingly exposes to the public, even in his own home, is not protected by the Fourth Amendment, but what he seeks to preserve as private, even in a public area, may be. The Government (P) stresses that Katz (D) was visible in the telephone booth because it was made partly of glass. However, what Katz (D) sought to exclude was not an intruding eye, but an intruding ear. A person who steps into a telephone booth, shuts the door, and pays a toll to place a call has the right to assume that the words he then utters will not be broadcast to the world. The Government (P) further argues that the Fourth Amendment should not apply in this case because its surveillance did not involve physical penetration of the telephone booth. When we interpreted the Fourth Amendment to limit only searches and seizures of tangible property, the absence of such physical penetration did foreclose Fourth Amendment protection. *Olmstead v. United States* [surveillance without trespass or seizure was outside the Fourth Amendment.] However, property interests no longer control our Fourth Amendment Analysis:. *Silverman v. United States* [Fourth Amendment governs recorded oral statements overheard without any technical trespass.] The "trespass doctrine" of *Olmstead* is overruled. The absence of physical penetration into the telephone booth is constitutionally insignificant. The Government's (P) electronic surveillance and recording of Katz's (D) words violated the privacy upon which Katz (D) justifiably relied while using the telephone booth and therefore constituted a "search and seizure" within the meaning of the Fourth Amendment. As to whether the search in this case was conducted according to constitutional standards, we find that a magistrate could have authorized this very limited surveillance if properly notified. However, because there was no presentation to or authorization by a magistrate prior to this search, it cannot withstand constitutional scrutiny. Judgment reversed.

■ CONCURRENCE

(Harlan) I read the Court's opinion to hold only that an enclosed telephone booth is an area where, like a home, and unlike a field, a person has a constitutionally protected reasonable expectation of privacy, and that electronic as well as physical intrusion into such a private place may violate the Fourth Amendment. While the Fourth Amendment "protects people, not places," the determination of what protection is afforded to those people generally requires reference to a "place." There is a twofold requirement for Fourth Amendment protection: first, that a person have exhibited an actual, subjective expectation of privacy, and, second, that this expectation be one that society is prepared to recognize as "reasonable." Thus, a home is generally "protected" because it is a place where a person can expect privacy, except for what is in "plain view," but conversations in the open are not protected because an expectation of privacy there would be unreasonable. In this case, the critical fact is not that the telephone booth is accessible to the public generally, but that when the booth is in use it is a place where society would recognize the occupant's expectations of privacy as reasonable.

■ DISSENT

(Black) I do not believe the words of the Fourth Amendment have the meaning given them by the Court. The first clause protects "persons, houses, papers and effects against unreasonable searches and seizures . . . ." These words connote the idea of tangible things capable of being searched, seized, or both. The second clause, which requires warrants to "particularly describ[e] the place to be searched, and the persons or things to be seized," further indicates the Framers' intent to limit the Amendment's protection to tangible things. A conversation is not tangible and, under the normally accepted meanings of the words, can neither be searched nor seized. The second clause not only refers to something tangible so that it can be seized, but also to something in existence so that it can be described. A future conversation is nonexistent until it takes place. The Framers were certainly aware of the practice of eavesdropping, and would have used appropriate language to prohibit or restrict the use of evidence obtained by this method if they desired to do so.

Analysis:

This landmark case redefined the scope of the Fourth Amendment. Before *Katz*, the Court required a physical intrusion into a "constitutionally protected area" before it would apply the Fourth Amendment. *Katz* replaced this with the two-pronged "reasonable expectation of privacy" test, which is found not in the majority opinion, but in Justice Harlan's concurring opinion. The subjective element of this test was clearly articulated by Justice Harlan as the "actual (subjective) expectation of privacy," but was also included in the Court's opinion as "privacy upon which [Katz (D)] . . . relied." The problem with the subjective element is that the police can affect subjective expectations simply by announcing their intentions. Justice Harlan later wrote that *Katz* must transcend subjective expectations because our expectations and the risks we assume reflect the laws and rules of society. Justice Harlan's second requirement, that the expectation of privacy be reasonable, fleshed out the Court's requirement that the reliance upon privacy be "justifiable." However, reasonableness, where it is based only on the probability of discovery, is insufficient. People who conduct criminal activity at night in a remote area of Central Park might be reasonable in expecting privacy insofar as the probability of discovery would be low, but if they are nonetheless discovered by police, their activity would not be protected by the Fourth Amendment. A justifiable expectation of privacy, then, must include more than reasonableness. As

Justice Harlan later suggested, it must also include a balancing of the value of individual security from intrusion against the value of effective law enforcement.

■ CASE VOCABULARY

PLAIN VIEW: The rule that if government agents, while acting lawfully, plainly see something which the agents have probable cause to believe is incriminating, the agents may search, seize and use it as evidence of a crime even without a search warrant.

REASONABLE EXPECTATION OF PRIVACY TEST: In order for the conduct of a government agent to constitute a search or seizure under the Fourth Amendment, there must be a manifest subjective expectation of privacy in the area of the search or the object seized, and this expectation must be one that society is willing to recognize as legitimate.

SEARCH: An examination of a person's property or body by a government agent, usually to discover a weapon or evidence of a crime, that invades the person's reasonable expectation of privacy.

SEIZURE: Some meaningful interference with a person's possessory interests in property by a government agent, usually because it will be needed as evidence of a crime.

Kyllo v. United States

(*Marijuana Grower*) v. (*Federal Agents*)

533 U.S. 27, 121 S.Ct. 2038, 150 L.Ed.2d 94 (2001)

PRIVACY IN THE HOME IS PROTECTED FROM ADVANCING TECHNOLOGY

■ **INSTANT FACTS** Without a warrant, federal agents (P) used a thermal imaging device to determine whether Kyllo's (D) home was emitting enough relative heat to indicate a marijuana grow.

■ **BLACK LETTER RULE** The Government (P) conducts a search when it uses sense-enhancing technology that is not in general public use to obtain information about the interior of a home that it could not otherwise obtain without physical intrusion into the home.

■ PROCEDURAL BASIS

Certiorari granted after appellate court affirmed the denial of motion to suppress evidence.

■ FACTS

Federal agents (P) suspected Kyllo (D) was growing marijuana in his home. Since this usually requires high-intensity heat lamps, they used a thermal imager to determine whether sufficient heat was emanating from Kyllo's (D) home to indicate his use of such lamps. Thermal imagers detect infrared radiation, which is not visible to the naked eye, and converts it into heat images, showing their relative warmth. The agents (P) scanned the triplex Kyllo (D) lived in and found that Kyllo's (D) garage was warmer than the rest of his home and the neighboring homes. Based on informants' tips, utility bills, and the thermal imaging, the agents (P) obtained a warrant, searched Kyllo's (D) home, and found a marijuana growing operation of more than 100 plants.

■ ISSUE

Does the Government (P) conduct a search when it uses sense-enhancing technology that is not in general public use to obtain information about the interior of a home that it could not otherwise obtain without physical intrusion into the home?

■ DECISION AND RATIONALE

(Scalia) Yes. The *Katz v. United States* [bugged phone booth case] test for whether Government (P) activity constitutes a search is whether the individual has an expectation of privacy that society recognizes as reasonable. Technology has expanded the scope of activity the Government (P) can use to obtain information without conducting a Fourth Amendment search. For example, airplanes now enable the Government (P) to observe uncovered portions of a house and its curtilage without conducting a "search" because this technology makes these areas open to public view. Here, we decide not how much the Government (P) may use technology to observe areas open to public view, but how much it may use technology to shrink the realm of guaranteed privacy. The expectation of privacy in the interior of a home is deeply rooted in the common law. Obtaining information about the interior of a home by using sense-enhancing technology, where the information would not otherwise be obtainable without a physical intrusion into the home, constitutes a search, at least where the technology is not in general public use. The information the thermal imager provided was therefore the product of a search. The Government (P) argues that the thermal imaging was proper because it detected only heat radiating from the external surface of the house. Similarly, the dissent argues that there is a fundamental difference between "off-the-wall" observations and "through-the-wall-surveillance." However, we rejected such arguments in *Katz*, where the eavesdropping device picked up only sound waves that reached the exterior of the phone booth. To reverse that approach would leave the homeowner at the mercy of advancing technology. Already, the Government (P) is developing thermal imaging devices that could conduct through-the-wall surveillance using only "off-the-wall" data. The Government (P) also argues that the thermal imaging here was constitutional because it did not detect private activities occurring in private areas. However, Fourth Amendment protection does not depend on the quality of the information the Government (P) obtains. In the home, all details are intimate details. Further, prohibiting only "intimate details" is impractical because this is not necessarily connected to the type of technology the Government (P) uses; we would have to define which details were intimate and which were not; and the Government (P) could not know in advance what information it would obtain from through-the-wall surveillance, and therefore could not know if it would be constitutional. The Fourth Amendment requires not only a firm line at the entrance of a house, but also a clear specification of those methods of surveillance that require a warrant. The thermal imaging here was an unlawful search. It remains for the District Court to determine whether, without the thermal imaging evidence, the Government's (P) search warrant was still supported by probable cause, or whether there was any other basis for admitting the evidence the search warrant produced. Reversed and remanded.

■ DISSENT

(Stevens) This case involves only off-the-wall surveillance to gather information exposed to the general public from outside Kyllo's (D) home. The thermal imager here only measured heat emitted from the exterior surfaces of Kyllo's (D) home, and revealed no details of its interior [except that some of it was unusually warm]. Unlike "through-the-wall" techniques, it was not a physical penetration into the home, and did not obtain information that was not obtainable by observation from outside the curtilage of the house. Neighbors might notice heat coming from the building or snow melting at different rates across the roof. Public officials should not have to avert their senses or equipment from detecting emissions in the public domain such as heat, smoke, odors, gases, or radioactivity. Such emissions could identify hazards to the community, and monitoring them is a reasonable public service. Further, the countervailing privacy interest is trivial. Homeowners who want to keep the amount of heat in their home private can keep their home well-insulated. Despite its attempt to draw a firm, bright line, the Court's new rule is uncertain because it does not apply where the technology is "in general public use." The Court does not define how much use is general public use. Further, the category of "sense-enhancing technology" is too broad. For example, it would apply to mechanical substitutes for dog sniffs that reveal only the presence or absence of narcotics. Since we have held that such dog sniffs do not constitute a search, sense-enhancing equipment that identifies only illegal activity must not be a search either. Under the Court's new rule, however, it would be. The Court's rule is also too narrow because it applies to information about the "interior" of the home. Protection against overly intrusive sense-enhancing equipment should apply not only to homes but also other private places, such as telephone booths and office buildings. The Court reasons that *Katz* compels its rule because there, as here, the surveillance only monitored waves emanating from a private area into the public domain. However, in *Katz* the device was the functional equivalent of intruding into the private area because it gathered information that otherwise would be obtainable only from within the private area. The Court also argues that the permissibility of "through-the-wall surveillance" cannot depend on whether it reveals intimate or nonintimate details. However, the thermal imager here did not and could not perform "through-the-wall surveillance," and could identify no details inside the house, intimate or nonintimate. We should leave it to the legislature to grapple with these issues rather than attempt to devise an all-encompassing rule for the future.

Analysis:

As Justice Stevens recognized in his dissent in *Kyllo*, the threat to privacy grows as technology advances and becomes more readily available. This, in turn, affects how much privacy it is reasonable to expect, and therefore, under *Katz*, how much privacy the Fourth Amendment protects. Noting criticism of this circularity of *Katz*, the Court stepped out of the circle, at least with respect to the interior of a home, to firm up the wall of the Fourth Amendment against intrusion by ever advancing technology. If the reasonableness of the privacy expectation were truly determinative, technology would be able to diminish our protected privacy by making it unreasonable to expect it. In *Kyllo* the Court decided that technology should not have that power, at least not over the privacy of the interior of the home. However, the Court only stepped out of the *Katz* circle with one foot. The Court's rule continues to make the question of whether there is a search dependent upon whether there is a reasonable expectation of privacy because it applies only to sense-enhancing technology that is not in general public use. As new surveillance technology becomes more widely available, the wall the Court firmed up begins to break down again. Thus, despite the Court's concern about technology's power "to shrink the realm of guaranteed privacy," it still has this power if it enters the realm of "general public use."

Andresen v. Maryland

(Attorney) v. *(State Government)*
427 U.S. 463, 96 S.Ct. 2737 (1976)

PERSONAL PAPERS AND DOCUMENTS ARE NOT PROTECTED FROM SEIZURE BY THE FIFTH AMENDMENT PRIVILEGE AGAINST SELF-INCRIMINATION

■ **INSTANT FACTS** Police seized papers pertaining to a fraudulent land sale from Andresen's (D) law office. Andresen (D) challenges the seizure as a Fifth Amendment violation.

■ **BLACK LETTER RULE** The Fifth Amendment does not prohibit government seizure of preexisting documents and other tangible items tending to inculpate the owner of those documents and items.

■ PROCEDURAL BASIS

Not stated.

■ FACTS

State government authorities, pursuant to a valid search warrant, searched Andresen's (D) law office for documents relating to a fraudulent land sale. The documents seized were used by the State of Maryland (State)(P) in obtaining a conviction at trial.

■ ISSUE

Does the Fifth Amendment guarantee against self incrimination prohibit the use in a criminal proceeding of personal documents and other tangible items seized from a defendant's property?

■ DECISION AND RATIONALE

(Blackmun, J.) No. The Fifth Amendment provides that "[n]o person . . . shall be compelled in any criminal case to be a witness against himself." The historic function of this privilege has been to protect a natural individual from compulsory incrimination through his own testimony or personal records. The records seized here were unquestionably incriminating and contain statements made by Andresen (D). The key question, then, is whether the seizure and subsequent admission into evidence of these records, compelled Andresen (D) to testify against himself in violation of the Fifth Amendment. We have previously stated in *Boyd v. United States*, another Fifth Amendment case, that "[w]e have been unable to perceive that the seizure of a man's private books and papers to be used in evidence against him is substantially different from compelling him to be a witness against himself." The continued validity of this statement, and others like it, has been discredited in later opinions. For instance, we've held that the compelled disclosure by an attorney of his client's tax records does not 'compel' the client to be a witness against himself. Similarly, in this case, Andresen (D) was not asked to say or to do anything. The records seized contained statements that Andresen (D) had voluntarily committed to writing. The search for and seizure of these records was conducted by law enforcement. Andresen (D) was not compelled to produce them. Finally, these records were authenticated at trial, not by Andresen (D), but by a handwriting expert. Any compulsion of Andresen (D) to speak was not present. Andresen (D) was therefore not compelled to bear witness against himself in violation of his Fifth Amendment rights.

■ DISSENT

(Brennan, J.) The Court chooses to resolve this matter by relying on the simplistic notion of compulsion. Search and seizure is as rife with elements of compulsion as subpoena. The intrusion occurs under the lawful process of the State. The individual is not free to resist that authority. The door to one's house, for example, is as much the individual's resistance to the intrusion of outsiders as his personal physical efforts to prevent the same. To refuse recognition of that sanctity of that door and, more generally, to confine the dominion of privacy to the mind compels an unconstitutional disclosure by denying to the individual a zone of physical freedom necessary for conducting one's affairs. Today's decision flies in the face of a long history of contrary precedent that teaches us that any forcible and compulsory extortion of a man's own testimony or his private papers to be used as evidence to convict him of crime is within the condemnation of the Fifth Amendment. We should not so lightly abandon this principle.

Analysis:

In *Andresen* the majority takes a strict constructionist approach to the Fifth Amendment. Specifically, it dwells on the word "compelled." Because Andresen (D) was not compelled to create, nor produce, the records that were seized and subsequently used to convict him there is no Fifth Amendment violation. Rather, he voluntarily created the documents for his own personal use. Notice also that the majority says, in dicta, that Andresen (D) was not forced to authenticate the records—a handwriting expert was used instead. Compelling Andresen (D) to do so would most certainly be a Fifth Amendment violation. A close evaluation of Justice Brennan's dissent reveals what seems to be flawed reasoning. His argument that the intrusion into a suspect's home is a violation makes little sense. Under this reasoning the police would never be able to enter and seize evidence from a suspect's home or office no matter how much probable cause there is. Criminals would be free to conduct any and all illegal business in their "individual . . . zone of physical freedom" called a home.

■ CASE VOCABULARY

SUBPOENA DUCES TECUM: An order to appear for a judicial proceeding with a specified item or document.

Spinelli v. United States

(Bookmaker) v. *(Federal Government)*
393 U.S. 410, 89 S.Ct. 584 (1969)

AN INFORMANT'S TIP MUST BE SUFFICIENTLY CORROBORATED TO BE THE BASIS FOR PROBABLE CAUSE

■ **INSTANT FACTS** Based on a sparsely corroborated tip from an informant the FBI obtained a search warrant that led to the discovery of evidence tending to indicate that Spinelli (D) was running an illegal bookmaking operation.

■ **BLACK LETTER RULE** To give rise to probable cause an informant's tip must either contain (1) a sufficient statement of the underlying circumstances from which the informant gained his knowledge, or (2) information supporting the applying officer's belief that the informant is reliable and credible.

■ PROCEDURAL BASIS

Certification to the U.S. Supreme Court after the Circuit Court of Appeals affirmed the Federal District Court's finding of probable cause supporting the issuance of the search warrant that led to the evidence used against Spinelli (D).

■ FACTS

Spinelli (D) was convicted of interstate travel with the intent of conducting illegal gambling activities. Evidence used against Spinelli (D) was seized pursuant to a search warrant issued based on an affidavit containing the following allegations: (1) The FBI had kept track of Spinelli (D) on five days in August 1965 and on four of these days he was seen crossing a bridge from illinois to Missouri; also on four of the days he parked his car at an apartment house; and on one of these days he was seen entering a particular apartment in the house; (2) An FBI check revealed that this apartment had two phones with the numbers Wydown 4–0029 and Wydown 4–0136; (3) that "Spinelli is known to this affiant . . . as a bookmaker, a gambler, and an associate of gamblers;" (4) that the FBI "has been informed by a confidential reliable informant that William Spinelli is operating a handbook and accepting wagers and disseminating wagering information by means of the telephones which have been assigned the numbers Wydown 4–0029 and Wydown 4–0136." Spinelli (D) made the appropriate challenges to the search warrant at every stage of the proceedings, but to no avail.

■ ISSUE

May a search warrant be properly issued without either (1) a sufficient statement of the underlying circumstances from which the informant gained his knowledge, or (2) information supporting the applying officer's belief that the informant is reliable and credible?

■ DECISION AND RATIONALE

(Harlan, J.) No. There is no question that the detailing of the informant's tip is a crucial ingredient in this warrant application and that without it probable cause could not be established. The first two items reflect only innocent activities and data and the assertion that Spinelli (D) is known to the affiant and other law enforcement officers as a gambler and associate of gamblers is but a bald and unilluminating assertion of suspicion that is entitled to no weight. These things the United States (Government)(P) does not deny. The Government (P) charges, however, that the tip lends a suspicious color to the reports of Spinelli's (D) innocent-seeming conduct and that the FBI's surveillance corroborates the informant's tip, entitling it to more weight. But where, as here, the informer's tip is a necessary element in a finding of probable cause, its proper weight must be determined by a more precise Analysis: than the "totality of the circumstances" approach applied by the Court of Appeals. The first step is to apply the *Aguilar* standard in assessing the tip's probative value. If the tip is found inadequate the other allegations that corroborate the information contained in the hearsay report should be considered by, once again, using the *Aguilar* standard. A magistrate must ask: Can it fairly be said that the tip, even when certain parts of it have been corroborated by independent sources, is as trustworthy as a tip which would pass *Aguilar*'s tests without independent corroboration? Applying these principles we first consider the weight given the informant's tip independent from the rest of the affidavit. It is clearly inadequate. The affiant swore his informant was "reliable," but offered the magistrate no reason for this conclusion. Nor has *Aguilar*'s other test been satisfied. The tip does not have a sufficient statement of the underlying circumstances from which the informer concluded that Spinelli (D) was running a bookmaking operation. There is no statement of how the FBI's source received this information. Also, there is nothing indicating why the informant believed his sources to be reliable. Without a statement detailing the manner in which the information was gathered, it is very important that the tip describe the accused's criminal activity in sufficient detail so the magistrate may know that he is relying on more than a casual rumor or an accusation based on the accused's general reputation. The details provided by the informant in *Draper v. United States* provides a good benchmark. There the informant did not provide information on how he obtained his information, but did provide details of how Draper had gone to Chicago and when, when he would return and how, what he would be carrying, the clothes he would be wearing, and so on. A magistrate confronted with such information could reasonably infer that the informant had gained his information in a reliable manner. This inference cannot be made here. Nor are the doubts *Aguilar* raises as to the report's reliability adequately resolved by a consideration of the allegations detailing the FBI's independent investigation. At most these allegation indicated that Spinelli (D) could have used phones specified by the informant for some purpose. This does not support the inference that the informant is reliable. In *Draper* the independent police investigation corroborated numerous details given by the informant—his dress and his arrival time corresponded perfectly to the informant's tip. It was thus apparent the informant was not fabricating his report out of whole cloth. Probable cause thus existed. We conclude here, however, that the informer's tip, even when corroborated to the extent it was, is not sufficient to provide a basis for a finding of probable cause. Reversed.

■ CONCURRENCE

(White, J.) The tension between *Draper* and the *Nathanson-Aguilar* line of cases is evident from the course followed by the majority opinion. If the *Draper* principle is to be given any scope at all shouldn't the fact that the informant's specific information, about the use of two phones with particular numbers, was verified give more credence to the gambling allegation? I would think so, especially since this information was not neutral, but was relevant to proving the gambling allegation. The *Draper* approach would reasonably justify the issuance of a warrant in this case, particularly since the police had some awareness of Spinelli's (D) past activities. Instead the majority confines *Draper* to its own facts. Pending full-scale reconsideration of that case, or of the *Nathanson-Aguilar* cases, I join the opinion of the Court especially since a vote to affirm would produce an equally divided Court.

Analysis:

The basic holding of this case is that there are two routes to take in using an informant's tip as a basis for probable cause. First, if the informant alone, without considering any information from other sources, provides a statement of the underlying circumstances of how he came by his information that leads to a reasonable inference that he is reliable, then the tip can be a proper basis for probable cause. The informant must provide reasons to support his reliability. If the informant does not provide sufficient underlying facts that give rise to a reasonable inference of reliability it is left to law enforcement to corroborate the informant's tip by verifying details of the tip, if there are such details. If the informant has provided such detail—as the informant in *Draper* did—then verification of the details by law enforcement will give rise to a reasonable inference that the informant is reliable and probable cause will follow. Moving on, Justice White criticizes the majority for confining *Draper* to the specific facts of that case. Is the majority guilty? The point the majority makes is simply that in *Draper* the informant provided several pieces of information, whether innocent or not, about the suspect. This information was so detailed and overwhelming that when verified it had to give rise to a reasonable inference that the informant was reliable. The information provided about Spinelli (D), when compared to that provided in *Draper*, falls well short. Justice White's criticism is thus unconvincing.

■ CASE VOCABULARY

AFFIANT: A person who signs an affidavit attesting to its accuracy.

AFFIDAVIT: A declaration of facts sworn to as true by the affiant before one qualified to administer oaths.

Illinois v. Gates

(*State Government*) v. (*Marijuana Distributor*)

462 U.S. 213, 103 S.Ct. 2317 (1983)

TWO-PRONG TEST FOR DETERMING PROBABLE CAUSE BASED ON INFORMANT'S TIP IS ABANDONED IN FAVOR OF A LESS TECHNICAL TOTALITY OF THE CIRCUMSTANCES TEST

■ **INSTANT FACTS** Based on a corroborated informant's tip regarding Gates' (D) travel plans police obtained a search warrant and discovered about 350 pounds of marijuana in Gates' (D) automobile, which the trial court excluded as fruits of an illegal search.

■ **BLACK LETTER RULE** A search warrant based on an informant's tip may be properly issued if, given the totality of the circumstances set forth in the warrant application, including the veracity and basis of knowledge of the informant and any corroboration of the informant's information, there is a fair probability that contraband or evidence will be found in the place to be searched.

■ PROCEDURAL BASIS

Certification to the U.S. Supreme Court after the State Supreme Court affirmed the decision of the State Appeals Court affirming the ruling of the trial court excluding the evidence under the Fourth Amendment.

■ FACTS

In May of 1978, the Bloomingdale, illinois police department received by mail an anonymous handwritten letter tipping off some illegal drug dealing activity. The letter said that Sue and Lance Gates (Gates) (D), a couple in the town, made their living exclusively off illegal drug distribution. It said where they lived and that they made most of their buys in Florida. It went on to state the usual routine of the Gates couple (D) is that Sue would drive their car to Florida where she leaves it to be loaded with drugs, and then Lance would fly down a couple days later and drive it back. The letter then stated that on May 3, Sue would be driving down to Florida and a few days later Lance would fly down to pick up the car; at the time it is driven back it has over $100,000 worth of drugs and that presently the Gates' (D) have over $100,000 worth of drugs in their basement. Mader, the detective assigned to the case, verified that a driver's license was issued to Lance Gates (D), who resided in Bloomingdale. Also learned from an airport police officer was that Lance Gates (D) had a reservation to fly to West Palm Beach, Florida on May 5. Mader then had the Drug Enforcement Agency (DEA) monitor the flight. The DEA reported that Lance Gates (D) did indeed board the flight and arrive in Florida where he went to the Holiday Inn. They also reported that Lance Gates (D) went to a room registered to Sue Gates (D) and that the next morning Lance Gates (D) and a woman left in a car bearing illinois plates and drove northbound on a highway used to travel to Chicago. In addition, the plate on the car registered to a car owned by Gates (D). Mader signed an affidavit setting forth these facts and, along with the anonymous letter, submitted it to a judge who issued a search warrant for the Gates' (D) residence and car. When the Gates (D) reached their residence their car and house were searched. The search revealed over 350 pounds of marijuana, some weapons and other contraband. The trial court ordered this evidence suppressed because the warrant application was insufficient. This ruling was affirmed by both the illinois Court of Appeals and the State Supreme Court.

■ ISSUE

Is an informant's tip a sufficient basis to issue a search warrant when its predictions are corroborated by independent police work, even though there is nothing to indicate the veracity or reliability of the informant, or the basis of his information?

■ DECISION AND RATIONALE

(Rehnquist, C.J.) Yes. As the Illinois Supreme Court correctly concluded, the informant's anonymous letter, standing alone, was not a sufficient basis for issuing a warrant. It provides nothing from which one might conclude that its author is either honest or its information reliable. It also gives no basis for the informant's predictions. Something more is required. The Illinois Supreme Court applied a two-prong test derived from our decision in *Spinelli v. United States.* This test requires that the informant's tip provide the basis of the informant's knowledge in addition to either facts establishing the veracity of the informant or the reliability of his report. Using this rule, that court held that the veracity prong was not satisfied because there was no basis for concluding the informant was credible; that independent corroboration of the tip might never satisfy the veracity requirement, and, in any event, could not do so when, as here, only "innocent" details are corroborated. It was also concluded that the letter provided no basis for inferring that it was truthful and accurate. Thus, it was ruled that there was no showing of probable cause. We agree that an informant's veracity, reliability and basis of knowledge are all highly relevant, but we do not agree that these considerations are to be rigidly applied in a mechanical way. Rather, they should be understood as closely intertwine?? issues to help illuminate the common sense, practical question of whether there is probable cause. This totality of the circumstances approach is far more consistent with our prior treatment of the probable cause inquiry with respect to an informant's tip, and recognizes that this inquiry is a fluid concept that cannot be readily reduced to a neat set of legal rules. Moreover, the "two pronged test" directs Analysis: into two largely independent channels—veracity or reliability and basis of knowledge. These elements should not be accorded such independent status. Instead, they are better understood as relevant considerations in the totality of the circumstances Analysis: that we've traditionally applied: a deficiency in one can be made up for by a strong showing in the other, or some other indicia of reliability. This approach is more appropriate when one considers the often informal and hurried manner in which warrant applications must be considered. Under such circumstances, the built-in subtleties of the "two-pronged test" are particularly unlikely to assist magistrates in determining probable cause. If such a mechanically demanding test were to be relied upon, police may very well resort to warrantless searches, with the hope of relying on consent or some other exception to the warrant clause that might develop at the time of the search. Finally, the direction taken by decisions following *Spinelli* poorly serves the most basic function of government—to provide for the security of the individual and his property—because it cannot avoid seriously impeding the task of law enforcement in that the value of anonymous tips would be severely reduced. For the foregoing reasons, we conclude that it is wiser to abandon the "two-pronged test" established by our decision in *Spinelli* and other cases like it. In its place we reaffirm the totality of the circumstances Analysis: that has traditionally informed probable cause determinations. Thus the task of the issuing magistrate is simply to make a practical, common-sense decision whether, given all of the circumstances set forth in the affidavit, including the "veracity" and "basis of knowledge" of the persons supplying the hearsay information, there is a fair probability that evidence of a crime will be found in a particular place. Such a requirement is not satisfied by mere conclusory statements by the affiant that he believes the informant to be truthful and reliable. The magistrate's determination cannot be a simple ratification of the bare conclusions of others. While Justice Brennan's dissent suggests that our holding somehow downgrades the role of the neutral magistrate, we believe it is to the contrary. Nothing in our opinion lessens the authority of the magistrate to draw such reasonable inferences as he will from material supplied by warrant applicants. Also, under our ruling, magistrates remain free to exact such assurances as they deem necessary, as well as those required by this opinion, in making probable cause inquiries. We also refute the assertion that our use of words such as "practical," "nontechnical" and "common sense" are but code words for an overly permissive attitude towards police practices in derogation of the Fourth Amendment. The task of this Court, as with other courts, is simply to hold the balance of private citizens' rights true with the valid interests of government in law enforcement. Our ruling today does this. Our decisions applying the totality of the circumstances Analysis: outlined above have consistently recognized the value of independent corroboration of details of an informant's tip. The decision in *Draper v. United States* is the classic case of independent police investigation corroborating a tip sufficiently to provide probable cause. The showing of probable cause in the present case was fully as compelling as that in *Draper.* Even standing alone, the facts ascertained by Mader and the DEA at least suggested the Gates (D) were involved in drug trafficking. Florida is a well-known source of narcotics and other illegal drugs. Lance Gates' (D) flight to Palm Beach, his brief overnight stay, and apparent immediate return north in the family car, conveniently awaiting him in Palm Beach, is as suggestive of a prearranged drug run, as it is of an ordinary vacation trip. This, in addition to the anonymous letter, excruciatingly corroborated by the police, leads quite logically to an inference that the Gates (D) were smuggling drugs. As we stated in *Spinelli,* "Because an informant is right about some things, he is more probably right about other facts." While the facts of this case may not be sufficient to satisfy the "reliability" or "veracity" prongs of *Spinelli*, we think it suffices for the practical, commonsense judgment called for in making a probable cause determination. The judgment of the Illinois Supreme Court therefore must be reversed.

■ CONCURRENCE

(White, J.) Although I agree that the warrant should be upheld, I reach this conclusion in accordance with the *Aguilar-Spinelli* framework. If a tip fails under either of the two *Aguilar-Spinelli* prongs, probable cause may yet be established by independent police investigatory work that corroborates the tip to such an extent that it supports "both the inference that the informer was generally trustworthy and that he made his charge on the basis of information obtained in a reliable way." The lower court's characterization of the Gates' (D) activity here as totally "innocent" is dubious. In fact, it was quite suspicious. The flight to Palm Beach, an area well known to be a source of narcotics, the brief overnight stay in the motel, and apparent immediate return North, suggest a pattern that trained law-enforcement officers have recognized as indicative of illicit drug-dealing activity. The critical issue is not whether the activities observed by the officers are innocent or suspicious. Instead, the proper focus should be on whether the actions of the suspects, whatever their nature, give rise to an inference that the informant is credible and that he obtained his information in a reliable manner. As in *Draper*, the police investigation in the present case satisfactorily demonstrated that the informant's tip was as trustworthy as one that would alone satisfy the *Aguilar* tests. I therefore conclude that the judgment of the Illinois Supreme Court must be reversed. This is true even in reliance of the *Aguilar* standard, and therefore I would not abandon *Aguilar-Spinelli* and their progeny. Instead, I would at least attempt to provide more precise guidance by clarifying *Aguilar-Spinelli* and the relationship of those cases with *Draper* before totally abdicating our responsibility in this area.

■ DISSENT

(Brennan, J.) Although I join Justice Steven's dissent, I write separately to dissent from the Court's unjustified and ill-advised rejection of the two-prong test for evaluating the validity of a warrant based on hearsay announced in *Aguilar v. Texas*, and refined in *Spinelli v. United States.* Properly understood, *Spinelli* stands for the proposition that corroboration of certain details in a tip may be sufficient to satisfy the veracity, but not the basis of knowledge, prong of *Aguilar.* *Spinelli* also suggests that in some limited circumstances considerable detail in an informant's tip may be adequate to satisfy the basis of knowledge prong of *Aguilar.* The Court's opinion seems to suggest that corroboration can satisfy both the basis of knowledge and veracity prongs. This is not the case and this is why the judgment below should be affirmed. In rejecting the *Aguilar-Spinelli* standards, the Court relies on the "practical, nontechnical" nature of probable cause. But one can concede that probable cause is a "practical, nontechnical" concept without betraying the values that *Aguilar* and *Spinelli* reflect. Those two cases preserve the role of magistrates as independent arbiters of probable cause, insure greater accuracy in probable cause determinations, and advance the substantive value of precluding findings of probable cause, and attendant intrusions, based on anything less than information from an honest or credible person who has acquired his information in a reliable way. The Court's additional assertion that abandonment of *Aguilar-Spinelli* is necessary because non-lawyers frequently serve as magistrates is flawed. To the contrary, those standards help to structure probable cause inquiries and, properly interpreted, may actually help non-lawyers make the determination. Furthermore, words like "practical," "nontechnical," and "commonsense," as used in the Court's opinion, are but code words for an overly permissive attitude towards police practices in derogation of the rights secured by the Fourth Amendment. We all share the Court's concern over the horrors of drug trafficking, but under our

Constitution only measures consistent with the Fourth Amendment may be employed by governments to cure this evil.

■ DISSENT

The informant indicated that Sue Gates (D) drives the car to Florida where she leaves it to be filled with drugs and then flies back after she drops the car off. Yet detective Mader's affidavit reported that she "left the West Palm Beach area driving the Mercury northbound." This discrepancy between the informant's predictions and the facts known to Detective Mader is significant for three reasons. First, the informant had suggested an itinerary that always kept one spouse in Bloomingdale, suggesting the Gates (D) did not want to leave their home unguarded because something valuable was hidden within. Such an inference cannot be drawn when in reality both of the Gates' (D) were in Florida. Second, the discrepancy makes the Gates' (D) activity substantially less unusual than predicted. The true facts show that they were both in Florida at the same time and drove back together, something that is neither unusual, nor probative of criminal activity. Third, the fact the anonymous letter contains a material mistake undermines the reasonableness of relying on it as a basis for making a forcible entry into a private home. Given that the note's predictions were faulty in one significant respect, and were corroborated by nothing except ordinary innocent activity, I must surmise that the Court's evaluation of the warrant's validity has been colored by subsequent events.

Analysis:

In *Gates*, the majority succeeds in watering down the probable cause standard as it applies to anonymous informants. Justice Brennan is correct when he asserts that the language used by the Court will lead to a relaxation of the probable cause requirement. The new "totality of the circumstances" test allows a magistrate to weigh all the facts, and feelings of the applicant, presented in support of the warrant application to decide whether there is a "fair probability" of criminal activity. This standard, by doing away with any real objective basis for conducting probable cause Analysis:, allows a magistrate to issue a warrant on the barest of supporting facts. It supplies no objective benchmark to be applied across the land and will thus lead to warrants being issued on the basis of facts that will run the gamut from extremely weak to very strong; in short, on the whim of the particular magistrate considering the application. The Court asserts that a contrary ruling would lead police to rely on warrantless searches in the hope that consent will be granted or "some other exception to the warrant clause that might develop at the time of the search." It supplies no supporting rationale for this assertion, instead relying on "mere conclusory statements" like the foregoing.

■ CASE VOCABULARY

VERACITY: The character trait of habitually telling the truth.

Maryland v. Pringle

(*Prosecuting Authority*) v. (*Drug Possessor*)

540 U.S. 366, 124 S.Ct. 795, 157 L.Ed.2d 769 (2003)

REASONABLE SUSPICION ESTABLISHES PROBABLE CAUSE

■ **INSTANT FACTS** Pringle (D) was arrested after cocaine was found in the rear seat of a vehicle in which Pringle (D) was riding, albeit in the front.

■ **BLACK LETTER RULE** Probable cause generally requires a reasonably particularized ground for belief of a defendant's guilt.

■ PROCEDURAL BASIS

Certiorari to review a decision of the Court of Appeals of Maryland reversing the defendant's conviction.

■ FACTS

Pringle (D) was the front-seat passenger in a vehicle driven by a friend. Another passenger was in the rear seat. When the vehicle was stopped for speeding, the officer noticed a large roll of money in the glove compartment. The officer searched the vehicle with the driver's consent and found cocaine behind the rear-seat armrest, which was folded up against the back seat of the car. All three men were arrested after none of them claimed ownership of the drugs. At the police station, Pringle (D) confessed to ownership of the drugs and claimed the other occupants were unaware of their existence. At trial, however, Pringle (D) moved to suppress his confession as the fruit of an illegal arrest, arguing that the officer had no probable cause to arrest him. The motion was denied and Pringle (D) was convicted. On appeal, the Court of Appeals of Maryland reversed, finding that the officer had no probable cause to arrest Pringle (D) because there was no indication that Pringle (D) had knowledge and dominion or control over the drugs at the time of arrest.

■ ISSUE

Did the officer have probable cause to arrest the defendant?

■ DECISION AND RATIONALE

(Rehnquist, C.J.) Yes. Probable cause generally requires a reasonably particularized ground for belief of a defendant's guilt. Here, there was no doubt that a crime had been committed. The officer found a large amount of money rolled up in the vehicle's glove compartment and thereafter discovered illegal narcotics concealed in the small vehicle in which the three men were riding. As nobody claimed personal responsibility for the drugs, there was a reasonable inference that any or all of the men had knowledge, dominion, or control of the drugs. The officer had probable cause to arrest Pringle (D) and his confession should not have been suppressed. Reversed and remanded.

Analysis:

Although there was no evidence at the time of arrest that Pringle (D) had actual control over the drugs in the car, the Court held here that probable cause for his arrest existed nonetheless. Fourth Amendment advocates have suggested that the Court's ruling gives law enforcement far too much power to arrest individuals under the mere suspicion of criminal activity. Because it was clear that a crime was committed, Pringle's (D) arrest without an individualized assessment of his involvement in the crime amounted to an arrest by association.

■ CASE VOCABULARY

LAWFUL ARREST: The taking of a person into legal custody either under a valid warrant or on probable cause that the person has committed a crime.

MOTION TO SUPPRESS: A request that the court prohibit the introduction of illegally obtained evidence at a criminal trial.

PROBABLE CAUSE: A reasonable ground to suspect that a person has committed or is committing a crime or that a place contains specific items connected with a crime.

United States v. Watson

(*Federal Government*) v. (*Thief*)
423 U.S. 411, 96 S.Ct. 820 (1976)

WARRANTLESS ARRESTS BASED ON PROBABLE CAUSE DO NOT VIOLATE THE FOURTH AMENDMENT

■ **INSTANT FACTS** A federal postal inspector, acting on a tip from a reliable informant, arrested Watson (D) without a warrant even though the inspector had time to secure a warrant. Watson (D) challenges the warrantless arrest on constitutional grounds.

■ **BLACK LETTER RULE** An officer with probable cause to make a felony arrest is not required, under the Fourth Amendment, to obtain an arrest warrant.

■ PROCEDURAL BASIS

Certification to the U.S. Supreme Court after the Circuit Court of Appeals held the arrest unconstitutional.

■ FACTS

Khoury, a reliable informant, told a federal postal inspector that Watson (D) was dealing in stolen credit cards and would be furnishing more credit cards to Khoury at their next meeting a few days later. At the next meeting Khoury signaled to the postal inspector that Watson had the stolen cards. The inspector then arrested Watson (D) without a warrant, as he was allowed to do under 18 U.S.C. § 3061 and the applicable postal regulations.

■ ISSUE

Does a warrantless felony arrest based on probable cause, but absent exigent circumstances, violate the Fourth Amendment?

■ DECISION AND RATIONALE

(White, J.) No. Section 3061 represents a judgment by Congress that it is not unreasonable under the Fourth Amendment for postal inspectors to arrest without a warrant provided they have probable cause to do so. Because there is a "strong presumption of constitutionality due to an Act of Congress, especially when it turns on what is 'reasonable'... the Court should be reluctant to decide that a search thus authorized by Congress was unreasonable and that the Act was therefore unconstitutional." Also, there is nothing in the Court's past indicating that the Fourth Amendment requires a warrant to make a valid felony arrest. Indeed, the relevant prior decisions are to the contrary. These cases reflect the old common-law rule that a warrant is not required to make an arrest for a misdemeanor or felony committed in an officer's presence, or a felony not committed in his presence so long as there is a reasonable basis for making the arrest. Furthermore, because this rule has also prevailed in the states it is important to note that in 1792 the Congress invested U.S. Marshals [not Tommy Lee Jones] and their deputies with "the same powers in executing the laws of the United States, as sheriffs and their deputies in their several states have by law, in executing the laws of their respective states." This rule allowing arrests for felonies based on probable cause has survived largely intact. This is the rule Congress has long directed its principal law enforcement officers to follow. Congress has plainly decided against conditioning warrantless arrest power on proof of exigent circumstances. While it may be wise to seek an arrest warrant when practicable to do so, we decline to transform this judicial preference into a constitutional rule when the judgment of the Nation and Congress has for so long been to authorize such warrantless arrests on probable cause. Reversed.

■ CONCURRENCE

(Powell, J.) The Fourth Amendment imposes a warrant requirement, absent exigent circumstances, on all searches and seizures. Today's decision seems therefore to be somewhat of an anomaly. After all, an arrest is a seizure and as an abstract matter an argument can be made that the restrictions upon an arrest should be greater. Logic therefore would seem to dictate that arrests be subject to the warrant requirement at least to the same extent as searches. But logic sometimes must defer to history and experience. The Court's opinion emphasizes the historical sanction accorded warrantless felony arrests. Moreover, a constitutional rule permitting felony arrests only with a warrant or in exigent circumstances could severely hamper effective law enforcement.

■ DISSENT

(Marshall, J.) Watson's (D) warrantless arrest here was perfectly valid. This is because the postal inspector had probable cause to believe an offense was taking place in his presence and that the suspect was at that moment in possession of the evidence, i.e. exigent circumstances existed. However, the substance of the ancient common-law rule provides no support for the far-reaching modern rule that the Court fashions on its model. At common law only the most serious crimes were felonies, and many crimes now classified as felonies were treated as misdemeanors. To make an arrest for any of these crimes at common law, the police officer was required to obtain a warrant, unless the crime was committed in his presence. But because many of these crimes are classified as felonies today, under the Court's holding a warrant is no longer needed to make such arrests, a result in contravention of the common law. Moving on, the Government (P) asserts that a warrant requirement would impose an intolerable burden because of the specious supposition that procurement of an arrest warrant would be necessary as soon as probable cause ripens. There is no requirement that a search warrant be obtained the moment police have probable cause to search. Only present probable cause to search need be shown and a warrant obtained before the search. This same rule should apply to arrest warrants where it makes even more sense. There is certainly less need for prompt procurement of a warrant in the arrest situation. Unlike probable cause to search, probable cause to arrest, once formed, will continue to exist, at least as long as no intervening exculpatory evidence comes to light. Such an approach would obviate most of the difficulties that have been suggested with an arrest warrant rule. A warrant could be obtained once probable cause exists and held without execution until the right time, to allow for the further gathering of evidence and investigation. Where a warrant has not been obtained, the police would still have the ability to arrest under exigent circumstances. The rule would invalidate an arrest only in the obvious situation: where police, with probable cause but without exigent circumstances, set out to arrest a suspect.

Analysis:

The Court states that there is a "strong presumption of constitutionality due to an Act of Congress, especially when it turns on what is reasonable." Do not confuse this approach with "rational basis" review. Under rational basis review the Court simply asks if Congress could have a rational basis for believing in the existence of a certain requirement that vests the Congress with jurisdictional authority. The civil rights cases of the 1960s provide a good example of rational basis review. In many of those cases the Court held that the Congress could have a rational basis for believing that Jim Crow laws hindered the national economy by dissuading minorities from engaging in interstate travel. Once this finding was made, Congress had jurisdiction to take steps to cure the ills that it led to, such as prohibiting segregation in public accommodations. In the instant case the Court is simply deferring to the judgment of the Congress on what is "reasonable." In the context of Fourth Amendment searches and seizures it is the judiciary that is tasked with determining what is reasonable. This is part of the separation of powers, a pillar of our Constitutional government. By deferring to the judgment of Congress on this issue, the Court chips away at this pillar. Moving on, Justice Marshall makes a good point regarding the expansion of felony coverage to include many crimes that were misdemeanors at common law. This has the effect of doing away with the arrest warrant requirement for a great many offenses, resulting in a marginalization of the Fourth Amendment's guarantees.

■ CASE VOCABULARY

EXIGENT CIRCUMSTANCES: Conditions that call for an immediate response, and that may excuse officials from following the usual, mandated procedures.

United States v. Robinson

(*Federal Government*) v. (*Heroin User*)
414 U.S. 218, 94 S.Ct. 467 (1973)

THE SUPREME COURT CREATES A BRIGHT LINE RULE ALLOWING THE SEARCH OF A PERSON INCIDENT TO ARREST

■ **INSTANT FACTS** During a pat-down incident to Robinson's (D) arrest for driving while his license was revoked, the officer (P) removed a crumpled cigarette pack from Robinson's (D) pocket, opened it, and found heroin.

■ **BLACK LETTER RULE** Any lawful custodial arrest justifies a full search of the arrestee's person.

■ PROCEDURAL BASIS

Certiorari granted after Court of Appeals reversed conviction.

■ FACTS

An officer (P) arrested Robinson (D) for driving while his license was revoked. During a routine pat-down incident to that arrest, the officer (P) felt an unidentifiable object in Robinson's (D) pocket, removed it, and found it to be a crumpled cigarette pack. The officer (P) felt objects inside the pack which he knew were not cigarettes, but could not identify. The officer (P) opened the cigarette pack and found and seized 14 capsules of heroin. The District Court admitted this heroin into evidence and Robinson (D) was convicted for its possession and concealment. The Court of Appeals reversed, holding that the heroin was the fruit of an illegal search.

■ ISSUE

Does any lawful custodial arrest justify a full search of the arrestee's person?

■ DECISION AND RATIONALE

(Rehnquist) Yes. A search incident to a lawful arrest is a well settled exception to the Fourth Amendment's warrant requirement. This exception includes two distinct propositions: that officers (P) may search the person of an arrestee on the basis of a lawful arrest, and that officers (P) may search the area within the arrestee's control. While there have been challenges to the second proposition and some changes as to the extent of the area which may be searched, none of the cases addressing this exception have expressed doubt as to an officer's (P) unqualified authority to search the person of an arrestee. Because these cases refer to this authority not simply in terms of an exception, but in terms of an affirmative authority to search, they clearly imply that these searches are reasonable under the Fourth Amendment. In this case the Court of Appeals decided that police (P) may not ordinarily fully search an arrestee, but may only conduct a limited frisk for weapons. The court recognized that *Terry v. Ohio* [a "stop and frisk" is permissible on reasonable suspicion] dealt with a frisk incident to an investigative stop based on less than probable cause to arrest. However, the court felt that the principles of *Terry* should also apply to this probable cause arrest for driving while one's license is revoked because a search of the arrestee could reveal no further evidence of such a crime, and therefore only a search for weapons was justified. In effect, the court decided that the only reason that would support a full search incident to arrest was the possibility of discovery of evidence or fruits. We disagree. In *Terry* we clearly recognized a difference between a search incident to arrest and a protective frisk, and held that different rules governed these two types of searches. Because the reason for the authority to search incident to arrest is as much to disarm the arrestee as it is to preserve evidence, the absence of probable fruits or evidence of a particular crime does not require application of the stricter *Terry* standards rather than those traditionally governing a search incident to arrest. Further, the danger to an officer (P) is far greater from extended exposure to a suspect while he is taken into custody and transported to the police station than from a relatively fleeting investigative stop. This is adequate basis for treating all custodial arrests alike for purposes of search justification. Even more fundamentally, we disagree with the suggestion that an officer's (P) authority to search an arrestee depends upon there being a sufficient probability of finding weapons or evidence on the arrestee's person. A custodial arrest based on probable cause is a reasonable intrusion under the Fourth Amendment. If the arrest is lawful, a search incident to that arrest requires no additional justification. It is the fact of the lawful arrest that establishes the authority to search. We hold that when there is a lawful custodial arrest, a full search of the arrestee is not only an exception to the warrant requirement of the Fourth Amendment, but is also a reasonable search under that Amendment. Because the officer (P) in this case made a lawful custodial arrest of Robinson (D), the search he conducted was permissible. Reversed.

■ DISSENT

(Marshall) The majority's attempt to avoid case-by-case adjudication of Fourth Amendment issues is both misguided in principle and impractical. The powers granted to the police (P) are strong ones and are subject to abuse. While not in this case, in most jurisdictions and for most traffic offenses the police (P) have discretion to decide whether to issue a citation or to effect a full arrest. There is thus the possibility that an officer (P) lacking probable cause to obtain a search warrant will use a traffic arrest as a pretext to conduct a search. The majority fails to recognize that the search in this case did not involve only a search of Robinson's (D) person, but also of effects found on his person. Even if it was reasonable to remove the object in Robinson's (D) pocket, once the officer (P) had the object in his hands, he had no reason to believe it contained a weapon, and even if it did, it was impossible for Robinson (D) to use it. Opening the package, therefore, did not further the protective purpose of the search. The majority suggests, however, that because the arrest itself is a significant intrusion into the privacy of the person, the additional intrusion of examining effects found on the person is not worthy of constitutional protection. We expressly rejected that approach in *Chimel v. California* [limited a search incident to arrest to the arrestee's person and the area within his immediate control]. The Government (P) argues that it is difficult to see what expectation of privacy a person has in the interior of a cigarette pack. Perhaps the result in this case would have been different if Robinson (D) was a businessman and the object searched was his wallet that might contain a razor blade, or if he was a lawyer and the object was a sealed envelope that might contain a razor blade or a pin. We would better serve the purpose of the Fourth Amendment and the legitimate needs of the police (P) by requiring the officer (P), if he has any question about what an object contains, to simply hold on to it until the arrestee is brought to the station.

Analysis:

In this case the Court established a bright line rule governing the search of a person incident to arrest. Under *Robinson's* bright line rule, police may conduct the search of a person incident to arrest as a matter of routine and without particular grounds. Scholars have praised the Court for choosing a bright line rule in this case, finding standardized procedures preferable for forms of police action which, like the search of an arrested person, involve relatively minor invasions of privacy, occur with great frequency in a great variety of circumstances, and usually involve circumstances that do not allow the arresting officer time to sort out different probabilities. Fourth Amendment doctrine, particularly the rules for searches incident to arrest, should provide adequate guidance for officers who must make quick decisions in potentially dangerous situations. Thus, the need for predictability and easy application justify *Robinson's* bright line rule. Like the Court, scholars find the search of a person to be a relatively minor intrusion when the person has already been subjected to the more serious intrusion of arrest.

Chimel v. California

(Burglar) v. *(State)*
395 U.S. 752, 89 S.Ct. 2034 (1969)

THE SUPREME COURT RESTRICTS THE SCOPE OF A SEARCH INCIDENT TO ARREST TO THE ARRESTEE'S "GRAB AREA"

■ **INSTANT FACTS** Based on Chimel's (D) arrest, officers (P) searched his entire home for evidence without a search warrant.

■ **BLACK LETTER RULE** A warrantless search incident to arrest may extend only to the person of the arrestee and the area within his immediate control.

■ PROCEDURAL BASIS

Certiorari granted after state conviction on evidence admitted over objection.

■ FACTS

Police officers (P) arrived at Chimel's (D) home with a warrant for his arrest for the burglary of a coin shop. Chimel's (D) wife let the officers (P) come in and wait a short time until Chimel (D) came home from work. When Chimel (D) arrived, one of the officers (P) arrested him and asked if he could "look around." Chimel (D) objected, but the officers (P) conducted a search anyway, without a search warrant, "on the basis of the lawful arrest." The officers (P) thoroughly searched the entire three-bedroom house and seized numerous coins and medals.

■ ISSUE

Does the arrest of a person in his home justify a warrantless search of the entire premises incident to that arrest?

■ DECISION AND RATIONALE

(Stewart) No. The decisions of this Court on this issue have been far from consistent. The state courts relied upon *United States v. Rabinowitz* [warrantless search incident to arrest may extend to the area in the arrestee's possession or control] to uphold the search of Chimel's (D) entire house as incident to his arrest. It is reasonable for an officer (P) to search the person he is arresting to remove weapons the person might use to resist arrest or to escape. It is also reasonable for an officer (P) to search for and seize any evidence on the arrestee's person to prevent its concealment or destruction. Likewise, it is reasonable for the officer (P) to search the area within the immediate control of the arrestee, meaning the area within which the arrestee might reach to grab a weapon or destructible evidence. However, there is no justification for routinely searching incident to an arrest any room other than that in which the arrest occurs, or for searching closed drawers or concealed areas. We reject the argument that it is reasonable to search a man's house when he is arrested in it. Although the reasonableness of a search depends upon the totality of the facts and circumstances, it must also be based on established Fourth Amendment principles, and not just on a subjective view of whether certain kinds of police (P) conduct are acceptable. The rationale of *Rabinowitz* [upheld search of a single room incident to arrest] and *Harris* [upheld search of a four-room apartment incident to arrest] would also allow the search of Chimel's (D) entire house. Under the Fourth Amendment, there is no point of rational limitation once the search is allowed to go beyond the area from which the arrestee might obtain weapons or evidentiary items. The only reasoned distinction is one between a search of the arrestee's person and the area within his reach on the one hand, and more extensive searches on the other. As Chimel (D) argues, *Rabinowitz* and *Harris* allow officers (P) to conduct searches not justified by probable cause simply by arranging to arrest suspects at home. If officers (P) arrested Chimel (D) at his place of employment rather than at home, they could not have searched his house without a search warrant. Because the search in this case went far beyond Chimel's (D) person and the area from within which he might have obtained a weapon or evidence, it was unreasonable in the absence of a search warrant. Reversed.

■ CONCURRENCE

(Harlan) Officials in every state, facing widely different law enforcement problems, must follow every change we make in Fourth Amendment law. We do not know the extent to which cities across the nation are prepared to administer the greatly expanded warrant system we require today.

■ DISSENT

(White) I agree that the search of an arrested person and of the items within his immediate reach is almost always reasonable because there is always the danger of the use of weapons to escape and of the destruction of vital evidence. I also agree that these justifications do not apply to the search of areas beyond the arrestee's physical access. However, when there is probable cause to believe seizable items are on the premises and it is impracticable to get a search warrant, then a warrantless search of the entire premises may be reasonable. While this is true regardless of whether an arrest is made at the time, an arrest often creates exigent circumstances that make it impracticable to obtain a warrant warrant before conducting a search. Therefore, when police (P) have probable cause to search certain premises and they are already legally there to make an arrest, I find it unreasonable to require them to leave the premises to obtain a warrant and risk that the arrestee's confederates will remove evidence before they return to conduct the search.

Analysis:

In *Chimel* the Supreme Court rejected the longstanding rule that the arrest of a person in his home automatically justified a warrantless search of the entire premises incident to that arrest. The Court found two underlying justifications for the "search incident to arrest" exception: (1) to prevent the arrestee from using weapons to escape or to harm the officer or others, and (2) to prevent the arrestee from concealing or destroying evidence. Based on these justifications, the Court limited the scope of this exception to a search of the arrestee's person and the area within his immediate control, or "grab area." The Court stated that reasonableness requires a case-by-case approach that looks to the totality of the facts and circumstances in light of Fourth Amendment principles. However, since the concerns underlying the search incident to arrest exception go only as far as the area within the arrestee's immediate control, the limits of the exception go no further.

■ CASE VOCABULARY

AREA OF IMMEDIATE CONTROL: The area from within which an arrestee might gain possession of a weapon or evidence, also called the "grab area."

SEARCH INCIDENT TO ARREST: Also called the "arrest power rule," this exception to the warrant requirement permits officers making an arrest to search the arrestee's person and grab area.

Payton v. New York

(Convicted Murderer) v. (State Government)
445 U.S. 573, 100 S.Ct. 1371 (1980)

THE FOURTH AMENDMENT REQUIRES POLICE TO HAVE AN ARREST WARRANT BEFORE ENTERING A SUSPECT'S HOME TO MAKE AN ARREST

■ **INSTANT FACTS** This involves companion cases in which police entered homes to make an arrest without arrest warrants, found evidence of crimes therein and used that evidence to convict the defendants. Both challenge the admission of such evidence on Fourth Amendment grounds.

■ **BLACK LETTER RULE** Absent exigent circumstances, police are required to have an arrest warrant before entering a suspects home to make an arrest, otherwise any evidence seized therein is inadmissible against the suspect.

■ PROCEDURAL BASIS

Certification to the U.S. Supreme Court after the New York Court of Appeals affirmed the convictions of Payton (D1) and Riddick (D2).

■ FACTS

After two days of investigating the murder of a gas station manager, New York detectives had assembled enough evidence to believe that Theodore Payton (D1) was the murderer. Subsequently, six officers went to Payton's (D1) apartment intending to arrest him. They had not obtained a warrant. After knocking on the door to no avail they pried the door open and entered. No one was present, but in plain view there was a .30 caliber shell casing that was seized and later admitted against Payton (D1) at trial. Payton (D1) was convicted. In the companion case, police had learned the address of Obie Riddick (D2), a suspect in two armed robberies. They did not obtain a warrant for his arrest. Four officers went to Riddick's (D2) residence and knocked on the door. When Riddick's (D2) young son answered the door the police could see Riddick (D2) sitting in bed. They entered the house and arrested Riddick (D2). Before permitting him to dress they opened a dresser drawer to search for weapons and [surprise, surprisel] discovered narcotics. Riddick (D2) was convicted of narcotic charges. The New York Court of Appeals affirmed both convictions.

■ ISSUE

Is evidence seized from a suspect's home while making a warrantless arrest, absent exigent circumstances, admissible against the suspect in criminal proceedings?

■ DECISION AND RATIONALE

(Stevens, J.) No. It is a "basic principle of Fourth Amendment law" that searches and seizures inside a home without a warrant are presumptively unreasonable. It is also well settled that objects found in public places may be seized by police without a warrant, as this Involves no invasion of privacy. This distinction has equal force when the seizure of a person is involved. There is a greater burden placed on officials who enter a home or dwelling without consent. Freedom from intrusion in the home is at the core of the Fourth Amendment. Absent exigent circumstances, a warrantless entry to search for weapons or contraband is unconstitutional even when a felony has been committed and there is probable cause to believe that incriminating evidence will be found within. This applies equally to a warrantless entry to make an arrest within for it is inherent in such an entry that a search for the suspect may be required before he can be apprehended. The New York Court of Appeals, however, has suggested that there exists a substantial difference in the relative intrusiveness of an entry to search and one to arrest because an entry to search for evidence is much more broad. This difference is more theoretical than real. Police may need to check an entire residence for safety reasons, and sometimes ignore restrictions on searches incident to arrest. But the important thing is the difference is one of degree rather than kind. The fundamental element—a breach of the entrance of the individual's home—is present in both. This is where the Fourth Amendment draws a firm line. Absent exigent circumstances that line may not be reasonably crossed without a warrant. Finally, the State (P) suggests that only a search warrant based on probable cause to believe the suspect is at home at a given time can adequately protect the privacy interests at stake, and since such a warrant requirement is manifestly impractical, there need be no warrant of any kind. We find this unpersuasive. An arrest warrant requirement may afford less protection than a search warrant requirement, but it will suffice to interpose the magistrate's determination of probable cause between the zealous officer and the citizen. Because no arrest warrant was obtained in either case, the judgments below must be reversed.

■ **DISSENT**

(White, J.) Under common law there are four restrictions on home arrests—a felony, knock and announce, in the daytime, and stringent probable cause. These restrictions constitute powerful and complimentary protections for the privacy interests associated with the home. Taken together, these requirements permit an individual suspected of a serious crime to surrender at the front door of his dwelling and thereby avoid most of the humiliation and indignity that the Court seems to believe necessarily accompany a house arrest entry. Such a front door arrest, in my view, is no more intrusive on personal privacy than the public warrantless arrests which we found to pass constitutional muster in *Watson.* All of these restrictions on warrantless arrest entries are satisfied on the facts of the present cases. Today's decision, therefore, sweeps away any possibility that warrantless home entries might be permitted in some limited situations other than those in which exigent circumstances are present. Some suggest that the opposite holding would lead to officers using their entry power as a pretext to make an otherwise invalid search. But such a search will rarely, if ever, be as complete as one under authority of a search warrant. Also, an arrest entry will inevitably tip off the suspects and likely result in destruction or removal of evidence not uncovered during the arrest. I therefore cannot believe that the police would take the risk of losing valuable evidence through a pretextual arrest entry rather than applying to a magistrate for a search warrant. The majority also fails to take account of the danger that its rule will severely hamper effective law enforcement. Faced with the task of making subtle discriminations that perplex even judges the police will sometimes delay making an arrest, even after probable cause is established, in order to ensure they have enough evidence to convict. If they have to make a sudden arrest they run the risk that the exigency will not excuse their prior failure to obtain a warrant. This problem cannot be cured by obtaining a warrant as soon as probable cause is established due to the chance the warrant will go stale before an arrest is made. It would be far preferable to adopt a clear and simple rule: after knocking and announcing their presence, police may enter the home to make a daytime arrest without a warrant when there is probable cause to believe that the felony suspect is present.

Analysis:

Justice White places great emphasis on the common law rule that officers knock and announce their presence when making a warrantless felony arrest at the suspects residence. What he seems to quite surprisingly, if not conveniently, overlook is the fact that not many felony suspects will be perfectly willing to come to the door once they know who is calling and for what purpose. So once the suspect fails to answer the door the police will automatically have carte blanche to enter the home and search every room on the basis that the suspect could be hiding. While conducting this "search" for the suspect the police will be able to seize anything in plain view and use it against the suspect or anyone else unfortunate enough to be living on the premises. Surely this is too much autonomy to give the police. What's to stop them from waiting until they know the suspect is gone, knocking and entering when the suspect does not answer? Clearly, Justice White misses the very important proposition made by the majority that the front door is a bulwark against unreasonable government intrusion. Justice White's assertion that the Court's requirement will hamper effective law enforcement is also flawed. He maintains that the rule will cause police to have to make subtle distinctions regarding the existence of exigent circumstances, resulting in the inadmissibility of evidence discovered when exigent circumstances do not, in fact, exist. Justice White also insists that the problem cannot be cured by obtaining an arrest warrant as soon as probable cause exists because the warrant may go stale in the interim before the arrest.

California v. Carney

(*State Government*) v. (*Marijuana Dealer*)
471 U.S. 386, 105 S.Ct. 2066 (1985)

VEHICLES MAY BE SEARCHED ON PROBABLE CAUSE EVEN IF IT IS PRACTICABLE TO OBTAIN A SEARCH WARRANT

■ **INSTANT FACTS** Police with probable cause to believe Carney (D) was dealing drugs searched his motor home without a warrant and discovered illegal narcotics therein.

■ **BLACK LETTER RULE** Any vehicle that is readily mobile and subject to the pervasive laws regulating motor vehicles may be searched, without first obtaining a search warrant, so long as there is probable cause supporting the search.

■ PROCEDURAL BASIS

Certification to the U.S. Supreme Court after the State Supreme Court reversed on Fourth Amendment grounds the ruling of the trial court admitting evidence seized from Carney's (D) motor home.

■ FACTS

An agent for the Drug Enforcement Agency witnessed Carney (D) approach a youth in downtown San Diego. The youth went back to Carney's (D) motor home parked in a nearby lot. The agent had received uncorroborated information that the same motor home was used by another person who was exchanging marijuana for sex. The youth came out of the motor home after just over an hour and was stopped by some agents. The youth told the agents that Carney (D) had given him some marijuana in exchange for sexual contacts. The agents then had the youth return to the motor home and knock on the door. When Carney (D) answered the door the agents identified themselves and entered the motor home where they observed marijuana and other evidence of drug dealing. At a preliminary hearing Carney's (D) motion to suppress the evidence found in the motor home was denied. The State Supreme Court later reversed the denial and held the search unconstitutional because no warrant was obtained.

■ ISSUE

Do law enforcement personnel need to obtain a search warrant when they have probable cause to believe a motor vehicle capable of traveling the public roadways contains evidence of a crime?

■ DECISION AND RATIONALE

(Burger, C.J.) No. There are exceptions to the general rule that a warrant must be secured before a search is commenced; one is the so-called "automobile exception." While the privacy interests in an automobile are constitutionally protected, the ready mobility of the automobile justifies a lesser degree of protection of those interests. This is so because it is not practicable to secure a warrant to search a vehicle because the vehicle can be quickly moved out of the locality or jurisdiction in which the warrant must be sought. While ready mobility was perhaps the original justification for the automobile exception, it is not the only one. The reasons for the exception are twofold. Besides the element of mobility, automobiles garner a lesser expectation of privacy than one's home or office. This reduced expectation of privacy derives not from the fact that the area to be searched is in plain view, but from the pervasive regulation of vehicles readily capable of traveling on the public highways. Autos, unlike homes, are subjected to pervasive and continuing governmental regulations and controls, including periodic inspections and licensing requirements. This is a compelling governmental need. Thus, a vehicle that is being used on the highways, or that is readily capable of such use, puts into play the two justifications for the automobile exception: ready mobility, and the reduced expectation of privacy stemming from its use as a licensed motor vehicle subject to a range of police regulations inapplicable to fixed dwellings. Even though Carney's (D) vehicle possessed many of the attributes it still falls clearly within the scope of the automobile exception—it was readily mobile, licensed to operate on public streets, and subject to extensive regulation and inspection. In addition, it was so situated that an objective observer would conclude that it was being used not as a residence, but as a vehicle. The fact that it is a motor "home" is irrelevant given its fulfillment of the requirements of the automobile exception. Our application of the automobile exception has never turned on the other uses to which a vehicle might be put. This search was therefore not unreasonable; it was plainly one that the magistrate could authorize if presented with these facts. Reversed.

■ DISSENT

(Stevens, J.) Until today the Court has never decided whether the practical justifications that apply to a vehicle that is stopped in transit on a public way apply with the same force to a vehicle parked in a lot near a court house where it could easily be detained while a warrant is issued. In this case, the motor home was parked in an off-the-street lot near a courthouse where dozens of magistrates could entertain a warrant application. The motor home offered no clues of imminent departure and the officers plainly had probable cause to search so it is inexplicable why they eschewed the safe harbor of a warrant. The Court relies on the inherent mobility of the motor home to create a conclusive presumption of exigency, but this Court has held that the mobility of the place to be searched is not a sufficient justification for abandoning the warrant requirement. Thus, in *United States v. Chadwick,* we held that a warrantless search of a footlocker violated the Fourth Amendment even though there was ample probable cause to believe it contained contraband. The fact that the footlocker was extremely mobile was not controlling. It is perfectly obvious that a citizen has a greater privacy interest in the interior of a motor home than in a piece of luggage such as a footlocker. It is true that a motor home seldom serves as a permanent lifetime abode. The one in this case, however, was quite lavish and designed to accommodate a breadth of everyday living. The size, shape, and mode of construction of the motor home should have indicated to the officers that it was a vehicle containing mobile living quarters, and this should have tipped the officers to the need for a search warrant. Searches of places that regularly accommodate a wide range of private human activity are fundamentally different from searches of passenger automobiles that serve primarily the public transportation function. The highest and most legitimate expectations of privacy associated with these temporary abodes should command the respect of this Court. In my opinion, a warrantless search of living quarters in a motor home is presumptively unreasonable absent exigent circumstances.

Analysis:

Justice Stevens makes a good point regarding the Court's decision in *Chadwick,* holding that a warrant was required to search a footlocker even though it was just as mobile as an automobile. On what other basis can a vehicle be distinguished from a footlocker? Perhaps this conundrum is what led the Court to invent the rationale that because automobiles are subject to pervasive regulation by the State their owners have a lesser expectation of privacy in them. So if state governments decided to pervasively regulate footlockers then they too would be subject to a warrant exception because they're both mobile and tightly regulated. In support of the majority it can be said that, unlike footlockers, automobiles are inherently mobile and can escape a jurisdiction in mere moments. While the majority opinion is certainly ripe for criticism, Justice Stevens' dissent is not beyond critique. He chooses to concentrate on the fact that many motor homes are quite palatial and serve as the owner's primary residence for at least some period of time. In doing so he completely ignores the fact that while motor homes can serve as a primary abode, they are still sitting on wheels that can very quickly carry it far away along with any "precious cargo" it happens to contain; and that they are, as the majority seems to rely on quite heavily, whether justified or not, pervasively regulated along with "sedans." In the end, law enforcement officials are left with the task of evaluating the mobility of a vehicle. Is it ready to roll?

What if it's up on blocks? What if it's got a flat tire or dead battery? At what point is the motor home mobile enough to fit within the rule's rationale?

California v. Acevedo

(*State*) v. (*Marijuana User*)

500 U.S. 565, 111 S.Ct. 1982 (1991)

THE SUPREME COURT ELIMINATES THE CAR/CONTAINER DISTINCTION AND ADOPTS ONE RULE FOR AUTOMOBILE SEARCHES: NO WARRANT REQUIRED

■ **INSTANT FACTS** Officers who had probable cause to search a bag in the trunk of Acevedo's (D) car for drugs stopped the car, opened the trunk and the bag, and found marijuana.

■ **BLACK LETTER RULE** Police may search a closed container in an automobile without a warrant if they have probable cause to search the container.

■ PROCEDURAL BASIS

Certiorari granted after Court of Appeals overturned trial court's denial of motion to suppress.

■ FACTS

A drug enforcement agent called a police officer and told him that he had seized a package of marijuana which was sent via Federal Express to J.R. Daza in the officer's city. The agent sent the package to the officer instead, and the officer took the package to the Federal Express office. Daza claimed and accepted the package, drove to his apartment, and brought the package inside. Two hours later Acevedo (D) arrived, entered Daza's apartment, and reappeared ten minutes later carrying a full brown paper bag about the size of one of the wrapped marijuana packages sent to Daza. Acevedo (D) walked to his car, put the bag in the trunk, and started to drive away. Officers stopped Acevedo (D), opened the trunk and the bag, and found marijuana. The Court of Appeals concluded that this marijuana should have been suppressed because, although the officers had probable cause to search the bag for drugs, they did not have probable cause to search the entire car. Since the probable cause was directed specifically at the bag, the court held that *United States v. Chadwick* [mobile containers may not be searched without a warrant absent exigent circumstances] rather than *United States v. Ross* [police may search containers within a car without a warrant if they have probable cause to search the entire car] controlled. The court agreed that the officers could seize the bag, but under *Chadwick* they could not open it without first obtaining a search warrant. The court then noted the dichotomy between *Chadwick* and *Ross* which dictates that if there is probable cause to search a car, police may search the entire car, including closed containers within it, without a warrant, but if there is only probable cause to search a container in the car, police may seize the container but may not search it until they obtain a warrant.

■ ISSUE

Must police obtain a warrant to search a container in an automobile when they have probable cause to search the container, but lack probable cause to search the entire automobile?

■ DECISION AND RATIONALE

(Blackmun) No. In *Ross* we held that a warrantless search of an automobile under the *Carroll v. United States* [warrantless automobile search is permissible if there is probable cause for the search] could include a search of containers found inside the car. In that case police had probable cause to believe there were drugs in the trunk of Ross' car. Police stopped the car, searched it, and found drugs in a paper bag in the trunk. We upheld the search, reasoning that when probable cause justifies the search of an automobile, it also justifies the search of every part of the automobile and its contents that may conceal the object of the search. In addition, *Ross* distinguished the *Carroll* doctrine from *Chadwick's* rule for the search of closed containers. In *Chadwick* police had probable cause to believe a certain locked footlocker contained drugs. Officers followed as the footlocker was carried from a train to a waiting car, seized it as soon as it was placed in the car's trunk, and searched it. The Government argued that the *Carroll* doctrine was applicable, not because of the footlocker's brief contact with the car, but rather because we should apply *Carroll's* rule for automobiles to movable luggage by analogy. We rejected this argument because there is a greater expectation of privacy in luggage and personal effects than in a car. We extended *Chadwick* to luggage actually being transported in the trunk of a car in *Arkansas v. Sanders* [*Carroll* does not apply to luggage simply because it is located in a car]. In *Sanders*, police had probable cause to believe a suitcase contained drugs, and watched Sanders place the suitcase in the trunk of a taxi and drive away. Officers stopped the taxi, found the suitcase in the trunk, and searched it. We did not apply *Carroll*, stating that the mere presence of the luggage in an automobile did not diminish the owner's heightened expectation of privacy in its contents. In *Ross* we tried to distinguish *Carroll* from *Chadwick*, explaining that *Carroll* covered searches of automobiles when the police had probable cause to search the entire vehicle, while *Chadwick* governed searches of luggage when the police had probable cause to search only a container within the vehicle. Thus in *Ross* and *Carroll* a warrantless search of a container within an automobile was permissible, but in *Sanders* and *Chadwick* it was not. In *Ross* we took the critical step of holding that police could search a closed container in a car without a warrant because of the container's presence within the car. Despite *Sanders*, the privacy interest in such containers yielded to the broad scope of an automobile search. In *Ross* we rejected *Chadwick's* distinction between containers and cars. Noting that a person's privacy interests in a car's trunk or glove compartment may be no less than his privacy interests in a movable container, we concluded that the expectation of privacy in the vehicle and the container are equal. We further concluded that the warrant process would be misdirected if the police could search an entire vehicle until they discovered a paper bag, but then had to ask a magistrate for permission to look inside. Today we hold that the Fourth Amendment does not require police to obtain a warrant to open a bag in an automobile simply because they lack probable cause to search the entire automobile. There is no difference in terms of privacy expectation or exigency between a container for which police are specifically searching and a container they find while searching an entire automobile. The containers are equally easy for police to store and for the suspect to hide or destroy. By attempting to distinguish between these containers, we have provided only minimal protection for privacy and have impeded effective law enforcement. Because it is not always clear whether police have probable cause to search an entire car or just a container in it, having separate rules to govern these situations may disserve privacy interests by enabling police to make more warrantless searches. For example, when officers stop an automobile, it may not be clear whether they have probable cause to believe the vehicle contains drugs in a bag or simply contains drugs. If they know they may open the bag only if they are searching the entire car, they may search the entire car just to establish the general probable cause required by *Ross.* We see no benefit in a rule that requires officers to conduct a more intrusive search to justify a less intrusive one. Further, the *Chadwick/Sanders* rule provides little protection for privacy because it permits officers to seize a container and hold it until they obtain a search warrant, and the warrant will almost always be issued if the police have probable cause to seize the container. In addition, police will often be able to search a container without a warrant despite the *Chadwick/Sanders* rule as a search incident to arrest. Finally, the search of a paper bag invades privacy far less than did the intrusion in *Carroll*, where officers slashed the upholstery of the car [never mind the invasion of possessory interests]. If destroying the interior of an automobile is not unreasonable, we cannot conclude that looking inside a closed container is. Because we seriously doubt that the *Chadwick/Sanders* rule substantially serves privacy interests, we hold that the Fourth Amendment does not require separate treatment for an automobile search that extends only to a container within the vehicle. In addition to failing to protect privacy, the discrepancy between the *Chadwick/Sanders* rule and the *Carroll* doctrine has confused law enforcement officers When an officer who has probable cause to search an entire vehicle for drugs finds a closed container as soon as he begins to search, some may argue that this indicates that his probable cause extended only to the container and that his search therefore required a warrant. On the other hand, the fact that he searched the most obvious location first should not restrict the propriety of the search. Under the *Chadwick/Sanders* rule, the more likely the police are to find drugs in a container, the less authority they have to search it. This rule is the antithesis of a clear and unequivocal guideline for law enforcement officers. To end the confusion this rule has bred, we interpret *Carroll* to provide one clear-cut rule to govern all automobile searches, and eliminate the warrant requirement for closed containers set forth in *Sanders.* In this case, police had probable cause to search the paper bag in the automobile's trunk, and this now permits a warrantless search of the paper bag. Reversed and remanded.

■ CONCURRENCE

(Scalia) I agree with the dissent that it is anomalous for a briefcase to be protected by the "general requirement" of a prior warrant when it is being carried along the street, but not once it is carried into an automobile. On the other hand, I agree with the Court that it would be anomalous for a locked compartment in an automobile to be unprotected by this requirement, but for an unlocked briefcase in the automobile to be protected. I join in the Court's judgment because I think its holding is more faithful to the text and tradition of the Fourth Amendment. The Fourth Amendment does not require a warrant for searches and seizures, but only that they be reasonable. However, it is possible to find a warrant requirement implied in the requirement of reasonableness, and following our announcement of the exclusionary rule, our jurisprudence lurched back and forth between imposing a categorical warrant requirement and looking to reasonableness alone. The preference for warrants seemed to win out, although it has become riddled with exceptions. Therefore, today's holding is not a momentous departure, but just more inconsistent jurisprudence. Cases like *Chadwick* and *Sanders* have taken our warrant preference seriously, while cases like *Ross* and *Carroll* have not. In my view, we should interpret the Fourth Amendment's reasonableness requirement in accordance with the common law. This may include a warrant requirement where the common law required one, and perhaps, due to changes in surrounding legal rules, even where it did not. However, a general warrant requirement has no basis in common law and hinders rather than helps attempts at developing rules of reasonableness, as the anomalies eliminated and created by today's holding demonstrate.

■ DISSENT

(White) I agree, for the most part, with Justice Stevens.

■ DISSENT

(Stevens) We based our holding in *Ross* not only on prior cases, but also on practical considerations involved when there is probable cause to search an entire vehicle. We explained that it would only exacerbate the invasion of privacy in such cases to prohibit police from immediately opening the container that is most likely to contain the contraband and to force them to comb the entire vehicle instead. In addition, to be certain that they did not miss the contraband, police would often need to seize the vehicle pending the warrant for the container. These concerns are not implicated in cases like *Chadwick* and *Sanders*, where the police do not have probable cause to search the entire vehicle, but only a particular container. Because the police can seize the container, they have no need or authority to search or seize the entire vehicle. In *Ross* we did not retreat from *Chadwick* and *Sanders.* As we explained in *Ross*, that case involved the scope of the automobile exception, while *Chadwick* and *Sanders* involved the applicability of the exception to closed containers. If there was an anomaly in our prior jurisprudence, the Court has cured it only by creating a more serious one. The Court now prohibits a search of a briefcase while the owner is carrying along a public street, but permits the search once the owner has placed the briefcase in the locked trunk of his car. A person's privacy interest in luggage does not decrease when he moves it from a public street to a privately owned vehicle. Likewise, the risk of loss of evidence does not increase when a person moves luggage from a street to a car [assuming the car can't move any faster than the street] because police with probable cause can seize the luggage from either place and hold it pending a warrant. Any boundary line around an exception to the warrant requirement will be blurred at the edges. The Court does not provide a clearer boundary by erasing one line and drawing another. To demonstrate that its holding minimizes intrusions on privacy, the Court suggests that if police know they may open a bag in a car only if they are searching the entire car, they may broaden their search to establish the general probable cause required in *Ross.* This fear is unfounded, since neither the evidence found nor the scope of a search can justify a search unsupported by probable cause. Today the Court shows that it is a loyal foot soldier in the Executive's war on drugs.

Analysis:

In this 6–3 opinion the Supreme Court reexamined and clarified the law applicable to searches of closed containers in automobiles. Under *Sanders*, police needed a warrant to search a container in a car if they had probable cause to search the container, but not the rest of the car. However, under *Ross*, if there was probable cause to search the entire car, police could conduct a warrantless search of any part of the car, including containers within it, that might conceal the object of the search. In *Acevedo* the Court overruled *Sanders* and held that police may conduct a warrantless search of a container located in an automobile even when they only have probable cause to search the container. The Court noted that police could broaden their search in order to justify a container search under *Ross*, that they could usually obtain a search warrant if they had probable cause to seize a container, and that they could often conduct a warrantless search of a container incident to an arrest. Finding that *Sanders* thus provided individuals only minimal protection for privacy, and provided police officers with confusion rather than guidance, the Court reasoned that it was better to adopt one clear rule for all automobile searches. The Court concluded by reaffirming the principle set forth in *Ross* that the scope of a warrantless search of an automobile is defined by the object of the search and the scope of the probable cause. Thus, while probable cause to search a container in an automobile is now sufficient to justify a warrantless search of that container, it does not justify a warrantless search of the entire automobile.

■ CASE VOCABULARY

A PRIORI: Deductively based on what came before.

ANOMALY: Something that seems inconsistent or improper.

CARROLL DOCTRINE: Also known as the automobile exception, this doctrine permits the warrantless search of an automobile if there is probable cause for the search.

DERELICT: Something abandoned or forsaken.

EXEMPLARY DAMAGES: Often called punitive damages, these damages are unrelated to the amount of the loss, but rather are awarded to punish and deter serious wrongdoing.

Thornton v. United States

(Drug Possessor) v. *(Prosecuting Authority)*
541 U.S. 615, 124 S.Ct. 2127, 158 L.Ed.2d 905 (2004)

POLICE OFFICERS MAY SEARCH A RECENTLY OCCUPIED VEHICLE INCIDENT TO A LAWFUL ARREST

■ **INSTANT FACTS** A police officer searched Thornton's (D) vehicle although he was arrested for drug possession outside his vehicle.

■ **BLACK LETTER RULE** A police officer may search a vehicle incident to lawful arrest once probable cause exists to arrest a recent occupant of the vehicle who had access to the interior of the vehicle.

■ PROCEDURAL BASIS

Certiorari to review the defendant's conviction.

■ FACTS

When a police officer discovered that the license tags on Thornton's (D) vehicle had been issued to another vehicle, the officer stopped Thornton (D). Thornton (D) parked and exited the vehicle. The officer approached him, informed him of the license violation, and asked if he had any illegal drugs on him. Thornton (D) produced some marijuana and crack cocaine and was placed in the police car. A search of the vehicle produced a handgun under the driver's seat. Thornton (D) was convicted of drug possession and possession of a firearm.

■ ISSUE

May a police officer search a vehicle incident to an arrest when the arrest occurs outside the vehicle?

■ DECISION AND RATIONALE

(Rehnquist, C.J.) Yes. In *New York v. Belton*, 453 U.S. 454 (1981), the Supreme Court established that a police officer may search the passenger compartment of a vehicle incident to a lawful arrest of the occupant because the occupant had access to and control over the interior of the vehicle. When the suspect has left the vehicle, the officer's right to search the vehicle is no different, for the immediate access to and control over the interior of the vehicle exists no less when the occupant has recently exited the vehicle than when he remains seated in the driver's seat. As a bright-line approach, "[o]nce an officer determines that there is probable cause to make an arrest, it is reasonable to allow officers to ensure their safety and to preserve evidence by searching the entire passenger compartment."

■ CONCURRENCE

(O'Connor, J.) While the Court's decision is a logical extension of *Belton*, the law in this area is unsettled and requires further definition. Justice Scalia's position appears the better approach, but should not apply in this case where neither party had an opportunity to comment upon its merits.

■ CONCURRENCE

(Scalia, J.) The type of search at issue can be reasonably justified as necessary to prevent the concealment or destruction of evidence of the commission of the crime for which the suspect has been arrested. Searches for this purpose find support in Court precedent as a narrow exception to the broad goal of collecting and preserving evidence. The Court's decision here moves away from the narrow purpose of avoiding the destruction of evidence toward the broader goal of collecting evidence, which risks violating a motorist's reasonable expectation of privacy in his vehicle, given the wide array of arrests that may occur. To balance this danger, the search of one's vehicle incident to an arrest must be limited to those cases in which the officer reasonably believes evidence relevant to the crime of arrest might be found.

■ DISSENT

(Stevens, J.) When a pedestrian is arrested for a crime, his constitutional interest in privacy should overcome the state's need to search his vehicle for any potentially valuable evidence. The law clearly provides that an officer may not search a pedestrian's home incident to arrest when the suspect is not in the home. There should be no distinction between a person's home and his vehicle when he is present in neither. Further, the bright-line test established by the court permits the police to search a vehicle in which an arrested suspect has been a "recent occupant," but fails to determine or define how recent is "recent." Without resolving such important issues, the Court's bright-line test threatens the unjustified expansion of searches of vehicles incident to arrest.

Analysis:

Once Thornton (D) was lawfully arrested for drug possession, one may wonder why the warrantless search of the vehicle was necessary. If Thornton (D) no longer had access to the vehicle to retrieve the handgun or any other contents, the threat to the officer's safety and the risk of the destruction of evidence appears minimal. On the facts of this case, sufficient time appears to have been available to obtain a proper warrant to search the vehicle.

■ CASE VOCABULARY

SEARCH: An examination of a person's body, property, or other area that the person would reasonably be expected to consider as private, conducted by a law-enforcement officer for the purpose of finding evidence of a crime.

Colorado v. Bertine

(*State Government*) v. (*Drug Dealer*)
479 U.S. 367, 107 S.Ct. 738 (1987)

AUTOMOBILE INVENTORY SEARCHES DO NOT VIOLATE THE FOURTH AMENDMENT

■ **INSTANT FACTS** Bertine (D) was pulled over and arrested for driving under the influence of alcohol. Before the tow truck arrived to take Bertine's (D) van, an officer inventoried the van's contents and discovered narcotics.

■ **BLACK LETTER RULE** An inventory of a motor vehicle and the containers therein pursuant to established police department administrative policy does not violate the Fourth Amendment's prohibition of unreasonable searches and seizures.

■ PROCEDURAL BASIS

Certification to the U.S. Supreme Court after the Colorado Supreme Court, basing its decision exclusively on the Federal Constitution, upheld the trial court's ruling that the search violated the State Constitution.

■ FACTS

A police officer in Boulder, Colorado arrested Bertine (D) for driving under the influence of alcohol. After Bertine (D) was taken into custody and before the arrival of the tow truck to take Bertine's (D) van to an impound lot, a backup officer inventoried the contents of the van. The officer opened a closed backpack in which he found controlled substances, cocaine paraphernalia, and a large amount of cash. Bertine (D) was charged with possession of cocaine with intent to distribute and other related charges. Bertine (D) challenged the admissibility of the evidence found in his backpack during the inventory search on the ground that the search of the closed backpack and containers therein exceeded the permissible scope of such a search under the Fourth Amendment. The trial court ruled that the search did not violate the Fourth Amendment, but did violate the Colorado Constitution. On appeal, the Colorado Supreme Court ruled that the search did not violate the State Constitution, but did violate the Federal Constitution.

■ ISSUE

Does an inventory search of a motor vehicle and any closed containers found therein, done pursuant to established police administrative policies, violate the Fourth Amendment?

■ DECISION AND RATIONALE

(Rehnquist, C.J.) No. Inventory searches are now a well-defined exception to the warrant requirement. The policies behind the warrant requirement are not implicated in an inventory search, nor is the related concept of probable cause. This is because probable cause is related to criminal investigation while the inventory search is an administrative caretaking function, not an investigatory function. For this reason the Colorado Supreme Court's reliance on *Arkansas v. Sanders* and *United States v. Chadwick* was incorrect. These cases concerned searches solely for the purpose of criminal investigation, with the validity of the searches therefore dependent on the application of the probable cause and warrant requirements of the Fourth Amendment. We have previously decided, in *South Dakota v. Opperman*, that inventory procedures serve to protect the owner's property while it is in the custody of the police, to insure it against claims of lost, stolen, or vandalized property, and to guard the police from potential danger. In light of these strong governmental interests and the diminished expectation of privacy in an automobile, we upheld the search. Here there has been no showing that the police, who were following standardized procedures, acted in bad faith or for the sole purpose of investigation. In addition, the police were potentially responsible for the property taken into their custody. Knowledge of the precise nature of the property helped guard against claims of theft, vandalism, or negligence, and also helped to avert any danger to police or others that may have been posed by the property. The Supreme Court of Colorado also suggests that because Bertine's (D) van was towed to a lighted and secured facility, and because Bertine (D) could have been offered a chance to make other arrangements for his van that the search is unreasonable. This assertion misses the remaining need for the police to protect themselves and others from potential dangers the van might pose. Also, the reasonableness of any particular government activity does not turn on the existence of alternative less intrusive means like allowing Bertine (D) to make other arrangements. Nor are the police required to, as the Colorado Supreme Court suggests, balance the individual's interest in the privacy of a container with the possibility that the container contains contraband. This is because it would be unreasonable to expect police officers in the everyday course of business to make fine and subtle distinctions in deciding which containers may be searched and which must be sealed as a unit. Bertine's (D) last argument is that the search was unreasonable because the departmental policy gave the officers discretion to decide to either impound the van or to park and lock it in a public lot. We reject this argument. Police may exercise discretion so long as it is done according to standard criteria and on the basis of something other than suspicion of evidence of criminal activity. The judgment of the Colorado Supreme Court must therefore be reversed.

■ CONCURRENCE

(Blackmun, J.) I write separately only to underscore that it is permissible for police officers to open closed containers in an inventory search only if they are following standard police procedures that mandate the opening of such containers in every impounded vehicle.

■ DISSENT

(Marshall, J.) As the Court acknowledges, inventory searches are only reasonable if conducted according to standardized procedures. In the past, the Court has relied on the absence of police discretion in determining that the inventory searches in question were reasonable. Here we have police exercising a vast amount of discretion in deciding to inventory Bertine's (D) vehicle when there as at least one viable and more appropriate alternative to impoundment. According to a Boulder Police Department directive, after placing a driver under arrest the officer may take three courses of action: (1) allow another driver to take the vehicle; (2) park the vehicle in a nearby public space and lock it up; or (3) impound the vehicle, in which case an inventory search is conducted. Bertine's (D) van was stopped in an area with ample public parking space available. A truly reasonable exercise of discretion would certainly have militated in favor of the park and lock option. Only if the police choose the third option are they entitled to search the vehicle. The police thus have unbridled discretion as to which procedure to use and it is no surprise that they chose the option allowing for the search. Furthermore, once this decision is made the police are given little guidance as to which areas to search and what sort of items to inventory. It is all up to the whim of the officer. This unfettered discretion is unreasonable because it poses the grave risk of abuse of discretion. In our past cases of this nature we balanced the individual's expectation of privacy against the government's interest to determine whether the search was reasonable. Under this Analysis: the search here is patently unreasonable. Of the three interests cited in support of the inventory search exception, only the first—the protection of the owner's property—is actually served by an inventory search. The use of secure impoundment facilities is enough to satisfy the interest in protecting the police against claims. As to false claims, inventories have little effect against them. Many inventories, like this one, are completely slipshod and inaccurate and thus provide little relief from property claims. As for the interest in protecting police and others from danger, as here, there is rarely any indication in the nature of the offense for which a person is arrested that would suggest danger. This leaves preservation of property as the only realistic justification for the inventory search, a justification that does not outweigh the privacy and security interests protected by the Fourth Amendment, especially in this case. Here Bertine (D) was present to make other arrangements for the safekeeping of his belongings, yet the police made no attempt to ascertain whether in fact he wanted them to "safeguard" his property. And, because Bertine (D) was likely to be in jail for but a few hours, he may very well have been willing to leave his valuables unattended in the locked van for the short period of time. Given this, the government's interests were clearly weaker than Bertine's (D) privacy interests.

Analysis:

Let us analyze the three justifications purportedly supporting the inventory search rule. First, the protection of the owner's property while in police custody. Most, if not all, impound lots are secured by enclosures and 24-hour watchmen. Given this, it is hard to take seriously the concern that valuables may be stolen while a vehicle is impounded. Further, it seems reasonable to assume that given the opportunity most people would readily sign a waiver releasing the police from liability for any property stolen from their car while its impounded. Such a requirement would cause very little burden to the police and would actually save time because cars would not have to be painstakingly inventoried. Second, the interest in protecting the police against claims over lost or stolen property. As Justice Marshall suggests, most inventories are done in such a haphazard manner that they do not accurately represent the contents of the vehicle. How do such inventories protect the police from claims? Once again, most citizens, knowing their vehicle will be impounded in a secure facility, will be quite willing to release the police from liability if it means avoiding an inventory search. Finally, the interest in protecting the police and others from potential dangers. This assertion has no basis. How often is a person who has been pulled over for a traffic violation, or a DUI/DWI, going to have articles in his car that would pose a danger to anyone? Are people commonly driving around these days with bombs strapped under their hoods? If these concerns are so real and important, why not just have a rule that allows the inventory search to go forward, but makes anything gathered during the search inadmissible? This way the purported interests underlying the search are satisfied and the suspect's interest in privacy, while violated, does not result in his facing the prospect of even more serious charges.

Terry v. Ohio

(*Suspected Burglar*) v. (*State Government*)

392 U.S. 1, 88 S.Ct. 1868 (1968)

REASONABLE SUSPICION THAT A SUSPECT IS ARMED ALLOWS AN OFFICER TO CONDUCT A LIMITED FRISK OF THE SUSPECT FOR WEAPONS

■ **INSTANT FACTS** A police officer observed Terry (D) and two other men casing out a store as if planning to rob it. When confronted the men acted suspiciously so the officer frisked them and discovered Terry (D) and another were armed.

■ **BLACK LETTER RULE** Where an officer observes conduct that, in light of experience and all other circumstances, would lead to an objectively reasonable belief that a suspect is armed and dangerous, the officer may conduct a frisk limited in scope to searching for weapons.

■ PROCEDURAL BASIS

Certification to the U.S. Supreme Court on appeal from the State Supreme Court's affirmation of the State Court of Appeal's affirmation of the Trial Court's denial of a motion to suppress evidence on Fourth Amendment grounds.

■ FACTS

Officer McFadden, a plainclothes cop, witnessed two men acting suspiciously on a downtown sidewalk. The two men, one of whom was Terry (D), were seen walking up and down the sidewalk, first one then the other, and repeatedly peering into a store. After each trip up and down the walk the two men would confer with each other. They did this about a dozen times between the two of them. They also talked with a third man, and then followed this man up the street about ten minutes after he departed. Officer McFadden, thinking they might be "casing" the store for a prospective robbery, followed and confronted the three men as they were again conversing. The officer identified himself and asked the three for their names. After the three mumbled something, Officer McFadden spun Terry (D) around and patted his breast pocket where he felt and removed a pistol. A frisk of Terry's (D) companion also uncovered a pistol. Terry (D) was charged with carrying a concealed weapon, and moved to suppress the weapon as evidence. The motion was denied. Both the State Appeals Court and the State Supreme Court also denied Terry's (D) appeals.

■ ISSUE

May an officer, lacking probable cause to seize and search, conduct a limited frisk for weapons under circumstances that would lead an officer, in light of training, experience, and all other circumstances, to have an objectively reasonable suspicion that a suspect is armed and dangerous?

■ DECISION AND RATIONALE

(Warren, C.J.) Yes. Police deal with rapidly unfolding, and possibly dangerous, situations everyday on the streets of this nation. Because of this it is urged that distinctions be made between a "stop" and an "arrest," and a "frisk" and a "search," and that police should be allowed to "stop" and briefly detain a person on suspicion that he may be connected with criminal activity. This position is justified on the basis that a momentary "stop" and "frisk" amounts to a mere minor inconvenience and petty indignity, which can properly be imposed in the interest of effective law enforcement on the basis of an officer's suspicion. On the other side it is contended that there cannot be a variety of police activity that doesn't depend solely upon the voluntary cooperation of the citizen and yet stops short of an arrest based upon probable cause. The State (P) has characterized the issue as the right of police to make a stop, interrogate and pat down for weapons, but this is only part of it. For the issue is not the abstract propriety of police conduct, but the admissibility of the evidence discovered in this frisk. A rule admitting evidence has the effect of legitimizing the conduct which produced the evidence. Exclusion of the evidence denies the conduct the imprimatur of constitutional approval and is used to deter such conduct in the future. But the exclusionary rule has its limitations and in some contexts is ineffective as a deterrent. Street encounters between individuals and police officers run the gamut from totally friendly exchanges to those that devolve into gun battles. Police are keenly aware of the dangers involved in their job and will not refuse to take actions aimed at their own safety simply because they may lose a conviction. In such situations the exclusionary rule is rendered somewhat meaningless. Proper adjudication of cases in which the exclusionary rule is invoked demands a constant awareness of these limitations. We turn our focus now to the quite narrow question posed by the facts before us: whether it is always unreasonable for a policeman to seize a person and make a limited search for weapons unless there is probable cause for an arrest. It must first be recognized that whenever a police officer "accosts" an individual and keeps him from leaving, he has "seized" that person. It is also easily recognized that even a patting down of the outer surfaces of a person's clothing is a "search." Therefore the Fourth Amendment is implicated even when the officer stops short of a full-blown search and/or arrest. It follows that Terry (D) was seized and searched by Officer McFadden. Now we must determine if Officer McFadden's actions were reasonable, both at inception and whether they were reasonably related in scope to the circumstances that justified the interference in the first instance. In doing so we must keep in mind the entire rubric of police conduct—necessarily swift action predicated upon the on-the-spot observations of the officer on the beat—which historically has not been subjected to the warrant procedure. Instead, such conduct must be tested against the standard of unreasonable searches and seizures. The first thing we must focus on is the government interest that allegedly justifies the intrusion, and balance this against the invasion which the search or seizure entails. In justifying a particular intrusion the police officer must be able to point to specific and articulable facts which, taken together with rational inferences from those facts, reasonably warrant the intrusion. In making this assessment we must judge the facts against an objective standard. Here the government interests are effective crime prevention and detection. These underlie the recognition that an officer may in appropriate circumstances and manner approach a person for investigative purposes even though there is no probable cause to arrest. Here Officer McFadden observed Terry (D) and the others go through a series of acts, each perhaps innocent in themselves, but which taken together warranted further investigation. The crux of this case is not the steps Officer McFadden took to investigate the suspicious behavior, but whether there was justification for McFadden's invasion of Terry's (D) personal security by searching him for weapons in the course of the investigation. Now we are dealing with the governmental interest of the officer in taking steps to assure himself that the person he is dealing with is not armed and dangerous. It would be patently unreasonable to require officers to take unnecessary risks while on duty. Police officers have a dangerous job and many are killed or wounded every year. It follows that there is a need for officers to protect themselves and others in situations, even though they lack probable cause to arrest. Such a search, however, must be strictly limited by the exigencies that justify it. It must therefore be limited to actions necessary to discover weapons and no further. Thus where a police officer has reason to believe he is dealing with an armed and dangerous person, even without probable cause to arrest, the officer must be free to take necessary actions to obviate, that danger. Absolute certainty the person is armed is not required; the test is whether a reasonably prudent man in the circumstances would be warranted in the belief that his safety or that of others is in danger. In making this determination due weight must be given to the specific reasonable inferences which he is entitled to draw from the facts in light of his experience. It is clear that under these standards Officer McFadden's actions were reasonable. The actions of Terry (D) and his cohorts were suspicious and, upon being approached by Officer McFadden, the men did nothing to dispel that suspicion. Officer McFadden had surely observed enough to believe the men could be armed and his steps in alleviating this fear—a quick patting down of the outer clothing of the men—were strictly limited in scope to those necessary. Each case of this sort will, of course, have to be decided on its own facts and we conclude on these facts that the revolver seized from Terry (D) was properly admitted into evidence against him. Affirmed.

■ CONCURRENCE

(Harlan, J.) Today's holding has two logical corollaries that I do not think the Court has fully expressed. In the first place, if the frisk is justified in order to protect the officer, the officer must first have constitutional grounds to insist on an encounter, to make a forcible stop. That right must be more than the mere liberty to address questions to other persons, for ordinarily the person addressed has an equal right to simply walk away. Where such a stop is reasonable, the right to frisk must be immediate and automatic if the reason for the stop is, as here, an articulable suspicion of a crime of violence. There is no reason why an officer, rightfully but forcibly confronting a person suspected of a serious crime, should have to ask one question and take the risk that the answer might be a bullet.

■ CONCURRENCE

(White, J.) There is nothing in the Constitution which prevents a policeman from addressing questions to anyone on the street. Normally, the person may simply go on his way. However, given the proper circumstances, such as those I this case, it seems to be the person may be briefly detained while pertinent questions are asked of him.

■ DISSENT

(Douglas, J.) We hold today that the police have greater authority to make a "seizure" and conduct a "search" than a judge has to authorize such action. We have said precisely the opposite over and over again. The infringement on personal liberty of any "seizure" of a person can only be "reasonable" under the Fourth Amendment if we require "probable cause" before the seizure. Only that line draws a meaningful distinction between an officer's mere hunch and the presence of real facts that would justify a search and seizure.

Analysis:

This case offers a classic illustration of the point that searches and seizures can be reasonable without a warrant. It is clear that when the police arrest a suspect on probable cause it is also reasonable to search that person, incident to arrest, for any weapons in order to guard against potential danger. Police deal with individuals all the time without having probable cause to arrest and search, but one of these individuals who happens to be armed poses as much danger to the officer as an individual for whom there is probable cause to arrest. To play games with officer safety based on the fine line between probable cause and lack of it is shear folly. The Constitution does not call for such hairsplitting in these situations. Notice the Court states that an objective standard is to be applied in analyzing *Terry*-type stops—reasonable suspicion. It goes on to say that the stop and frisk must be reasonable in light of the officer's experience. Now it is obvious that every officer possesses differing experience, so how is this an objective standard? Justice Douglas' dissent makes much of the fact that the *Terry* decision files in the face of numerous precedents. But had the Court ever been faced with a situation like this before? Such cases, as the Court stated, must be decided on their individual facts—there is no hard and fast rule.

■ CASE VOCABULARY

IMPRIMATUR: Sanction, approval; license to print or publish.

REASONABLE SUSPICION: Specific and articulable facts that give rise to a particularized and objective basis for suspecting an individual of criminal activity; required before a police officer may stop an individual in public.

TERRY STOP: The brief stop and frisk of a person whose behavior a police officer reasonably considers suspicious and dangerous.

Schneckloth v. Bustamonte

(Not Stated) v. *(Consent Provider)*

412 U.S. 218, 93 S.Ct. 2041 (1973)

SUSPECTS NEED NOT BE INFORMED OF THEIR RIGHT TO REFUSE CONSENT TO SEARCH FOR SUCH CONSENT TO BE DEEMED VOLUNTARY

■ INSTANT FACTS Bustamonte (D) was a passenger in a car owned by his brother that was stopped by the police for an equipment violation. Bustamonte (D) gave the police permission to search the car and now seeks to have the evidence excluded.

■ BLACK LETTER RULE For a consent search to be valid the State need only prove consent was voluntarily given and not the result of duress or coercion, either express or implied; the consent giver need not know his right to refuse consent, although such knowledge is one factor in determining if the consent was voluntary.

■ PROCEDURAL BASIS

Certification to the U.S. Supreme Court after the conviction was overturned by the Federal Circuit Court of Appeals which ruled that consent was not voluntary.

■ FACTS

A police officer pulled over for equipment violations a car in which Bustamonte (D) was a passenger. Bustamonte (D) told the officer that the car belonged to his brother. Bustamonte (D), at the officer's request, granted consent to search the car. Stolen checks were found under the seat leading to charges against Bustamonte (D). Bustamonte's (D) motion to suppress the evidence on the ground that the consent was not voluntary was denied and he was convicted. The conviction was affirmed on appeal. The federal district court denied Bustamonte's (D) petition for a writ of habeas corpus, but the 9th Circuit Court of Appeals set aside the district court's order.

■ ISSUE

Must the State prove that one who consents to a search had knowledge of the right to refuse consent in order for the search to be valid?

■ DECISION AND RATIONALE

(Stewart, J.) No. The most extensive exploration of what "voluntary" means has been in the context of voluntary confessions. It is that body of law to which we turn. In none of these decisions did the result turn on the presence or absence of a single controlling criterion; each reflected a careful scrutiny of all the surrounding circumstances. The question of whether consent to a search was in fact "voluntary" or was the product of duress or coercion, express or implied, is a question of fact to be determined from the totality of all the circumstances, with knowledge of the right to refuse consent being only one factor to be considered. There are two competing interests to be accommodated in the inquiry—the legitimate need for such searches and the equally important requirement of assuring the absence of coercion. In some situations a search authorized by valid consent may be the only means of obtaining important and reliable evidence. It also may result in considerably less inconvenience for the subject of the search, and, properly conducted, is a constitutionally permissible and wholly legitimate aspect of effective police activity. But the Fourth and Fourteenth Amendments require that consent not be coerced, by explicit or implicit means, by implied threat or covert force. There is no hard and fast rule for reconciling the legitimacy of consent searches with the requirement that they be free from coercion. But the requirement of a "voluntary" consent reflects a fair accommodation of the constitutional requirements involved. In making the inquiry account must be taken of all factors, including subtly coercive police questions, as well as the possibly vulnerable subjective state of the person who consents. Searches based on coerced consent can thus be filtered out. In sum, there is no reason to depart in the area of consent searches from the traditional definition of "voluntariness." The Court of Appeals ruling, that the State must prove the subject of the search knew he had a right to refuse consent, would create serious doubt whether consent searches could continue. A defendant faced with conviction could frustrate his prosecution simply by failing to testify that he in fact knew he could refuse consent. Such a result is unacceptable. One alternative would be to require police to inform suspects of this right, but we feel it would be impractical to impose on the normal consent search the detailed requirements of an effective warning. Our ruling in *Miranda v. Arizona* does not demand a contrary result. In that case we held that a valid "waiver" could only be established by showing "an intentional relinquishment or abandonment of a known right or privilege." But almost without exception the requirement of a knowing and intelligent waiver has been applied only to those rights which the Constitution guarantees to criminal defendants in order to preserve a fair trial. The protections of the Fourth Amendment are of a wholly different order, and have nothing to do with promoting fairness in a criminal trial. Nor can it be said that a search, as opposed to an eventual trial, is unfair when one consents to it. Also, the community interest in encouraging consent searches that lead to crime solving outweighs the interest that any consent be given knowingly and intelligently. Further, it would be unrealistic to expect a policeman, upon pain of tainting the evidence obtained, to make the kind of examination of all the circumstances required in evaluating waivers of trial rights. Similarly, a "waiver" approach would be inconsistent with our decisions that have approved "third party consents" since such consent cannot, by definition, be knowing and intelligent. Besides, the considerations that informed the Court in Miranda—for instance, that police custodial interrogation is inherently coercive—are simply inapplicable in the present case. Consent searches normally occur on a person's own familiar territory where the spectre of incommunicado police interrogation in some remote station house is simply inapposite. We therefore hold that when the subject of a search is not in custody and the State tries to justify a search based on consent, the Fourth and Fourteenth Amendments require that it show that the consent was in fact voluntarily given, and not the result of duress or coercion, express or implied. Voluntariness is a question of fact to be determined from all the circumstances, with the subject's knowledge of the right to refuse being one of many factors to be taken into account. The prosecution is not required to demonstrate such knowledge as a prerequisite to establishing a voluntary consent. Reversed.

■ DISSENT

(Marshall, J.) If consent to search means that a person has chosen to give up his right to exclude the police from the place they seek to search, it follows that his consent cannot be considered a meaningful choice unless he knew that he could in fact exclude the police. The burden on the prosecutor would disappear, of course, if the police told the subject that he has a right to refuse consent and that his decision to refuse consent would be respected. The Court's assertion to the contrary notwithstanding, there is nothing impractical about this method of satisfying the prosecution's burden of proof. The Federal Bureau of Investigation has been informing suspects of their right to refuse consent for some time with no significant problems. I would therefore hold, at a minimum, that the prosecution may not rely on a purported consent to search if the subject of the search did not know that he could refuse to give consent.

Analysis:

There are flaws in the majority's reasoning in this case. For starters, it asserts, "it would be thoroughly impractical to impose on the normal consent search the detailed requirements of an effective warning." What is so hard about simply stating to a suspect whose property an officer desires to search, "Sir, may I have your consent to search your car? You have the right to refuse consent with no adverse results." Police officers have been administering *Miranda* warnings for decades with no difficulties. Some urban police departments, in response to concerns regarding racial profiling, have begun to inform suspects of their right to refuse consent. Informing an individual of his right to refuse consent to search is even less complicated than giving the *Miranda* warning and takes even less time. Furthermore, providing such information, like the *Miranda* warning, would most likely not result in a significant barrier to effective law enforcement. This belies the Court's concerns about providing such a warning regarding consent searches. The Court also maintains that, unlike custodial interrogation, asking for consent to search is not inherently coercive. However, for many people, just the sight of a police officer makes them nervous, while having one stop you and ask to search your car is cause to be even more nervous and results in compliancy. There is a certain psychological dynamic that compels people to want to cooperate with police.

Illinois v. Rodriguez

(*State Government*) v. (*Cocaine Dealer*)
497 U.S. 177, 110 S.Ct. 2793 (1990)

A WARRANTLESS ENTRY MADE WITH CONSENT OF A THIRD PARTY IS VALID IF RELIANCE ON THE CONSENT IS OBJECTIVELY REASONABLE

■ **INSTANT FACTS** Rodriguez's (D) former girlfriend used her key to Rodriguez's (D) apartment to let police in to arrest him. While inside the police discovered evidence of narcotics trafficking. Rodriguez (D) challenges the entry as a Fourth Amendment violation.

■ **BLACK LETTER RULE** A warrantless entry based on consent of a third party is reasonable, and thus valid under the Fourth Amendment, so long as it was objectively reasonable for law enforcement to believe the third party had authority to give consent.

■ PROCEDURAL BASIS

Certification to the U.S. Supreme Court after the State Court of Appeals upheld the trial court's granting of a motion to suppress evidence based on a Fourth Amendment violation.

■ FACTS

Police were summoned to a location where they met Gail Fischer, who showed signs of a severe beating. Fischer told police that she'd been assaulted by Edward Rodriguez (D) earlier that day in an apartment on South California. Fischer also stated that Rodriguez (D) was then asleep in the apartment and she consented to travel there with the police in order to unlock the door with her key so that the officers could enter and arrest him. Fischer several times referred to the apartment as "our" apartment, and said that she had clothes and furniture there. It is unclear whether she indicated that she currently lived at the apartment, or only that she used to live there. The police went to the apartment where Fischer unlocked the door and allowed them entry. While inside the police discovered large amounts of cocaine and other evidence of narcotics trafficking. At no time did police possess an arrest or search warrant.

■ ISSUE

Is the Fourth Amendment violated where police make a warrantless consent entry based on a reasonable belief, based on all the circumstances, that the person giving consent has the authority to do so?

■ DECISION AND RATIONALE

(Scalia, J.) No. The Fourth Amendment generally prohibits the warrantless entry of a person's home, whether to make an arrest or to search for evidence. The prohibition does not apply, however, where voluntary consent is given either by an individual whose property is to be searched, or by one who possesses common authority over the premises. The State of Illinois (the State) (P) asserts that the exception applies to this case. As we have previously stated, common authority rests on mutual use of the property by persons having joint access or control for most purposes. The burden of establishing this common authority rests upon the Government. Here it is clear this burden was not sustained because Ms. Fischer had long since left Rodriguez's (D) apartment to live with her mother. Her name was not on the lease nor did she help with rent. Fischer did not have "joint access or control for most purposes." Rodriguez (D) contends that permitting a reasonable belief of common authority to validate an entry would cause a "vicarious waiver" of his Fourth Amendment rights. We disagree. One must distinguish between, on the one hand, trial rights that derive from the violation of constitutional guarantees and on the other hand, the nature of those constitutional guarantees themselves. Rodriguez (D) is assured of his trial right that no evidence seized in contravention of the Fourth Amendment will be admitted against him. What he is assured of by the Fourth Amendment itself, however, is not that no government search of his house will occur unless he consents; but that no such search will occur that is "unreasonable." In order to satisfy the "reasonableness" requirement of the Fourth Amendment, what is generally demanded of the many factual determinations that must be made by government agents is not that they always be correct, but that they always be reasonable. The Constitution is not violated by a warrantless entry when the officers reasonably believe that the person who has consented to their entry is a resident of the premises. As with other factual determinations bearing upon search and seizure, determination of consent to enter must be judged against an objective standard: would the facts available to the officer at the moment warrant a man of reasonable caution to believe that the consenting party had authority over the premises? If so, the search is valid. Since we find the ruling from below to be in error, we remand for consideration of the reasonableness of the officer's belief in this case.

■ DISSENT

(Marshall, J.) Unlike searches conducted under the recognized exceptions to the warrant requirement, third-party consent searches are not based on an exigency and therefore serve no compelling social goal. Police officers, when faced with the decision of either relying on a third person's consent or obtaining a warrant should get a warrant. They must otherwise accept the risk for error. The majority seeks to rely on cases suggesting that reasonable but mistaken factual judgments by police will not invalidate otherwise reasonable searches. The majority reads these cases as establishing a "general rule" that "what is generally demanded of the many factual determinations that must regularly be made by agents of the government is not that they always be correct, but that they always be reasonable. The majority's assertion, however, is premised on the erroneous assumption that third-party consent searches are generally reasonable, something the cases it cites do not bear out. These cases make clear that the possibility of factual error is built into the probable cause standard, and such a standard, by its very definition, will in some cases result in the arrest of a suspect who has not actually committed a crime. Thus, a search or seizure outside the home is reasonable whenever the probable cause standard is met, notwithstanding the possibility of "mistakes" on the part of police. In contrast, our cases have already struck the balance against warrantless home intrusions in the absence of an exigency. Because reasonable factual errors by law enforcement officers will not validate unreasonable searches, the reasonableness of an officer's mistaken belief that the third party had authority to consent is irrelevant.

Analysis:

Under the majority's rule it is clear that for police officers wanting to enter a residence without a warrant, but with "consent" from a third-party, ignorance is most assuredly bliss. So long as the third party has a key and does not say anything to tip the officers off to the fact that they do not, in fact, exercise domain over the residence, the officers will be free to bury their heads in the sand and rely on the "reasonable" belief that the third party has common authority over the abode. Would it be possible to formulate a rule that places upon the officers a duty to inquire into the authority to consent issue? Police officers are very good at asking questions. After all, this is a fundamental part of their job. Why can't they simply ask the third party if he or she has common authority over the premises? Do you help pay rent? Are you on the lease? Do you live here right now? These are all very simple and straight forward questions that will give the officers a clear and accurate picture of the situation.

CHAPTER SEVEN

Wiretapping, Electronic Eavesdropping, Secret Agents, And the Fourth Amendment

United States v. White

Instant Facts: A narcotics defendant sought to challenge his conviction on the ground that the government violated the Fourth Amendment when its informant transmitted conversations with the defendant to narcotics agents by way of a concealed radio transmitter.

Black Letter Rule: A defendant's expectation of privacy is not invaded when an agent of the government electronically transmits his conversation with the defendant.

United States v. White

(*Government*) v. (*Convicted Narcotics Dealer*)
401 U.S. 745, 91 S.Ct. 1122 (1971)

THE FOURTH AMENDMENT DOES NOT PROHIBIT UNDERCOVER AGENTS OR INFORMANTS FROM SECRETLY TRANSMITTING THEIR CONVERSATIONS WITH THE DEFENDANT DURING AN INVESTIGATION

■ **INSTANT FACTS** A narcotics defendant sought to challenge his conviction on the ground that the government violated the Fourth Amendment when its informant transmitted conversations with the defendant to narcotics agents by way of a concealed radio transmitter.

■ **BLACK LETTER RULE** A defendant's expectation of privacy is not invaded when an agent of the government electronically transmits his conversation with the defendant.

■ PROCEDURAL BASIS

Certiorari granted by United States Supreme Court to review decision of Seventh Circuit Court of Appeals, which reversed the defendant's conviction on the ground that the Fourth Amendment prohibited testimony about electronically overheard conversations.

■ FACTS

On several occasions a government informer used a concealed radio to transmit conversations he had with White (D) in several locations, including a restaurant, in the informer's car and White's (D) home. The transmissions were received and overheard by narcotics agents stationed inside and outside the home. No search warrant was ever sought by or issued to the agents. Although the informer was not called to testify, the testimony of the agents who overheard the transmission led to a narcotics-related conviction.

■ ISSUE

Does the Fourth Amendment protect a defendant's privacy from the electronic transmission of a conversation between the defendant and an agent of the government who monitors the conversation?

■ DECISION AND RATIONALE

(White, J.) No. A defendant's expectation of privacy is not invaded when an agent of the government electronically transmits his conversation with the defendant. [Drug dealers, beware of whom you talk to—it could land you in jail.] Thus, the Fourth Amendment is inapplicable under such circumstances. In *Hoffa v. United States* [case involving a government informant whose testimony regarding conversations with the defendant was used to obtain a conviction] we held that a government agent can conceal his true identity and engage in incriminating conversations with the defendant, and thereafter, write down the contents of that conversation. In *Lopez v. United States* [case involving an IRS agent who recorded the defendant's bribe offers by means of a concealed wire], we held that a government agent could use electronic equipment to simultaneously record his conversations with the defendant. In *On Lee v. United States* [regarding a Chinese laundromat owner who made incriminating statements to an acquaintance who was transmitting the conversation with the defendant to government agents by use of a concealed wire] we upheld the government's right to simultaneously transmit to a recorder or other agents a conversation between the defendant and an agent of the government, without the need for a search warrant. Although *On Lee* was partially decided on the grounds of the defendant's property rights, a basis which has since been rejected by this Court, the decision there was also grounded in the facts that the defendant "was talking confidentially and indiscreetly with one he trusted, and he was overheard." Our decision in *Katz v. United States* [Supreme Court overrules the "trespass" doctrine announced in *Olmstead*] does not affect these cases, which stand for the proposition that, if revelations of an undercover agent who does not use electronic equipment do not invade the defendant's expectation of privacy, then those expectations are not invaded when an agent of the government electronically transmits his conversation with the defendant. The problem we are faced with here is what expectations of privacy are constitutionally "justifiable." If the law gives no protection to the defendant whose trusted accomplice is a police agent, neither should it protect him when that same agent records or transmits the conversations later offered in evidence to prove the State's case. It makes no sense to hold as unreasonable the conduct of a government agent who uses a recorder when that conduct would be reasonable were it not for the recorder. Reversed.

■ DISSENT

(Douglas, J.) *Katz* established, with only a few exceptions, that searches conducted outside the judicial process are *per se* unreasonable under the Fourth Amendment. Furthermore, prevalent monitoring kills free discourse and spontaneous utterances. The individual must keep some facts to a small zone of people, but at the same time he must be free to speak. The First, Fourth and Fifth Amendments protect the individual's right to judge what must be spoken and what may not.

■ DISSENT

(Harlan, J.) The plurality makes a giant logical leap between those cases permitting a government agent to verbally relay information a defendant has entrusted to him and allowing the government agent to simultaneously transmit that information to a third party. The contention that the two situations are indistinguishable is based on the mistaken assumptions that there is no greater invasion of privacy when the transmission occurs and that uncontrolled consensual surveillance is a tolerable technique of law enforcement. Basing the Fourth Amendment Analysis: on subjective expectations or the risks one can expect to assume ignores the fact the assumed risks and subjective expectations are formed, in part, by what the law is. The critical question should be whether under our system of government, as reflected in the Constitution, we should impose upon our citizens the risks of the electronic listener or observer without the protections of the warrant requirement. I believe the answer is no. The societal impact of government monitoring goes beyond the usual criminal case, for such conduct undermines the security citizens enjoy when dealing with each other. It is important to remember that the protections of the Fourth Amendment would not abolish all electronic monitoring. The Constitution merely guarantees that such monitoring will not occur extra-judicially. The Fourth Amendment does not shield "wrongdoers," it secures privacy and personal security throughout our society.

■ DISSENT

(Marshall, J.) I believe that *On Lee* was overruled by our decision in *Katz.* The Fourth Amendment's warrant requirement applies to electronic surveillance that occurred in this case.

Analysis:

The plurality bases its opinion, in part, on a "wrongdoer's" reasonable expectations of privacy when relaying information to third parties. The plurality concludes that, because those expectations are not invaded when a defendant communicates information to a government agent the defendant has mistakenly entrusted, the Fourth Amendment should offer no protection when those same communications are recorded or transmitted. Justice Harlan's poignant dissent offers an alternate basis for answering the question of whether electronic monitoring falls within the ambit of the Fourth Amendment's warrant requirement. He notes that the question is not whether the Fourth Amendment protects the privacy expectations of a "wrongdoer," but whether, in light of the aims of the Fourth Amendment, the citizenry at large should expect that the government will monitor its conversations extra-judicially. After so reframing the issue, Justice Harlan determines that, because third-party bugging has a psychological impact in undermining the security and privacy of citizens, electronic eavesdropping requires the issuance of a judicial warrant. Most importantly, Justice Harlan stresses that the Fourth Amendment does not outlaw particular investigative techniques, it merely requires judicial approval of them.

CHAPTER EIGHT

Police "Encouragement" and the Defense of Entrapment

United States v. Russell

Instant Facts: A man convicted of unlawfully manufacturing methamphetamine sought to challenge his conviction on the ground that government agents entrapped him by providing him with an essential ingredient in the manufacturing process.

Black Letter Rule: The prosecution of a defendant is not per se precluded when it is shown that the criminal conduct would not have been possible unless an agent of the government has supplied an indispensable means to the commission of the crime that could not have been obtained otherwise.

United States v. Kelly

Instant Facts: A congressman who was convicted of taking bribes sought to challenge his conviction on the ground that the FBI's conduct in hatching and carrying out the entire scheme was a violation of due process.

Black Letter Rule: For a defendant to successfully challenge his conviction based on law enforcement's overinvolvement in a criminal enterprise he is required to show that the conduct of the government's agents involved coercion, violence or brutality.

Jacobson v. United States

Instant Facts: A man convicted of receiving child pornography through the mails sought to challenge his conviction on the ground that the government entrapped him by making repeated inquiries into his sexual preferences over two and one-half years before making any offer to purchase the illicit materials.

Black Letter Rule: Under a claim of entrapment, the defendant's predisposition must be independent and not the product of the conduct of the government.

United States v. Russell

(*Government*) v. (*Convicted Methamphetamine Manufacturer*)

411 U.S. 423, 93 S.Ct. 1637 (1973)

THE DEFENSE OF ENTRAPMENT FOCUSES ON THE CONDUCT AND PROPENSITIES OF THE DEFENDANT

■ **INSTANT FACTS** A man convicted of unlawfully manufacturing methamphetamine sought to challenge his conviction on the ground that government agents entrapped him by providing him with an essential ingredient in the manufacturing process.

■ **BLACK LETTER RULE** The prosecution of a defendant is not *per se* precluded when it is shown that the criminal conduct would not have been possible unless an agent of the government has supplied an indispensable means to the commission of the crime that could not have been obtained otherwise.

■ PROCEDURAL BASIS

Certiorari granted by the United States Supreme Court from decision of the Ninth Circuit Court of Appeal, which reversed the defendants drug conviction on the ground that the government's involvement in the criminal enterprise reached an intolerable level.

■ FACTS

In 1969, Joe Shapiro, a federal agent, approached Russell (D) and his codefendants and told them that he was with an enterprise interested in controlling the manufacture and distribution of methamphetamine. Shapiro offered to supply Russell (D) and the others will the chemical phenyl-2-propanone (propanone), an essential ingredient in the manufacturing of methamphetamines, in exchange for one-half the end product. Some testimony showed that propanone was difficult to obtain and that some chemical supply companies had, at the insistence of the government, stopped selling the chemical. Nonetheless, Shapiro was given a bag containing a sample of what one of the men claimed was methamphetamine from the "last batch." When shown the laboratory where Russell (D) and his codefendants had been making the drug, Shapiro observed an empty bottle labeled "phenyl-2-propanone." Two days later, Shapiro returned with the propanone he had promised and witnessed the manufacturing process. When the process was completed the next morning, Russell (D) and the others gave Shapiro one-half of the finished product and sold to him part of the remainder. A month later, the men provided Shapiro with some additional methamphetamine. Shortly thereafter, Shapiro returned with a search warrant [much to the surprise of Russell (D)], seizing an empty 500 gram bottle of propanone and a partially filled 100 gram bottle of propanone. The District Court gave the jury a standard entrapment instruction, and Russell (D) was convicted on all counts. The Ninth Circuit Court of Appeals reversed on the ground that the Government's (P) involvement in the enterprise went too far.

■ ISSUE

Is a prosecution precluded when the government provides the means by which the criminal conduct was undertaken?

■ DECISION AND RATIONALE

(Rehnquist, C.J.) No. The prosecution of a defendant is not *per se* precluded when it is shown that the criminal conduct would not have been possible unless an agent of the government has supplied an indispensable means to the commission of the crime that could not have been obtained otherwise. When this Court first recognized and applied the defense of entrapment in *Sorrells v. United States* [case involving a prohibition agent who gained the defendant's confidence, asked for some liquor from the defendant, was twice refused, and insisted until he succeeded in getting the defendant to capitulate] it held as a matter of statutory construction that the defense prohibits law enforcement officers from instigating a criminal act by persons "otherwise innocent in order to lure them to its commission and to punish them." The focus of the defense was on the intent or predisposition of the defendant. In a concurring opinion, Justice Roberts wrote that the defense of entrapment should focus not on the predisposition of the defendant, but on whether the government instigated the crime. In *Sherman v. United States* [case involving a defendant who was convicted of selling narcotics to an undercover agent only after repeated solicitation from the agent], this Court affirmed the theory in *Sorrells* and held that entrapment involves drawing a line "between the trap for the unwary innocent and the trap for the unwary criminal." In a concurring opinion, Justice Frankfurter reiterated the position that the entrapment defense should focus on whether the government's conduct fell below acceptable standards. Russell (D) would have us formulate an entrapment defense that embodies the views of Justices Roberts and Frankfurter and which is grounded in the fundamental principles of due process. However, even were we to adopt an entrapment defense based on due process, Russell (D) would not qualify. [In other words, he's just flat out of luck and guilty!] The evidence clearly shows that Russell (D) and his partners had previously obtained phenyl-2-propanone and that the chemical was available without any assistance from Shapiro. Although there might be cases where the government's involvement in a criminal enterprise is so outrageous as to offend due process, such is not the case here. Shapiro did nothing more that supply a legal substance to gain the confidence of the Russell (D) and his partners. Infiltration is essential to the detection and punishment of drug rings. If infiltration is a permissible investigation tool then the supply of some item of value to the criminal in an effort to gain his confidence should also be permissible. As to the statutory defense of entrapment, we refuse to overrule *Sorrells* and *Sherman* and adopt the view of the concurring opinions in those cases. If Congress wishes, it can so modify the defense. The defense of entrapment announced in those two cases did not give federal courts the authority to veto law enforcement practices of which it did not approve. We believe that the jury was warranted in finding that Russell was, in the words of *Sherman*, an "unwary criminal" and not an "unwary innocent." Reversed.

■ DISSENT

(Stewart, J.) I believe that the central inquiry in the entrapment defense is whether the government agents have acted in such a way as is likely to instigate or create a criminal offense, the predisposition of the defendant notwithstanding. This view, also known as the objective approach to the entrapment defense, is most consistent with the purpose of the defense. The focus on "innocent" versus "predisposed" makes no sense because the fact that the defendant committed the crime establishes that he is not innocent. Furthermore, inducement by the government makes a defendant no less guilty than inducement by a private citizen. Another problem with placing the focus on the defendant's predisposition is that it allows for the introduction of evidence which may be prejudicial to the defendant, leading a jury to convict on the basis of defendant's character and not his guilt. More fundamentally, the focus on predisposition or innocence gives the government the green light to entrap a person with a past record or bad reputation, prosecute the person of the manufactured crime and then rely on his reputation as evidence that he would have committed the crime anyway. I find misplaced the majority's reliance on the fact that phenyl-2-propanone was otherwise obtainable. The fact remains that the propanone supplied by the agent was the one involved in all three counts of the indictment. The chemical was available only to licensed persons, yet the government readily offered a supply in exchange for production of the drug, the very conduct which the government now seeks to prosecute. I believe this is the type of activity the defense of entrapment is aimed at eradicating.

Analysis:

When it first expressly recognized the defense of entrapment, the Supreme Court inferred that Congress' intent was to exclude prosecution of those who were induced by the government to commit the crime. There exists two major approaches to the entrapment defense. The "subjective approach" is the one favored by federal courts and it involves a two-step Analysis:. First, courts must be asked whether the government induced the defendant to commit the crime. If this question is answered in the affirmative, then the court must ask whether the defendant was predisposed to commit the crime. If the defendant was so predisposed, the entrapment defense is wholly unavailable. In contrast, the objective approach involves only a more focused inquiry into the government's conduct. The objective approach asks whether the government's conduct went beyond an acceptable level. The Court here attempted to lay to rest the issue of whether the defense of entrapment involved a subjective inquiry into the predisposition of the defendant vis-à-vis the alleged crime or an objective Analysis: of the government's conduct vis-à-vis a hypothetical defendant. As this case illustrates, the question of which approach to apply really depends on how one views the purposes of the entrapment defense. Those who believe the defense is intended as a restraint against "overzealous law enforcement" will favor the objective approach supported by Justice Stewart's dissent. On the other hand, the subjective approach adopted by the majority will be favored most by those who view the defense as protecting the innocent against unfair inducement by the government.

■ CASE VOCABULARY

ENTRAPMENT: The act of government agents who induce a person to commit a crime in order to prosecute the commission of the very crime the defendant was induced to commit.

METHAMPHETAMINE: Also known as "speed," a narcotic that acts as a stimulant on the central nervous system.

United States v. Kelly

(*Government*) v. (*United States Congressman*)

707 F.2d 1460 (D.C. Cir. 1983)

A DUE PROCESS DEFENSE BASED ON THE GOVERNMENT'S OVERINVOLVEMENT IN A CRIMINAL ENTERPRISE INVOLVES AN INQUIRY INTO WHETHER THE GOVERNMENT'S CONDUCT REACHED AN EXTREME LEVEL OF OUTRAGEOUSNESS

■ **INSTANT FACTS** A congressman who was convicted of taking bribes sought to challenge his conviction on the ground that the FBI's conduct in hatching and carrying out the entire scheme was a violation of due process.

■ **BLACK LETTER RULE** For a defendant to successfully challenge his conviction based on law enforcement's overinvolvement in a criminal enterprise he is required to show that the conduct of the government's agents involved coercion, violence or brutality.

■ PROCEDURAL BASIS

Appeal to the District of Colombia Circuit Court of Appeals to review the decision of the district court, which dismissed indictment and entered a judgment of acquittal on due process grounds.

■ FACTS

In an effort to identify "corrupt" members of Congress, the FBI and Weinberg, a convicted con-man, hatched a plan whereby word would be spread that wealthy Arabs were willing to bribe congressmen to ensure that they would introduce legislation favorable to the Arabs. When word reached Cuizio, he told Congressman Kelly (D) that he had some Arab clients with immigration difficulties. Kelly (D) agreed to help, partly because Cuizio indicated that the Arabs would invest in Kelly's district. The word was then passed back through the "middlemen" until it reached Weinberg and the FBI that a candidate had been found. Cuizio then met with Weinberg and Amoroso, an FBI agent, and told the two men that Kelly (D) was willing, but that Cuizio was left to make the arrangements. Cuizio sought to dissuade Weinberg and Amoroso from directly offering the bribe to Kelly (D). It was eventually agreed that payment would be made to Cuizio, but that Kelly (D) would acknowledge that the money was in exchange for political assistance. When Kelly (D) met with Amoroso, who was posing as a representative of the "Arabs," Kelly (D) told him that he was interested in investment in his district and that he was not involved in, and had no knowledge of, any arrangement with Cuizio. After some pressing, Kelly (D) agreed that he instead of Cuizio would take the money. Amoroso handed $25,000 to Kelly (D), who placed the money in his pocket. [Big mistake!] Kelly (D) was indicted and convicted of bribery and other federal offenses. The district court then granted Kelly's (D) motion to dismiss the indictment on the ground that the FBI's actions violated due process.

■ ISSUE

Does the government violate due process when it attempts to root out political corruption by engaging in a scheme that offers public officials the opportunity to take bribes?

■ DECISION AND RATIONALE

(MacKinnon, Cir. J.) No. Where the government simply provides the opportunity to commit a crime, prosecution of a defendant does not violate due process. A due process claim that is based on an entrapment-like theory or the Government's (P) overinvolvement in a criminal enterprise requires us to determine whether the FBI's conduct reached a demonstrable level of outrageousness. Abscam was nothing more than an offer to public officials to commit a crime. After sending word through the grapevine, the FBI merely waited for takers. There were no particular targets. Abscam was no different than when law enforcement officials set up an operation looking to buy drugs or stolen goods. [Except the catch was a much bigger fish.] We also find that no specific act by the FBI reached that level of outrageousness required for a successful due process challenge. First, we do not agree with the district court that Abscam's Arab scheme was not triggered by any suspicion of corruption. Assuming that reasonable suspicion is even required to instigate a sting operation (a requirement expressly rejected by other Circuits), the record shows that the FBI had some evidence that Kelly (D) was corrupt. Second, we find nothing outrageous in the FBI's use of a convicted con-man to devise and carry-out the scheme. True criminals are often needed to provide police sting operations with an aura of credibility. Finally, we disagree with Kelly's (D) argument that Amoroso violated due process in insisting that Kelly (D) take the bribe, after what Kelly (D) describes as his initial rejection. The evidence clearly shows that Kelly (D) never rejected the proposal. The only thing Kelly (D) rejected was the method of payment, not the acceptance of a bribe. Furthermore, Amoroso's conduct was not a series of bribe offers. Amoroso merely engaged in the type of negotiation which would take place while a public official was being bribed. Considering the need to root-out political corruption and the inherent difficulties in doing so, we find the FBI did not cross the threshold of intolerable government conduct required by the Supreme Court.

■ DECISION AND RATIONALE, PART 2

(Ginsburg, Cir. J.) We disagree that Abscam was nothing more than your run-of-the-mill undercover operation. The scheme did more than spread the word. Furthermore, the FBI had no "reasonable" suspicion that Kelly (D) was corrupt. Accordingly, the district court applied an objective test which asked: Was the crime-inducing conduct in which the government engaged, the temptation presented to the target, modeled on reality? In the view of the court this test was necessary when the government had no knowledge of prior wrongdoing and no reason to believe the target was about to commit a crime. This real-world test has it merits and its drawbacks. Our inclination toward such a test is tempered by the fact that we are not writing on a cleanslate. Lower courts cannot alter the entrapment defense under the rubric of the due process clause. It is plain that a due process claim based on "overinvolvement" in crime requires the government's conduct to meet an extraordinary threshold of outrageousness. This level is reached when there is "coercion, violence or brutality to the person." None of these has been alleged. Thus, we are required to reverse the district court.

Analysis:

In *United States v. Russell* [case involving a narcotics officer who provided the defendants with an ingredient essential to the manufacture of methamphetamine, which the defendants were convicted of manufacturing] the Supreme Court left open the possibility that there might exist a due process claim based on law enforcement's overinvolvement with a criminal enterprise. As the *Kelly* case illustrates, the due process claim requires a high threshold of outrageous conduct on the part of the government. Now Supreme Court Justice Ginsburg, whose whole opinion also constituted part of the opinion of the court, held that the Supreme Court has limited the due process "overinvolvement" claim to those cases where there is "coercion, violence or brutality to the person." So narrowly stated, it would seem that the due process claim is not really based on overinvolvement at all. Some cases suggest a broader interpretation of the due process claim. In *United States v. Twigg* (a case involving a methamphetamine lab) the Third Circuit reversed a conviction where the government's informant supplied the equipment, materials and laboratory site and managed operation of the lab. The court held that such involvement reached a "demonstrable level of outrageousness." The *Twigg* court's holding was partly based on the fact that the defendant was not engaged in any criminal activity until approached by the informant. This rationale gives rise to one of the issues, raised by Judge MacKinnon's opinion, as to whether the government must have a reasonable suspicion that the defendant is engaged in unlawful activity before it approaches him. The *Kelly* case did not address the question squarely; and as Judge MacKinnon points out, other Circuits have held that reasonable suspicion is not required. The due process cases show that there is no bright-line rule for determining when the government's conduct has reached an intolerable level of outrageousness. It simply is one of those "I know when I see it" inquiries.

■ CASE VOCABULARY

ABSCAM: A federal sting operation of the late 1970s and early 80s aimed at rooting-out corruption in Congress.

Jacobson v. United States

(*Defendant Convicted of Receiving Child Pornography*) v. (*Government*)

503 U.S. 540, 112 S.Ct. 1535 (1992)

A DEFENDANT'S PREDISPOSITION TO COMMIT A CRIME CANNOT BE CAUSED BY GOVERNMENT CONDUCT

■ **INSTANT FACTS** A man convicted of receiving child pomography through the mails sought to challenge his conviction on the ground that the government entrapped him by making repeated inquiries into his sexual preferences over two and one-half years before making any offer to purchase the illicit materials.

■ **BLACK LETTER RULE** Under a claim of entrapment, the defendant's predisposition must be independent and not the product of the conduct of the government.

■ PROCEDURAL BASIS

Certiorari granted by the United States Supreme Court from decision of the Eighth Circuit Court of Appeals to review the appellate court's decision to affirm a conviction on the ground that the defendant was not entrapped as a matter of law.

■ FACTS

In February of 1984, Jacobson (D), a Nebraskan farmer, ordered and received two magazines containing photos of nude preteen and teenage boys from an adult bookstore in California. At that time, no applicable law prohibited Jacobson (D) from ordering or receiving magazines of such content. Several months later, Congress enacted the Child Protection Act of 1984, which criminalized the knowing receipt through the mails of depictions of minors engaged in sexual activity. Postal inspectors subsequently found Jacobson's (D) name on a mailing list in the possession of the California bookstore. The Government (P) sent Jacobson (D) a letter from a fictitious organization. Jacobson (D) enrolled in the organization and filled out a questionnaire stating his enjoyment of "pre-teen sex," but indicating his opposition to pedophilia. Over a year later, the Government (P) again came across Jacobson's (D) name from its own files and sent him a letter from another fictitious organization, seeking a response from those who enjoyed what the letter termed as an awareness of "lusty and youthful lasses and lasses of neophyte age." Jacobson (D) responded with a request for more information. The Government (P) then sent a letter from another fictitious organization indicating that the organization was involved in lobbying efforts, to be funded by sales of a future catalogue, and stating that it was Jacobson's (D) constitutional right to receive such material. Thereafter the Government (P) sent a letter to Jacobson (D) from a fictitious pen pal, "Carl Long." Jacobson (D) replied to the letter, stating that he preferred pictures of young men in their late teens and early twenties. The correspondence with "Carl Long" ceased after two letters. Twenty-six months after the Government (P) first targeted Jacobson (D), the Customs Service included him in its own sting operation. Jacobson (D) filled an order for pictures of young boys engaging in sex from a brochure sent by the Customs Service under the guise of a fictitious organization. That order was never filled. The Postal Service then sent Jacobson (D) a letter from a fictitious Canadian organization. [What took it so long?] Jacobson (D) responded by ordering a magazine containing child pornography. After making a controlled delivery of the magazine, the Government (P) arrested Jacobson (D). No other illicit materials, save for the legally received magazines, were found in Jacobson's (D) possession.

■ ISSUE

When entrapment is at issue, must the government prove that the defendant's predisposition to commit the crime was not the result of the government's efforts?

■ DECISION AND RATIONALE

(White, J.) Yes. Under a claim of entrapment, the defendant's predisposition must be independent and not the product of the conduct of the government. The government failed to prove this beyond a reasonable doubt. The only piece of evidence of Jacobson's (D) predisposition prior to the Government's (P) 26 month operation were the magazines from the California bookstore. However, these magazines only establish Jacobson's inclination to view sexually-oriented photos containing children [ONLY!]. The magazines were lawfully obtained. Evidence of predisposition to do what was once lawful is insufficient to show criminal predisposition, for it is understood that people obey the law even when they disapprove of it. The evidence gathered during the investigation also falls to establish such predisposition. Jacobson's (D) responses to the Government's (P) solicitations merely establish that he was inclined to view the prohibited materials, not to break the law. Furthermore, it can be inferred that the Government (P) exerted pressure on Jacobson (D) by reference to his constitutional rights and lobbying efforts to change the law. The evidence only shows that Jacobson (D) was willing to unlawfully receive the materials after the Government's (P) lengthy campaign; no rational juror could have found otherwise beyond a reasonable doubt. Reversed.

■ DISSENT

(O'Connor, J.) The facts clearly show that the Government (P) twice offered Jacobson (D) the opportunity to purchase child pornography through the mails and that Jacobson (D) accepted both times. The first order was never filled. The delivery of the second order formed the basis of Jacobson's (D) conviction. The Court holds that the Government (P) must prove not only that a suspect was predisposed to commit the crime before the opportunity to commit it arose, but also before the Government (P) came on the scene. The defense of entrapment requires an assessment of predisposition prior to the government suggesting the crime, not prior to contacting the defendant. The rule that Government (P) contact can "create" predisposition has the potential to be misread as requiring that the Government (P) have reasonable suspicion of a defendant's predisposition prior to contacting him. So interpreted the rule might act to prevent the Government (P) from advertising the seductions of criminal activity as part of its sting operation. In this case, the Government (P) did not coax, threaten or persuade Jacobson (D). All it did was to send some letters which could have been ignored or discarded. Also troubling is the Court's redefinition of predisposition. The Court seems to require that the Government (P) show that the defendant was predisposed to engage in the illegal activity, here, receiving child pornography in the mail, and that the defendant was predisposed to break the law knowingly in order to do so. The problem is that the crime at issue is not one that requires specific intent to break the law. The Court has usurped the province of the jury by holding as a matter of law that the Government (P) did not prove that Jacobson (D) was predisposed to participate in the criminal activity.

Analysis:

In defining the contours of the predisposition requirement of the entrapment defense, as announced by the progenitors of *United States v. Russell* [case involving a narcotics officer who provided the defendants with an ingredient essential to the manufacture of methamphetamine, which the defendants were convicted of manufacturing], the Court has left lower courts struggling to figure what exactly is required of the government in entrapment cases. The dissent suggests that the majority's rule might be read as requiring the Government (P) to have a reasonable suspicion that the defendant was predisposed prior to contacting him. A plain reading of the Court's opinion exposes as unreasonable the dissenters' fear on this point. At most, the case can be read as restricting what the Government (P) can do during its sting operation. Indeed, that the Government (P) must prove disposition prior to its coming to the scene is exactly what the dissent reads as the holding of the Court. However, a much narrower interpretation is just as likely. The Court's opinion could be read as stating that, when the Government's (P) conduct is sufficient to "create" predisposition, it must prove that the defendant's predisposition existed prior to the Government's (P) conduct. In this case, the majority believed that the Government's (P) repeated mailings, some of which hinted at the legality of the materials, and the length of the operation were sufficient to conclude that the Government (P) created Jacobson's (D) predisposition.

CHAPTER NINE

Police Interrogation and Confessions

Miranda v. Arizona

Instant Facts: A rapist who confessed during custodial interrogation appeals his conviction, contending he was not informed of his constitutional privilege against self-incrimination and right to counsel.

Black Letter Rule: Confessions produced by custodial interrogation are inadmissible unless the suspect was informed of (i) his right to silence, (ii) the consequences of waiving that right, and (iii) his right to retained or appointed counsel, and (iv) waived those rights knowingly and intelligently.

Yarborough v. Alvarado

Instant Facts: Alvarado (D), a minor, confessed to committing murder and attempted robbery during pre-custody questioning.

Black Letter Rule: Whether a suspect is in custody under *Miranda* is determined objectively by how a reasonable person in the suspect's situation would understand his ability to terminate questioning and leave.

Rhode Island v. Innis

Instant Facts: After a murder suspect in police custody requested counsel, one officer remarked the lost murder weapon might injure nearby children, which induced the suspect to locate the weapon.

Black Letter Rule: Even if a suspect is in police custody, police officers' statements are not deemed "interrogation" unless they are either express questions or equivalent statements which are reasonably likely to elicit an incriminating response, and in fact elicit such a response.

New York v. Quarles

Instant Facts: After police arrested an armed suspect who hid his gun, they asked him where the gun was before reciting Miranda. At trial, the suspect moved to exclude the gun and his answer.

Black Letter Rule: Police may ask questions reasonably necessary to ensure public safety without reciting Miranda warnings, and suspects' replies are admissible.

Minnick v. Mississippi

Instant Facts: After a suspect demanded counsel, the police allowed him to consult an attorney but then re-started questioning without the attorney present.

Black Letter Rule: Once a suspect requests counsel, police may not re-initiate questioning unless counsel is present.

Moran v. Burbine

Instant Facts: After the police failed to tell a suspect that a lawyer had been appointed for him, and falsely told the lawyer the suspect would not be interrogated, the suspect moved to suppress his confession.

Black Letter Rule: A confession is not rendered inadmissible merely because the police failed to inform the suspect that a lawyer tried to contact him, or because the police did not grant the lawyer access, although egregious police misconduct may violate constitutional due process.

Dickerson v. United States

Instant Facts: Supreme Court considered whether *Miranda* was a constitutional holding, and thus, not subject to being superseded by Congressional legislation, originating from the granting of Dickerson's (D) motion to suppress because he had not received *Miranda* warnings before interrogation.

Black Letter Rule: *Miranda v. Arizona* announced a constitutional rule, which Congress may not supersede legislatively.

Chavez v. Martinez

Instant Facts: After being shot in a police altercation, Martinez (P) requested that Chavez (D), a patrol officer, cease interrogation until he could receive medical treatment.

Black Letter Rule: The Fifth Amendment right against self-incrimination does not attach until criminal proceedings have been initiated.

United States v. Patane

Instant Facts: Patane (D) was convicted of possession of a firearm as a felon after he voluntarily admitted possession without being read his *Miranda* rights.

Black Letter Rule: Nontestimonial evidence obtained as a result of a defendant's voluntary statement without the benefit of *Miranda* warnings need not be excluded at the defendant's trial.

Missouri v. Seibert

Instant Facts: After Seibert (D) made an incriminating statement without a *Miranda* warning, she was read her *Miranda* rights and repeated the statement.

Black Letter Rule: Incriminating statements initially made before *Miranda* warnings are given are not admissible simply because they are repeated after proper warnings are given.

Brewer v. Williams

Instant Facts: Police elicited statements during long automobile ride from very religious mental patient accused of murder, and represented by counsel, resulting in body being found.

Black Letter Rule: The right to counsel is violated if incriminating statements are obtained from the accused after judicial proceedings have been initiated and counsel retained.

Texas v. Cobb

Instant Facts: Cobb (D), charged with burglary and represented by counsel, confessed to an uncharged murder and thereafter claimed his right to counsel attached for the murder as well.

Black Letter Rule: After the Sixth Amendment right to counsel attaches to an offense, it also attaches to other offenses that, even if not formally charged, would be considered the same offense because each requires the same proof of facts.

Miranda v. Arizona

(A Confessed Criminal(s)) v. *(Prosecutor(s))*
384 U.S. 436, 86 S.Ct. 1602, 16 L.Ed.2d 694 (1966)

IN CUSTODIAL INTERROGATION, POLICE MUST WARN SUSPECTS OF RIGHT TO REMAIN SILENT AND RIGHT TO COUNSEL

■ **INSTANT FACTS** A rapist who confessed during custodial interrogation appeals his conviction, contending he was not informed of his constitutional privilege against self-incrimination and right to counsel.

■ **BLACK LETTER RULE** Confessions produced by custodial interrogation are inadmissible unless the suspect was informed of (i) his right to silence, (ii) the consequences of waiving that right, and (iii) his right to retained or appointed counsel, and (iv) waived those rights knowingly and intelligently.

■ PROCEDURAL BASIS

Consolidated opinion for 4 separate criminal appeals from appellate affirmation of convictions, on writ of certiorari.

■ FACTS

Ernesto Miranda (D), an indigent, semi-educated, and possibly schizophrenic Mexican, was suspected of kidnaping and rape, and arrested. At the police station, Miranda (D) was identified by a witness. While in police custody, Miranda (D) was interrogated. Miranda (D) was not advised of his right to counsel. After the interrogation, Miranda (D) signed a confession, on a preprinted form stating the confession was made voluntarily, without threats or immunity offers, and "with full knowledge of . . . legal rights, understanding any statement [made] may be used against me." At trial, the state prosection (P) introduced the confession, and Miranda (D) was convicted of kidnaping and rape. Miranda (D) appealed. The appellate court affirmed, finding that Miranda (D) never specifically requested counsel. [Is an indigent, semi-educated, and possibly schizophrenic person really supposed to know this?] Miranda (D) appeals. [This case also consolidates the cases of defendants Vignera (D), Westover (D), and Stewart (D), who, in unrelated cases, confessed during custodial interrogation by police which did not include a warning on their right to counsel or privilege against self-incrimination.]

■ ISSUE

Is a confession admissible when produced after custodial interrogation in which the suspect was not informed of his privilege against self-incrimination and right to counsel?

■ DECISION AND RATIONALE

(Warren) No. Confessions produced by custodial interrogation are inadmissible unless the suspect was informed of (i) his right to silence, (ii) the consequences of waiving that right, and (iii) his right to retained or appointed counsel, and (iv) waived those rights knowingly and intelligently. The *Fifth Amendment* provides "No person . . . shall be compelled in any criminal case to be a witness against himself" and "the accused [shall] have the Assistance of Counsel." These cases implicate those constitutional guarantees when defendants are questioned while in police custody or otherwise significantly deprived of free action. While interrogations are private and thus secretive, we can obtain information about actual interrogation practices from police manuals on interrogation. Notably, the interrogation is psychologically intimidating, since the defendant is alone, in isolated unfamiliar surroundings, against the authority of the state and police. The manuals state interrogators should suggest they believe the suspect is guilty, and to dismiss and discourage contrary explanations. These manuals recommend the "good cop, bad cop" technique, and may instruct the interrogator to induce confessions by trickery (e.g., false witness identifications in a lineup, or false accusations of more serious crimes). The manuals state that, when a suspect requests an attorney, the interrogator should discourage it, suggest that consulting an attorney suggests his guilt, or recommend he confess before seeing the attorney. Thus, the very fact of custodial interrogation exacts a heavy toll on individual liberty and individuals' weakness, even absent deception, brutality, or the "third degree." Obviously, such an interrogation environment is created solely to subjugate individuals' wills to the examiners' will; this atmosphere carries its own badge of intimidation. In such cases, a defendant's confession may be "voluntary" in traditional terms, but we hold the *Fifth Amendment* provides additional safeguards to individual liberty. Incommunicado interrogation is at odds with our cherished common law principle, the privilege against self-incrimination, which was adopted to force the state to respect individual dignity, to level the balance between state and individual, and to require the prosecution to produce evidence by its independent labors. We are convinced the privilege against self-incrimination applies to police custodial questioning, as well as to trial, since the compulsion during interrogations is greater. The *Fifth Amendment* requires that, during police custodial interrogation, the police must observe proper safeguards. We recommend the following safeguards; while the police or Congress may enact other safeguards, they must prove their alternative procedures are at least as effective in apprising suspects of their right to silence. When a person is subjected to custodial interrogation, he must be informed clearly and unequivocally that he has the right to remain silent, even if he is (or should be) aware of that right. This warning must be accompanied by the explanation that anything they say can and will be used against him in court. Also, the suspect must be informed clearly that he has the right to consult a lawyer and have the lawyer with him during interrogation, and that if he cannot afford a lawyer, the state will appoint one. If the suspect requests the assistance of an attorney but cannot afford one, the state must appoint one to represent him. The failure to request an attorney is not deemed a waiver unless the suspect is informed of his right to counsel, and chooses to confess anyway. If the suspect indicates he wishes to remain silent, before or during questioning, the interrogation must cease. If the interrogation is continued against his wishes, all statements made after the suspect invoked his right to silence are inadmissible. If the suspect requests an attorney, the interrogation must cease until an attorney is present, at which time the suspect must have an opportunity to confer with the attorney and have him present during any subsequent questioning. If the suspect indicates he wants an attorney before speaking with police, but cannot obtain one, the police cannot question him, though they may continue investigating by other means. The police need not provide an attorney immediately if they need a reasonable period of time to investigate. If the suspect requests counsel, but the police continue interrogating him without counsel, any statement taken is *presumed* inadmissible, unless the state meets the heavy burden of proving the defendant knowingly and intelligently waived his privilege against self-incrimination and right to counsel. A waiver may be proven by showing an express statement that the suspect is willing to make a statement and does not want an attorney, followed by a statement (confession). However, if the suspect is merely silent after hearing the warnings, or eventually gives a confession, no waiver is presumed. Similarly, if the suspect first answers some questions or volunteers some information before invoking his right to remain silent, he is not deemed to waive his rights for any post-invocation statements [though presumably the information he volunteered before remaining silent is admissible]. If the suspect confessed after lengthy interrogation, protracted incommunicado incarceration, threat, trick, or cajole, the confession is presumably invalid. Any statement obtained in violation of these procedures is inadmissible, be it a confession, admission of limited facts, inculpatory, or exculpatory. These procedures are required for custodial interrogation only, not for on-the-scene questioning or general questioning of non-suspects, since in such circumstances the inherently compelling atmosphere is not necessarily present. Volunteered statements of any kind are not barred by our holding. While we are not unmindful of the burdens policemen must bear, we believe this holding is necessary to safeguard individual liberties, and will not hinder police interrogation unduly. Here, Miranda's (D) confession was invalid, since he was never informed of his privilege against self-incrimination or right to counsel, and the mere fact he signed a confession on paper containing a boilerplate clause stating he had "full knowledge" of his legal rights is not nearly the "knowing and intelligent waiver" required. Reversed.

■ **DISSENT**

(Clark) I disagree with the majority's grim characterization of custodial interrogation as practiced, and I fear its mandate, inserted at the nerve center of crime detection, may kill it. Instead, I would follow the more pliable dictates of the Due Process Clause.

■ **DISSENT**

(Harlan) The majority opinion goes beyond banning just improper interrogation techniques, and aims for utopian "voluntariness," disregarding past practice and pragmatism. The *Fifth Amendment* was never interpreted to forbid *all* pressure. The majority's reading overstates interrogation's coercive quality, and makes obtaining confessions nearly impossible, since if the suspect is allowed a lawyer before questioning, the lawyer will always instruct him to say nothing. This is an unrealistic response to our fairly progressive interrogation techniques, and no other country has adopted such measures.

■ **DISSENT**

(White) The majority opinion is at odds with common law and the *Fifth Amendment*'s past interpretation. Its new law is predicated on antiquated views of interrogation procedure, and is more cumbersome than necessary, assuming as it does that practically every jailhouse statement is coerced. This new rule is deliberately calculated to reduce confessions, even if they are reliable and uncoerced. The requirement of hiring a lawyer will add delay and increase litigation.

Analysis:

The *Miranda* decision gave rise to the eponymous Miranda warnings, which police now read to suspects upon arrest: "You have the right to remain silent. Anything you say can and will be used against you in a court of law. You have the right to an attorney. If you cannot afford one, one will be appointed for you." It is widely unpopular among police, since it reduces greatly the number of confessions and sets strict procedures which must be followed during the interrogation; failure will result in all statements being rendered inadmissible. The majority opinion is predicated on the assumption, perhaps overstated, that the very act of custodial interrogation is inherently coercive, even absent trickery, threat, or torture. However, some version of Miranda is procedurally necessary if we truly desire to implement the constitutional privilege against self-incrimination and right to counsel. If these rights exist but suspects are not informed of them and instead directed to answer police questioning despite their existence, then these constitutional privileges will benefit only the rich and educated, or recidivists and career criminals. However, practically, if suspects are provided an attorney, few will confess, since any lawyer will instruct them not to make any statements to police. But that is the very aim of the privilege against self-incrimination.

■ **CASE VOCABULARY**

CAJOLING: Persuasion by coaxing (or, sometimes, by flattery). Here, this presumably refers to a situation where the suspect indicated a desire not to answer further questions, but the interrogator kept asking, and eventually elicited a response.

CUSTODIAL INTERROGATION: Police interrogation where the person has been taken into police custody or otherwise significantly deprived of his freedom. "Custody" usually means the person (suspect) is not free to leave the police station.

INCOMMUNICADO: "Without any means of communication." Without the ability to talk to others (i.e., an attorney).

"THIRD DEGREE": Police interrogation through threats, protracted questioning, and/or torture. Here, the majority opinion uses "third degree" to mean threats.

Yarborough v. Alvarado

(Prison Warden) v. *(Convicted Murderer)*

541 U.S. 652, 124 S.Ct. 2140, 158 L.Ed.2d 938 (2004)

A SUSPECT'S AGE AND EXPERIENCE ARE NOT TO BE CONSIDERED IN A *MIRANDA* CUSTODY INQUIRY

■ **INSTANT FACTS** Alvarado (D), a minor, confessed to committing murder and attempted robbery during pre-custody questioning.

■ **BLACK LETTER RULE** Whether a suspect is in custody under *Miranda* is determined objectively by how a reasonable person in the suspect's situation would understand his ability to terminate questioning and leave.

■ PROCEDURAL BASIS

Certiorari to review a decision of the Ninth Circuit Court of Appeals reversing the defendant's conviction on a writ of habeas corpus.

■ FACTS

Alvarado (D), a minor, assisted another person in attempting to steal a truck, leading to the shooting of the truck's owner. The investigating officer notified Alvarado's (D) parents that she wanted to speak with Alvarado (D). Alvarado's (D) parents brought him to the police station, where they remained in the lobby while the officer interrogated Alvarado (D) in a solitary room without *Miranda* warnings. After first denying his involvement, Alvarado (D) later admitted to helping the other person attempt to steal the truck and hide the murder weapon. At the conclusion of questioning, Alvarado (D) was returned to his parents. Alvarado (D) was charged with murder and attempted robbery. The trial court denied Alvarado's (D) request to suppress the incriminating statements because he was not in custody during questioning, so no *Miranda* warnings were required. On appeal, the California District Court of Appeal agreed. Alvarado (D) filed a petition for a writ of habeas corpus with the federal district court, which denied the writ. The Ninth Circuit Court of Appeals reversed, however, holding that because of his youth and inexperience, Alvarado (D) could not have reasonably appreciated his right to leave during questioning. The Ninth Circuit further concluded that Alvarado's (D) juvenile status was relevant to habeas relief under the federal Antiterrorism and Effective Death Penalty Act of 1996, because his status "resulted in a decision [that] involved an unreasonable application [of] clearly established Federal law."

■ ISSUE

Is a suspect's age and experience with the judicial system relevant to an inquiry of his "in-custody" status during pre-arrest questioning?

■ DECISION AND RATIONALE

(Kennedy, J.) No. Under clearly established Court precedent, custody is determined by how a reasonable person in the suspect's situation would perceive his circumstances. If a reasonable person in the suspect's position would appreciate his ability to freely leave, the suspect is not in custody. Here, Alvarado (D) was not brought to the police station by the police, was never placed under arrest or threatened with arrest, the questioning focused on another person's conduct rather than his own, and his parents remained in the lobby. Under these objective facts, a reasonable person would feel free to terminate the questioning and leave at any time.

On the other hand, Alvarado (D) was questioned at the police station, he arrived at the initiative of his legal guardians rather than of his own volition, and his parents were not permitted to participate in the questioning. From these facts, a reasonable person may feel in custody. Because of the differing perspectives, the state court's application of federal law was reasonable, for this Court cannot second-guess whether the state court was correct in fact. The *Miranda* custody inquiry is an objective one and does not consider subjective elements such as the suspect's age and experience with the judicial system. The proper standard is that of a reasonable person, not a reasonable person of the suspect's age and experience. Because the state court properly considered the correct factors, its decision was reasonable.

■ CONCURRENCE

(O'Connor, J.) While a suspect's age may be relevant in some circumstances, the suspect was so close to the age of majority that requiring police to recognize that a suspect was a juvenile would be difficult. In other situations, however, a suspect's obvious minority may be relevant.

■ DISSENT

(Breyer, J.) No reasonable person in Alvarado's (D) position would have felt free to terminate the police questioning. Alvarado (D) was told by his parents that he needed to submit to police questioning, and his parents took him to the police station. He was separated from his parents, after they were denied participation, and taken to a small interrogation room. For two hours, the officer questioned Alvarado (D) concerning evidence they had against him and gave him an opportunity to tell the truth and "take care of himself." No reasonable person in his position would feel free to leave at any time. The majority sees a reasonable difference of opinion as to whether Alvarado (D) was in custody, but points only to things the police *did not* do. A focus on what *did* happen, however, demonstrates he acted as a reasonable person would. His age is not a subjective component of the standard, for a person of advanced age would not feel the pressure Alvarado (D) did when faced with his parents' role in the questioning. The reasonable person standard must account for personal characteristics, such as age, that ensure that Alvarado's beliefs (D) are properly compared to the expected beliefs of those similarly situated.

Analysis:

The Court's conclusion that age and inexperience are subjective factors that are unknowable by the police at the time of questioning is questionable. With today's intricate police network, background checks on suspects are easily obtained and reviewed by police before an interrogation commences. While a suspect may lie about such factors, objective data within an officer's possession can easily satisfy the knowledge requirement of the objective standard.

CASE VOCABULARY

CUSTODY: The care and control of a thing or person for inspection, preservation, or security.

MIRANDA RULE: The doctrine that a criminal suspect in police custody must be informed of certain constitutional rights before being interrogated. The suspect must be advised of the right to remain silent, the right to have an attorney present during questioning, and the right to have an attorney appointed if the suspect cannot afford one. If the suspect is not advised of these rights and does not validly waive them, any evidence obtained during the interrogation cannot be used against the suspect at trial (except for impeachment purposes).

Rhode Island v. Innis

(*State Prosecution*) v. (*Confessed Murderer*)

446 U.S. 291, 100 S.Ct. 1682, 64 L.Ed.2d 297 (1980)

POLICE "INTERROGATION" MEANS QUESTIONS OR STATEMENTS REASONABLY LIKELY TO ELICIT INCRIMINATING REPLY

■ **INSTANT FACTS** After a murder suspect in police custody requested counsel, one officer remarked the lost murder weapon might injure nearby children, which induced the suspect to locate the weapon.

■ **BLACK LETTER RULE** Even if a suspect is in police custody, police officers' statements are not deemed "interrogation" unless they are either express questions or equivalent statements which are reasonably likely to elicit an incriminating response, and in fact elicit such a response.

■ FACTS

Innis (D) was arrested on suspicion he robbed and shot fatally a taxi driver. Innis (D) was read his *Miranda* warning, and he asked to consult a lawyer. Innis (D) was placed in the police car's backseat, to be taken to the police station. En route, two police officers in the car discussed the missing murder weapon, a shotgun, and expressed concern it might be found by nearby schoolchildren. At that point, Innis (D) interrupted their conversation and told them he would point out where the gun was. Innis (D) was again read *Miranda*, and replied he understood but wanted to get the gun out of the children's way. Innis (D) then pointed out the shotgun hidden under rocks. Innis (D) was tried for murder, and convicted on evidence including the shotgun and testimony about how he located it. On appeal, the court held the evidence inadmissible, finding his ride in the police car's backseat constituted custodial interrogation without counsel. The prosecution (P) [not pleased that the conviction was overturned] appeals.

■ ISSUE

If a suspect is in police custody, is a police officer's statement which elicits an incriminating response from the suspect an "Interrogation" which requires *Miranda* safeguards?

■ DECISION AND RATIONALE

(Stewart) No. Even if a suspect is in police custody, police officers' statements are not deemed "interrogation" unless they are either express questions or equivalent statements which are reasonably likely to elicit an incriminating response, and in fact elicit such a response. The parties agree that Innis (D) was properly informed of his *Miranda* rights, asserted his right to counsel, and was "in custody" while driven to the police station. The issue is whether he was being "interrogated." Some commentators opined that *Miranda* equates "interrogation" with express police questioning, but we disagree. *Miranda* was concerned about any "interrogation environment" which subjugates individual will, and expressly referred to police practices other than direct questioning as amounting to interrogation. However, mere custody does not require *Miranda* warnings, so "interrogation" must involve compulsion beyond that inherent in custody itself. We conclude the *Miranda* safeguards are required whenever a person in custody is subject to either express questioning or its functional equivalent, which is words or actions that the police should know are reasonably likely to elicit an incriminating response, and which in fact elicited an incriminating response. This latter definition focuses primarily on suspects' perceptions, not the police's intent. Here, we conclude Innis (D) was not "interrogated," since he was not questioned expressly in the officers' dialogue, and it cannot be concluded fairly that the officers should have known their conversation would move Innis (D) to make an incriminating response. [It must have been guilt that moved him.] There is no evidence on record suggesting the officers' remarks were designed to elicit a response from Innis (D). Also, Innis' (D) incriminating statement was not caused by the police's words. Reversed.

■ CONCURRENCE

(Burger) I concur to the extent the result is consistent with *Miranda*, but would not introduce new uncertainty by articulating a new test.

■ DISSENT

(Marshall) I agree with the holding, but believe the officers' appeal to Innis' (D) conscience is a classic technique which constitutes "interrogation."

■ DISSENT

(Stevens) In my view, any statement which would normally be understood by average listeners as calling for a response is the functional equivalent of a question, as there is no reason to exclude continued attempts to extract information via statements rather than questions. Here, the police's statements were intended and likely to elicit Innis' (D) response.

Analysis:

One interesting factual question which remains unclear from the record is whether the officer's statement was *designed* to appeal to Innis' (D) conscience and encourage him to locate the murder weapon. This may be seen as highly relevant to the issue of whether Innis's (D) continued questioning was a deliberate trampling of his *Miranda* right to discontinue questioning until counsel is provided. However, the court dismisses this as irrelevant, noting the proper test is the statement's effect on the suspect, not the intent with which it was made. As with the nebulous earlier "voluntariness" test of confessions, it is indeterminate whether an incriminating statement made in response to such an appeal to conscience is "caused" by the appeal, since the suspect "chose" to make it when he might have remained silent, but was certainly encouraged to speak by psychological pressure.

New York v. Quarles

(*State Prosecution*) v. (*Gun Possessor*)
467 U.S. 649, 104 S.Ct. 2626, 81 L.Ed.2d 550 (1984)

MIRANDA ALLOWS "PUBLIC SAFETY" EXCEPTION

■ **INSTANT FACTS** After police arrested an armed suspect who hid his gun, they asked him where the gun was before reciting *Miranda.* At trial, the suspect moved to exclude the gun and his answer.

■ **BLACK LETTER RULE** Police may ask questions reasonably necessary to ensure public safety without reciting *Miranda* warnings, and suspects' replies are admissible.

■ PROCEDURAL BASIS

In criminal prosecution for gun possession, appeal from appellate exclusion of evidence, on writ of certiorari.

■ FACTS

Police received reports a rapist armed with a gun had entered a supermarket. They arrested Quarles (D), who fit the description. Quarles (D) was wearing an empty gun holster. The police asked Quarles (D) where the gun was, and he said, "the gun is over there," indicated it was hidden in a carton. Then, Quarles (D) was formally arrested and read *Miranda.* Quarles (D) was not prosecuted for rape, but was prosecuted for gun possession. At trial, the prosecution attempted to present as evidence the gun and fact that Quarles (D) knew where it was, but the court excluded both, finding they were obtained in violation of Quarles' (D) *Miranda* rights. On appeal, the appellate court affirmed. The prosecution [i.e., they'll sure try hard to find a "public safety" situation] appeals.

■ ISSUE

If a police officer asks an arrestee where his gun is hidden, is the arrestee's answer and the gun admissible?

■ DECISION AND RATIONALE

(Rehnquist) Yes. Police may ask questions reasonably necessary to ensure public safety without reciting *Miranda* warnings, and suspects' replies are admissible. The *Miranda* requirements recognize a "public safety" exception. Here, we find the officers' failure to provide *Miranda* warnings was justified by overriding considerations of public safety. In this kaleidoscopic situation, the arresting officers necessarily acted outside standard procedure, and we should not second guess their motivations. Whatever the officers' motivations in such situations, we believe *Miranda* must be modified to include situations where officers ask questions reasonably prompted by concerns for public safety. Here, the officers acted to ensure public safety, since they immediately needed to find the gun they reasonably believed Quarles (D) had discarded in the supermarket. So long as the gun was concealed there, it posed a danger to public safety if discovered by an accomplice or another. In such situations, if police are required to recite *Miranda* warnings, suspects might be deterred from responding. We conclude the need to ask questions necessary to protect public safety outweighs the need for *Fifth Amendment* privileges against self-incrimination. We believe this exception will be easy to apply, because police will instinctively recognize questions necessary to secure their safety, or the public's. Reversed.

■ CONCURRENCE

(O'Connor) *Miranda* requires suppression of testimonial evidence obtained improperly, but not nontestimonial evidence. Thus, I would suppress the statement, "the gun is over there," but admit the gun itself. Also, I believe the majority's "public safety" exception blurs *Miranda*'s clear requirements.

■ DISSENT

(Marshall) The majority opinion falsely assumes the public was at risk during Quarles' (D) interrogation, whereas in fact Quarles (D) lacked accomplices, and the police knew the gun was in the immediate vicinity a few feet away. This difference of opinion illustrates the chaos the "public safety" exception will unleash. I feel the police may protect public safety without violating the *Fifth Amendment.*

Analysis:

Quarles features an extremely nebulous holding. While the majority recognizes a "public safety" exception to *Miranda* in some form, it never articulates what is necessary to trigger the exception, except perhaps that the arresting officer must reasonably (or unreasonably?) perceive a threat to the safety of the police or public. In fact, the court gladly delegates to the police the task of assessing what constitutes a threat. However, reasonable people may differ on whether a particular factual scenario constitutes an emergency, as the dissenting opinions show.

■ CASE VOCABULARY

POST HOC: From the Latin phrase "Post hoc, ergo propter hoc" meaning "After this, therefore because of this."

Minnick v. Mississippi

(*Confessed Murderer*) v. (*State Prosecution*)

498 U.S. 146, 111 S.Ct. 486, 112 L.Ed.2d 489 (1990)

ONCE SUSPECT REQUESTS COUNSEL, POLICE MAY NOT RE-INITIATE QUESTIONING WITHOUT COUNSEL PRESENT

■ **INSTANT FACTS** After a suspect demanded counsel, the police allowed him to consult an attorney but then re-started questioning without the attorney present.

■ **BLACK LETTER RULE** Once a suspect requests counsel, police may not re-initiate questioning unless counsel is present.

■ PROCEDURAL BASIS

In criminal prosecution for capital murder, review by U.S. Supreme Court from appellate affirmation of conviction.

■ FACTS

Prisoners Minnick (D) and Dykes escaped from jail and killed two people while robbing them. Later, Minnick (D) was arrested. Minnick (D) was read *Mirnada* and questioned. Minnick (D) refused to sign a confession, but stated Dykes killed one victim and forced him to shoot the other. Then, Minnick (D) requested a lawyer. A lawyer was appointed, and spoke with Minnick (D) several times. Later, sherriffs again came to question Minnick (D), telling him he would "have to talk" and "could not refuse." Minnick (D) answered their questions, incriminating himself. Minnick (D) was tried for murder, and moved to suppress his statements, contending they violated *Edwards'* protection against repeated questioning. The trial court admitted the statements, and Minnick (D) was convicted and sentenced to death. Minnick (D) appealed, but the appellate court affirmed. Minnick (D) appeals again.

■ ISSUE

If a suspect demands counsel and is allowed to consult with an attorney, may the police re-initiate questioning without the attorney present and admit any incriminating statements?

■ DECISION AND RATIONALE

(Kennedy) No. Once a suspect requests counsel, police may not re-initiate questioning unless counsel is present. *Edwards v. Arizona* (S.Ct. 1981) held that, if the suspect demands a lawyer, the police cannot re-question him before providing one. *Edwards'* rule is designed to prevent police from badgering suspects into waiving their previously-asserted *Miranda* rights, and its clear and unequivocal command conserves judicial resources by not requiring courts to determine "voluntariness." Previously, we interpreted *Edwards* as barring police-initiated interrogation unless the accused has counsel present. We now resolve any ambiguities by holding that, when counsel is requested, interrogation must cease, and officials may not reinitiate interrogation without counsel present, even if the accused has consulted his attorney. A single consultation with counsel does not remove suspects from police's persistent attempts to persuade them to relinquish their rights, nor from the coercive pressures of prolonged custody. Also, brief consultation may be insufficient to instruct the suspect of his rights, which is why *Edwards* allows counsel to be present during interrogation. Here, we believe Minnlck (D) may have been coerced into making incriminating statements, and may have misunderstood counsel's advice, believing oral confessions were inadmissible. Reversed.

■ DISSENT

(Scalia) *Edwards* should not be read to create an irrebuttable presumption that suspects can never waive their right to counsel, even after actually consulting an attorney. Once a suspect consults with an attorney, he will receive warnings about the effect of incriminating statements, and continued statements may constitute a waiver of the right to counsel. The majority opinion makes it impossible for suspects to change their minds, and sacrifices principle for simplicity's sake.

Analysis:

Whether *Minnick*'s expansion of the *Edwards* rule is justified depends on the desirable role of counsel. If the right to counsel envisions that any counsel will advise the suspect not to confess or answer any police questions, then the right to counsel is satisfied by a single consultation, and continued police questioning should be deemed proper, since the suspect already acquired the benefit of counsel. However, if the right to counsel is the right to have counsel present during all interrogations to provide continuous advice, then *Minnick* is correct. The fact that *Edwards* allows counsel to be present during interrogation suggest the latter view.

Moran v. Burbine

(*Not Stated*) v. (*Confessed Murderer*)
475 U.S. 412, 106 S.Ct. 1135, 89 L.Ed.2d 410 (1986)

MIRANDA IS NOT VIOLATED WHEN POLICE DENY LAWYERS ACCESS TO A SUSPECT

■ **INSTANT FACTS** After the police failed to tell a suspect that a lawyer had been appointed for him, and falsely told the lawyer the suspect would not be interrogated, the suspect moved to suppress his confession.

■ **BLACK LETTER RULE** A confession is not rendered inadmissible merely because the police failed to inform the suspect that a lawyer tried to contact him, or because the police did not grant the lawyer access, although egregious police misconduct may violate constitutional due process.

■ PROCEDURAL BASIS

In criminal prosecution for murder in the first degree, review of habeas corpus reversal of conviction, on writ of certiorari.

■ FACTS

Burbine (D) was arrested for murdering a woman with a pipe, and for a separate burglary. While Burbine (D) was in custody, he refused counsel, but his sister called the Public Defender's Office and obtained a lawyer for him. When the lawyer called the police and asked to be present at Burbine's (D) questioning, they told her (falsely) that they would not question him. [In other words, the cops lied!] The police also never told Burbine (D) that a lawyer had been obtained for him. Instead, the police interrogated Burbine (D) properly, inducing his confession. Burbine (D) was tried for murder. At trial, Burbine (D) moved to suppress his statements, contending he was deprived of the ability to knowingly waive counsel, and that the police's actions were improper. The trial court denied his motion, finding he refused counsel. Burbine (D) was convicted. On appeal, the state supreme court affirmed. Burbine (D) appealed on a writ of habeas corpus. The circuit court overturned his conviction. The prosecution (P) appeals.

■ ISSUE

Is an otherwise validly-obtained confession inadmissible because police did not inform a suspect that a lawyer tried to contract him, and falsely told the lawyer the suspect was not being interrogated?

■ DECISION AND RATIONALE

(O'Connor) No. A confession is not rendered inadmissible merely because the police failed to inform the suspect that a lawyer tried to contact him, or because the police did not grant the lawyer access, although egregious police misconduct may violate constitutional due process. *Miranda* holds that defendants may waive their rights to counsel and silence, provided such waiver is made voluntarily, knowingly, and intelligently. This inquiry has 2 dimensions; the waiver must have been the product of free choice rather than coercion, and must have been made with full awareness of both the nature of the right abandoned and the consequences of abandoning it. Events entirely unknown to the defendant have no bearing on his capacity to comprehend and knowingly relinquish those rights. Nor is the police's culpability relevant to the validity of his waiver, unless it deprives him of knowledge necessary to understand his *Miranda* rights. We have never read the Constitution to require police to supply suspects with information to guide their decisions, or to advise suspects of attorneys' attempts to contact them, and believe such a reading would undermine police interrogation's effectiveness without significantly protecting suspects' rights. Furthermore, how police treat suspects' *attorneys* is outside the scope of *Miranda.* While here we find the police's deliberate deception distasteful [to say the least], we find this does not change the fact that Burbine (D) knowingly waived his rights to counsel and silence, while fully understanding those rights. Burbine (D) also contends the interrogation violated his *Sixth Amendment* right [to have the assistance of counsel in all criminal prosecutions], but we find the interrogation occurred before adversarial judicial proceedings began, and decline to hold that the *Sixth Amendment* applies earlier. Finally, Burbine (D) contends the police's treatment of his public defender was so offensive as to deprive him of due process. While we concede that police deception might rise to the level of due process violations, we do not find the police's actions here to be that egregious. Reversed.

■ DISSENT

(Stevens) Police interference with attorneys' access to their clients should make their clients' subsequent waiver of rights inadmissible. Prior cases viewed incommunicado questioning with strictest scrutiny. Police interference is a pervasive problem, which requires clear and adequate safeguards. *Miranda* prohibits police trickery, and this should apply to police misstatements or omissions regarding counsel. Under agency law, the police's deception of Burbine's (D) attorney was tantamount to deceiving Burbine (D) himself. Also, the majority holding seemingly permits police to deny lawyers access to clients being interrogated; such interference with the attorney-client relationship violates the *Due Process Clause.*

Analysis:

Moran offers a "personal" definition of the *Miranda* warnings, under which the police must inform suspects of their abstract legal rights, but need not inform them of circumstances and facts which might well cause them to change their minds about speaking to police. Thus, though a suspect has the right to request an attorney, he has no right to be told a lawyer has been appointed for him, or is trying to contact him. Even more disturbingly, the Court permits the police to lie to the lawyer in a way which discourages the lawyer from being present during interrogation, which apparently undermines the right to counsel. As such, it reflects the Court's changed reading of *Miranda*, which initially seemed to prohibit all police trickery used to induce confessions.

■ CASE VOCABULARY

ARRAIGNMENT: Formal courtroom procedure where the suspect is charged with crimes.

HABEAS CORPUS: "Must have the body." Writ used to challenge illegal imprisonment.

Dickerson v. United States

(*Bank Robber*) v. (*Government*)
530 U.S. 428, 120 S.Ct. 2326 (2000)

SUPREME COURT DECLARES THAT CONGRESS MAY NOT, THROUGH LEGISLATION, SUPERSEDE *MIRANDA*

■ **INSTANT FACTS** Supreme Court considered whether *Miranda* was a constitutional holding, and thus not subject to being superseded by Congressional legislation, originating from the granting of Dickerson's (D) motion to suppress because he had not received *Miranda* warnings before interrogation.

■ **BLACK LETTER RULE** *Miranda v. Arizona* announced a constitutional rule, which Congress may not supersede legislatively.

■ PROCEDURAL BASIS

Review by Supreme Court of U.S. Court of Appeal's reversal of District Court's granting of criminal defendant's motion to suppress.

■ FACTS

Dickerson (D) was indicted for bank robbery and conspiracy to commit bank robbery. Before trial, he moved to suppress a statement he had made to the FBI, on the grounds that he had not received *Miranda* warnings [certain warnings must be given before a suspect's statement made during custodial interrogation can be admitted in evidence before being interrogated]. The trial court granted the motion and the Government (P) took an interlocutory appeal to the court of appeals, which reversed the decision of the lower court. The court of appeals held that § 3501 [*Crime Control Act of 1968,* which limits *Miranda* and the *McNabb-Mallory* rule in federal prosecutions, by giving judges the option of admitting confessions obtained without informing the suspect of his right to silence and/or counsel, if they are deemed "voluntary."] was satisfied. It also concluded that *Miranda* was not a constitutional holding, and thus Congress, by statute, could supersede the decision. Dickerson (D) [perhaps realizing his case was of great constitutional importance] sought review by the United States Supreme Court.

■ ISSUE

Does the decision in *Miranda v. Arizona* constitute a constitutional rule, which may not be legislatively superseded by Congress?

■ DECISION AND RATIONALE

(Rehnquist) Yes. We hold that *Miranda v. Arizona* announced a constitutional rule, which Congress may not supersede legislatively. Moreover, we decline to overrule *Miranda* ourselves. Prior to *Miranda,* we evaluated the admissibility of a suspect's confession under a voluntariness test, based upon the Fifth Amendment right against self-incrimination and the Due Process Clause of the Fourteenth Amendment. The due process test takes into consideration the totality of all the surrounding circumstances—both the characteristics of the accused and the details of the interrogation. We have never abandoned this due process jurisprudence, and thus continue to exclude confessions that were obtained involuntarily. Two years after *Miranda* was decided, Congress enacted § 3501, which expressly designates voluntariness as the touchstone of admissibility, and omits any warning requirements. It is clear that Congress intended to overrule *Miranda.* We must determine whether Congress has the authority to supersede *Miranda*; if it does, § 3501 will prevail over *Miranda,* and if it does not, the section must yield to *Miranda's* more specific requirements. Congress has supervisory authority over federal courts, and we may use that authority to prescribe rules of evidence and procedure that are binding in those tribunals; however, we do not have the power to judicially create and enforce nonconstitutional rules of procedure and evidence, absent an Act of Congress. However, Congress may not legislatively supersede our decisions interpreting and applying the Constitution. Thus, we must decide whether the *Miranda* Court announced a constitutional rule or merely exercised its supervisory authority to regulate evidence in the absence of congressional direction. This Court has repeatedly referred to the *Miranda* warnings as "prophylactic" and not rights protected by the Constitution. However, we believe that *Miranda* is a constitutional decision. We have consistently applied it to state court prosecutions, and our authority in state courts is limited to enforcing the commands of the United States Constitution. In addition, the *Miranda* opinion itself begins by stating that the Court granted certiorari "to give concrete constitutional guidelines for law enforcement agencies and the courts to follow." The opinion is replete with statements indicating that the majority thought it was announcing a constitutional rule. Additionally, the opinion invites legislative action to protect the constitutional right against coerced self-incrimination. Finally, *Miranda* has become embedded in routine police practice to the point where the warnings have become part of our national culture. Experience suggests that the totality-of-the-circumstances test which § 3501 seeks to revive is more difficult than *Miranda* for law enforcement officers to conform to, and for courts to apply in a consistent manner. Thus, we conclude that *Miranda* announced a constitutional rule and therefore Congress may not supersede it. Following the rule of stare decisis, we decline to overrule *Miranda.*

■ DISSENT

(Scalia) Today's decision is not a reaffirmation of *Miranda,* but a radical revision of the most significant element of *Miranda*: the rationale that gives it a permanent place in our jurisprudence. *Marbury v. Madison* held that an Act of Congress will not be enforced by the courts if what it prescribes violates the Constitution of the United States. To justify today's decision, the Court must adopt a significant *new,* if not entirely comprehensible, principle of constitutional law—statutes of Congress can be disregarded, not only when what they prescribe violates the Constitution, but when what they prescribe contradicts a decision of this Court that "announced a constitutional rule." The only thing that can possibly mean in the context of this case is that this Court has the power, not merely to apply the Constitution but to expand it, imposing what it regards as useful "prophylactic" restrictions upon Congress and the States. That is an immense and frightening antidemocratic power, and it does not exist. The power we recognized in *Marbury* will require us to disregard § 3501—a duly enacted statute governing the admissibility of evidence in federal courts—only if it be in opposition to the Constitution, which in this case is the dictates of the Fifth Amendment. This Court has long since abandoned the notion that failure to comply with *Miranda's* rules is itself a violation of the Constitution. What today's decision will stand for, whether the Justices can bring themselves to say it or not, is the power of the Supreme Court to write a prophylactic, extraconstitutional Constitution, binding on Congress and the States. Thus, while I agree with the Court that § 3501 cannot be upheld without also concluding that *Miranda* represents an illegitimate exercise of our authority to review state-court judgments, I do not share the Court's hesitation in reaching that conclusion. Today's judgment converts *Miranda* from a milestone of judicial overreaching into the very Cheops' Pyramid (or perhaps the Sphinx would be a better analogue) of judicial arrogance. In imposing its Court-made code upon the States, the original opinion at least asserted that it was demanded by the Constitution. Today's decision does not pretend that it is—and yet still asserts the right to improve it against the will of the people's representatives in Congress. Far from believing that stare decisis compels this result, I believe we cannot allow to remain on the books even a celebrated decision—especially a celebrated decision—that has come to stand for the proposition that the Supreme Court has power to impose extraconstitutional constraints upon Congress and the States. I dissent from today's decision, and, until § 3501 is repealed, will continue to apply it in all cases where there has been a sustainable finding that the defendant's confession was voluntary.

Analysis:

This very significant case could have resulted in the overruling of the landmark *Miranda v. Arizona* case. However, the majority held that *Miranda* was a constitutional rule, and therefore Congress could not supersede it by enacting the § 3501 legislation. This legislation sought to reintroduce the former totality-of-circumstances approach and to mandate that, as long as suspect's statements were voluntary, they would be admissible. Over the strong objection from dissenting justice Scalia, the majority reaffirmed *Miranda's* constitutional status, leaving in tack over 35 years, and nearly 60 cases, of post *Miranda* decisions. The majority faced with post-*Miranda* cases that referred to it as "prophylactic" and not involving rights protected by the Constitution, asserted in a cursory manner that *Miranda* nevertheless set forth a constitutional rule, relying upon its subsequent application to the States, and the language from the opinion referencing the Constitution. This decision also demonstrates that basic principle that Congress has authority to modify *or* set aside any judicially created rules of evidence and procedure that are not required by the Constitution, but it may not legislatively supersede Supreme Court decisions that interpret and apply the Constitution.

■ CASE VOCABULARY

AMICUS CURIAE: A "friend of the court" brief, submitted by interested non-parties.

INTERLOCUTORY APPEAL: An appeal of a matter which does not resolve the entire controversy, but which relates to an intervening matter.

MOTION TO SUPPRESS: Formally requesting the court to declare certain evidence inadmissible based upon any number of legal grounds.

STARE DECISIS: Latin for "to stand by things decided." A rule requiring the court to follow prior judicial decisions that have already decided the same principles of law.

Chavez v. Martinez

(*Patrol Officer*) v. (*Injured Criminal Suspect*)

538 U.S. 760, 123 S.Ct. 1994, 155 L.Ed.2d 984 (2003)

POLICE MAY QUESTION A MATERIAL WITNESS DURING MEDICAL TREATMENT

■ **INSTANT FACTS** After being shot in a police altercation, Martinez (P) requested that Chavez (D), a patrol officer, cease interrogation until he could receive medical treatment.

■ **BLACK LETTER RULE** The Fifth Amendment right against self-incrimination does not attach until criminal proceedings have been initiated.

■ PROCEDURAL BASIS

Certiorari to review a decision of the Ninth Circuit Court of Appeals for the plaintiff.

■ FACTS

Martinez (P) was shot several times in an altercation with police, causing partial blindness and paralysis. Chavez (D), a patrol officer on the scene, accompanied Martinez (P) to the hospital, where he questioned Martinez (P) while Martinez (P) received medical treatment. Martinez (P) was never given *Miranda* warnings. Initially, Martinez's (P) responses to Chavez's (D) questions included mainly complaints of pain. Later, Martinez (P) admitted drawing the officer's pistol from his holster and aiming it at him. Despite answering questions, Martinez (P) continued to complain of pain and request medical treatment. Martinez (P) was never charged with a crime, but he filed a civil suit against Chavez (D) under 42 U.S.C. § 1983 for violations of his Fifth Amendment right against self-incrimination and Fourteenth Amendment due process rights. The court concluded that Martinez's (P) constitutional rights were firmly established and that Chavez (D) "would have known that persistent interrogation" violated Martinez's (P) Fifth and Fourteenth Amendment rights.

■ ISSUE

Does continued police questioning of a material witness or criminal suspect after the suspect asks to terminate the questioning violate the Fifth Amendment right against self-incrimination?

■ DECISION AND RATIONALE

(Thomas, J.) No. Even before determining whether a police officer is entitled to qualified immunity, it must be determined whether a constitutional violation occurred. If not, there is no need to consider whether the plaintiff's rights are "clearly established." The Fifth Amendment requires that "[n]o person . . . shall be compelled *in any criminal case* to be a *witness* against himself." But a criminal case requires the initiation of legal proceedings and is not so broad as to include police interrogation. Until a criminal case is initiated and a defendant's statements introduced against him, the Fifth Amendment right against self-incrimination does not attach. Here, no charges were ever brought against Martinez (P) and he was never compelled to be a witness against himself. At most, Chavez's (D) actions violate various prophylactic rules established to protect Fifth Amendment rights in noncriminal cases. In such cases, a person may invoke an evidentiary privilege before giving incriminating testimony, to exclude the testimony in a future criminal trial against the person. Violations of these protective rules, however, do not extend the scope of the constitutional right itself and cannot support a § 1983 claim. Similarly,

Chavez's (D) questioning did not deprive Martinez (P) of a liberty interest within the meaning of the Due Process Clause. Martinez (P) was not denied medical treatment during the questioning and his injuries were not exacerbated by the questioning. Chavez (D) merely furthered the need to investigate the matter to determine whether there was any police misconduct that required additional investigation. Had Martinez (P) died, such evidence would have been forever lost.

■ CONCURRENCE IN PART

(Souter, J.) If police questioning that results in incriminating statements before charges are brought can support a constitutional violation in this case, all police questioning resulting in admissions or confessions constitutes a constitutional violation. Moreover, beyond evidentiary issues in a criminal case, police interrogation would effectively be eliminated by the threat of civil liability for the constitutional violation.

■ CONCURRENCE IN PART

(Scalia, J.) Section 1983 liability requires proof of a constitutional violation, not a violation of the prophylactic evidentiary rules judicially established to protect the constitutional right. Without proof of a constitutional violation, no civil liability exists.

■ DISSENT IN PART

(Stevens, J.) The defendant's questioning amounts to police action to obtain a confession by tortuous methods. The record demonstrates that Martinez (P) was in severe pain and mental anguish. Under such circumstances, continuing police questioning violates his protected liberty interest.

■ DISSENT IN PART

(Kennedy, J.) While a constitutional violation does not arise by the simple failure to give *Miranda* warnings before interrogation ensues, the Fifth Amendment is violated as soon as a police officer uses torture or coercive conduct in the course of interrogation. The violation depends upon the conduct displayed, not the future use of the fruits of the conduct, if any. While interrogation of a suspect in pain or anguish is not necessarily unconstitutional, there are police actions that amount to inappropriate coercion. When an officer inflicts pain or threatens to prolong pain or anguish, the officer should be civilly liable to the suspect for his actions. Here, the record shows that Martinez (P) thought that medical attention would be withheld and his pain increased until he responded to Chavez's (D) questioning. This evidence sustains the § 1983 action.

■ DISSENT IN PART

(Ginsburg, J.) The right against self-incrimination applies not only at the initiation of criminal proceedings, but also whenever a suspect is subjected to coercive measures to solicit a statement. Regardless of any benign intent, Chavez (D) should have reasonably known that his conduct was constitutionally impermissible.

Analysis:

While *Chavez* turned on the issue of a Fifth Amendment violation, the availability of § 1983 liability for a substantive due process violation in this case was reserved for remand. On remand, the Ninth Circuit Court of Appeals held that, if supported by the evidence, Chavez's (D) conduct "shocks the conscience" and "interferes with rights implicit in the concept of ordered liberty." Thus, although Martinez' (P) Fifth Amendment rights were not violated, substantive due process violations establish the requisite unconstitutional acts in the § 1983 suit.

■ CASE VOCABULARY

DUE PROCESS: The conduct of legal proceedings according to established rules and principles for the protection and enforcement of private rights, including notice and the right to a fair hearing before a tribunal with the power to decide the case.

SELF–INCRIMINATION: The act of indicating one's own involvement in a crime or exposing oneself to prosecution, especially by making a statement.

United States v. Patane

(Prosecuting Authority) v. *(Convicted Felon)*

542 U.S. 630, 124 S.Ct. 2620, 159 L.Ed.2d 667 (2004)

THE FAILURE TO GIVE *MIRANDA* WARNINGS IS NOT A CONSTITUTIONAL VIOLATION

■ **INSTANT FACTS** Patane (D) was convicted of possession of a firearm as a felon after he voluntarily admitted possession without being read his *Miranda* rights.

■ **BLACK LETTER RULE** Nontestimonial evidence obtained as a result of a defendant's voluntary statement without the benefit of *Miranda* warnings need not be excluded at the defendant's trial.

■ PROCEDURAL BASIS

Certiorari to review the defendant's conviction.

■ FACTS

Patane (D), a convicted felon, was handcuffed and arrested outside his home by a federal agent for possession of a handgun. As the agent began reading Patane (D) his *Miranda* rights, Patane (D) interrupted him, claiming to know his rights. No further *Miranda* warnings were given. Patane (D) then told the agent that the handgun was in his bedroom. The agent searched the home, found the handgun, and seized it. Patane (D) was convicted for possession of a firearm by a felon.

■ ISSUE

Is nontestimonial evidence obtained following a suspect's voluntary statement, made without being read his *Miranda* rights, inadmissible at trial?

■ DECISION AND RATIONALE

(Thomas, J.) No. Although the failure to continue with a reading of Patane's (D) rights is a violation of *Miranda* rules, those rules serve to protect the right against self-incrimination. The Self–Incrimination Clause protects a defendant's right not to testify against himself at trial, but does not affect the admission of nontestimonial evidence obtained as a result of a voluntary statement. The Self–Incrimination Clause does not rely upon the *Miranda* exclusionary rule, for it contains its own exclusionary rule. "No person [shall] be compelled in any criminal case to be a witness against himself." Since the Clause contains its own exclusionary principles, the Court may not expand the textual scope to include the *Miranda* rule. Police failure to give *Miranda* warnings is not a constitutional violation. "Potential violations occur, if at all, only upon the admission of unwarned statements into evidence at trial." The Self–Incrimination Clause, however, applies only to testimonial evidence presented at trial, and the policy of protecting the defendant's right not to testify against himself is not furthered by excluding nontestimonial evidence obtained through a voluntary statement.

■ DISSENT

(Kennedy, J.) Because there is no constitutional violation under these facts, the Court need not have determined whether the agent's actions in this case violated the *Miranda* rules. It suffices to hold that no constitutional violation exists.

■ DISSENT

(Souter, J.) The Court's decision gives police an evidentiary advantage to exclude physical evidence obtained without providing a defendant his *Miranda* warnings. When a *Miranda* violation occurs, a presumption of police coercion exists, and the defendant's right against self-incrimination requires the exclusion of all derivative evidence under the fruit-of-the-poisonous-tree doctrine.

■ DISSENT

(Breyer, J.) Under the fruit-of-the-poisonous-tree approach, the Court should exclude all physical evidence obtained from unwarned questioning unless the *Miranda* violation was in good faith. Because the lower court made no such determination, the case should be remanded for further consideration.

Analysis:

From a practical standpoint, the exclusion of evidence obtained through voluntary statements made before *Miranda* warnings are given could cripple effective law enforcement. In fact, a suspect could voluntarily interrupt his *Miranda* warning, confess to the crime, disclose the existence and location of all incriminating evidence, and thereby virtually ensure the later exclusion of the evidence such that the prosecution has no meaningful way to convict the defendant.

■ CASE VOCABULARY

FRUIT–OF–THE–POISONOUS–TREE DOCTRINE: The rule that evidence derived from an illegal search, arrest, or interrogation is inadmissible because the evidence (the "fruit") was tainted by the illegality (the "poisonous tree"). Under this doctrine, for example, a murder weapon is inadmissible if the map showing its location and used to find it was seized during an illegal search.

MIRANDA RULE: The doctrine that a criminal suspect in police custody must be informed of certain constitutional rights before being interrogated. The suspect must be advised of the right to remain silent, the right to have an attorney present during questioning, and the right to have an attorney appointed if the suspect cannot afford one. If the suspect is not advised of these rights and does not validly waive them, any evidence obtained during the interrogation cannot be used against the suspect at trial (except for impeachment purposes).

Missouri v. Seibert

(*Prosecuting Authority*) v. (*Murder Defendant*)

542 U.S. 600, 124 S.Ct. 2601, 159 L.Ed.2d 643 (2004)

"QUESTION–FIRST TACTICS" FRUSTRATE THE PURPOSES UNDERLYING *MIRANDA* WARNINGS

■ INSTANT FACTS After Seibert (D) made an incriminating statement without a *Miranda* warning, she was read her *Miranda* rights and repeated the statement.

■ BLACK LETTER RULE Incriminating statements initially made before *Miranda* warnings are given are not admissible simply because they are repeated after proper warnings are given.

■ PROCEDURAL BASIS

Certiorari to review a decision of the Missouri Supreme Court reversing the defendant's conviction.

■ FACTS

When Seibert (D), a murder suspect, was arrested, the arresting officer received specific instructions not to read her *Miranda* rights. Seibert (D) was questioned, made an incriminating statement, and was left alone. Thereafter, the interrogating officer read Siebert (D) her *Miranda* rights, which she waived. Seibert (D) then repeated the incriminating statement. At trial, the court excluded only the first statement made without the *Miranda* warning, but allowed the second statement. The Missouri Supreme Court reversed, holding that the second statement must be suppressed as well.

■ ISSUE

Is a confession given by a suspect who has not been read her *Miranda* warnings admissible if it is later repeated after *Miranda* warnings are given?

■ DECISION AND RATIONALE

(Souter, J.) No. Under *Miranda*, a custodial confession is admissible only if the suspect is informed of her rights. When the suspect has been read her *Miranda* rights, the admissibility of a confession is generally unquestionable. The practice of questioning a suspect first and providing warnings only after a confession challenges the purpose of the *Miranda* warnings. When the warnings are given only after an incriminating statement is made, the suspect's ability to effectively choose between invoking her rights and waiving them is limited. Telling a suspect that "anything you say can and will be used against you" suggests that the previous incriminating statement will be used as evidence, so there is little to gain by remaining silent. Especially when the successive questioning occurs in the same environment as the initial questioning, the suspect is left with the impression that the successive questioning is a continuation of the earlier questioning and no reasonable expectation that her initial statements would not be used against her. Because the "question-first tactic" frustrates the purpose of *Miranda* warnings, any successive statements are inadmissible at trial.

■ CONCURRENCE

(Breyer, J.) "Courts should exclude the 'fruits' of the initial unwarned questioning unless the failure to warn is in good faith." This approach comports to prosecutors' and judges' understanding of well-known evidentiary principles by limiting evidence collected as a product of illegal government conduct.

■ CONCURRENCE

(Kennedy, J.) While not every violation of the *Miranda* rule requires the suppression of evidence, evidence is inadmissible when it frustrates the purpose of *Miranda*. Here, the pre-warning statement was deliberately used to obtain the post-warning confession, and both statements should be excluded because no countervailing interests outweigh *Miranda*'s central purpose. The Court, however, uses an objective test to determine whether such is the case by viewing the situation from that of a reasonable suspect in Siebert's (D) position. *Miranda*'s strength is in its clarity, and the objective approach threatens to create a per se rule of inadmissibility when question-first tactics are employed. If such tactics are used deliberately to circumvent *Miranda*, the Court's approach reaches the correct result. However, there may be occasions when two-step questioning does not result in a substantial *Miranda* violation. When the police take curative measures to ensure that the suspect understands her rights and the consequences of her earlier statements, a subsequent confession may not offend *Miranda*'s purposes.

■ DISSENT

(O'Connor, J.) A suspect's confession should not be suppressed because she "let the cat out of the bag." To do so immunizes a suspect from the effects of incriminating statements made after receiving her *Miranda* warnings, considerably hampering law enforcement investigations. The important consideration when determining the admissibility of a suspect's statement is the voluntariness with which the statement was made. If the first statement was made without her *Miranda* warnings, it cannot be voluntary and must be suppressed. When the statement is reiterated with the full benefit of her *Miranda* warnings, however, the issue concerns whether the later statement was made voluntarily to permit its use against her at trial.

Analysis:

Much debate among the Justices revolves around whether a *Miranda* violation should turn on the bad-faith intent of the interrogating officers. While the concurring opinions of Justices Breyer and Kennedy embrace an intent-based inquiry, the Court relies instead on objective principles to determine the *Miranda* violation, noting the impact the question-first technique has on the effectiveness of the *Miranda* warning.

■ CASE VOCABULARY

INCRIMINATING STATEMENT: A statement that tends to establish the guilt of an accused.

Brewer v. Williams

(*People*) v. (*Religious Child-Murderer*)

430 U.S. 387, 97 S.Ct. 1232, 51 L.Ed.2d 424 (1977)

SIXTH AMENDMENT RIGHT TO COUNSEL ATTACHES ONCE JUDICIAL PROCEEDINGS HAVE BEEN INITIATED

■ **INSTANT FACTS** Police elicited statements during long automobile ride from very religious mental patient accused of murder, and represented by counsel, resulting in body being found.

■ **BLACK LETTER RULE** The right to counsel is violated if incriminating statements are obtained from the accused after judicial proceedings have been initiated and counsel retained.

■ PROCEDURAL BASIS

Appeal to Supreme Court from lower court's affirming judgment granting writ of habeas corpus reversing criminal conviction.

■ FACTS

Williams (D), an escaped mental patient, was suspected of murdering a young girl. A warrant was issued for his arrest. He retained an attorney who contacted the police in Des Moines, Iowa, where the crime occurred, to arrange the details for his surrender. Williams (D) surrendered to the police in Davenport, Iowa, and was charged with the crime. He was given his Miranda warnings by the police in Davenport. Williams (D) talked on the telephone with his attorney who was at the Des Moines police station. His attorney, while in the presence of the Des Moines police, told him not to talk about the matter until after he returned to De Moines and talked to the attorney. Williams (D) was arraigned in Davenport, and the judge advised him of his Miranda rights. He was then taken to jail. While being arraigned in court in Davenport, Williams (D) talked with another attorney who also told him not to make any statements until talking with his other attorney in De Moines. Later, when De Moines police arrived in Davenport to drive Williams (D) back to De Moines, they met with Williams (D) and the local Davenport attorney. He was again advised of his *Miranda* rights and the police expressly acknowledged to Williams (D) that he was being represented by an attorney in De Moines and another one in Davenport. The local Davenport attorney told the police not to question Williams (D) about the crime during the 160 mile automobile ride back to De Moines. During the ride back to De Moines, the police engaged in conversation with Williams (D), including the subject of religion. They knew that he was a former mental patient and was deeply religious. While referring to Williams (D) as Reverend, the police told him to think about the bad weather and the prediction for snow that evening. The Detective said that since Williams (D) was the only one who knew where the girl's body was, he might be unable to find it after it snows. The Detective further said that they should stop and locate the body, so the girl's parents could have a Christian burial for their child who was murdered on Christmas Eve. After Williams (D) had the police make several unsuccessful stops in an attempt to located the girl's shoes and blanket, he then directed the police to the girl's body. At trial, the judge denied Williams' (D) motion to suppress all evidence relating to his statements made during the automobile ride. The judge denied the motion on the ground that Williams (D) had waived his right to counsel. The jury [thank goodness] convicted [the dirt bag, scum bucket] Williams (D), and the state Supreme Court affirmed. Williams (D) was successful in his federal habeas corpus action.

■ ISSUE

Is the right to counsel violated if incriminating statements are obtained from the accused after judicial proceedings have been initiated and counsel retained?

■ DECISION AND RATIONALE

(Stewart). Yes. Clearly Williams (D) was deprived of the right to assistance of counsel. Judicial proceedings had been initiated against Williams (D) because an arrest warrant had issued, arraignment had occurred, and he had been confined in jail. The Detective, by drawing upon Williams' (D) religious background, set out to elicit information from him, which was probably more effective than a formal interrogation. [Smart guy that Detective]. The Detective knew that Williams (D) was represented by counsel in two cities. The state court concluded that although Williams (D) had been denied the right to counsel, he nevertheless waived the right during the course of the automobile trip. We do not agree. Waiver requires an intentional relinquishment or abandonment. The record reflects that Williams (D) consulted with his lawyers on numerous occasions. Despite the assertions of his right to counsel, the [very clever and tricky] Detective elicited incriminating statements from Williams (D). Judgment affirmed.

■ CONCURRENCE

(Marshall). I concur in order to comment on the dissenting opinions. They indicate that the actions of the Detective were proper, and examples of good police work. I disagree. The intentional police conduct of isolating Williams (D) from the protection of his lawyers during the time he gave his statement is misconduct, not good police practice.

■ CONCURRENCE

(Powell). I agree that the methods used by the Detective to elicit the testimony from Williams (D) was skillful and effective. The entire setting was conducive to the psychological coercion that was successfully exploited.

■ DISSENT

(Burger). The majority opinion continues the course of punishing the public for the mistakes and misdeeds of the police, instead of punishing the officer directly. Williams (D) was given his rights to remain silent and to counsel no fewer than five times. He spoke and acted voluntarily, and was not threatened or coerced. The facts of the case establish a valid waiver by Williams (D) of his rights.

■ DISSENT

(White). I am of the opinion that Williams (D) intentionally relinquished his right to counsel. He did not talk to the police when the car approached the area where the victim's clothes were hidden. The Detective told Williams (D) not to respond to what he was saying, just to think about it, and was it said hours before Williams (D) decided to make a statement.

■ DISSENT

(Blackman). Williams (D) was not deliberately separated from his counsel; rather, it was a necessary incident of transporting him to the county where the crime occurred. The Detective's purpose in talking to Williams (D) was to find the girl, not to deprive Williams (D) of his right to counsel. It appears from the majority opinion that the right to counsel is violated whenever police engage in any conduct, in the absence of counsel, with the subjective desire to obtain information from the subject. Such a rule is far too broad.

Analysis:

This case picks up where *Massiah v. United States* [obtaining incriminating statements from an accused after an indictment has been returned violates the right to counsel, even if statements are not made directly to the police] left off years earlier. The right to counsel approach with respect to confessions was uncertain following *Miranda*. *Massiah* was not even mentioned by the court in *Miranda*. The

Brewer case reconfirmed the right to counsel in confession cases and recognized its attachment once the adversary proceedings commence. The court also acknowledged that the right to counsel could be waived upon showing an intentional relinquishment or abandonment. Thus, the Sixth Amendment right to counsel may, if violated, cause incriminating statements to be inadmissible even though the Miranda warnings were properly given. The majority concluded that the police used improper methods because they intentionally obtained incriminating statements knowing that Williams (D) was represented by counsel and had repeatedly been told not to provide them with information concerning the murder. The court also analyzed whether or not there was a valid waiver of the right to counsel. In so doing, it acknowledged that waiver could occur under the right circumstances. The importance of this case is the solidifying of the right to counsel in matters where judicial proceedings have commenced.

■ CASE VOCABULARY

HABEAS CORPUS: A writ procedure seeking release from custody, alleging that being in custody violates the law or the Constitution.

Texas v. Cobb

(*Government*) v. (*Confessed Murderer*)

532 U.S. 162, 121 S.Ct. 1335 (2001)

SUPREME COURT REJECTS "CLOSELY RELATED" TEST FOR DETERMINING IF RIGHT TO COUNSEL ATTACHES TO UNCHARGED CRIME

■ **INSTANT FACTS** Cobb (D), charged with burglary and represented by counsel, confessed to an uncharged murder and thereafter claimed his right to counsel attached for the murder as well.

■ **BLACK LETTER RULE** After the Sixth Amendment right to counsel attaches to an offense, it also attaches to other offenses that, even if not formally charged, would be considered the same offense because each requires the same proof of facts.

■ PROCEDURAL BASIS

Review by U.S. Supreme Court following appellate court's reversal of criminal conviction based upon violation of Sixth Amendment right to counsel.

■ FACTS

Cobb (D) confessed to the burglary of a home, and was thereafter indicted. Counsel was appointed to represent him on the burglary charge. While in custody, Cobb (D) waived his *Miranda* rights and confessed to the murders of the woman and child who had disappeared from the home he had burglarized. He was convicted of capital murder and sentenced to death. [Realizing that he should not have confessed] Cobb (D) challenged the conviction asserting that his Sixth Amendment right to counsel had been violated because the right had attached to the murder charge at the time of his confession even though he had not been charged with that offense. The court of appeal reversed his conviction.

■ ISSUE

After the Sixth Amendment right to counsel attaches to an offense, does it also attach to other offenses that, even if not formally charged, would be considered the same offense because each requires the same proof of facts?

■ DECISION AND RATIONALE

(Rehnquist) Yes. We have previously explained that when the Sixth Amendment right to counsel arises it is offense specific. It cannot be invoked once for all future proceedings, for it does not attach until a prosecution is commenced. Some lower courts, however, have read into the "offense-specific" definition an exception for crimes that are "factually related" to a charged offense. We decline to do so. Although it is clear that the Sixth Amendment right to counsel attaches only to charged offenses, we have recognized in other contexts that the definition of an "offense" is not necessarily limited to the four corners of a charging instrument. In *Blockburger v. United States,* we explained that "where the same act or transaction constitutes a violation of two distinct statutory provisions, the test to be applied to determine whether there are two offenses or only one, is whether each provision requires proof of a fact which the other does not." Accordingly, we hold that when the Sixth Amendment right to counsel attaches, it does encompass offenses that, even if not formally charged, would be considered the same offense under the *Blockburger* test. We reject the "closely related to" or "inextricably intertwined with" test. Applying the *Blockburger* test to the facts at hand, the statutory definitions of burglary and capital murder are not the same offense. Thus, the Sixth Amendment right to counsel did not bar police from interrogating Cobb (D) regarding the murders [even though the two crimes were closely related and inextricably intertwined]. Cobb's (D) confession was therefore admissible.

■ CONCURRENCE

(Kennedy) Contrary to the dissent's assertion that once a suspect has accepted counsel at the commencement of adversarial proceedings he should not be forced to confront police interrogation without the assistance of counsel, the question remains: acceptance of counsel for what? It is quite possible that a suspect, who wants counsels for hearings and trial, might choose to disclose to the police his account of the events that occurred. A court made rule that prevents a suspect from doing this serves little purpose.

■ DISSENT

(Breyer) This case focuses on the meaning of the words "offense specific," and requires us to determine whether "offense" includes factually related aspects of a single course of conduct other than those few facts that make up the essential elements of the crime charged. The majority's rule permits law enforcement officials to question those charged with a crime without first approaching counsel, through the simple device of asking questions about any other related crime not actually charged in the indictment. Thus, the police could ask the individual charged with robbery about the not yet charged assault of the cashier who was robbed. Such an approach will remove a significant portion of the protection that this Court has found inherent in the Sixth Amendment. Moreover, the simple-sounding *Blockburger* test has proved extraordinarily difficult to administer in practice, and now police officers in the field must attempt to navigate it when they question suspects. The better approach is to define "offense" in terms of the conduct that constitutes the crime that the offender committed on a particular occasion, including criminal acts that are "closely related to" or "inextricably intertwined with" the particular crime set forth in the charging instrument. In this case, the police officers should have spoken to Cobb's (D) counsel before questioning him.

Analysis:

This case concerns the issue of whether the right to counsel attaches to all other offenses closely related to the charged offense (for which the right to counsel has already attached). Although, according to the dissent, virtually every lower court in the United States to consider the issue has defined "offense" in the Sixth Amendment context to encompass "closely related" acts, the Supreme Court rejected that approach and instead held that it encompasses only those offenses considered to be the same offense because each requires the same proof of facts, even if not formally charged. The dissent makes the following compelling arguments: 1) law enforcement may now ask the suspect about all related crimes not yet charged without notifying counsel retained for the charged offense; 2) the role of the lawyer as a "medium" between the defendant and the government will be undermined; 3) the *Blockburger* test is extraordinarily difficult to administer, especially for police officers in the field. The majority notes that the Constitution does not forbid the ability of the police to talk to suspects and witnesses, even those who have been charged with other offenses. It also asserts that if the "closely related" test were used, the police likely would refrain from questioning certain defendants altogether in fear of possibility violating the Sixth Amendment.

■ CASE VOCABULARY

CHARGING INSTRUMENT: A formal pleading that accuses the defendant with a crime, such as an indictment.

INDICTED: Being charged with a crime.

CHAPTER TEN

Lineups, Showups, and Other Pre–Trial Identification Procedures

United States v. Wade

Instant Facts: A man charged with robbing a bank was subjected to a lineup without his counsel present.

Black Letter Rule: Conducting a lineup without the defendant's counsel present violates the defendant's right to counsel.

Kirby v. Illinois

Instant Facts: Defendants arrested for robbery, but not formally charged, were identified at the police station by the victim without their counsel present.

Black Letter Rule: A criminal defendant's right to counsel does not attach for purposes of a witness identification until the government initiates criminal proceedings against the defendant.

United States v. Ash

Instant Facts: A criminal defendant objected to the government's use of a photographic lineup without the presence of defense counsel.

Black Letter Rule: A criminal defendant has no right to have counsel attend a photographic lineup conducted by the government.

Manson v. Brathwaite

Instant Facts: An undercover police officer identified a suspect from a photograph two days after the officer bought drugs from the suspect.

Black Letter Rule: Even if a witness's identification is based on suggestion and is unnecessary, it does not violate the defendant's due process rights if it is reliable based on the totality of the circumstances.

United States v. Wade

(*Federal Government*) v. (*Bank Robber*)
388 U.S. 218, 87 S.Ct. 1926 (1967)

PRETRIAL LINEUP WITHOUT COUNSEL PRESENT VIOLATES DEFENDANT'S RIGHT TO COUNSEL

■ **INSTANT FACTS** A man charged with robbing a bank was subjected to a lineup without his counsel present.

■ **BLACK LETTER RULE** Conducting a lineup without the defendant's counsel present violates the defendant's right to counsel.

■ PROCEDURAL BASIS

Certification to the U.S. Supreme Court after the Court of Appeals granted the defendant a new trial.

■ FACTS

Wade (D) was charged with robbing a bank. After Wade (D) was arrested, the FBI, without notice to Wade's (D) court-appointed lawyer, arranged for the two bank employees who witnessed the robbery to view a lineup consisting of Wade (D) and several other prisoners. The person who robbed the bank had a small strip of tape on each side of his face [good disguise]. Each person in the lineup wore tape on the sides of their faces and was required to say something like "put the money in the bag." Both bank employees identified Wade (D) as the robber. On direct examination at trial, both employees identified Wade (D) as the robber. The prior lineup identification was elicited on cross-examination.

■ ISSUE

Is an in-court identification of an accused at trial admissible if the government conducted a pretrial lineup without the defendant's counsel present?

■ DECISION AND RATIONALE

(Brennan, J.) No, unless the defendant knowingly waives his right to counsel. Despite the Government's (P) argument, a lineup is not the same type of preparatory step in evidence gathering as analyzing fingerprints or blood samples, at which counsel is not required. Those types of evidence gathering can more easily be attacked at trial than a lineup. Eyewitness identifications are notoriously unreliable, and any prejudice in the lineup, such as a subtle suggestion by the police, may taint a witness's identification. A pretrial lineup is a particularly crucial event because it is unlikely that a witness will go back on his word later after picking out someone at the lineup. In addition, it would be very difficult for a defendant to reconstruct a prejudicial lineup and convince a jury that the lineup was in fact prejudicial. Insofar as a defendant's conviction is based upon a courtroom identification based on a suspect lineup, the defendant is deprived of his right of cross-examination. Thus, the first line of defense must be the prevention of unfairness in the lineup itself. The Government (P) has not offered substantial countervailing policy considerations against requiring the presence of counsel. The Government (P) has not presented any evidence that notifying counsel would cause prejudicial delay in the identification process. If this were to be the case, substitute counsel may suffice. Any local legislation or regulations that eliminate the risks of abuse and suggestion at lineups may eliminate the need for counsel to be present, but Congress and the federal authorities have not so acted. As to the question of whether a new trial is required, we do not hold that in-court identifications after a pretrial lineup must always be excluded. Before excluding an in-court identification after a pretrial lineup at which counsel was not present, courts should look at factors such as the opportunity to observe the criminal act, any identification prior to the lineup of another person, the identification by picture of the defendant prior to the lineup, the witness's failure to identify the defendant on a prior occasion, and the lapse of time between the crime and the lineup. We vacate the conviction pending a hearing by the district court to determine whether the in-court identifications had an independent source or were otherwise harmless error.

■ CONCURRENCE AND DISSENT

(Black, J.) I would reverse Wade's conviction without hesitation if the prosecution had made use of his lineup identification either in place of courtroom identification or to bolster in a harmful way crucial courtroom identification. But the prosecution here did neither of these things. Indeed, here it was the defense that brought up the prior lineup. I am further concerned that while stating that "a *per se* rule of exclusion of courtroom identification would be unjustified," the Court nevertheless remands the case for "a hearing to determine whether the in-court identifications had an independent source," or whether they were the tainted fruits of the invalidly conducted lineup. I think that this rule is unsound; the tainted fruit determination required by the Court involves more than considerable difficulty. Moreover, how is a witness going to probe the recesses of his mind to draw a sharp line between a courtroom identification due exclusively to an earlier lineup and a courtroom identification due to memory not based on the lineup? I think that the 5th and 6th Amendments are satisfied if the prosecution is precluded from using lineup identification as either an alternative to or corroboration of courtroom identification. If the prosecution does neither and the witness under oath makes an in-court identification, there is no justification for stopping the trial in midstream to hold a lengthy "tainted fruit" hearing.

■ CONCURRENCE AND DISSENT

(White, J.) Today the Court has propounded a broad constitutional rule barring the use of a wide spectrum of relevant and probative evidence, solely because a step in its discovery occurs outside the presence of defense counsel. The Court's opinion is far-reaching. It proceeds first by creating a new *per se* rule of constitutional law: a criminal suspect cannot be subjected to a pretrial identification process in the absence of counsel without violating the Sixth Amendment. If he is, the State may not buttress a later courtroom identification by any reference to the previous identification. Furthermore, the courtroom identification is not admissible at all unless the State can establish by clear and convincing proof that the testimony is not the fruit of the earlier identification made in the absence of defendant's counsel—admittedly a heavy and likely impossible burden. For all intents and purposes, courtroom identifications are now barred if pretrial identifications have occurred without counsel being present. Also disconcerting is the fact that this rule will apply regardless of when or where the pretrial identification occurs, how well the witness knows the suspect, and how long the witness observed the defendant at the scene of the crime. Additionally, the rule does not bar courtroom identifications where there have been no previous identifications in the presence of the police, although when identified in the courtroom, the defendant is known to be in custody and charged with the commission of a crime. And courtroom identification may be barred, absent counsel at a prior identification, regardless of the extent of counsel's information concerning the circumstances of the previous confrontation between witnesses and defendant. In sum, I doubt that the Court's new rule will measurably contribute to more reliable pretrial identifications. My fears are that it will have precisely the opposite result.

Analysis:

Despite what Justice White calls a broad, prophylactic new rule, the Court does not really go as far as it appears. The Court ultimately holds that an in-court identification, even if it follows a pretrial identification at which counsel was not present, may be admissible so long as it is not based on the pretrial identification. In addition, a violation will not result in reversal if it is found to be harmless error. Thus, if the witness had a particularly good view of the defendant during the commission of the crime, such as a kidnap victim who was with the defendant for several hours or days, any violation of the defendant's right to counsel will likely be considered harmless error. Another issue to think about is what role the lawyer will play at the lineup to prevent the prejudice the Court worries about. As a passive observer, the lawyer may not do much good. On the other hand, the lawyer's mere presence may make officials act more fairly.

Kirby v. Illinois

(*Robber*) v. (*State*)
406 U.S. 682, 92 S.Ct. 1877 (1972)

RIGHT TO COUNSEL DURING CRIMINAL IDENTIFICATION DOES NOT ATTACH UNTIL AFTER DEFENDANT IS FORMALLY CHARGED

■ **INSTANT FACTS** Defendants arrested for robbery, but not formally charged, were identified at the police station by the victim without their counsel present.

■ **BLACK LETTER RULE** A criminal defendant's right to counsel does not attach for purposes of a witness identification until the government initiates criminal proceedings against the defendant.

■ PROCEDURAL BASIS

Certification to the U.S. Supreme Court.

■ FACTS

Kirby (D) and another defendant were arrested for robbery. The victim identified Kirby (D) at the police station without Kirby's (D) counsel present. Kirby (D) was later indicted. The victim identified Kirby (D) at trial and also testified about the previous identification.

■ ISSUE

Is an identification that took place before the defendant was formally charged admissible if the defendant's counsel was not present?

■ DECISION AND RATIONALE

(Stewart, J.) Yes. It is firmly established that the right to counsel attaches only after adversary judicial criminal proceedings have been formally initiated against the defendant, whether by way of formal charge, preliminary hearing, indictment, information, or arraignment. Only then does the whole system of criminal justice begin. As such, a routine police investigation does not warrant an absolute constitutional guarantee of the presence of defense counsel. This is not to say that the Constitution does not protect against pre-criminal proceeding procedures. Any abuses of lineups before criminal proceedings have been initiated against a defendant will be remedied by the due process clauses of the Fifth and Fourteenth Amendments. Affirmed.

■ DISSENT

(Brennan, J.) The rule set forth in *Wade* was not dependent on the initiation of formal criminal proceedings against the defendant. Counsel is required to protect against the dangers inherent in eyewitness identification in any stage of the investigation process, as it is plain that there inheres in a confrontation for identification conducted after arrest the same hazards to a fair trial that inhere in such a confrontation conducted "after the onset of formal prosecutorial proceedings." Moreover, the plurality apparently considers an arrest to be nothing more than a part of a "routine police investigation," however they offer no reason for concluding that a post-arrest confrontation for identification, unlike a post-charge confrontation, is not among those "critical confrontations of the accused by the prosecution at pretrial proceedings where the results might well settle the accused's fate and reduce the trial itself to a mere formality." In short, it is fair to conclude that rather than "declin[ing] to depart from [the] rationale" of *Wade* and *Gilbert,* the plurality refuses even to recognized that rationale.

■ DISSENT

(White, J.) *Wade* and *Gilbert* govern this case and compel reversal of the judgment.

Analysis:

If *Wade* were intended to protect against the problems inherent in eyewitness identifications, these problems are not lessened merely because the defendant has not yet been formally charged with a crime. This case severely limits *Wade,* insofar as most lineups and identifications are conducted before the defendant has been formally charged. This case makes *Wade* only a right to counsel case, and ignores the fact that *Wade* was also based on the defendant's right to confrontation at trial. However, this case may be more in keeping with the realities of police investigations. Police often need to conduct on-the-scene identifications or identifications soon after a crime was committed when witness's memories are still fresh. Finally, the Court does not address exactly what constitutes an adversarial criminal proceeding that would trigger the right to counsel. Some states hold that the proceeding begins when a defendant is taken into custody under an arrest warrant, whereas other states hold that judicial proceedings begin when an arrest warrant is issued.

■ CASE VOCABULARY

INDICT: To formally charge someone with a crime.

United States v. Ash

(*United States Government*) v. (*Criminal Defendant*)

413 U.S. 300, 93 S.Ct. 2568, 37 L.Ed.2d 619 (1973)

A PHOTOGRAPHIC LINEUP IS NOT A "CRITICAL STAGE" OF A CRIMINAL PROCEEDING REQUIRING THE PRESENCE OF DEFENSE COUNSEL

■ **INSTANT FACTS** A criminal defendant objected to the government's use of a photographic lineup without the presence of defense counsel.

■ **BLACK LETTER RULE** A criminal defendant has no right to have counsel attend a photographic lineup conducted by the government.

■ PROCEDURAL BASIS

Appeal to the United States Supreme Court of a D.C. Court of Appeals ruling that a defendant has a right to have his or her attorney attend a photographic lineup.

■ FACTS

Long after criminal proceedings had been initiated against Ash (D), the government (P), without notifying Ash's (D) attorney, conducted a photographic lineup in which three of four witnesses identified Ash (D) as the perpetrator of the crime to which they had been witnesses. (The fourth witness was unable to select any of the photographs.) When he found out about the lineup, Ash (D) complained that under *Wade* his attorney should have been present at the lineup.

■ ISSUE

Does a defendant have a constitutional right to have his or her attorney attend a photographic lineup conducted by the government?

■ DECISION AND RATIONALE

(Blackmun, J.) No. Although the defendant's right to counsel guarantee has been expanded such that it applies in more than just the formal criminal trial, the function of the lawyer has remained essentially the same at those other proceedings as his function at trial. In all cases considered by this Court, counsel has continued to act as a spokesman for, or advisor to, the accused. The accused's right to the assistance of counsel has meant just that—the right of the accused to have counsel acting as his assistant. The function of counsel in rendering assistance continued to exist at the lineup under consideration in *Wade* and its companion cases. Although the accused was not confronted there with legal questions, the lineup offered opportunities for prosecuting authorities to take advantage of the accused. A substantial departure from the historical test would be necessary if the Sixth Amendment were interpreted to give Ash (D) a right to counsel at the photographic identification in this case. Since the accused himself is not present at the time of the photographic display, no possibility arises that the accused might be misled by his lack of familiarity with the law or overpowered by his professional adversary. Similarly, the counsel guarantee would not be used to produce equality in a trial-like adversary confrontation. Even if we were willing to view the counsel guarantee in broad terms as a generalized protection of the adversary process, we would be unwilling to go so far as to extend the right to a portion of the prosecutor's trial-preparation interviews with witnesses. The traditional counterbalance in the American adversary system for these interviews arises from the equal ability of defense counsel to seek and interview witnesses himself. That adversary mechanism remains as effective for a photographic display as for other parts of pretrial interviews. Finally, pretrial photographic lineups are hardly unique in offering possibilities for the actions of the prosecutor to unfairly prejudice the accused. A prosecutor, should he so desire, has many other opportunities to improperly influence the outcome of a trial at which defense counsel has no right of attendance. As such, there should be no special right to have defense counsel present at these lineups. Reversed.

■ CONCURRENCE

(Stewart, J.) A photographic identification is quite different from a lineup, for there are substantially fewer possibilities of impermissible suggestion when photographs are used, and those unfair influences can be readily reconstructed at trial. In short, an accused would not be foreclosed from an effective cross-examination of an identification witness simply because his counsel was not present at the photographic display. For this reason, a photographic display cannot fairly be considered a "critical stage" of the prosecution.

■ DISSENT

(Brennan, J.) Today's decision marks another step towards the complete evisceration of the fundamental constitutional principles established only six years ago in *Wade, Gilbert,* and *Stovall.* The risks of misidentification are as great at a photographic display as at a lineup. Moreover, contrary to the suggestion of the majority, the conclusion in *Wade* that a pretrial lineup is "critical stage" of the prosecution did not in any sense turn on the fact that a lineup involves the physical presence of the accused at a trial-like confrontation with the Government. And that conclusion most certainly did not turn on the notion that presence of counsel was necessary so that counsel could offer legal advice or guidance to the accused at the lineup. On the contrary, *Wade* envisioned counsel's function at the lineup to be primarily that of a trained observer, able to detect the existence of any suggestive influences and capable of understanding the legal implications of the events that transpire. Having witnessed the proceedings, counsel would then be in a position effectively to reconstruct at trial any unfairness that occurred at the lineup, thereby preserving the accused's fundamental right to a fair trial on the issue of identification. As in the lineup situation, the possibilities for impermissible suggestion in the context of a photographic display are manifold. As with lineups, the defense can seldom reconstruct at trial the mode and manner of photographic identification. It is true that the photos used might be preserved for examination at trial, yet this does not justify a lineup without counsel. In reality, preservation of the photos cannot in any sense reveal to defense counsel the more subtle, and therefore more dangerous, suggestiveness that might derive from the manner in which the photographs were displayed or any accompanying comments or gestures.

Analysis:

Ash stands for the proposition that the government does not have to invite defense counsel to attend or even notify defense counsel of its plans to conduct a photographic lineup. To put it another way, no Sixth Amendment right to counsel attaches when a photographic lineup is presented to a witness. Instead, the *Ash* majority states that the defendant's general right to due process under the Fifth and Fourteenth Amendments and the prosecutor's ethical obligation to seek justice guarantee fairness in the conducting of the photographic lineup. One interesting aspect of this decision is the use and interpretation of the *Wade* decision by each side of the Court. (Once again, *Wade* held that a criminal defendant has a right to have his or her attorney present at any lineup in which the defendant is involved.) Both are interpreting the same Supreme Court precedent, but they do so in drastically different ways. The majority reads *Wade* to mean that the right to counsel attaches when the prosecution has any opportunity "to take advantage of the accused," because of a lack of familiarity with the law or the workings of the legal system. (This necessarily requires the presence of the accused as he or she cannot be taken advantage of if he or she is absent.) Because the defendant is not present when a photographic lineup is held, the majority determined that *Wade* did not require an attorney to be present. The dissent put a different spin on *Wade.* Specifically, the dissent states that *Wade* does not guarantee the presence of an attorney for the sole purpose of providing legal advice or guidance to the defendant during a lineup. Instead, Justice Brennan states, the presence of a defense attorney is guaranteed so that suggestive influences can be detected and kept away from the proceeding. Further, the presence of an attorney, according to the dissent, serves to provide the defense with the knowledge necessary to reconstruct any unfairness at trial.

■ CASE VOCABULARY

PHOTOGRAPHIC LINEUP: A pretrial identification procedure in which a witness is shown an array of photographs which may or may not include a picture of the accused, and is then asked to identify, if possible, the perpetrator of the crime; the physical presence of the defendant is not required as it is with a traditional lineup.

Manson v. Brathwaite

(*Not Stated*) v. (*Not Stated*)
432 U.S. 98, 97 S.Ct. 2243 (1977)

A RELIABLE IDENTIFICATION, EVEN IF UNNECESSARY AND BASED ON SUGGESTION, DOES NOT VIOLATE DUE PROCESS

■ **INSTANT FACTS** An undercover police officer identified a suspect from a photograph two days after the officer bought drugs from the suspect.

■ **BLACK LETTER RULE** Even if a witness's identification is based on suggestion and is unnecessary, it does not violate the defendant's due process rights if it is reliable based on the totality of the circumstances.

■ PROCEDURAL BASIS

Certification to the U.S. Supreme Court after the Second Circuit Court of Appeals excluded the identification.

■ FACTS

Glover, an undercover policeman, bought drugs from a suspect. Glover observed the suspect at the door of an apartment. While the entire transaction took several minutes, it is unclear how long Glover actually observed the suspect. Glover then drove directly to police headquarters where he described the suspect to another officer, D'Onofrio. D'Onofrio thought the suspect might be the defendant in this case, and obtained a photograph of him. He left the photograph at Glover's office. Glover viewed the photograph two days later and identified the defendant as the seller of the drugs. The prosecution did not explain why the police did not use a photographic array or conduct a lineup.

■ ISSUE

Does a witness identification that may be based on suggestion and that is unnecessary violate a defendant's due process rights?

■ DECISION AND RATIONALE

(Blackmun, J.) No, as long as the identification is reliable. We resolved a similar issue in *Neil v. Biggers* [due process not violated if identification is reliable even though procedure is suggestive] with respect to identifications that occurred prior to our decision in *Stovall v. Denno* [due process approach is used to assess identifications not governed by *Wade* and *Gilbert*, i.e., pre-indictment]. This opinion applies to identifications to which *Wade* does not apply. The identification procedure here was suggestive because only one photograph was used, and unnecessary because there were no exigent circumstances. With respect to such identifications, courts have been using two approaches: the *per se* approach and the totality-of-the-circumstances approach. The *per se* approach absolutely excludes out-of-court identifications based on suggestive procedures without regard to their reliability. We reject this approach because it keeps from the jury evidence that is reliable and relevant. We endorse the totality-of-the-circumstances approach. This approach will still deter police misconduct and is less likely to result in the guilty going free. Thus, to assess reliability, we look at the following factors: 1) The opportunity to view. Here, Glover stood only a couple of feet from the respondent in good light and looked directly at him. 2) The degree of attention. Glover was an on-duty police officer and was trained to pay scrupulous attention to detail. 3) The accuracy of the description. No claim has been made that the respondent does not have the physical characteristics Glover described. Both Glover and the suspect were black, and thus Glover was unlikely to perceive only the suspect's general features. 4) The witness's level of certainty. Glover stated that he was positive that the photograph was of the suspect from whom he bought the drugs. 5) The time between the crime and the confrontation. Glover described the suspect to D'Onofrio within minutes of the crime and identified the photograph only two days later. Finally, there was little pressure on Glover to acquiesce in the suggestive procedure. Reversed.

■ DISSENT

(Marshall, J.) Here, the Court continues to chip away at the protections against mistaken eyewitness testimony. I believe the *per se* approach is better than the totality-of-the-circumstances approach for the following reasons: The *per se* rule would better deter police misconduct. Also, the Court totally ignores the lessons of *Wade* [right to counsel in lineups]. In addition, the *per se* rule is not "inflexible." The evidence to be excluded is not forever lost. Even if an out-of-court identification is excluded, an in-court identification is permitted if it has an independent source. Similarly, a prosecutor may conduct another lineup if a previous identification was based on a suggestive procedure. Furthermore, excluding suggestively-obtained eyewitness testimony makes sense precisely because it is unreliable. Finally, even under the totality-of-the-circumstances approach, the identification here should be excluded. Glover only saw the suspect for 15–20 seconds and, during that period, Glover made other observations about the scene, so he could not have seen the suspect's face for very long. In addition, the fact that Glover was a trained police officer is no guarantee that he was correct in this case. Furthermore, it is unlikely Glover would admit that he was unsure about his identification. Also, the greatest loss of memory about an incident occurs within hours after the event. Thus, the reliability of an identification is increased only if it was made within several hours after the crime. Finally, Glover gave only a general description of the suspect. He failed to state that the suspect was from the West Indies, which would be immediately recognizable by a black man.

Analysis:

Manson v. Brathwaite is a part of the Supreme Court's continued chipping away at the blanket rule set forth in *United States v. Wade.* (*Manson* was decided ten years after *Wade*; the Court began retreating from *Wade* just five years after it was decided.) In doing so, the Supreme Court rejected a per se exclusion test in favor of one that allows the admission of identification evidence despite the possibility of some police misconduct. While some have argued that the *Manson* majority ignores the warnings about the dangers of eyewitness identifications as presented in *Wade*, the Court is simply trying to balance a defendant's due process rights against the ability of the police to investigate crime. In its view, the Court is imposing a rule that, like the per se rule, will continue to deter police misconduct in identification procedures, but at the same time will not completely bind their hands. To put it another way, the Court is trying to give the police some flexibility in carrying out their duties.

CHAPTER ELEVEN

Grand Jury Investigations

Boyd v. United States

Instant Facts: An importer, charged by civil forfeiture proceeding with evading customs, objected to a judicial "notice" compelling production of records as violating the Fourth Amendment ban on unreasonable search and seizure.

Black Letter Rule: In criminal or forfeiture proceedings, courts may not order defendants to produce documents which will be used to incriminate them, under the Fourth Amendment's ban on unreasonable search and seizure.

United States v. Dionisio

Instant Facts: When a grand jury investigating gambling subpoenas mafioso's voice exemplars, the bookies refuse, claiming the subpoena constitutes unreasonable seizure.

Black Letter Rule: Grand juries may subpoena witnesses' personal testimony and voice exemplars, without showing such subpoenas are reasonable.

United States v. R. Enterprises, Inc.

Instant Facts: When a grand jury investigating obscenity subpoenaed a porn publisher's companies' records, he moved to quash, contending the documents would likely be inadmissible.

Black Letter Rule: Grand juries may subpoena items which are likely inadmissible, irrelevant, or broad, as long as the subpoena is not arbitrary or malicious.

Fisher v. United States

Instant Facts: Tax cheats gave their sole proprietorships' tax records to their attorneys for review. When the IRS subpoenaed the lawyers to produce the records, they refused.

Black Letter Rule: If incriminating non-personal documents are given to a lawyer for legal advice, a grand jury may subpoena the lawyer to produce those documents if it could have subpoenaed the client to produce them.

United States v. Hubbell

Instant Facts: A defendant moved to dismiss a grand jury indictment that he argued violated his grant of immunity with respect to documents he produced in response to a subpoena duces tecum.

Black Letter Rule: The constitutional privilege against self-incrimination protects the target of a grand jury investigation from being compelled to produce documents designed to elicit information about the existence of sources of potentially incriminating evidence.

Doe v. United States (Doe II)

Instant Facts: When a grand jury investigating a tax evader orders him to sign a form authorizing his banks to disclose his accounts, he claims the order amounts to compelled self-incriminating testimony.

Black Letter Rule: If a grand jury subpoena demands documentary evidence, witnesses must provide it, even if it is self-incriminating, including a consent to release incriminating information.

Boyd v. United States

(*Smuggler*) v. (*Federal Prosecution*)
116 U.S. 616, 6 S.Ct. 524, 29 L.Ed. 746 (1886)

COMPELLED DOCUMENT PRODUCTION IN CRIMINAL OR FORFEITURE ACTIONS VIOLATES *FOURTH AMENDMENT* RULE AGAINST UNREASONABLE SEARCH

■ **INSTANT FACTS** An importer, charged by civil forfeiture proceeding with evading customs, objected to a judicial "notice" compelling production of records as violating the *Fourth Amendment* ban on unreasonable search and seizure.

■ **BLACK LETTER RULE** In criminal or forfeiture proceedings, courts may not order defendants to produce documents which will be used to incriminate them, under the *Fourth Amendment's* ban on unreasonable search and seizure.

■ PROCEDURAL BASIS

In civil customs action seeking forfeiture, appeal from judgment against defendant.

■ FACTS

Customs officials charged the partnership of Boyd and Sons (D) with evading customs duties, and seized 35 cases of its glass. Under then-current customs laws, importers who defrauded the government by evading duties were subject to fine, jail, and forfeiture of the goods in question. The prosecution (P) instituted a forfeiture proceeding, and obtained a court "notice" directing Boyd (D) to produce an invoice for the glass. Under the then-current "notice" statute, in *civil* prosecutions, trial judges could issue a "notice" directing defendants to produce documents described by the prosecution. The defendant could refuse to produce without incurring contempt sanctions, but refusal was deemed an admission of whatever the prosecution (P) claimed the documents said. Boyd (D) produced the invoice, but objected to the court order's validity, and the introduction of the invoice into evidence. At trial, the jury found against Boyd (D), and his glass was seized. Boyd (D) appeals, contending the "notice" violated the *Fourth Amendment's* prohibition of unreasonable search and seizure.

■ ISSUE

May courts in civil forfeiture proceedings order the defendant to produce documents or else admit the contents?

■ DECISION AND RATIONALE

(Bradley) No. In a criminal or forfeiture proceeding, courts may not order defendants to produce documents which will be used to incriminate themselves, under the *Fourth Amendment's* ban on unreasonable search and seizure. It is our opinion that compulsory production of a man's private papers to establish a criminal charge against him or forfeit his property is within the *Fourth Amendment's* scope. Here, the act authorizing the "notice" is tantamount to compulsory production, since the failure to produce is deemed an admission of whatever the prosecution claims it says. The "notice" accomplishes the substantial object of actual search and seizure by forcing from a party evidence against himself, though it lacks certain aggravating incidents of search. Thus, the remaining issue is whether effectively compulsory production of personal papers, to be used as evidence in forfeiture proceedings, are *unreasonable.* Here, the act authorizing "notices" is the first to compel production of personal papers as evidence. The celebrated English decision *Entick v. Carrington and Three Other King's Messengers* (U.K. 1765) [suspect sues monarchial officials for breaking into house to examine his personal papers] held personal papers are so personal they may never be inspected or seized, even by court order. This famous decision is still good law, and its principles affect all government invasion of individuals' personal rights to security and property, and apply to any forcible or compulsory extortion of a man's own testimony or private papers to be used to convict him or forfeit his property. Thus, the *Fourth Amendment's* ban on unreasonable search is intertwined with the *Fifth Amendment's* privilege against self-incrimination in criminal prosecutions. While the act applies to "civil" forfeiture, we believe that all forfeiture proceedings for fraud against the government are inherently criminal, and thus are within the scope of the *Fourth* and *Fifth Amendments.* Here, the "notice" is equivalent to compelled search for self-incrimination, and is unconstitutional. Reversed.

■ CONCURRENCE

(Miller) I agree the "notice" is equivalent to a subpoena duces tecum, which is prohibited in criminal cases, or cases where failure to produce is deemed an admission of criminal acts. But I see no reason why court orders directing parties to produce papers are necessarily searches or seizures, since the owner is not deprived of them.

Analysis:

Boyd's narrow holding was later overruled by later cases holding that a partnership may be compelled to produce records. *Bellis v. United States* (S.Ct. 1974). However, *Boyd* was seen as landmark protection of civil liberties, and many later Supreme Court opinions followed its broad constitutional protections, though they rejected its Analysis: of the *Fourth Amendment* and *Fifth Amendment*, e.g., that defendants' legal property and business documents are immune from search.

■ CASE VOCABULARY

SUBPOENA DUCES TECUM: A subpoena (order to produce) of documents, rather than testimony.

United States v. Dionisio

(*Federal Prosecution*) v. (*Bookie*)
410 U.S. 1, 93 S.Ct. 764, 35 L.Ed.2d 67 (1973)

GRAND JURY SUBPOENAS FOR PERSONAL TESTIMONY OR EXEMPLARS NEED NOT BE REASONABLE

■ **INSTANT FACTS** When a grand jury investigating gambling subpoenas mafioso's voice exemplars, the bookies refuse, claiming the subpoena constitutes unreasonable seizure.

■ **BLACK LETTER RULE** Grand juries may subpoena witnesses' personal testimony and voice exemplars, without showing such subpoenas are reasonable.

■ PROCEDURAL BASIS

In grand jury investigation, appeal from contempt citation for failure to produce subpoenaed evidence.

■ FACTS

A grand jury investigating illegal gambling subpoenaed 20 mafiosi defendants, including Dionisio (D), and demanded they provide voice exemplars, for comparison with recorded conversations. Dionisio (D) refused, claiming the subpoena violated his rights under the *Fourth Amendment* [unreasonable seizure] and *Fifth Amendment* [compelled self-incrimination]. The district court rejected Dionisio's (D) argument and ordered compliance; when Dionisio (D) refused, the court adjudged him in civil contempt and ordered him imprisoned. When Dionisio (D) appealed, the Court of Appeals reversed, holding the *Fourth Amendment* applies to grand jury investigations, and finding the subpoenas here were unreasonable because of the large number of witnesses. The prosecution (P) appeals.

■ ISSUE

May a grand jury subpoena voice exemplars from numerous witnesses?

■ DECISION AND RATIONALE

(Stewart) Yes. Grand juries may subpoena witnesses' personal testimony and voice exemplars, without showing such subpoenas are reasonable. Obtaining physical evidence from persons involves 2 potential *Fourth Amendment* violations: the "seizure" of the person necessary to bring him into contact with government agents, and the subsequent search and seizure of evidence. Subpoenas to appear before a grand jury are "seizures," even if inconvenient. Case law has long held citizens are not constitutionally immune from grand jury subpoenas, since personal sacrifice is necessary for the public welfare, and responding is not unduly stigmatic or burdensome. This is not to say a grand jury subpoena is some talisman that dissolves all constitutional protections; grand juries cannot require witnesses to testify against themselves, require persons to produce private records that would incriminate themselves, issue subpoenas duces tecum which are too sweeping to be reasonable, or take steps to harass witnesses. Here, Dionisio (D) has no constitutional claim, since there is no order to produce private papers, no sweeping subpoena duces tecum, and no indication of harassment. That the subpoena was issued to 20 people is irrelevant, since grand juries have a duty to identify all witnesses. Thus, Dionisio's (D) compulsory appearance before the grand jury is not an unreasonable "seizure." Next, we consider whether the subpoena of a voice sample is an unreasonable "seizure."

We find it is not, since prior cases hold that the *Fourth Amendment* provides no protection for what a person knowingly exposes to the public, and we find a person's voice itself is publicly exposed, and no one can have a reasonable expectation that it will not be (though this does not necessarily permit a subpoena of any specific conversation). The grand jury's subpoena of a voice exemplar need not even be reasonable, since the grand jury necessarily has broad investigative powers, and may act on tips and rumors to collect possible evidence. Holding otherwise would interfere with the grand jury's mandate to investigate, frustrating the public's interest in fair administration of criminal laws. Reversed.

■ DISSENT

(Marshall) Our prior case *Hale v. Henkel* (S.Ct. 1906) held subpoenas duces tecum to obtain business records may not be so overbroad as to be unreasonable. By implication, subpoenas compelling personal appearance before a grand jury are subject to the Fourth Amendment's standards of reasonableness. Since the *Fourth Amendment* protects not just papers but also "persons, "houses," and [personal] "effects," it follows personal subpoenas must be reasonable, especially since they are stigmatic and inconvenient. Holding otherwise encourages prosecutorial exploitation of the grand jury, at the expense of individual liberty and grand juries' neutrality.

Analysis:

Dionisio is contrasted with *Hale.* While *Hale*'s overbreadth doctrine that a subpoena duces tecum—one for documents—must be reasonable and not overbroad, or otherwise unreasonable, *Dionisio* applies a looser standard to subpoenas of personal testimony (and also of exemplars), holding that such subpoenas are enforceable even if unreasonable, as long as they fall short of being deliberately oppressive. For policy reasons, it is unclear why the court accords greater protection to documents than to people, since personal appearance before a grand jury is as stigmatic as arrest, and can be highly inconvenient. While there is nothing in *Dionisio*'s facts to suggest the grand jury's subpoenas were overbroad, policy reasons dictate that all subpoenas should be invalid if overbroad.

■ CASE VOCABULARY

EXEMPLAR: A standard sample. Here, the subpoena demanded a voice sample; namely, for the mafiosos involved to read a transcript of taped conversations, so the speakers could be identified. However, the subpoena did not demand the mafiosos turn over any records of their actual conversations.

SUBPOENA DUCES TECUM: Subpoena of documents, rather than of live testimony.

United States v. R. Enterprises, Inc.

(*Prosecution*) v. (*Grand Jury Investigatee*)

498 U.S. 292, 111 S.Ct. 722, 112 L.Ed.2d 795 (1991)

GRAND JURY MAY SUBPOENA INADMISSIBLE EVIDENCE

■ **INSTANT FACTS** When a grand jury investigating obscenity subpoenaed a porn publisher's companies' records, he moved to quash, contending the documents would likely be inadmissible.

■ **BLACK LETTER RULE** Grand juries may subpoena items which are likely inadmissible, irrelevant, or broad, as long as the subpoena is not arbitrary or malicious.

■ PROCEDURAL BASIS

In grand jury investigation for shipping obscene materials illegally, appeal from quash of subpoena for documents.

■ FACTS

A federal grand jury investigated illegal interstate transport of obscene materials by Rothstein (D) and 3 of his wholly-owned companies, Model Magazine ("Model") (D), R. Enterprises (D), and MFR Books (D). The grand jury subpoenaed various corporate records and copies of videos Model (D) had shipped across state lines. The defendants moved to quash their subpoena, contending it demanded irrelevant materials, and that compliance would infringe defendants' *First Amendment* rights. The district court denied, finding the subpoena for records was sufficiently specific, that production would not constitute prior restraint, that there was sufficient connection with Model's (D) shipment to Virginia for further investigation, and that the items subpoenaed were relevant. When the defendants appealed, the Court of Appeals quashed the business records subpoena to R. Enterprises (D) and MFR (D), applying *United States v. Nixon* (S.Ct. 1974) [*trial* subpoenas must be shown by the prosecution to be relevant, admissible, and specific] and finding the documents subpoenaed were likely inadmissible and irrelevant. The prosecution (P) appeals, contending *Nixon* is inapplicable to grand jury subpoenas.

■ ISSUE

May a grand jury subpoena records and merchandise which is likely inadmissible as evidence?

■ DECISION AND RATIONALE

(O'Connor) Yes. Grand juries may subpoena items which are likely inadmissible, irrelevant, or broad, as long as the subpoena is not arbitrary or malicious. Grand jury subpoenas are much different from trial subpoenas, since the grand jury occupies the unique role of being able to investigate merely on suspected violations. This Court often emphasized that many trial restrictions are inapplicable to grand jury proceedings, especially evidentiary restrictions. Such restrictions would not advance the grand jury's mission, which is to conduct *ex parte* investigations to determine probable cause to prosecute. Thus, *Nixon* is inapplicable to grand juries, since it would impose delay and impede grand jury investigations' secrecy. Grand juries' investigative powers are not unlimited; they cannot conduct arbitrary fishing expeditions, or select targets with malice or intent to harass. Also, they are limited by *Federal Rule of Criminal Procedure 17(c)*, which provides "the court on motion ... may quash or modify the subpoena if compliance would be unreasonable or oppressive." In the context of grand jury investigations, "reasonable" cannot mean "relevant," since grand juries routinely cannot know what crime will be charged until they finish investigating. Grand jury subpoenas issued through normal channels are presumed reasonable, absent *defendants'* strong showing to the contrary. We hold *17(c)*'s "reasonableness" standard means that, where the subpoena's relevancy is challenged, the court may quash only if it determines there is no reasonable possibility the category of materials sought will produce information relevant to the general subject of the grand jury's investigation. We do not consider whether the subpoenas are too indefinite or burdensome. However, we recognize that subpoenaed parties face a difficult situation, since they do not know whether they are suspects or witnesses, and may have no conception of the prosecution's purpose in seeking information. Thus, we believe that where the party alleges unreasonableness, courts *may* be justified in requiring the prosecution to reveal the general subject of the grand jury's investigation, though we need not resolve this question now. Also, we express no view on *First Amendment* concerns. Here, we find the appellate court quashed incorrectly, since there is sufficient cause for investigating: the 3 companies are all owned by the same person and do business in the same area, and one of them shipped sexually-explicit materials across state lines, thus raising the reasonable possibility that any one's business records would shed light on the shipping. Reversed.

■ CONCURRENCE

(Stevens) I believe the holding should include adequate guidance on applying *Federal Rule of Criminal Procedure 17(c).* I would add that the movant should have the initial task of demonstrating some valid objection to compliance, e.g., volume, cost, effort, invasion of privacy, compelled disclosure of trade secrets or confidential information, *First Amendment* implications, etc.

Analysis:

On remand, the Fourth Circuit rejected defendants' *First Amendment* claim. *R. Enterprises* illustrates courts' differing treatment of trial subpoenas and grand jury subpoenas, predicated on the latter's broad investigatory powers. While *Nixon* held trial subpoenas may be quashed if they seek evidence which is likely inadmissible, *R. Enterprises* holds that grand jury subpoenas may rarely be quashed at all, and then only if they are malicious or totally unconnected to the investigation. True, the grand jury's ongoing investigation may well require it to look at evidence which cannot yet be deemed "relevant" or "irrelevant" until the charges are formulated. However, *R. Enterprises'* holding makes it virtually impossible to quash its subpoena for irrelevance.

■ CASE VOCABULARY

PRIOR RESTRAINT: Censorship practice whereby the government gives advance notice of the type of items which may/may not be published. Prior restraint is unconstitutional. Here, Rothstein (D) apparently argues that the grand jury's viewing of his porn would allow it to dictate what type of porn was acceptable.

QUASH: To void [a subpoena].

Fisher v. United States

(*Lawyers*) v. (*Federal Prosecution*)

425 U.S. 391, 96 S.Ct. 1569, 48 L.Ed.2d 39 (1976)

ACT OF PRODUCING DOCUMENTS MAY CONSTITUTE SELF-INCRIMINATING TESTIMONY THAT IS PROTECTED BY FIFTH AMENDMENT

■ **INSTANT FACTS** Tax cheats gave their sole proprietorships' tax records to their attorneys for review. When the IRS subpoenaed the lawyers to produce the records, they refused.

■ **BLACK LETTER RULE** The act of producing documents in response to a subpoena has communicative aspects that may constitute self-incriminating testimony that is protected by the Fifth Amendment.

■ PROCEDURAL BASIS

In (consolidated) enforcement actions for failure to answer subpoena, appeal from judgement for defendants.

■ FACTS

The IRS investigated several taxpayers for their sole proprietorships' civil and criminal tax violations. When the taxpayers received from their accountants their tax papers (accountants' work sheets, returns, and correspondence), they forwarded the papers to their attorneys, including Fisher (D). The IRS served summonses on Fisher (D) and the other attorneys, demanding the papers. When the attorneys (D) refused, the prosecution (P) commenced enforcement actions against them. [Presumably, the trial court found against the defendant attorneys, and they appealed.] On appeal, the Court of Appeals held the requested documents need not be produced, because the defendant attorneys' clients retained a reasonable expectation of privacy for the records when they transferred the records to their attorneys (D) for advice, per the attorney-client privilege. The prosecution (P) appeals.

■ ISSUE

Is the act of producing documents in response to a subpoena a communication that may constitute self-incriminating testimony that is protected by the Fifth Amendment?

■ DECISION AND RATIONALE

(White) Yes, under certain circumstances. If incriminating non-personal documents are given to a lawyer for legal advice, a grand jury may subpoena the lawyer to produce those documents if it could have subpoenaed the client to produce them. The *Fifth Amendment* provides "No person . . . shall be *compelled* in any criminal case to be a *witness against himself.*" Compelling an accused's lawyer would not "compel" the *accused* to do anything, much less become a "witness" against himself. That the attorney is the accused's agent is irrelevant, since the *Fifth Amendment* protects only the accused himself against the extortion of information. While the *Fifth Amendment* serves the purpose, inter alia, of protecting personal privacy (as the Court of Appeals suggested), it only prohibits evidence-gathering which involves compelled testimonial self-incrimination, not merely any privacy violation. We feel obliged to inquire whether a lawyer who possesses documentary evidence which would be privileged under the *Fifth Amendment* in the client's hands may refuse to surrender such evidence under the attorney-client privilege. Prior cases held that, if evidence is obtainable from the accused, it continues to be obtainable even after being transferred to a lawyer. We now hold that, if evidence is not obtainable from the accused, and is transferred to an attorney for legal advice, the attorney-client privilege dictates it cannot be obtainable from the attorney; holding otherwise would discourage clients from seeking legal advice. Here, since each taxpayer transferred his documents to his attorney (D) to seek legal advice, the documents are obtainable by summons from the attorneys (D) only if they were obtainable while in the taxpayers' possession. Accordingly, we proceed to the issue of whether such documents were obtainable from the accuseds, over their *Fifth Amendment* privilege against self-incrimination. While our early case *Boyd v. United States* held courts may not order defendants to produce documents which will be used to incriminate them, under the *Fourth Amendment*'s ban on unreasonable search and seizure, this rule's foundations have been washed away over time, and is no longer good law. A subpoena requiring taxpayers to produce accountants' work papers in their possession is permissible under the *Fifth Amendment*, unless the act of producing the document would amount to "incriminating" "testimonial" evidence [e.g., if the defendant falsely claimed he never filed a return, forcing him to produce the return would amount to an admission that he lied]. This is so because such a subpoena does not compel oral testimony, nor require the taxpayer to affirm the documents' truth. Here, we find that requiring the taxpayers to produce their papers does not amount to an incriminating testimonial, since the papers' existence and location are foregone conclusions which are not incriminating, and producing the papers would not have the effect of authenticating them. We do not rule on whether the *Fifth Amendment* permits the subpoena of accuseds' personal tax records. Reversed.

■ CONCURRENCE

(Brennan) I concur in the conclusion that the papers here were obtainable, since they were wholly business-related rather than personal, and were viewed by the accountants. However, I believe the majority opinion cripples *Boyd*'s protection against compelled production of private books and papers. While it is probably impossible to catalogue all papers which should be protected by privilege, sole proprietorships' business records should generally be privileged, since such records are at least an extension of an aspect of the owners' activities. [What?!] Individuals' non-business economic records should also be privileged, since they constitute an integral aspect of a person's private enclave. [When a concurrence starts sounding like a yoga manual, you know the author is making up justifications from whole cloth.]

■ CONCURRENCE

(Marshall) I believe the majority's theory will provide substantial protection for documents, though I would have preferred for the Court to recognize the import of the documents' contents themselves.

Analysis:

Here the Court holds that, under certain circumstances, the mere act of producing documents in response to a subpoena communicates several things. First, it communicates that the requested documents exist. It also communicates that the documents are in the subpoenaed party's custody or control. Finally, it communicates that the subpoenaed party believes that the documents produced are those documents requested in the subpoena, thus, that the documents are authenticated. However, in *Fisher*, the Court holds that producing the accountant's work papers is not testimonial because it is a "foregone conclusion" that the taxpayers would have documents of that sort. The Court further held that, even if producing the documents could be considered testimonial, it was not incriminating. First, the Court noted that the existence and possession of the documents was not incriminating because it was not illegal to hire an accountant to prepare tax returns. There also was no authentication issue because the taxpayer did not prepare the documents and could not vouch for their authenticity. In the next case in the book, *United States v. Hubbell*, the Court holds that the production did constitute a form of self-incriminating testimony that was protected by the Fifth Amendment.

■ CASE VOCABULARY

AUTHENTICATE: To establish as genuine and authored by a particular person.

United States v. Hubbell

(*Government*) v. (*Indicted Tax Evader*)
530 U.S. 27, 120 S.Ct. 2037 (2000)

PRODUCTION OF DOCUMENTS MAY CONSTITUTE TESTIMONY THAT BARS INDICTMENT BASED ON THEIR PRODUCTION

■ **INSTANT FACTS** A defendant moved to dismiss a grand jury indictment that he argued violated his grant of immunity with respect to documents he produced in response to a subpoena duces tecum.

■ **BLACK LETTER RULE** The constitutional privilege against self-incrimination protects the target of a grand jury investigation from being compelled to produce documents designed to elicit information about the existence of sources of potentially incriminating evidence.

■ PROCEDURAL BASIS

Certiorari to review prosecution's appeal of dismissal of indictment.

■ FACTS

In 1994, Webster Hubbell (D) pleaded guilty to charges of mail fraud and tax evasion arising from his billing practices in his law firm, and was sentenced to 21 months in prison. In the plea agreement, Hubbell (D) promised to provide the Independent Counsel (P) with full and accurate information about the Whitewater investigation. In 1996, while in prison, Hubbell (D) was served a subpoena duces tecum requesting the production of 11 categories of documents before a grand jury. Hubbell (D) appeared before the grand jury and invoked his Fifth Amendment privilege against self-incrimination and refused to state whether he had any documents responsive to the subpoena. Hubbell (D) was then granted immunity "to the extent allowed by law" under 18 U.S.C. § 6003(a) [federal statute providing for use immunity] and ordered to comply with the subpoena. Hubbell (D) then produced 13,120 pages of documents, and stated that those were all the responsive documents in his custody or control except for a few privileged documents. As a result of Hubbell (D) producing these documents, a grand jury returned an indictment against Hubbell (D) for various tax-related crimes and mail and wire fraud. Hubbell (D) challenged his indictment as a violation of the immunity granted to him. The Independent Counsel (P) admitted he was not investigating tax-related crimes when he issued the subpoena. The district court dismissed the indictment on the ground that all the evidence the Independent Counsel (P) would use against Hubbell (D) would be derived from Hubbell's (D) testimonial and immunized act of producing the documents. The Court of Appeals reversed, holding that the district court should have inquired into the extent of the Government's (P) knowledge of Hubbell's (D) financial affairs and supporting documents on the day it issued the subpoena. If the Government (P) could prove with "reasonable particularity" that it had specific knowledge about the documents, then the indictment was appropriate. If it did not, the indictment is tainted. On remand to the district court, the Independent Counsel (P) conceded it could not satisfy the "reasonable particularity" requirement. The Independent Counsel (P) and Hubbell (D) entered into a conditional plea agreement. They agreed that if the Supreme Court ruled that Hubbell's (D) act of production immunity barred his prosecution, the charges against him would be dismissed. Otherwise, Hubbell (D) agreed to plead guilty. The Court granted certiorari to determine the precise scope of a grant of immunity with respect to the production of documents in response to a subpoena.

■ ISSUE

Does the constitutional privilege against self-incrimination protect the target of a grand jury investigation from being compelled to produce documents designed to elicit information about the existence of sources of potentially incriminating evidence?

■ DECISION AND RATIONALE

(Stevens, J.) Yes. First, we note that the privilege against self-incrimination applies only to testimonial communications. It does not apply to putting on a shirt, recording one's voice, or providing a blood or handwriting sample. In addition, a person may be compelled to produce documents that contain incriminating statements because the creation of those documents was not compelled. On the other hand, we have held that the act of producing documents may itself constitute a communication that the documents exist, are in the defendant's possession or control, and are authentic. In addition, the person who produces the documents may be required to testify about whether he has produced everything demanded by the subpoena. Finally, the Fifth Amendment also protects against compelled testimony that may not be incriminating but that leads to the discovery of incriminating evidence. We have previously held that the use immunity set forth in § 6002 is constitutional (*Kastigar v. United States*). We emphasized the importance of the prosecution's duty to prove that the evidence it proposes to use is derived from a legitimate source wholly independent of the compelled testimony. Here, the compelled testimony is the act of producing the responsive documents. The Government (P) claims that the only testimonial aspect of a response to a subpoena is to establish the existence, authenticity, and custody of the produced items, and that it would not have to refer to Hubbell's (D) act of production in order to prove these things. In fact, the Government (P) claims it would not have to use the documents in order to prove the charges against Hubbell (D). However, the Government (P) has already made a derivative use of the testimonial aspect of producing the documents in obtaining the indictment. Because the 11 categories of documents requested were so broad, collecting and assembling the responsive documents was like responding to a series of interrogatories or deposition questions regarding the existence and location of the documents. Providing a catalog of these documents could provide a prosecutor with a link in the chain of evidence needed to prosecute. Here, the documents were produced before a grand jury in Arkansas to determine whether Hubbell (D) had violated his promise to assist in the Whitewater investigation. The documents were then used by a grand jury in the District of Columbia to indict Hubbell (D) for tax crimes. The documents that led to that indictment did not magically appear on the prosecutor's desk. They arrived only after Hubbell (D) asserted his constitutional privilege, received a grant of immunity, and took the physical and mental steps necessary to truthfully respond to the subpoena. The Government (D) is incorrect that producing the documents was merely a physical act with no testimonial aspect. Therefore, we hold that the constitutional privilege against self-incrimination protects the target of a grand jury investigation from being compelled to produce documents designed to elicit information about the existence of sources of potentially incriminating evidence. It was not a "foregone conclusion" that Hubbell (D) would have these documents. We affirm the judgment of the Court of Appeals.

■ CONCURRENCE

(Thomas, J.) I agree with the Court, but I write separately to note that the Fifth Amendment may protect not just against the compelled production of incriminating testimony, but of any incriminating evidence at all. There is support for the view that, at the time of the founding, the term "witness" meant a person who gives or furnishes evidence, not just testimony. In a proper case, I am open to reconsidering the scope of the self-incrimination clause.

Analysis:

This case arises from the Whitewater investigation by Independent Counsel Kenneth Starr against former president Bill Clinton and his friends and business partners. More importantly for our purposes, this case is the Court's latest word on the act-of-production doctrine set forth in *Fisher* [the act of producing documents in response to a subpoena has communicative aspects that may constitute self-incriminating testimony that is protected by the Fifth Amendment], that is, the idea that the mere act of producing documents is a communication that may be protected by the Fifth Amendment. Here, the Government (P) claimed that it would not even use the documents Hubbell (D) produced at a trial against him, and that it did not need the documents to prove the existence, custody, or authentication of the documents. Nonetheless, the Court held that the documents led the Government (P) to investigate whether Hubbell (D) may have committed various tax-related crimes. It also held that Hubbell (D) used his mental faculties or "the contents of his own mind" to catalog and assemble the documents, thus creating a communication separate from the mere act of producing the documents.

■ CASE VOCABULARY

DEPOSITION: Part of the pre-trial discovery process, where the sworn testimony of a witness is recorded before trial, out of court, with no judge present.

DERIVATIVE USE: A use of evidence that derives from the use of evidence that is protected by a privilege or immunity, such as using protected evidence to discover other evidence that is otherwise not protected.

INDEPENDENT COUNSEL: A lawyer hired by the government to investigate and prosecute crimes committed by a specific person or a group of persons.

INTERROGATORY: Part of the pre-trial discovery process in which a party provides written answers under oath to written questions from another party.

Doe v. United States (Doe II)

(*Grand Jury Target*) v. (*Federal Prosecution*)
487 U.S. 201, 108 S.Ct. 2341, 101 L.Ed.2d 184 (1988)

PHYSICAL EVIDENCE AND DOCUMENTS CARRY NO PRIVILEGE AGAINST SELF-INCRIMINATION

■ **INSTANT FACTS** When a grand jury investigating a tax evader orders him to sign a form authorizing his banks to disclose his accounts, he claims the order amounts to compelled self-incriminating testimony.

■ **BLACK LETTER RULE** If a grand jury subpoena demands documentary evidence, witnesses must provide it, even if it is self-incriminating, including a consent to release incriminating information.

■ PROCEDURAL BASIS

In grand jury investigation for fraud and tax evasion, appeal from appellate affirmation of contempt order for failure to provide evidence.

■ FACTS

John Doe (D) was investigated by a federal grand jury for fraudulently manipulating oil cargoes and not reporting income. When the grand jury directed Doe (D) to produce records of his transactions at 3 named banks in the Cayman Islands and Bermuda, Doe (D) produced some records, claimed no others existed, and invoked the *Fifth Amendment* when questioned about the others' existence. Then, the grand jury subpoenaed the foreign banks, but they refused, contending their governments' laws prohibited disclosing account records without customer consent. Thus, the prosecution (P) moved to order Doe (D) to sign consent directives. The directives were drafted to avoid admitting that Doe (D) actually had an account at any bank, and noted their purpose was to comply with a court order and bank secrecy laws. Doe (D) refused to sign on self-incrimination grounds, and was held in contempt. Doe (D) appealed, and the Court of Appeals affirmed. Doe (D) appeals again, contending that his compelled signature would amount to self-incriminating testimony, since the government could use the derived information to prosecute him.

■ ISSUE

If a grand jury subpoena demands documentary evidence, must witnesses provide a consent to release incriminating information?

■ DECISION AND RATIONALE

(Blackmun) Yes. If a grand jury subpoena demands documentary evidence, witnesses must provide it, even if it is self-incriminating, including a consent to release incriminating Information. The *Fifth Amendment* protects persons against compelled incriminating testimonial communications. Here, signing the consent directives would be compelled. We assume that signing will incriminate Doe (D). The question is whether signing the form would amount to a "testimonial communication." We previously held that requiring production of subpoenaed documents might sometimes amount to compelled testimony, if producing them would implicitly admit such documents existed, were in the defendant's control, or were authentic. *Fisher v. United States* (1976). We now apply *Fisher*'s test to both written and oral statements. We also hold that for a communication to be "testimonial," it must itself relate a factual assertion or disclose information, implicitly or explicitly. This holding is consistent with precedent, which allows suspects to be compelled to furnish non-testimonial evidence, e.g., blood samples, voice or handwriting exemplar, lineup appearance. Traditionally, only the "extortion of information from the accused" which forces him "to disclose the contents of his own mind" counts as "testimony" protected by the *Fifth Amendment* privilege against self-incrimination. Such an interpretation is also consistent with the policies underlying the *Fifth Amendment*, which was aimed at sparing the accused from being compelled to testify on his thoughts and beliefs to the Government. Next, we consider whether Doe's (D) signing of the consent directive here would have testimonial significance. We find it would not, since it is carefully drafted to avoid admitting the existence of any particular account or documents, nor their ownership. Although the signed form would allow the prosecution (P) access to potential sources of evidence, the form itself does not point to any hidden accounts or other evidence; the Government (P) must still locate such evidence "by the independent labor of its officers." Similarly, Doe's (D) signature on the directive has no testimonial significance, since it does not amount to admitting any fact, and does not claim he (voluntarily) consents to the investigation, meaning it does not provide access to Doe's (D) knowledge.

■ DISSENT

(Stevens) Defendants can be compelled to produce incriminating material evidence, but cannot be compelled to use their minds to assist their prosecution. Here, the directive purports to show a Doe's (D) decision to permit (and order) others to provide evidence against him, which amounts to making him a witness against himself.

Analysis:

Doe II illustrates the general principle that subpoenas duces tecum—ones for documentary or physical evidence—are rarely subject to the privilege against self-incrimination, and must be obeyed on penalty of contempt. This case notes that the distinction between (protected) live testimony and (unprotected) written evidence is largely historical rather than principled; the privilege against self-incrimination was formulated as a response to questioning in the King's Star Chamber, to prevent the government from forcing witnesses to disclose their thoughts. However, there is no practical difference between the witness' mental thoughts and those same thoughts reduced to paper, though the latter would be admissible.

■ CASE VOCABULARY

STAR CHAMBER: English royal court founded in the 16th century by King James to persecute enemies of the crown. It quickly acquired a reputation for rubber-stamping royal decisions, and was eventually disbanded.

CHAPTER TWELVE

The Scope of the Exclusionary Rules

Minnesota v. Carter

Instant Facts: A police officer looked through a window and observed three people bagging cocaine, two of which were guests and now challenge the search as unreasonable.

Black Letter Rule: A person must be more than a casual day-guest in a home to challenge a search of the home as being unreasonable under the Fourth Amendment.

Nix v. Williams

Instant Facts: A dispute arose over the admissibility of evidence related to a murder victim's body located as a result of illegal police conduct when the prosecution was able to show that the body would have been discovered shortly without the illegal police conduct.

Black Letter Rule: If the prosecution can establish by a preponderance of the evidence that illegally obtained information ultimately or inevitably would have been discovered by lawful means, the evidence should not be excluded.

People v. Berrios

Instant Facts: A criminal defendant argued that on a motion to suppress evidence the burden of proof should be on the prosecution to prove the legality of a search, and not on the defendant to prove the illegality of it.

Black Letter Rule: Where a defendant challenges the admissibility of physical evidence or makes a motion to suppress, he bears the ultimate burden of proving that the evidence should not be used against him.

Minnesota v. Carter

(*People*) v. (*Cocaine Dealer*)
525 U.S. 83, 119 S.Ct. 469 (1998)

MERE PRESENCE IN ANOTHER'S HOME WITH THEIR PERMISSION, WITHOUT MORE, DOES NOT CONSTITUTE SUFFICIENT CONTACT WITH THE HOME TO CONFER FOURTH AMENDMENT STANDING

■ **INSTANT FACTS** A police officer looked through a window and observed three people bagging cocaine, two of which were guests and now challenge the search as unreasonable.

■ **BLACK LETTER RULE** A person must be more than a casual day-guest in a home to challenge a search of the home as being unreasonable under the Fourth Amendment.

■ PROCEDURAL BASIS

Certification to the U.S. Supreme Court after the State Supreme Court reversed both the appeals court's and trial court's holdings that the evidence was admissible.

■ FACTS

[This case involves two defendants who will be referred to as "Carter and Johns."] Carter and Johns (D) and the lessee of an apartment were in one of its rooms bagging cocaine. An informant told police that he'd walked by the window of the apartment and saw the bagging operation in progress. A police officer then looked through the drawn blinds of the same window and also witnessed the operation for several minutes. He then notified headquarters to start preparing affidavits for a search warrant. When Carter and Johns (D) left the apartment in their car the police stopped them and eventually searched the car and found several items of contraband, including pagers, a scale, and 47 grams of bagged cocaine. After seizing the car, the police went back to the apartment and arrested the occupant, Thompson, who is not a party to this appeal. During a search of the apartment pursuant to the warrant police found cocaine residue and plastic baggies similar to those found in the car. It was later learned that while Thompson was the lessee of the apartment, Carter and Johns (D) had never been there before and had been in the apartment for two and a half hours. In return for the use of the apartment, Thompson was given one-eighth of an ounce of cocaine. Carter and Johns moved to suppress all evidence obtained from the apartment and their car on the ground that the initial peering of the officer into the apartment was an unreasonable search under the Fourth Amendment and, as a result, all the evidence was the fruit of the poisonous tree. Both the trial court and appeals court disagreed, but the State Supreme Court reversed and held the evidence inadmissible.

■ ISSUE

Does being a casual social guest in another's home, without more, confer a right to object to an illegal search of that home?

■ DECISION AND RATIONALE

(Rehnquist, C.J.) No. The Minnesota Supreme Court analyzed this case under the rubric of "standing" doctrine, an Analysis: this Court expressly rejected 20 years ago in *Rakas.* We held in that case that in order to claim the protection of the Fourth Amendment, a defendant must show that he personally has a reasonable expectation of privacy, as recognized by society, in the place searched. It must be remembered that rights under the Fourth Amendment are personal rights that can be invoked only by an individual whose rights have been violated. These rights are violated when the person has a legitimate expectation of privacy in the invaded place. While the text of the Amendment suggests the right extends only to people in "their" houses, we have held that in some circumstances a person may have a legitimate expectation of privacy in the home of another. For example, in *Minnesota v. Olson*, we held that an overnight guest had a sort of expectation of privacy under the Fourth Amendment. In *Jones v. United States* we held that one who is given the use of a friend's apartment in the role of caretaker, and who slept in the apartment "maybe a night" has a legitimate expectation of privacy. However, the statement in *Jones* that "anyone legitimately on the premises where a search occurs may challenge its legality," was expressly repudiated in *Rakas.* Thus, an overnight guest may claim Fourth Amendment protection, but one who is merely present with the owner's consent may not. Carter and Johns (D) were obviously not overnight guests, but were only present for a business transaction and then, only for a matter of hours. They did not have any previous relationship with Thompson, and there is no indication of them having any other purpose for their visit. While the apartment was a dwelling place for Thompson, it was for Carter and Johns (D) simply a place to do business. The purely commercial transaction engaged in here, the relatively short period of time on the premises, and the la?? of any previous connection between Carter and Johns (D) and the householder, all lead us to conclude that Carter and Johns (D) did not have a legitimate and reasonable expectation of privacy in the apartment. Therefore, their Fourth Amendment rights were not violated by the search. We do not decide if the officer's observations were a "search" because we conclude there was no expectation of privacy that could have been violated by a search. Reversed and remanded.

■ CONCURRENCE

(Scalia, J.) I write separately to express my view that the case law gives short shrift to the text of the Fourth Amendment, and to the well and long understood meaning of that text. Under a proper reading of the Amendment the present case is not even remotely difficult. The portion of the Amendment "their houses" in isolation, is ambiguous. It could mean "their respective houses," so that the protection extends to each person only in his own house, or it could mean "their respective and each other's houses," so that each person would be protected even when visiting the house of someone else. But it is easy to see, as even today's opinion shows, that the latter interpretation is impossible unless it is also given to the rest of the Amendment's nouns, "persons, papers, and effects." This would give me the constitutional right not to have your person unreasonably searched. This is absurd. The obvious meaning is, therefore, the former. [Justice Scalia then goes into an exhaustive presentation of founding era material that tends to support his position.] Of course this is not to say that the Fourth Amendment protects only the Lord of the Manor who owns the estate in fee simple. It extends to those whose legal title is in the bank, those who rent, and even those who occupy a dwelling rent-free—so long as they actually live there. This is clear from the text of the Fourth Amendment, the common-law background against which it was adopted, and the understandings consistently displayed after its adoption. We took the Amendment to its absolute limit of what text and tradition permit in Minnesota v. Olson, when we protected a mere overnight guest against an unreasonable search of his host's apartment. Today's case falls far below the bar set in *Olson* though. The dissent's position would require us to stretch the Fourth Amendment well beyond its clear foundation. But that provision did not guarantee some generalized "right to privacy" and leave it to this Court to determine which particular manifestations of the value of privacy society is prepared to recognize as reasonable. Any expansion beyond the text is for the people to decide through their elected representatives, not the courts. We go beyond our proper role as judges in a democratic society when we restrict the people's power to govern themselves over the full range of policy choices that the Constitution has left available to them.

■ CONCURRENCE

(Kennedy, J.) I join the Court's opinion because it is consistent with my view that almost all social guests have a legitimate expectation of privacy in their host's home. Fourth Amendment rights are personal, and anyone objecting to a search must have the requisite connection with the place searched. I would expect that most, if not all, social guests legitimately expect that, in accordance with social custom, the homeowner will exercise her discretion to include or exclude others for the guest's benefit. Where these social expectations exist, as they did in *Olson*, they are sufficient to create a legitimate expectation of privacy. In this respect, the dissent must be correct that the reasonable expectations of the owner are shared, to some extent, by the guest. This suggests that, as a general rule, social guests will have an expectation of privacy in their host's home. This is not the case here, however. Here, Carter and Johns (D) had only a fleeting and insubstantial connection with Thompson's home. They were there for business and business only, had never been there before, and even left it before their arrest. They therefore did not have a reasonable and legitimate expectation of privacy. With these observations, I join the Court's opinion.

■ DISSENT

(Ginsburg, J.) In my view, when a householder invites a guest into her home to share a common endeavor, even if for business purposes licit or illicit, that guest should share his host's shelter against unreasonable searches and seizures. The home has a unique importance, it is the most essential bastion of privacy recognized by the law. This does not mean I support a position that would allow a "casual visitor who has never seen, or been permitted to visit, the basement of another's house to object to a search of the basement if the visitor happened to be in the kitchen at the time of the search. Further, I would here decide only the case of the homeowner who chooses to share the privacy of her home with a guest, and would not reach classroom hypotheticals like the milkman or pizza deliverer. Our decisions indicate that people have a reasonable expectation of privacy in their homes in part because they have the prerogative to exclude others. This implies as well the power to include. Our Fourth Amendment decisions should reflect these complementary prerogatives. Today's decision places the homeowner's privacy at risk when she invites someone into her home. This is because human frailty suggests that this decision will tempt police to pry into private dwellings without warrant, to find incriminating evidence against guests who do not rest there through the night. *Rakas* tolerates that temptation with respect to automobile searches. I see no impelling reason to extend this risk into the home. People cannot be secure in their homes against unreasonable government searches if their invitations to others will increase the risk of government peering and prying. One should not have to stay overnight in his host's home in order to be free of government sponsored disturbances.

Analysis:

As illustrated by the many opinions in this case, the "rule" of when a houseguest can assert Fourth Amendment rights against unreasonable searches and seizures is extremely fuzzy—so fuzzy that it lends itself to inconsistent rulings. For instance, what if someone comes to your home for both personal and business purposes? What if a longtime friend visits you at your new house? Does he have a reasonable expectation of privacy even though he's never been there? The ultimate decision seems to be more dependent on the makeup of the Court than on any rule of law. When you ask yourself whether you feel you would have a legitimate expectation of privacy when accompanying a friend to the house of your friend's friend that you do not know, what is your answer? Most people would probably say 'yes,' they would have such an expectation. If what Justice Scalia says is true—that it is the role of the people, through their legislators, to decide what kind of expectation of privacy society should recognize as legitimate—then why shouldn't the casual visitor, present for a summer barbecue, enjoy such an expectation? It appears that the Supreme Court is out of touch with the views of the majority of the American people, at least when it comes to privacy expectations.

■ CASE VOCABULARY

FEE SIMPLE: A complete and full legal interest in land that does not expire until the current owner dies without heirs.

Nix v. Williams

(Not Stated) v. *(Convicted Murderer)*

467 U.S. 431, 104 S.Ct. 2501, 81 L.Ed.2d 377 (1984)

THE SUPREME COURT ACCEPTS THE INEVITABLE DISCOVERY DOCTRINE

■ **INSTANT FACTS** A dispute arose over the admissibility of evidence related to a murder victim's body located as a result of illegal police conduct when the prosecution was able to show that the body would have been discovered shortly without the illegal police conduct.

■ **BLACK LETTER RULE** If the prosecution can establish by a preponderance of the evidence that illegally obtained information ultimately or inevitably would have been discovered by lawful means, the evidence should not be excluded.

■ PROCEDURAL BASIS

Appeal to the Supreme Court of the United States of an Eighth Circuit Court of Appeals decision holding that the inevitable discovery doctrine does not apply when the police acted in bad faith in illegally obtaining evidence.

■ FACTS

Williams (D) murdered a child and disposed of the body. Later he was confronted by the police, who illegally obtained incriminating statements from him. These statements included reference to the location of the body. Prior to Williams' (D) disclosure, a search party had been organized and had begun searching. The search party included approximately 200 volunteers who were searching in organized grids. The party was specifically instructed to look for the body in ditches and culverts along the sides of roads, which is where the body was eventually found. The search party was terminated when Williams (D) promised to lead police to the body. Using the grid system, had the search continued the body likely would have been found a matter of hours after the search was stopped. Williams (D) was tried for murder and convicted. His statements to the police were used at trial. Later the Supreme Court, on appeal, ruled 5–4 that the police (and a Detective Learning in particular) had acted in bad faith in obtaining statements from Williams (D), and that the evidence disclosed by Williams (D) therefore should have been excluded. On retrial, the trial court nevertheless allowed the prosecution to bring forth evidence of the condition of the body as it was found, articles and photographs of the child's clothing, and the results of post mortem medical and chemical tests. (The prosecution did not attempt to show that Williams (D) had directed the police to the body. Nor did it bring up any statements made by Williams (D).) The trial court admitted the evidence under the inevitable discovery doctrine, finding that because the search party would have continued had Williams (D) not confessed, the body would inevitably have been found in the same condition in which it was found when Williams (D) disclosed its location. The Supreme Court of Iowa affirmed, and a federal district court denied a petition for habeas relief. Both invoked the inevitable discovery doctrine. On appeal, the Eighth Circuit reversed, holding that if there is an inevitable discovery doctrine it does not apply when the police have acted in bad faith. Appeal was taken to the Supreme Court—the second time the Court had heard something relating to Williams' (D) prosecution.

■ ISSUE

Can evidence obtained illegally nevertheless be admitted at trial if the prosecution can show that it inevitably would have been discovered regardless of police misconduct?

■ DECISION AND RATIONALE

(Burger, J.) Yes. The core rationale consistently advanced for extending the exclusionary rule to evidence that is the fruit of unlawful police conduct has been that this admittedly drastic and socially costly course is needed to deter police from violations of constitutional and statutory protections. Under this rationale, the prosecution is not to be put in a better position than it would have been in had no illegality occurred. By contrast, the derivative evidence Analysis: ensures that the prosecution is not put in a worse position simply because of some earlier police error or misconduct. The independent source doctrine allows admission of evidence that has been discovered by means wholly independent of any constitutional violation, because when the challenged evidence has an independent source, exclusion would put the police in a worse position than they would have been in absent any error or violation. That doctrine, however, does not apply here. The inevitable discovery doctrine, on the other hand, does. There is a functional similarity between these two doctrines in that exclusion of evidence that would inevitably have been discovered would also put the government in a worse position, because the police would have obtained that evidence if no misconduct had taken place. Thus, while the independent source exception would not justify admission of evidence in this case, its rationale is wholly consistent with and justifies our adoption of the ultimate or inevitable discovery exception to the exclusionary rule. As such, we now hold that if the prosecution can establish by a preponderance of the evidence that the information inevitably would have been discovered by lawful means—here the volunteers' search—then the deterrence rationale has so little basis that the evidence should be received. Anything less would reject logic, experience, and common sense. The requirement that the prosecution must prove the absence of bad faith, imposed by the Court of Appeals in this case, would place courts in the position of withholding from juries relevant and undoubted truth that would have been available to police absent any unlawful police activity. Of course, that view would put the police in a worse position than they would have been in if no unlawful conduct had transpired. And, of equal importance, it wholly fails to take into account the enormous societal cost of excluding truth in the search for truth. Nothing in this Court's prior holdings supports any such formalistic, pointless, and punitive approach. The Court of Appeals concluded that if an absence of bad faith requirement were not imposed, "the temptation to risk deliberate violations of the Sixth Amendment would be too great, and the deterrent effect of the Exclusionary Rule reduced too far." We reject that view. A police officer who is faced with the opportunity to obtain evidence illegally will rarely, if ever, be in a position to calculate whether the evidence sought would inevitably be discovered. On the other hand, when an officer is aware that the evidence will inevitably be discovered, he will try to avoid engaging in any questionable practice. In that situation, there will be little to gain from taking any dubious shortcuts to obtain the evidence. Significant disincentives to obtaining evidence illegally—including the possibility of departmental discipline and civil liability—also lessen the likelihood that the ultimate or inevitable discovery exception will promote police misconduct. In these circumstances, the societal costs of the exclusionary rule far outweigh any possible benefits to deterrence that a good-faith requirement might produce. The Court of Appeals did not find it necessary to consider whether the record fairly supported the finding that the volunteer search party would ultimately or inevitably have discovered the victim's body. However, three courts independently reviewing the evidence have found that the body of the child inevitably would have been found by the searchers. On this record, it is clear that the search parties were approaching the actual location of the body and we are satisfied, along with the three earlier courts, that the volunteer search teams would have resumed the search had Williams (D) not earlier led the police to the body and the body inevitably would have been found. Reversed.

■ CONCURRENCE

(White, J.) I write separately only to point out that many of Justice Stevens' remarks are beside the point when it is recalled that *Brewer v. Williams* was a 5–4 decision and that four members of the Court, including myself, were of the view that Officer Learning had done nothing wrong at all, let alone anything unconstitutional.

■ CONCURRENCE

(Stevens, J.) The majority refers to the "societal cost" of excluding probative evidence. In my view, the more relevant cost is that imposed on society by police officers who decide to take procedural shortcuts instead of complying with the law. What is the consequence of the shortcut that Detective Learning took when he decided to question Williams in this case and not to wait an hour or so until he arrived in Des Moines? Instead of having a 1969 conviction affirmed in routine fashion, the case is still alive 15 years later. Thanks to Detective Learning, the State of Iowa has expended vast sums of money and countless hours of professional labor in his defense. That expenditure surely provides an adequate deterrent to similar violations; the responsibility for that expenditure lies not with the Constitution, but rather with the constable.

■ DISSENT

(Brennan, J.) Today the Court concludes that unconstitutionally obtained evidence may be admitted at trial if it inevitably would have been discovered in the same condition by an independent line of investigation that was already being pursued when the constitutional violation has occurred. I agree. I would require, however, that the prosecution prove the inevitable discovery of illegally obtained evidence by clear and convincing evidence, and not just by a preponderance of the evidence.

Analysis:

The significance of *Nix* lies in its acceptance of the inevitable discovery doctrine. Prior to *Nix*, many state and lower federal courts had accepted and applied the doctrine, but in *Nix* the Supreme Court put its stamp of approval on the doctrine. Significantly, even the two dissenters in the case. Justices Brennan and Marshall did not dispute the viability of the doctrine—they simply disputed the standard of proof that the prosecution should have to meet to invoke the doctrine. In that regard, the *Nix* majority states that the proper standard of proof to be applied when determining the applicability of the doctrine is the preponderance of the evidence standard, which simply requires that the prosecution show that it is more likely than not that the evidence would inevitably have been discovered. While the *Nix* decision solidified the place of the inevitable discovery doctrine in American criminal procedure jurisprudence, it did not fully explain the parameters and details of the doctrine.

■ CASE VOCABULARY

INDEPENDENT SOURCE DOCTRINE: Exception to the exclusionary rule under which evidence discovered by means wholly independent of any preceding constitutional violation can be admitted despite the preceding illegality.

INEVITABLE DISCOVERY DOCTRINE: Exception to the exclusionary rule under which evidence discovered as a result of a constitutional violation can nevertheless be admitted at trial; in order for the evidence to qualify for admission, the prosecution must show by a preponderance of the evidence that the evidence obtained illegally would have inevitably been found had the illegality not occurred.

PRIMARY EVIDENCE: As used in the context of the inevitable discovery doctrine, evidence found as a direct result of unconstitutional police activity (e.g., drugs found in a suitcase that was illegally searched).

SECONDARY EVIDENCE: As used in the context of the inevitable discovery doctrine, evidence found as an indirect or derivative result of unconstitutional police activity (e.g., drugs found in the home of a person for which a warrant was obtained after the owner's drug dealing activities were discovered through the illegal search of a suitcase that contained drugs).

People v. Berrios

(*State of New York*) v. (*Drug User/Seller*)
270 N.E.2d 709 (1971)

THE FACT THAT GOVERNMENT WITNESSES MIGHT LIE DURING A SUPPRESSION HEARING DOES NOT REQUIRE A SHIFT IN THE BURDEN OF PROVING THE ILLEGALITY OF THE SEARCH FROM THE DEFENDANT TO THE PROSECUTION

■ **INSTANT FACTS** A criminal defendant argued that on a motion to suppress evidence the burden of proof should be on the prosecution to prove the legality of a search, and not on the defendant to prove the illegality of it.

■ **BLACK LETTER RULE** Where a defendant challenges the admissibility of physical evidence or makes a motion to suppress, he bears the ultimate burden of proving that the evidence should not be used against him.

■ PROCEDURAL BASIS

Not Stated.

■ FACTS

Berrios (D) was charged with possession of heroin and, at trial, the arresting officers testified that glassine envelopes containing narcotics were dropped on the ground as Berrios (D) and his companions were approached by police.

■ ISSUE

Does the prosecution bear the burden of proving the legality of a challenged search and seizure?

■ DECISION AND RATIONALE

(Scileppi, J.) No. Berrios (D) contends that the police testimony in the "dropsy" cases is inherently untrustworthy and the product of fabrication. As such, he argues that we should require that the People (P) bear the burden of proving admissibility, and thus depart from our present rule which places the burden to show inadmissibility on the defendant. No argument has been made showing that such a switch is required by either the State or Federal Constitutions; rather it is simply asserted that the change is needed to alleviate the possibility of perjured police testimony. We are not persuaded that such a change is necessary. Where a defendant challenges the admissibility of physical evidence or makes a motion to suppress, he bears the ultimate burden of proving that the evidence should not be used against him. The very words of § 813-c of our Code of Criminal Procedure make this point clear. They read: "A person claiming to be aggrieved by an unlawful search and seizure and having reasonable grounds to believe that the property . . . claimed to have been unlawfully obtained may be used as evidence against him [may] move for the return [or] suppression of its use as evidence." Since such a person makes the claim because he contends that he is aggrieved and requests the court to give redress to an alleged wrong, it is most reasonable to require him to bear the burden of proof of that wrong. The People (P), of course, must always show that police conduct was reasonable. Thus, though a defendant who challenges the legality of a search and seizure has the burden of proving illegality, the People (P) are nevertheless put to the burden of going forward to show the legality of the police conduct in the first instance. These considerations require that the People (P) show that the search was made pursuant to a valid warrant, consent, incident to a lawful arrest, or, in cases such as those here, that no search at all occurred because the evidence was dropped by the defendant in the presence of the police officer. Berrios (D) has argued that with the advent of *Mapp v. Ohio* [extending the exclusionary rule to the states], there has been a great incidence of "dropsy" testimony by police officers. Hence, this court has been asked to infer that the police are systematically evading the mandate of *Mapp* by fabricating their testimony. We cannot embrace this *post hoc ergo propter hoc* reasoning, for it would be a dismal reflection on our society to say that police testimony is inherently suspect. There is no valid proof that all members of law enforcement who testify are perjurers. Therefore, all policemen should not be singled out as suspect as a matter of law. Furthermore, we feel that a change in the burden of proof would be ineffective to combat the alleged evil about which the defendants complain. As such, principles of *stare decisis* do not allow a departure from our present rule of burden of proof. Where a judge determines that the testimony of the police officer is untrustworthy, he should conclude that the People (P) have not met their burden of coming forward with sufficient evidence and grant the motion to suppress. Similarly, appellate courts that carefully review evidence can effectively curtail any alleged abuses. Additionally, there are more appropriate methods of dealing with the abuses of police perjury. Internal procedures and policies within a police department, as well as training on the subject, can work to eliminate such abuses. Also, district attorneys should evaluate the testimony of the police officers, as they do the testimony of all witnesses to determine what pro?? will be offered in a case. Affirmed.

■ DISSENT

(Fuld, J.) There is significant evidence—more than the majority will admit—that police perjury, particularly in dropsy cases, is a serious problem in America as police often tailor their testimony to meet the search and seizure requirements of the Fourth Amendment. Underlying the Fourth and the Fourteenth Amendments is the basic proposition that "no man is to be convicted on unconstitutional evidence." The present rule, which imposes upon the accused the burden of proving the illegality of a seizure, subverts this principle by making it possible for some defendants to be convicted on unconstitutionally obtained evidence. Specifically, a trial judge who is unsure which side's account is correct must resolve doubts in favor of the People and admit the evidence; this is true even when law enforcement has presented perjured testimony about which the judge does not know. To thus increase the likelihood of a conviction on proof of questionable constitutionality is highly unfair. A change in the rule would assure that there was less of a chance that a defendant's constitutional rights will be violated since, by placing the burden on the People, the judge will be permitted to suppress evidence where he finds the testimony of each side evenly balanced.

Analysis:

People v. Berrios addresses the allocation of the burdens of going forward and persuasion in the context of motions to suppress evidence allegedly obtained in violation of the Fourth Amendment. As the dissent points out, where the burden is placed can be of great significance to a defendant. In *Berrios*, the New York Court of Appeals adopts the view that the prosecution should bear the burden of going forward, and if it carries its burden, the burden of persuasion is then placed upon the defendant, who must rebut the prosecution's evidence and show that a particular search and/or seizure was illegal. This is a legitimate way to allocate the burdens of proof on a motion to dismiss or suppress. However, it is not the only way to do so. For example, some states place both burdens on the defendant. Others place both on the prosecution. Neither way is improper. Most states, however, as well as the federal courts, allocate the burdens according to whether a warrant is involved. In these jurisdictions, the burden is on the defendant if the search was made pursuant to a warrant. In non-warrant cases, the government bears the burden, though the defendant must first make a prima facie showing of fact before the prosecution is required to prove its burdens. It is this latter view that the *Berrios* dissent advocates.

■ CASE VOCABULARY

BURDEN OF GOING FORWARD: The burden of introducing enough evidence to require the trier of fact to consider a given issue. This is also termed the burden of production.

BURDEN OF PROOF: The duty placed upon a party to a lawsuit requiring the party to prove a particular assertion. Both the burden of going forward and the burden of persuasion are encompassed by the burden of proof.

BURDEN OF PERSUASION: The burden of introducing enough evidence to convince the trier of fact to rule or decide in one's favor; if this burden is not met, then the trier of fact must necessarily rule in favor of the party not carrying the burden.

DROPSY CASES: Cases in which suspects drop evidence such as narcotics to the ground when approached by police so that they cannot be found in possession of the evidence.

GLASSINE ENVELOPE: A container made of thin transparent or semi-transparent paper, often used to store small quantities of narcotics.

POST HOC ERGO PROPTER HOC: Latin phrase meaning "after this, therefore because of this."

CHAPTER THIRTEEN

Pretrial Release

United States v. Salerno

Instant Facts: Salerno (D) was jailed without bail pursuant to the Bail Reform Act of 1984, which allows for the pretrial detention without bail of persons believed to pose a danger to individuals or the community if released.

Black Letter Rule: If the Government has a sufficiently compelling reason, shown by clear and convincing evidence that a criminal defendant is a danger to individuals or the community, it may detain the defendant prior to trial without bail.

United States v. Salerno

(*Federal Government*) v. (*Mafia Boss*)
481 U.S. 739, 107 S.Ct. 2095 (1987)

CRIMINAL SUSPECTS MAY BE HELD WITHOUT BAIL IF THEY POSE A DANGER TO INDIVIDUALS OR THE COMMUNITY

■ **INSTANT FACTS** Salerno (D) was jailed without bail pursuant to the Bail Reform Act of 1984, which allows for the pretrial detention without bail of persons believed to pose a danger to individuals or the community if released.

■ **BLACK LETTER RULE** If the Government has a sufficiently compelling reason, shown by clear and convincing evidence that a criminal defendant is a danger to individuals or the community, it may detain the defendant prior to trial without bail.

■ PROCEDURAL BASIS

Facial challenge of the Bail Reform Act certified to the Supreme Court after the Circuit Court found the Act to be unconstitutional.

■ FACTS

As a response to the high number of crimes being committed by defendants on pretrial release Congress enacted the Bail Reform Act of 1984 (the Act). The Act allowed for the pretrial detention, without bail, of criminal defendants being prosecuted for certain dangerous crimes or who posed a danger to individuals or the community if released. The Act required defendants to be given a full adversarial hearing at which the Government has the burden of proving by clear and convincing evidence that no release conditions will assure the safety of the community. Anthony Salerno (D) and his fellow defendant, Vincent Cafaro, were arrested and charged with various counts of violating the Racketeer Influenced and Corrupt Organizations Act (RICO), and also mail and wire fraud, extortion, and some gambling violations. Pursuant to the Act, the Government moved for pretrial detention without bail. At the hearing, evidence and testimony was proffered to show that Salerno (D) was the "boss" of the Genovese crime family. The court granted the Government's detention motion. The Act does provide for an immediate appeal and Salerno (D) exercised this option. On appeal, the Second Circuit Court of Appeals ruled the Act unconstitutional as a violation of substantive due process.

■ ISSUE

May defendants in a criminal prosecution be detained without bail upon a showing that they pose a danger to individuals or the community without violating constitutional safeguards?

■ DECISION AND RATIONALE

(Rehnquist, C.J.) Yes. A facial challenge to a statute will only be successful if the challenger can establish that there are no circumstances under which the statute is valid. Just because the Act is unconstitutional in some instances does not mean it is wholly invalid. Salerno (D) first argues that the Act violates substantive due process because it acts as punishment before trial. However, the Court of Appeals determined that pretrial detention under the Act is regulatory, not penal, and we agree. In making this determination, the first thing to be looked at is legislative intent. Unless Congress expressly intended to impose punitive restrictions, the punitive/regulatory distinction turns on whether there is an alternative purpose to which the restriction may rationally be connected, and whether it appears excessive in relation to the alternative purpose assigned to it. The legislative history of the Act clearly shows that it was not intended to punish dangerous individuals. Rather, Congress' intent was to solve a pressing national problem—preventing danger to the community—that is a legitimate regulatory goal. The incidents of pretrial detention are not excessive in relation to Congress' goal. The Act carefully limits the circumstances in which pretrial detention without bail is allowed by prescribing it only for certain crimes, and by providing for a quick adversarial hearing. What's more, there are stringent time limits on such pretrial detention pursuant to the Speedy Trial Act. All of this shows that the Act is regulatory in nature. The Court of Appeals' assertion that such detention violates the Due Process Clause is erroneous. We have repeatedly held that the government's regulatory interest in community safety can, in appropriate circumstances, outweigh an individual's liberty interest. One example of this is the government's power to detain individuals thought to be dangerous during time of war. Also, as Salerno (D) admits, the government may detain an individual before trial if he presents a flight risk or is a danger to witnesses. Here, the government's interest in preventing crime by arrestees is both legitimate and compelling. What's more, the Act is narrowly drawn in that it permits such detention only for certain dangerous crimes and provides for a full adversarial hearing where the government has the burden by clear and convincing evidence to show that no conditions of release will reasonably assure the safety of the community. Of course there is the individual's strong interest in personal liberty and we do not minimize this interest. But this right may be subordinated to the greater needs of society by a sufficiently weighty governmental interest. Salerno (D) also claims that the Act violates the Excessive Bail Clause of the Eighth Amendment. We disagree. The clause does prohibit excessive bail, but it does not say anything about whether bail shall be available at all. Salerno (D) concedes that the right to bail is not absolute: A court may, for example, refuse bail in capital cases. The claim that the sole purpose of bail is to ensure the integrity of the judicial process is inaccurate. While this is a primary function of bail, there are other sufficiently compelling interests the government is allowed to pursue through regulation of pretrial release. The only arguable substantive limitation of the Bail Clause is that the conditions of release not be excessive in light of the perceived evil. This requires a comparison of the governmental interest with the conditions. We believe that when Congress has mandated detention on the basis of compelling interests other than prevention of flight, as it has here, the Eighth Amendment does not require release on bail. Reversed.

■ DISSENT

(Marshall, J.) Suppose that a defendant is indicted, as the Act requires, and the government makes a sufficient showing that the defendant is dangerous and should be detained pending trial, at which trial the defendant is acquitted. May the defendant be further detained pursuant to the prior showing that he is dangerous? The answer cannot be yes because that would mean that a person could be imprisoned for uncommitted crimes based upon "proof" not beyond a reasonable doubt. However, under the Act an untried indictment somehow acts to permit a detention, based on other charges, which after an acquittal would be unconstitutional. Does the fact that a defendant who is being detained without bail decides to help the government investigate other crimes suddenly make him less dangerous to the community so that he may be released? Throughout the world there are countless men, women, and children incarcerated while awaiting trials that may be a mockery of the word, because their governments believe them to be dangerous. Our Constitution was meant to shield us from such abuses, but today a majority of this Court applies itself to an ominous exercise in demolition. This decision will undoubtedly go forth without authority, and come back without respect. I dissent.

Analysis:

Notice in Chief Justice Rehnquist's majority opinion the deference given Congress: "Congress specifically found that these individuals are far more likely to be responsible for dangerous acts in the community after arrest," and, "[W]e believe that when Congress has mandated detention on the basis of a compelling interest other than prevention of flight, as it has here, the Eighth Amendment does not require release on bail." These statements are an example of the Court giving Congress broad discretion in deciding what is a compelling interest. The Court does not inquire into how Congress came to the conclusion that crimes committed by defendants awaiting trial is a pressing national problem. Maybe there are statistics indicating this and maybe there are not. None are mentioned by the Court. This indicates that rational basis review is being applied to the Act. Is this appropriate considering the important liberty interests at stake? Also, the Court bases its assertion that the Eighth Amendment does not mandate a bail setting on the fact that, while the Amendment prohibits excessive bail, it does not address whether bail must be set at all. Basically the Court is saying that only when bail is set does the excessive provision kick in. But when no bail is set at all it is impossible for bail to be excessive. What kind of logic is this? Is it more logical to conclude that the Eighth Amendment assumes that bail is required and that it must not be excessive?

■ CASE VOCABULARY

FACIAL CHALLENGE: Legal challenge of an entire law, as written, not necessarily as enforced.

OVERBREADTH DOCTRINE: The doctrine that a law that chills free expression because it is broadly written is unconstitutional even if it is valid in other respects.

CHAPTER FOURTEEN

The Decision Whether to Prosecute

United States v. Armstrong

Instant Facts: As a result of being indicted under federal statutes for distributing cocaine, the defendants filed a motion for discovery or for dismissal of the indictment, alleging that they were selected for federal prosecution because they were black.

Black Letter Rule: In order to obtain discovery in support of a claim of selective prosecution the defendant must make a credible showing of different treatment of similarly situated persons.

United States v. Armstrong

(*Government*) v. (*Crack Dealer*)

517 U.S. 456, 116 S.Ct. 1480 (1996)

DEFENDANTS BRINGING SELECTIVE PROSECUTION CLAIM REQUIRED TO MEET HIGH THRESHOLD IN ORDER TO OBTAIN DISCOVERY

■ **INSTANT FACTS** As a result of being indicted under federal statutes for distributing cocaine, the defendants filed a motion for discovery or for dismissal of the indictment, alleging that they were selected for federal prosecution because they were black.

■ **BLACK LETTER RULE** In order to obtain discovery in support of a claim of selective prosecution the defendant must make a credible showing of different treatment of similarly situated persons.

■ PROCEDURAL BASIS

Appeal to the United States Supreme Court by the United States government, challenging the 9th Circuit Court of Appeals en banc decision to affirm the District Court's dismissal of the case.

■ FACTS

Armstrong and others (D) were indicted on charges of conspiring to possess with intent to distribute cocaine base ("crack") in violation of federal statutes. In response, Armstrong and others (D) filed a motion for discovery and for dismissal, alleging that they were selected for federal prosecution because they were black. As support, Armstrong and others (D) offered an affidavit by an employee of the Federal Public Defender, which alleged that all the defendants, in similar cases closed by the Federal Public Defender, were black. Accompanying the affidavit was a list of the 24 defendants, their race, whether they were prosecuted for dealing cocaine as well as crack, and the status of each case. The District Court granted the motion and ordered the Government (P) to provide information relating to the claim. The Government (P) refused to comply and the charges were dropped. After being reversed by a three judge panel, the decision of the District Court was upheld by an en banc panel for the 9th Circuit. This apeal followed.

■ ISSUE

In order to obtain discovery in support of a claim of selective prosecution, must the defendant demonstrate that the government failed to prosecute others who are similarly situated?

■ DECISION AND RATIONALE

(Rehnquist, C.J.) Yes. A selective prosecution claim is not a defense on the merits to the criminal charge itself, but an independent assertion that the prosecutor had brought the charge for reasons forbidden by the Constitution. Thus Federal Rule of Criminal Procedure 17 may not be used to obtain discovery for such a claim. Our cases dealing with claims of selective prosecution have established a "background presumption" that the showing necessary to obtain discovery should itself be a significant barrier to the litigation of insubstantial claims. Courts have afforded decisions to prosecute a "presumption of regularity" because the decision to prosecute is within the "special province" of the

Executive Branch. Moreover, executive officers are more competent than courts at assessing factors such as the strength of the case, the Government's enforcement priorities, and the case's relationship to the overall enforcement plan. This deference notwithstanding, the prosecutor's discretion is subject to constitutional constraints. The Due Process Clause of the Fifth Amendment prohibits decisions to prosecute that are based on race, religion, or other arbitrary classification. In order to succeed, a selective prosecution claim must demonstrate that the federal prosecutorial policy had a discriminatory effect and that it was motivated by a discriminatory purpose. Discriminatory effect is established by showing that similarly situated individuals of a different race were not prosecuted. Accordingly, because discovery in support of such a claim may impose a large burden on the Government, we require a rigorous standard for discovery in aid of such a claim. The Courts of Appeals which have considered the matter, require "some evidence tending to show the existence of the essential elements of the claim." Contrary to the holding of the lower court, our cases require that in order to make a preliminary showing as to the discriminatory effect element, the defendant must produce some evidence that similarly situated defendants of other races could have been prosecuted, but were not. We think this adequately balances the Government's interest in vigorous prosecution and the defendant's interest in avoiding selective prosecution. In applying this standard to the present case, we find that Armstrong (D) has failed to meet the threshold. The affidavit and the accompanying list fail to identify individuals who were not black, could have been prosecuted for the same offenses, but were not. Moreover, much of the information provided is either irrelevant or based on hearsay. Reversed and remanded.

■ DISSENT

(Stevens, J.) I believe the District Judge did not abuse her discretion in concluding that the factual showing was sufficiently disturbing to require some response from the Government (P). The decision should be viewed in light of three factors. First, federal legislation has established higher penalties for the possession and distribution of "crack" cocaine than those for powder cocaine. Second, this is matched by the disparity between the severity of punishment imposed by federal law and that imposed by state law. Finally, blacks have borne the brunt of the elevated federal penalties. The severity of the imposed penalties and the troubling racial patterns of enforcement give rise to a special concern about the fairness of charging practices for crack offenses.

Analysis:

The Court here sets forth the preliminary showing that must be made before a court grants a defendant a discovery motion in support of a claim of selective prosecution. The Court notes that in order to succeed in such a claim two elements must be proved: discriminatory intent and discriminatory effect. The court goes on to hold that effect can only be proved by showing that similarly situated individuals of a different race could have been, but were not prosecuted. Correspondingly, the Court holds that in order to obtain discovery, the defendant must make some showing that both elements are met. The Court ultimately rejects Armstrong's (D) motion because the evidence he offered did not prove discriminatory effect by the appropriate means—a showing that similarly situated individuals of a different race could have been, but were not prosecuted. In adopting its rule the Court was faced with a simple choice: adopt a rigorous threshold, maintaining respect for the separation of powers; or create a less exacting standard for discovery, thus advancing the equal protection rights of citizens. Although it believed it was adequately balancing the two interests, it seems the Court was more concerned with preserving respect for the Executive Branch. Selective prosecution claims have rarely been successful, and the Court's opinion here will only continue that trend.

■ CASE VOCABULARY

EN BANC: "By the full court"; a case decided by the full court, at the request of a litigant or on the court's own motion.

CHAPTER FIFTEEN

The Preliminary Hearing

State v. Clark

Instant Facts: A district court dismissed bindovers because the State (P) failed to establish probable cause at the preliminary hearing.

Black Letter Rule: A defendant may be bound over for trial upon the State's (P) showing of probable cause that the defendant committed the crime charged.

State v. Clark

(*Prosecuting Authority*) v. (*Forgery Suspect*)
20 P.3d 300 (Utah 2001)

PROBABLE CAUSE IS A UNIFORM STANDARD

■ **INSTANT FACTS** A district court dismissed bindovers because the State (P) failed to establish probable cause at the preliminary hearing.

■ **BLACK LETTER RULE** A defendant may be bound over for trial upon the State's (P) showing of probable cause that the defendant committed the crime charged.

■ PROCEDURAL BASIS

On appeal to review decisions of a state district court dismissing bindover orders.

■ FACTS

In separate proceedings, Clark (D) and another defendant were charged with forgery for attempting to cash a check written to Clark (D) from a stolen checkbook. Each defendant was initially bound over upon a magistrate's finding of probable cause, but the district court quashed the bindovers because the State (P) failed to meet its burden of proof at the preliminary hearing. The State (P) appealed from both decisions.

■ ISSUE

Did the district court err in quashing the magistrate's findings that there was probable cause to bind the defendants over for trial?

■ DECISION AND RATIONALE

(Durrant, J.) Yes. To bind a defendant over for trial, the State (P) must establish at the preliminary hearing probable cause that the suspects committed the crimes charged. The State's (P) burden at this stage is minimal, and the magistrate must consider all the evidence in a light most favorable to the prosecution to determine whether probable cause exists. To prevail at a preliminary hearing, the State (P) must provide credible evidence to support the elements of the crime charged, but need not establish each element beyond a reasonable doubt. Based on this standard, there is no distinction between the State's (P) burden to establish probable cause for an arrest warrant and the State's burden at a preliminary hearing.

Applying this standard here, the State's (P) evidence demonstrated that the defendants attempted to cash forged checks shortly after the checks were reported stolen. After the bank declined to cash the checks, each defendant left the bank and abandoned the checks. Taking this evidence in a light most favorable to the State (P), a reasonable inference of the intent to defraud exists, and the State (P) has established probable cause. Reversed.

Analysis:

By equating the probable cause standard at the preliminary hearing with that required to obtain an arrest warrant, it is difficult to imagine a magistrate or trial judge determination at a preliminary hearing that probable cause is lacking. Because an arrest warrant requires a showing of credible evidence to issue, the same evidence supporting the warrant will suffice at the later stage.

■ CASE VOCABULARY

BIND OVER: To hold (a person) for trial; to turn (a defendant) over to a sheriff or warden for imprisonment pending further judicial action.

PROBABLE CAUSE: A reasonable ground to suspect that a person has committed or is committing a crime or that a place contains specific items connected with a crime. Under the Fourth Amendment, probable cause—which amounts to more than a bare suspicion but less than evidence that would justify a conviction—must be shown before an arrest warrant or search warrant may be issued.

CHAPTER SIXTEEN

Grand Jury Review

Costello v. United States

Instant Facts: A defendant challenged his indictment for tax evasion on the grounds that the only evidence presented to the grand jury was testimony of investigators, which was allegedly based on hearsay.

Black Letter Rule: Defendants cannot challenge the validity of a grand jury indictment based upon the contention that all evidence presented to the grand jury was hearsay.

United States v. Williams

Instant Facts: A criminal defendant, indicted by a grand jury, sought dismissal of his indictment on the grounds that the prosecution had not shown the grand jury certain evidence which the defendant alleged exculpated him of the charges.

Black Letter Rule: A prosecutor has no duty to present substantial exculpatory evidence to a grand jury about the target of its investigation.

Costello v. United States

(*Tax Evader*) v. (*Government*)
350 U.S. 359, 76 S.Ct. 406 (1956)

THE CONSTITUTION DOES NOT PRESCRIBE THE KINDS OF EVIDENCE UPON WHICH A GRAND JURY MAY INDICT

■ **INSTANT FACTS** A defendant challenged his indictment for tax evasion on the grounds that the only evidence presented to the grand jury was testimony of investigators, which was allegedly based on hearsay.

■ **BLACK LETTER RULE** Defendants cannot challenge the validity of a grand jury indictment based upon the contention that all evidence presented to the grand jury was hearsay.

■ PROCEDURAL BASIS

Appeal to the United States Supreme Court challenging the decision to deny the defendant's motion to dismiss the indictment.

■ FACTS

Frank Costello (D) was indicted for tax evasion. At his trial the United States (Government) (P) offered evidence designed to show increases in Costello's net worth to prove he had received more income than he reported. The government called and examined 144 witnesses and introduced 368 exhibits to establish its case. The last three Government witnesses were government agents who collected the evidence, summarized the same at trial, and testified that according to their computations, Costello (D) received far greater income than reported. Costello's (D) attorney asked each government witness whether they had appeared before the grand jury. All but the three agents responded in the negative. After the government concluded its case Costello (D) moved to dismiss the indictment, claiming that it was based on hearsay because the government agents had no first hand knowledge of the transaction upon which their conclusions were based. The District Court denied the motion and the Court of Appeals affirmed Costello's (D) conviction.

■ ISSUE

Is a defendant entitled to a dismissal of the indictment when only hearsay evidence is presented to the grand jury?

■ DECISION AND RATIONALE

(Black, J.) No. Neither the Fifth Amendment nor any other constitutional provision prescribes the kind of evidence upon which grand juries must act. Historically, the basic purpose of the grand jury was to provide a fair method for instituting criminal proceedings. Their work was rarely hampered by procedural or evidentiary rules. There is every reason to believe that the Framers intended to incorporate the historical function of the grand jury into the Constitution. If indictments were subject to challenge based upon the evidence proffered, the delay would be great. Such a rule would permit a defendant to insist on a hearing regarding the evidence weighed by the grand jury. The Fifth Amendment merely requires that the grand jury be legally constituted and unbiased. Any indictment returned by such a grand jury is per se valid. Furthermore, we cannot accede to Costello's suggestion that this Court, under its supervisory authority, should create a rule authorizing a defendant to challenge indictments based on inadequate evidence. Such a rule would run counter to the notion that grand juries should be unfettered by technical rules and would add nothing to the assurance of a fair trial. Affirmed.

■ CONCURRENCE

(Burton, J.) I agree with the denial of the motion to quash the indictment. However, I believe that the Courts rule is too broad. If it is shown that the grand jury had before it no substantial or rationally persuasive evidence upon which to base its indictment, that indictment should be quashed.

Analysis:

The Court here creates a blanket rule which permits a grand jury to indict on any kind of evidence that is presented to it. Several justifications for the rule can be offered. First, inadmissible evidence often has probative value. Second, the grand jury is an accusatorial body, yet evidentiary rules are designed to ensure fairness in adversarial proceedings. Third, the guarantees afforded a defendant at trial will remedy any shortfall in the grand jury process. Fourth, the Court also points out that any other rule would severely burden grand jury proceedings with unnecessary delay. Finally, if the grand jury were subject to rules of evidence, who would object to the use of improper evidence? Neither witnesses nor those under investigation have a right to counsel at grand jury proceedings. Moreover, the proceedings are usually secret, making scarce any knowledge of the types of evidence used. Notice that the Court also places a great deal of emphasis on the historical development of the grand jury. What role the history of the grand jury should play in today's cases regarding the quality of grand jury indictments is subject to much debate.

■ CASE VOCABULARY

QUASH AN INDICTMENT: Vacate, overthrow or annul a formal accusation against a defendant.

HEARSAY: A rule that declares not admissible as evidence any statement other than that by a witness while testifying at the hearing, offered to prove the truth of the matter stated.

United States v. Williams

(*Federal Government*) v. (*Criminal Defendant*)
504 U.S. 36, 112 S.Ct. 1735 (1992)

U.S. SUPREME COURT HOLDS THAT PROSECUTOR HAD NO DUTY TO PRESENT SUBSTANTIAL EXCULPATORY EVIDENCE TO A GRAND JURY ABOUT THE TARGET OF ITS INVESTIGATION

■ **INSTANT FACTS** A criminal defendant, indicted by a grand jury, sought dismissal of his indictment on the grounds that the prosecution had not shown the grand jury certain evidence which the defendant alleged exculpated him of the charges.

■ **BLACK LETTER RULE** A prosecutor has no duty to present substantial exculpatory evidence to a grand jury about the target of its investigation.

■ PROCEDURAL BASIS

Appeal to the U.S. Supreme Court, following a grant of certiorari, of a judgment of the U.S. Court of Appeals for the Tenth Circuit, affirming a U.S. District Court's dismissal of a criminal indictment.

■ FACTS

A federal grand jury indicted John H. Williams, Jr. ("Williams") (D), an investor, on seven counts of knowingly making a false statement or report for the purpose of influencing the action of a federally insured financial institution. According to the indictment, in an effort to influence their decisions on loan requests he had made, Williams (D) had supplied four banks with materially false statements contained in two financial statements he had prepared that overstated the value of his assets and income. Following his arraignment, Williams successfully moved for disclosure of all exculpatory portions of the grand jury transcripts in his case. After reviewing the material provided by the prosecution, Williams (D) asked the trial court to dismiss the indictment, asserting that the United States (P) had failed to present to the grand jury his general ledgers and tax returns and his testimony in a bankruptcy proceeding, which would have shown that, for tax purposes and otherwise, he had regularly accounted for his assets and income in a manner consistent with the financial statements he had provided the banks. Williams (D) argued that this evidence showed that he had no intent to mislead the banks when he gave them the statements, negating an essential element of the offense charged. Williams (D) asserted that the prosecution had a duty to present "substantial exculpatory evidence" to the grand jury under a prior decision of the Tenth Circuit Court of Appeals, the circuit in which he had been indicted. After a hearing on the withheld evidence, the trial court agreed with Williams (D) and dismissed the indictment. The Tenth Circuit affirmed. The prosecution then appealed the dismissal of the indictment to the U.S. Supreme Court, which granted certiorari.

■ ISSUE

Does a prosecutor have a duty to present substantial exculpatory evidence to a grand jury about the target of its investigation?

■ DECISION AND RATIONALE

(Scalia, J.) No. Williams (D) does not argue that the Fifth Amendment itself requires a prosecutor to disclose substantial exculpatory evidence in his possession to the grand jury. Instead, he asserts that the Tenth Circuit's disclosure rule is supported by the inherent supervisory power of the courts. We disagree. Our cases that rely on the supervisory power of courts deal strictly with the courts' power to control their own procedures. While we have held that the courts' supervisory power can be used to dismiss an indictment because of misconduct before the grand jury, we have said that such misconduct must amount to a violation of the Federal Rules of Criminal Procedure or a federal statute. We have not held that the courts' supervisory power could be used, not merely as a means to enforce legally compelled standards of prosecutorial conduct before the grand jury, but as a means of setting those standards of conduct in the first place. Because the grand jury is an institution that is separate from the courts, over whose functioning the courts do not preside, we think it clear that no such supervisory judicial authority exists and that the disclosure rule applied here exceeded the Tenth Circuit's authority. The grand jury is assigned to no branch of government. It serves as a kind of referee between the government and the people. Although it generally operates in a courthouse and under judicial auspices, judges' direct involvement with its functioning has generally been confined to calling grand jurors together and administering their oaths of office. The grand jury require no authorization from its constituting court to initiate an investigation and in its day-to-day operations, it generally operates without the interference of a presiding judge, swearing in its own witnesses and deliberating in total secrecy. Any supervisory power the courts possess over the grand jury is limited and not remotely comparable to the power courts maintain over their own proceedings Williams (D) argues that judicial supervision of the quantity and quality of evidence relied on by the grand jury facilitates the grand jury's performance of its twin historical responsibilities; bringing to trial those who are justly accused and shielding the innocent from unfounded accusations and prosecution. We do not agree. Rather than preserving the traditional functioning of the grand jury, to require the prosecutor to present exculpatory evidence would alter the grand jury's historical role, changing it from an accusatory to an adjudicatory body. The grand jury sits not to determine guilt or innocence, but to assess whether there is an adequate basis to bring a criminal charge. To make that assessment it has always been thought sufficient to hear only the prosecutor's side. Neither in this country nor in England, has the suspect under investigation ever been thought to have a right to testify or to have exculpatory evidence presented. To impose on the prosecutor a legal obligation to present exculpatory evidence when there is not even a legal requirement for the target of the investigation to tender his own defense is absurd. Williams (D) admits that the grand jury itself could choose to hear no more evidence than that which convinces it an indictment is proper. Thus, even if the prosecutor had delivered boxes of exculpatory evidence, the grand jury could have ignored it. We reject the attempt to convert a nonexistent duty of the grand jury itself into an obligation of the prosecutor. Reversed.

■ DISSENT

(Stevens, J.) Yes. The United States (P) should not be concerned with winning a criminal case, but should be concerned that justice is done in the case. The costs of unchecked prosecutorial misconduct before the grand jury are particularly substantial because the prosecutor operates there without the check of a judge or a trained legal adversary, virtually immune from public scrutiny. Our prior rulings hold that the standard for judging prosecutorial misconduct during grand jury proceedings is essentially the same as the harmless error standard applicable to trials. If the misconduct played a critical role in persuading the jury to return the indictment, dismissal is required. Today, the majority repudiates the assumptions underlying our past holdings and seems to suggest that a court has no authority to supervise the conduct of a prosecutor in grand jury proceedings so long as he follows the dictates of the Constitution, applicable statutes, and the Federal Rules of Criminal Procedure. I disagree with this approach and its reasoning. Throughout its life, from the moment it is convened, until it is discharged, the grand jury is subject to the control of the court. While this Court's cases have previously acknowledged that the grand jury's operation is generally unrestrained by the technical procedural and evidentiary rules governing criminal trials, this is simply because Congress and this Court have generally thought it best not to impose procedural restraints on the grand jury; it is not because they lack all power to do so. To the contrary, this Court has held that it has the authority to create and enforce limited rules applicable in grand jury proceedings. For example, we have said that the grand jury may not itself violate a valid privilege whether established by the Constitution, statutes, or the common law. Unlike the majority, I am unwilling to hold that countless forms of prosecutorial misconduct must be tolerated, no matter how prejudicial they may be, or how seriously they distort the legitimate function of the grand jury, simply because they are not prohibited by the Federal Rules of

Criminal Procedure or an applicable statute. I do agree that a prosecutor is not required to place all exculpatory evidence before the grand jury. Requiring the prosecutor to ferret out and present all evidence that could be used at trial to create a reasonable doubt as to the defendant's guilt would be inconsistent with the grand jury's purpose and place too great a burden on the investigation. But that does not mean that a prosecutor may mislead the grand jury into believing that there is probable cause to indict by withholding clear evidence to the contrary of which he is personally aware. I would affirm.

Analysis:

Prior to the Court's decision in *Williams*, many lower federal court rulings, including the Tenth Circuit mentioned in the *Williams* opinion, had held that federal courts, through their supervisory power, could define prohibited conduct by the prosecution in the presentation of evidence before the grand jury that could lead to the dismissal of an indictment. In *Williams*, the majority effectively limits the ability of federal courts to supervise a prosecutor's conduct before a grand jury to ensuring that the prosecution did not violate any constitutional prohibitions, the Federal Rules of Criminal Procedure, and any federal statutes relating to conduct before the grand jury. According to the majority, a federal court has no inherent supervisory authority over a grand jury. Under the standard promulgated in *Williams*, certain actions by the prosecutor before the grand jury such as inflammatory comments, incorrect legal advice, and even conflicts of interest, all of which are not addressed under the Federal Rules of Criminal Procedure or a federal statute, may now be beyond the reach of the courts.

■ CASE VOCABULARY

ARRAIGNMENT: A proceeding before a judge or magistrate where a criminal defendant initially pleads guilty or not guilty to the criminal charges with which he has been indicted.

EXCULPATORY EVIDENCE: Evidence that would clear or excuse a criminal defendant of guilt for a crime.

SUPERVISORY POWER: Control exercised by a court over its own proceedings and the proceedings of lower courts or other entities under its authority.

CHAPTER SEVENTEEN

The Charging Instrument

Russell v. United States

Instant Facts: Russell (D) and others refused to answer questions posed by a congressional subcommittee and were convicted of violating a federal statute, but the indictment did not state the subject matter under congressional committee inquiry.

Black Letter Rule: An indictment, charging a violation of a federal statute making it a crime to refuse to answer certain questions before a congressional subcommittee, must state the subject matter under congressional committee inquiry as found by the grand jury.

United States v. Cotton

Instant Facts: The defendants were sentenced to a higher penalty than that prescribed for the offenses charged in the indictment.

Black Letter Rule: An appellate court may correct an error not raised at trial if the error is plain, affects substantial rights, and seriously affects the fairness, integrity, or public reputation of judicial proceedings.

United States v. Miller

Instant Facts: Miller (D) challenged sufficiency of indictment because the trial proof was narrower and more limited than the fraudulent scheme alleged in the indictment.

Black Letter Rule: The Fifth Amendment's grand jury guarantee is not violated when a defendant is tried under an indictment that alleges a certain fraudulent scheme but is convicted based on trial proof that supports only a significantly narrower and more limited, though included, fraudulent scheme.

Russell v. United States

(*Persons Questioned by Congress*) v. (*United States*)
369 U.S. 749, 82 S.Ct. 1038, 8 L.Ed.2d 240 (1962)

A CRIMINAL INDICTMENT MUST CONTAIN THE ELEMENTS OF THE OFFENSE INTENDED TO BE CHARGED, AND SUFFICIENTLY APPRISE THE DEFENDANT OF WHAT HE MUST BE PREPARED TO MEET

■ **INSTANT FACTS** Russell (D) and others refused to answer questions posed by a congressional subcommittee and were convicted of violating a federal statute, but the indictment did not state the subject matter under congressional committee inquiry.

■ **BLACK LETTER RULE** An indictment, charging a violation of a federal statute making it a crime to refuse to answer certain questions before a congressional subcommittee, must state the subject matter under congressional committee inquiry as found by the grand jury.

■ PROCEDURAL BASIS

Review by United States Supreme Court of criminal conviction for refusing to answer congressional subcommittee questions in violation of federal statute.

■ FACTS

Russell (D) and others were convicted of violating a federal statute after they refused to answer certain questions before a congressional subcommittee concerning the investigations of un-American propaganda activities in the United States and all other questions in relation thereto. [Otherwise known as a witch hunt.] In each case, a motion was filed to quash the indictment before trial on the ground that the indictment failed to state the subject matter under investigation at the time of the interrogation of Russell (D) and the other defendants. Each motion was denied. The matter came before the Supreme Court for review.

■ ISSUE

Must an indictment, charging a violation of a federal statute making it a crime to refuse to answer certain questions before a congressional subcommittee, state the subject matter under congressional committee inquiry as found by the grand jury?

■ DECISION AND RATIONALE

(Stewart) Yes. We hold that an indictment, charging a violation of a federal statute making it a crime to refuse to answer certain questions before a congressional subcommittee, must state the subject matter under congressional committee inquiry as found by the grand jury. In *Sinclair v. U.S.* we held that 1) the question which the witness refused to answer must pertain to a subject then under investigation by the congressional body which summoned him, 2) the United States must plead and show that the question he refused to answer pertained to some matter under investigation, and 3) the question of pertinency is one for determination by the court as a matter of law. With respect to determining whether the questions asked were pertinent to the subject under inquiry, there must be an identification of the subject matter. Moreover, with respect to the sufficiency of the indictment, it must contain the elements of the offense intended to be charged, and sufficiently apprise the defendant of what he must be prepared to meet. The indictments have failed to satisfy this requirement. This failure violates that basic principle that the accused must be apprised by the indictment, with reasonable certainty, of the nature of the accusation against him. An example of one of the cases now before us illustrates the unfairness and uncertainty that occur where the indictment has failed to specify the subject under inquiry. In No. 12, *Price v. U.S.,* the petitioner (D) refused to answer a number of questions. The Chairman had said that the investigation was of such attempt as may be disclosed on the part of the Communist Party to influence or subvert the American Press. It was also said that "we are simply investigating communism wherever we find it." It was previously denied that the purpose of the subcommittee was to investigate Communist infiltration of the press and other forms of communication. But when Price (D) was called to testify, no one told him what subject was under inquiry. [Maybe they were trying to trick him into providing incriminating answers.] At trial the Government (P) took the position that the subject had been Communist activities generally. The judge found that the questions put were pertinent to the matter under inquiry, and the court of appeals affirmed the conviction, neither of which indicated what the subject of inquiry was. In this Court, the Government (D) contends that the subject was "Communist activity in news media." It is difficult to imagine a case in which an indictment's insufficiency resulted so clearly in the indictment's failure to fulfill its primary office—to inform the defendant of the nature of the accusation against him. An important corollary purpose of requiring an indictment to set out the specific offense charged is to inform the court of the facts alleged, so that it may decide whether they are sufficient in law to support a conviction, if one should be had. We disagree with the argument that any deficiency in the indictments could have been cured by bills of particulars. Congress has decided that only a grand jury can determine whether one should be held for criminal trial for refusing to give testimony in response to a congressional committee inquiry. The grand jury must determine what the question under inquiry was. It would be improper to allow the prosecutor or court to make a subsequent guess as to what was in the minds of the grand jury when they returned the indictment. Thus, an indictment under the statute at issue here must state the subject matter under congressional committee inquiry as found by the grand jury.

■ DISSENT

(Harlan) The majority's holding throws the federal courts back to an era of criminal pleading from which it was thought they had finally emerged. It seems that the pertinency allegations of the indictments should be deemed sufficient. The indictments were sufficient to advise Russell (D) and the others of the nature of the charge they would have to meet. The proposition advanced by the majority that a statement of the subject under inquiry is necessary in the indictment in order to fend against the possibility that a defendant may be convicted on a theory of pertinency based upon something different from that which may have been found by the grand jury is unsound.

Analysis:

This case demonstrates that an indictment must properly advise the defendant of the charges against him. The elements of the offense must be presented, and in this case, the subject matter under congressional committee inquiry must be stated as found by the grand jury. Although there is a requirement that the indictment must contain the elements of the offense, it is not necessary that it contain the factual proof that will be relied upon. *See United States v. Crippen.* Notice that the majority and dissent came to different conclusions regarding the sufficiency of the information contained in the indictment. The dissent argued that the holding would throw the courts back to the era where indictments had to contain detailed facts and the actual legal theory of the case or else the indictment could be quashed. The true basis for the majority's holding was that the indictments failed to Inform Russell (D) and the others of the nature of the accusation so that they could be sufficiently apprised of what they must be prepared to meet. Merely referring to the statute would not be enough. The indictment needed to contain the subject of the questioning so that the court could determine if the conviction was based upon facts presented to the grand jury.

■ CASE VOCABULARY

BILL OF PARTICULARS: A document provided by a civil plaintiff or a criminal prosecutor, upon request of the defendant, which states detailed information concerning the complaint or criminal charge.

MOTION TO QUASH: To void the effect of a legal document.

United States v. Cotton

(*Prosecuting Authority*) v. (*Drug Conspirator*)
535 U.S. 625, 122 S.Ct. 1781, 152 L.Ed.2d 860 (2002)

THE REVIEWING COURT MAY CONSIDER THE EVIDENCE TO DETERMINE WHETHER TO IMPOSE A GREATER SENTENCE

■ **INSTANT FACTS** The defendants were sentenced to a higher penalty than that prescribed for the offenses charged in the indictment.

■ **BLACK LETTER RULE** An appellate court may correct an error not raised at trial if the error is plain, affects substantial rights, and seriously affects the fairness, integrity, or public reputation of judicial proceedings.

■ PROCEDURAL BASIS

Certiorari to review a decision of the Fourth Circuit Court of Appeals vacating the defendants' convictions.

■ FACTS

Cotton (D) and others were indicted for conspiracy to distribute and possession with intent to distribute of five kilograms or more of cocaine and fifty grams or more of cocaine base in violation of federal statutes. Several months later, a superseding indictment was issued adding five additional defendants, extending the time of the conspiracy, and charging a conspiracy to distribute and possession with intent to distribute a "detectable amount" of cocaine and cocaine base. The superseding indictment did not allege the threshold quantity of drugs necessary for enhanced penalties under the federal statute. The court instructed the jury that as long as the evidence demonstrated a defendant was involved in the conspiracy or possessed drugs with intent to distribute, the amount involved was unimportant. The defendants were convicted. Under the appropriate federal statute, the defendants could be imprisoned for up to twenty years for offenses involving a detectable amount of drugs. The court, however, applied the sentencing provision of another statute, providing for up to life imprisonment for offenses involving at least fifty grams of cocaine base. Reviewing the trial evidence, the court found that it supported enhanced penalties and sentenced the defendants to prison terms ranging from thirty years to life. The defendants did not object to the court's sentencing method, but instead appealed to the Fourth Circuit Court of Appeals. While the appeal was pending, the Supreme Court decided *Apprendi v. New Jersey*, which held that any fact that increases a penalty beyond the maximum statutory penalty must be submitted to the jury and proven beyond a reasonable doubt. The Fourth Circuit vacated the convictions because the court was not authorized to sentence the defendants for a crime not alleged in the indictment.

■ ISSUE

Does the omission from a federal indictment of a fact that enhances the statutory maximum sentence justify vacating the enhanced sentence, even though the defendant did not object in the trial court?

■ DECISION AND RATIONALE

(Rehnquist, C.J.) No. Although Court precedent has suggested that a deficiency in an indictment constitutes a jurisdictional defect, that notion has receded through time given the growing availability of direct appeal from a defendant's conviction. To the extent that a defective indictment may deprive a court of jurisdiction over the criminal proceeding, Court precedent is overruled. Because the defendants failed to object to the court's sentencing method, thus preserving the issue for appeal, an appellate court is guided by the requirements of Federal Rule of Criminal Procedure 52(b). Under the rule, an error not raised at trial may be corrected only the error is "plain" and "affect[s] substantial rights." When these circumstances exist, the court may exercise its discretion to correct the error if it "seriously affect[s] the fairness, integrity, or public reputation of judicial proceedings." While the Government (P) concedes that the indictment's deficiencies constitute plain error, the shortcomings are merely a structural error that did not materially affect the outcome of the trial. When the evidence supporting the outcome is "overwhelming" and "essentially uncontroverted," the fairness and integrity of the judicial proceedings are not compromised.

Here, although the indictment neglected to quantify the amount of drugs at issue, the evidence at trial overwhelmingly demonstrated an amount exceeding the threshold for enhanced sentences. There is no reason to believe that the grand jury would not have issued the indictment on the higher charges based on the evidence presented. The fairness and integrity of the judicial system would be frustrated if the defendants, having committed aggravated drug offenses, received a lesser penalty than others committing more severe violations. Reversed.

Analysis:

Permitting trial courts to sentence a defendant on a conviction greater than that charged in the indictment presents a significant threat to constitutional rights. For instance, suppose Cotton (D) chose not to testify on his own behalf because the evidence clearly supported his possession of a "detectable amount" of drugs. While he may concede that the Government's (P) evidence supports that charge, he may have important evidence to offer that would reduce the quantity possessed below the enhanced-penalty threshold. Yet, because he was not placed on notice that the crime was being charged, he has effectively been denied the opportunity to present evidence favorable to his defense. If such evidence exists, it would be relevant to the plain-error analysis on appeal.

■ CASE VOCABULARY

SENTENCE: The judgment that a court formally pronounces after finding a criminal defendant guilty; the punishment imposed on a criminal wrongdoer.

INDICTMENT: The formal written accusation of a crime, made by a grand jury and presented to a court for prosecution against the accused person.

United States v. Miller

(*Government*) v. (*Mail Fraud Defendant*)

471 U.S. 130, 105 S.Ct. 1811, 85 L.Ed.2d 99 (1985)

SUPREME COURT LIMITS *BAIN* RULE AND HOLDS THAT IT IS PERMISSIBLE TO STRIKE OUT PARTS OF AN INDICTMENT WITHOUT INVALIDATING THE WHOLE OF THE INDICTMENT

■ **INSTANT FACTS** Miller (D) challenged sufficiency of indictment because the trial proof was narrower and more limited than the fraudulent scheme alleged in the indictment.

■ **BLACK LETTER RULE** The Fifth Amendment's grand jury guarantee is not violated when a defendant is tried under an indictment that alleges a certain fraudulent scheme but is convicted based on trial proof that supports only a significantly narrower and more limited, though included, fraudulent scheme.

■ PROCEDURAL BASIS

Review by Supreme Court of reversal by Court of Appeal of criminal conviction of mail fraud.

■ FACTS

A federal grand jury indicted Miller (D) for several violations of the mail fraud statute, by alleging that he had defrauded an insurance company by both arranging for a burglary at his place of business and by lying to the insurer as to the value of the loss. The trial proof, however, concerned only the value of loss allegation and the Government (P) moved to strike that part of the indictment that alleged prior knowledge of the burglary. The [very cleaver] defense opposed the amendment and the entire indictment was submitted to the jury. The jury found Miller (D) guilty. Miller (D) then appealed on the ground that the trial proof had fatally varied from the scheme alleged in the [original and entire] indictment. [See why he opposed the motion to strike parts of the indictment.] The Court of Appeals agreed, stating that the grand jury quite possibly would have been unwilling or unable to return an indictment based solely on Miller's (D) exaggeration of the amount of his claimed loss even though it had concluded than an indictment could be returned based on the overall scheme involving a use of the mail caused by his knowing consent to the burglary.

■ ISSUE

Is the Fifth Amendment's grand jury guarantee violated when a defendant is tried under an indictment that alleges a certain fraudulent scheme but is convicted based on trial proof that supports only a significantly narrower and more limited, though included, fraudulent scheme?

■ DECISION AND RATIONALE

(Marshall) No. The Fifth Amendment's grand jury guarantee is not violated when a defendant is tried under an indictment that alleges a certain fraudulent scheme but is convicted based on trial proof that supports only a significantly narrower and more limited, though included, fraudulent scheme. The Court of Appeals held that Miller (D) had been prejudiced in his right to be free from a trial for any offense other than that alleged in the indictment. It reasoned that a grand jury's willingness to indict an individual for participation in a broad criminal plan does not establish that the same grand jury would have indicted the individual for participating in a substantially narrower, even if wholly included, criminal plan. [The big criminal versus little criminal defense.] We have long recognized that an indictment may charge numerous offenses or the commission of any one offense in several ways. As long as the crime and elements of the offense are fully and clearly set out in the indictment, the right to a grand jury is not normally violated by the fact that the indictment alleges more crimes or other means of committing the same crime. The decision in *Stirone v. United States* [admitting evidence that resulted in a variance between proof and the charge was error] is unlike the case now before us because in *Stirone* the offense proved at trial was not fully contained in the indictment. However, there is some support for the Court of Appeal's ruling in *Ex parte Bain* [amendment of an indictment could only be done by the grand jury and not by the trial court], where there was a deletion from an indictment of allegations that would not have been necessary to prove the offense. The opinion reasoned that the court could not assume that the narrower indictment would have been returned by the grand jury that returned the broader one. The decision in *Bain* can support the proposition that the striking out of parts of an indictment invalidates the whole of the indictment, for a court cannot speculate as to whether the grand jury had meant for any remaining offense to stand independently, even if that remaining offense was included in the original test. Thus, the narrowing of an indictment is no different from the adding of a new allegation that had never been considered by the grand jury; both are treated as amendments that alter the nature of the offense charged. This holding of *Bain* has been limited or distinguished by this Court. Modern criminal law has generally accepted that an indictment will support each offense contained within it. To the extent *Bain* stands for the proposition that it constitutes an unconstitutional amendment to drop from an indictment those allegations that are unnecessary to an offense that is clearly contained within it, we reject that proposition. [What happened to the doctrine of stare decisis, *i.e.*, let the decision stand?] The variance complained of in the case now before us added nothing new to the grand jury's indictment and constituted no broadening. Judgment reversed.

Analysis:

This case modified the rule laid down in *Ex parte Bain.* It limited the holding of *Bain* to stand for the proposition that a conviction cannot stand if based on an offense that is different from that alleged in the indictment. Under the facts of *Miller*, however, the indictment contained the offense charged, but the facts supporting the conviction were much more limited and narrower than those contained in the indictment. The evidence submitted at trial only referred to Miller's (D) defrauding the insurance company as to the value of the loss, and not to the allegations concerning arranging for a burglary at his place of business. The court held that it was permissible to strike out of parts of an indictment without invalidating the whole of the indictment. The Supreme Court held that it would have been permissible for the Government (P) to amend the indictment to the proof presented at trial. Note that the Court's ruling does not affect that portion of the *Bain* rule that provides that a conviction cannot stand if based upon an offense that is different from that alleged in the indictment.

■ CASE VOCABULARY

MOVED TO STRIKE: Referring to a "motion to strike" whereby a request is made to the court to delete all or a portion of a pleading, or evidence offered at trial.

CHAPTER EIGHTEEN

The Location of the Prosecution

United States v. Rodreguez–Moreno

Instant Facts: Defendant charged with carrying a firearm during commission of kidnapping challenged right to bring charge in New Jersey since he only carried the gun in Maryland.

Black Letter Rule: Where venue is proper for the underlying crime of violence, so it is too for the crime of carrying a firearm during the commission of a crime of violence.

United States v. Rodriguez-Moreno

(*Government*) v. (*Criminal Defendant*)

526 U.S. 275, 119 S.Ct. 1239, 143 L.Ed.2d 388 (1999)

CONVICTION FOR USE OF GUN IN NEW JERSEY UPHELD EVEN THOUGH GUN WAS ONLY USED IN MARYLAND

■ **INSTANT FACTS** Defendant charged with carrying a firearm during commission of kidnapping challenged right to bring charge in New Jersey since he only carried the gun in Maryland.

■ **BLACK LETTER RULE** Where venue is proper for the underlying crime of violence, so it is too for the crime of carrying a firearm during the commission of a crime of violence.

■ PROCEDURAL BASIS

Appeal from conviction for carrying a firearm during the commission of a crime of violence obtained in New Jersey.

■ FACTS

During a drug deal that took place in Houston, Texas, a New York drug dealer stole 30 kilograms of a Texas drug distributor's cocaine. The distributor hired Jacinto Rodriguez-Moreno (D) (Rodriguez) and others to find the dealer who stole the drugs and to hold a middleman captive until they did so. In pursuit of the dealer, the distributor and his henchmen, including Rodriguez (D), drove from Texas to New Jersey with the middleman in tow. They then moved to a house in New York and then a house in Maryland, taking the middleman with them. Shortly after arriving at the Maryland house, the owner passed around a .357 magnum revolver, which Rodriguez (D) took possession of. As it became clear that their efforts to find the dealer were fruitless, Rodriguez (D) suggested that they kill the middleman. Rodriguez (D) put the gun to the back of the middleman's head, but at the behest of his cohorts, he did not kill him. The middleman eventually escaped [so much for listening to the cohorts] and neighbors called the police. Rodriguez (D) and the rest were arrested. The police also found the gun with Rodriguez (D) fingerprints. All of the men were tried together in the United States District Court for the District of New Jersey. Rodriguez (D) was tried with conspiring to kidnap the middleman, kidnapping and using and carrying a firearm during the commission of a crime of violence. At the conclusion of the government's case, Rodriguez (D) moved to dismiss the gun charge on the grounds that venue was improper. The trial court denied his motion and the jury found him guilty on all counts. Rodriguez (D) was sentenced to 87 months in prison and a mandatory consecutive sentence of 60 months for the gun charge. On appeal, the Court of Appeals reversed the gun conviction, and this appeal followed.

■ ISSUE

For a charge of carrying a firearm during the commission of a crime of violence, is venue proper in any jurisdiction in which the underlying crime of violence occurred, even if the gun was not used in all of the jurisdictions?

■ DECISION AND RATIONALE

(Thomas) Yes. Applying the verb test, the Court of Appeals concluded that a defendant violates § 924(c)(1) only when he "uses" or "carries" a firearm. As such, they concluded that the only proper place to try a § 924(c)(1) case is in the jurisdiction in which the statute was violated. Since it was undisputed that Rodriguez (D) only used and carried the firearm in Maryland, the Court of Appeals concluded that his conviction, obtained in New Jersey, must be reversed. We disagree. The location of the charged offense must be determined from the nature of the crime and the location of the acts constituting the crime. While the verb test is a proper tool of statutory interpretation, it is not the sole means and should never be the only means. It should never be applied rigidly to the exclusion of other language in the statute. Here, in addition to carrying and using a firearm, the essential elements of the crime include violent acts. To prove a violation of the statute here, the government must show that Rodriguez (D) used a firearm and that he committed all of the acts necessary to subject him to punishment for kidnapping, the underlying crime of violence. The statute thus has two distinct elements: the using and carrying of a gun and the commission of the crime of violence. Rodriguez (D) argues that for venue purposes, the kidnapping is completely irrelevant. It is thus his position, and that of the amicus curie, that § 924(c)(1) is a point of time offense. We disagree. Kidnapping is a unitary crime, once begun, it does not end until the victim is free. It does not make sense, then, to consider it in only geographic fragments. Here, the crime with which Rodriguez (D) was charged prohibited the use of a firearm during the commission of a crime of violence. It makes no difference that he used the gun only during the final phase of the commission of that underlying crime. The kidnapping was begun in Texas, continued in New Jersey and New York and completed in Maryland. Having used a gun during the commission of the kidnapping, Rodriguez (D) can be charged with violating § 924(c)(1) in any of those states. Where a crime consists of distinct parts, all of which occur in different localities, the whole may be charged in any location where any part took place. Reversed.

■ DISSENT

(Scalia) In my view, the statute prohibits the carrying and using of a firearm *during* the commission of an underlying crime of violence. Thus, only when the underlying crime of violence is occurring at the same time the defendant is carrying or using a gun is the statute violated and only in those jurisdictions in which both events are taking place may the defendant be tried for having violated the statute. Here, it is conceded that Rodriguez (D) only used the firearm during the kidnapping in Maryland, as such, he can only be tried for violating § 924(c)(1) in Maryland. I therefore dissent.

Analysis:

In this case we are concerned with applying the crime-committed formula for determining where venue is proper. As the majority points out, where a crime is committed is dependent on the nature of the crime itself, which often involves an interpretation of the statute defining the offense. Here, the language of the statute is the key point of contention. The Court of Appeals, relying on "carries" and "uses" in the statute, concluded that only when a defendant is actually carrying or using a gun can he be deemed to have committed this offense and, consequently, can only be charged in the jurisdiction in which he has done so. The majority, focusing on both the carries and uses language in conjunction with "crime of violence", disagrees. Rather, in the majority's view, since the gun offense requires a crime of violence, the defendant can be charged in any jurisdiction in which the underlying crime occurred, regardless of where he actually carried or used the gun. The dissent offers up yet another interpretation of the same language. The dissent focuses on the word "during" in the statute, concluding that only when both the elements of the underlying offense are present and the element of the gun charge are present is venue proper. For our purposes, the key here is to recognize that for offenses that rely on an underlying offense, such as the gun charge here, the majority view is that the defendant can be charged in any jurisdiction in which the underlying offense took place.

■ CASE VOCABULARY

18 U.S.C. § 924(c)(1): Federal statute that prohibits the carrying of a firearm during the commission of a crime of violence.

LOCUS DELECTI: Refers to the location of the crime.

VERB TEST: A statutory interpretation tool under which the meaning of a statute is determined from the verbs used within the statute itself.

CHAPTER NINETEEN

Joinder and Severance of Offenses and Defendants

Cross v. United States

Instant Facts: The Court refused to separate the two counts against the defendant for trial, and the defendant was subsequently convicted on one count and acquitted on the other.

Black Letter Rule: Prejudice may develop when an accused wishes to testify on one but not the other of two joined offenses which are clearly distinct in time, place and evidence.

Drew v. United States

Instant Facts: A defendant arrested at the scene of an attempted robbery was also accused of and tried in the same proceeding for another robbery which had occurred under similar circumstances.

Black Letter Rule: In any given case the court must weigh prejudice to the defendant caused by the joinder against the obviously important considerations of economy and expedition in judicial administration.

United States v. Dixon

Instant Facts: Dixon (D) and Foster (D) were found guilty of criminal contempt and were later charged with the underlying crimes for which they were found guilty of contempt.

Black Letter Rule: The Double Jeopardy Clause bars prosecution of a defendant on substantive criminal charges based upon the same conduct for which he previously has been held in criminal contempt.

United States v. Ash

Instant Facts: A criminal defendant objected to the government's use of a photographic lineup without the presence of defense counsel.

Black Letter Rule: A criminal defendant has no right to have counsel attend a photographic lineup conducted by the government.

Schaffer v. United States

Instant Facts: The defendants were charged with conspiracy as well as the substantive offense, however the conspiracy count was dismissed at the close of the prosecution's case, and the substantive count alone went to the jury.

Black Letter Rule: Under Rule 14 of the Federal Rules of Criminal Procedure, defendants are not entitled to separate trials unless prejudice from joinder is demonstrated.

Gray v. Maryland

Instant Facts: Gray (D) was convicted of murder after the prosecution used a redacted confession of a codefendant which implicated Gray (D).

Black Letter Rule: Under Bruton, certain powerfully incriminating extrajudicial statements of a codefendant those naming another defendant considered as a class, are so prejudicial that limiting instructions cannot work.

Cross v. United States

(*Career Robber*) v. (*Prosecution*)
335 F.2d 987 (1964)

JOINDER MAKES IT IMPOSSIBLE FOR THE JURY TO WEIGH THE EVIDENCE SEPARATELY AS TO EACH COUNT OF THE INDICTMENT

■ **INSTANT FACTS** The Court refused to separate the two counts against the defendant for trial, and the defendant was subsequently convicted on one count and acquitted on the other.

■ **BLACK LETTER RULE** Prejudice may develop when an accused wishes to testify on one but not the other of two joined offenses which are clearly distinct in time, place and evidence.

■ PROCEDURAL BASIS

Appeal from the District Court's denial of the defendant's motion for severance of the two counts against him, and the jury's subsequent conviction of the defendant on one count and acquittal on the other.

■ FACTS

Cross (D) was charged in Count I with robbery of a church rectory, and in Count II with robbery of a tourist home over two months later. He filed a pretrial motion for severance of the counts, however the motion was denied. The jury returned a verdict of guilty on Count I and not guilty on Count II. Cross (D) is appealing, claiming that the District Court erred in refusing to sever the counts for trial.

■ ISSUE

Was the defendant prejudiced by the District Court's refusal to separate the counts in the indictment for trial?

■ DECISION AND RATIONALE

(Bazelon, C.J.) Yes. Prejudice may develop when an accused wishes to testify on one but not the other of two joined offenses which are clearly distinct in time, place and exigence. In the present case, Cross (D) did not specify at trial the counts upon which he wished to remain silent and why. It does appear that, when the trial court asked Cross (D) whether he wished to testify in his own behalf, Cross (D) answered: "Which case, Your Honor?" Cross (D) repeatedly tried to elaborate upon his objections to the joinder, but the court precluded this by insisting that the issue of joinder had been determined in the pre-trial denial of severance, and demanded a categorical answer to its original query. In this situation, it is not necessary to decide whether this invades his constitutional right to remain silent, since we think it constitutes prejudice within the meaning of Rule 14 of the Federal Rules of Criminal Procedure. An examination of Cross' (D) testimony on both counts supports his claim in this court that he wished to testify on Count II and remain silent on Count I. His testimony on Count II was convincing even in the face of cross-examination and attempts at impeachment, while his testimony on Count I was plainly evasive and unconvincing. Thus it would appear that Cross (D) had ample reason not to testify on Count I and would not have done so if that count had been tried separately. In a separate trial of that count, the jury would not have heard his admissions of prior convictions and unsavory activities; nor would he have been under duress to offer dubious testimony on that count in order to avoid the damaging implication of testifying on only one of two joined counts. Since the joinder embarrassed and confounded Cross (D) in making his defense, the joinder was prejudicial within the meaning of Rule 14. The judgment on Count I is vacated and the case is remanded to the District Court for a new trial on that count.

■ DISSENT

(Bastian, C.J.) The jury was apprized of its responsibility to consider each count separately. That the jury acquitted the defendant on one count while convicting on the other demonstrates that it did, in fact, consider the evidence as it related to each count separately.

Analysis:

This case discusses the right of a defendant to severance of offenses for trial where the joinder of offenses would prejudice the defendant Under Fed. R. Civ. P. 8(a), offenses may be joined for trial if they arise from the same criminal scheme or occurrence, or if they are similar in nature regardless of when they occurred. In this case, the offenses were not part of one criminal scheme. However, since both offenses were robberies, they were of the same or similar character. There are limits to when offenses may be joined, or when they must be severed. Offenses should not be joined for trial if the joinder will violate some constitutional right of one of the defendants. Offenses should also not be joined if the joinder will be prejudicial to the ability of the defendant to put forward his defense, pursuant to Fed. R. Crim. P. 14.

■ CASE VOCABULARY

IMPEACHMENT: The calling into question the veracity of a witness, by means of evidence adduced for such purpose, or the adducing of proof that a witness is unworthy of belief.

JOINDER: The charging of two or more offenses in the same indictment or information in a separate count for each offense.

Drew v. United States

(*Robber*) v. (*Prosecution*)
331 F.2d 85 (D.C. Cir. 1964)

COURTS MUST BALANCE THE PREJUDICE OF JOINDER AGAINST THE BENEFITS OF JUDICIAL ECONOMY

■ **INSTANT FACTS** A man accused of robbing two convenience stores was tried for both robberies in the same trial and was convicted of both.

■ **BLACK LETTER RULE** To determine whether severance should be granted, the economy of joining two unrelated but similar offenses must be weighed against the prejudice and confusion that the joinder will create.

■ PROCEDURAL BASIS

Appeal from criminal conviction.

■ FACTS

Two High's Neighborhood Stores were robbed by a man with the same general description—a black male wearing sunglasses. In both cases, the store's clerk was female. The robberies occurred two and a half weeks apart. During the first robbery, the robber demanded money from the clerk and, when she refused, he threatened her with a gun. During the second robbery, the robber also demanded money from the clerk, but when she refused and then another customer came into the store, the robber simply fled the store. Drew (D) was arrested near the second store about 25 minutes after the attempted robbery. The clerk at the second store identified him as the robber. At the same trial, Drew (D) was tried for the robbery of the first store and the attempted robbery of the second store. Drew (D) objected to joinder of the offenses both before and after trial.

■ ISSUE

Must two offenses be severed for trial where they are not part of the same criminal scheme and the joinder will confuse the jury and prejudice the defendant?

■ DECISION AND RATIONALE

(McGowan) Yes. Joinder of offenses for trial is desirable from the standpoint of judicial economy. However, joinder is undesirable if it prejudices the defendant. There are several situations where prejudice may occur. The defendant may become embarrassed or confounded in presenting separate defenses in the same trial. Where the jury becomes convinced that the defendant committed one of the offenses, it may then decide that the defendant has a criminal disposition, and on that basis alone convict the defendant of the other offense. The jury may cumulate the evidence as to all offenses and find guilt when, if the evidence of each offense had been considered separately, it could not have so found. Thus, the court must, in each case, weigh the prejudice of joinder against the economy that joinder achieves. Evidence of a prior criminal history cannot be presented to a jury in the hopes that they will infer that the defendant has a disposition to commit crimes. Since juries are likely to assume such a disposition, courts presume prejudice and exclude evidence of prior crimes unless there is another purpose for admitting it. Traditionally, prior crimes of the defendant can be admitted into evidence to prove motive, intent, absence of mistake or accident, common scheme or plan, or identity. Under this reasoning, joinder of separate offenses is permissible where evidence of the offenses would be independently admissible if introduced in separate trials. In addition, joinder of separate offenses is also permissible if the evidence for each offense is simple and distinct. This rests on the assumption that, with a proper jury instruction, the jury will be able to deliberate separately with respect to each charge. In the present case, however, the facts do not show such a close similarity in manner of committing the crimes as would make them admissible in separate trials as proof of identity. Nor is there any proof that the robberies, which came two and a half weeks apart, were part of a common scheme or plan. In addition, this is not a case where the offenses and the evidence can be called "simple and distinct." Here the record shows that witnesses at trial were often confused as to which robbery counsel was discussing during questioning, the two robberies were referred to as the same type of crime, and the prosecutor often lumped both crimes together in his closing. Because of superficial similarities in the two crimes, the jury may easily have been confused. For these reasons, there was prejudice in the joinder, and the offenses should have been severed for trial. Reversed.

Analysis:

Here, the court purports to weigh the prejudice to the defendant against the needs of judicial economy (another way to put it might be the prejudice to the court and prosecution in having to conduct a separate trial). However, the court does not explain exactly how to determine how much weight is to be given to the needs of judicial economy, or how to measure those needs against prejudice to the defendant. The court does give two tests to determine when the defendant has *not* been prejudiced: 1) If evidence of the first crime would be admissible in a trial for the second, then there is no prejudice in trying the offenses at the same time; and 2) Is the evidence of both crimes so separate and distinct that the jury will not get confused and can be successfully instructed to consider the offenses separately? In applying the first test, the court points to the rule of evidence that a previous crime cannot be used to demonstrate a propensity to act criminally. There are many other instances where evidence is inadmissible for its truth or probative value (such as hearsay evidence). However, evidence of a previous crime, like many other types of normally inadmissible evidence, may be introduced for other purposes (as long as the jury is later told to consider the evidence for only the purpose for which it was introduced.) Other purposes include impeachment, proof of motive, proof of intent, proof of absence of mistake or accident, proof of common scheme, proof of identity. The court reasons that the facts in this case are not so similar (there is merely a "superficial similarity") as would make them admissible in separate trials.

United States v. Dixon

(*Government*) v. (*Accused*)

509 U.S. 688, 113 S.Ct. 2849 (1993)

A DEFENDANT CANNOT BE PROSECUTED ON CRIMINAL CHARGES BASED ON THE SAME CONDUCT FOR WHICH HE WAS PREVIOUSLY HELD IN CRIMINAL CONTEMPT

■ **INSTANT FACTS** Dixon (D) and Foster (D) were found guilty of criminal contempt and were later charged with the underlying crimes for which they were found guilty of contempt.

■ **BLACK LETTER RULE** The Double Jeopardy Clause bars prosecution of a defendant on substantive criminal charges based upon the same conduct for which he previously has been held in criminal contempt.

■ PROCEDURAL BASIS

Writ of certiorari granted after subsequent prosecutions were barred.

■ FACTS

This case involves two cases which were combined on appeal. Dixon (D) was arrested for murder and released on bond. He was warned not to commit any criminal offense or he would be subject to prosecution for contempt. Dixon (D) was subsequently arrested for possession of cocaine with intent to distribute. He was prosecuted and found guilty of contempt. The court concluded that the Government had proven beyond a reasonable doubt that he possessed drugs with the intent to distribute. Dixon (D) was then indicted for possession of cocaine with intent to distribute. His motion to dismiss on double jeopardy grounds was granted by the trial court. Foster (D), the second petitioner, was prosecuted for contempt for violating a civil restraining order obtained by his estranged wife. Foster's wife prosecuted the action claiming that Foster (D) had threatened her on three occasions and assaulted her twice in violation of the order. The court found Foster (D) guilty beyond a reasonable doubt of criminal contempt for the two assaults, but acquitted him of the alleged threats. The U.S. Attorney's Office later indicted Foster (D) for simple assault, threats, and assault with intent to kill. Some of these counts were based on the events for which Foster (D) had been held in contempt. Foster (D) moved to dismiss, claiming a double jeopardy bar to all counts. On appeal, the court found that both Dixon's (D) and Foster's (D) subsequent prosecutions were barred by the Double Jeopardy Clause.

■ ISSUE

Does the Double Jeopardy Clause bar prosecution of a defendant on criminal charges based on the same conduct for which he previously has been held in criminal contempt of court?

■ DECISION AND RATIONALE

(Scalia, J.) Yes. Criminal contempt is a crime in the ordinary sense. The double jeopardy bar applies where the two offenses for which the defendant is punished cannot survive the "same-elements" test. This test, referred to as the *Blockburger* test, asks whether each offense contains an element not contained in the other; if not, they are the same offense and double jeopardy prevents additional punishment. The crime of violating a condition of release is not separate from the violated condition.

Dixon's (D) court order incorporated the entire criminal code. Here, the underlying criminal offense is a species of lesser-included offense. Dixon's (D) drug offense did not include any element not contained in his previous contempt offense; therefore, the Double Jeopardy Clause prevents further prosecution. Except for the assault charge, the counts against Foster (D), however, are not barred under the *Blockburger* test. The contempt actions required proof that Foster (D) knew of a civil protective order and committed a willful violation of one of its conditions, here simple assault. Foster's (D) subsequent indictment was for assault with intent to kill which requires an intent to kill which simple assault does not. Applying the *Blockburger* test, Foster's (D) crimes required additional elements and constitute different offenses. Therefore, the subsequent prosecution of Foster (D) for assault with intent to kill is allowed. We must also consider whether the counts at issue here are barred by the additional double jeopardy test of *Grady v. Corbin.* They would be barred by this test since *Grady* prohibits a subsequent prosecution if, to establish an essential element of an offense charged in that prosecution, the government will prove conduct that constitutes an offense for which the defendant has already been prosecuted. We conclude, however, that *Grady* must be overruled. *Grady* lacks historical and constitutional roots. *Grady* has also proven unstable in application, and the case was clearly a mistake. Dixon's (D) subsequent prosecutions therefore violate the Double Jeopardy Clause. Except for the assault charge, Foster's subsequent prosecutions do not violate the Double Jeopardy Clause.

■ CONCURRENCE AND DISSENT

(Rehnquist, J.) I do not join the majority because I think that none of the criminal prosecutions in this case were barred under *Blockburger.* The *Blockburger* test requires us to focus on the elements of contempt of court in the ordinary sense rather than on the terms of the particular court order involved. Because the generic crime of contempt of court has different elements than the substantive criminal charges in this case, they are separate offenses under *Blockburger.* Two offenses are different for purposes of double jeopardy if each provision requires proof of a fact the other does not. Contempt of court involves two elements: 1) a court order known to the defendant, and 2) a willful violation of that order. Neither of these elements is satisfied by proof that a defendant has committed assault or drug distribution. The crimes here cannot be viewed as greater and lesser included offenses. The crime of possession with intent to distribute is a felony that cannot easily be seen as a lesser included offense of criminal contempt, which is a relatively minor offense. However, I agree that *Grady* must be overruled. I would uphold the substantive criminal prosecutions which followed the convictions for criminal contempt. I join the court in overruling *Grady.*

■ CONCURRENCE AND DISSENT

(White, J.) I concur in the portion of the judgment which holds that the subsequent prosecutions were barred. However, I would not overrule *Grady.*

■ CONCURRENCE AND DISSENT

(Blackmun, J.) I cannot agree that contempt of court is the "same offense" for double jeopardy purposes as either assault or possession of cocaine with intent to distribute. Contempt of court is an important tool for a trial court to enforce its orders. The decision today will undermine a court's ability to respond to threats on its authority. The interests of contempt litigators and criminal prosecutors are different. I would allow the subsequent prosecutions for the substantive offenses.

■ CONCURRENCE AND DISSENT

(Souter, J.) I would hold that both the prosecution of Dixon (D) and the prosecution of Foster (D) under all the counts of the indictment against them to be barred by the Double Jeopardy Clause. The interests at stake in avoiding successive prosecutions are different from those at stake in the prohibition against multiple punishments, and our cases reflect this reality. The protection against successive prosecutions is the central protection provided by the Clause. Consequently, while the government may punish a person separately for each conviction of at least as many different offenses as meet the *Blockburger* test, we have long held that it must sometimes bring its prosecutions for these offenses together. If a separate prosecution were permitted for every offense arising out of the same conduct, the government could manipulate the definitions of offenses, creating fine distinctions among them and permitting a zealous prosecutor to try a person again and again for essentially the same criminal conduct. The limitation on successive prosecution is thus a restriction on the government different in kind from that contained in the limitation on multiple punishments, and the government cannot get around the restriction on repeated prosecution of a single individual merely by precision in the way it defines its statutory offenses.

Analysis:

This case explores the question of when it is impermissible to hold separate trials on related offenses. In other words, when *must* two offenses be joined for trial. Sometimes, it is necessary to join offenses that are the result of the same criminal act, transaction, or occurrence. This is because the Double Jeopardy Clause prevents a defendant from being tried twice for the same crime, but does not prevent multiple charges, and therefore multiple punishments, arising from the same criminal act if the act constitutes more than one crime. The Double Jeopardy clause is designed to prevent the prosecution from holding "dress rehearsals" until it can finally obtain a conviction. The test adopted in Dixon is known as the "same elements" test - do both offenses have at least one unique statutory element each? However, prior to this decision the courts had been using the "same conduct" test - has the defendant already been prosecuted for this conduct? Notice that the "same conduct" test will better protect the defendant against dress rehearsals. However the same elements test insures that a defendant is held fully accountable for all of the consequences of his criminal actions.

Ashe v. Swenson

(Accused) v. *(Prosecution)*
397 U.S. 436, 90 S.Ct. 1189 (1970)

AFTER AN ISSUE HAS BEEN NECESSARILY AND ACTUALLY DECIDED, THAT ISSUE CANNOT AGAIN BE LITIGATED BETWEEN THE SAME PARTIES

■ **INSTANT FACTS** Ashe (D) was acquitted of robbing one victim but was brought to trial and convicted for robbing another victim during the same event.

■ **BLACK LETTER RULE** After an issue of ultimate fact has been finally determined, the same issue cannot be re-litigated between the same parties in any future proceeding.

■ PROCEDURAL BASIS

Writ of certiorari granted after an acquittal and then a conviction for a related crime.

■ FACTS

Six men were playing poker in the basement of a home. Suddenly three or four masked men, armed with a shotgun and pistols, broke in and robbed each of the players of money and personal property. The robbers fled in a car belonging to one of the victims. The car was found abandoned later that day, and Ashe (D) and three others were found nearby and arrested. All four were charged with seven separate offenses, the armed robbery of six of the seven poker players and the theft of the car. Ashe (D) went to trial on the charge of robbing one of the victims, Donald Knight. The State's evidence that Ashe (D) was one of the robbers was weak. The State's witnesses had difficulty identifying Ashe (D), one claiming he "sounded like" one of the robbers, and some thought there were only three robbers. Ashe (D) was found not guilty due to insufficient evidence. Weeks later, Ashe (D) was brought to trial again for the robbery of another participant in the poker game, Roberts. The witnesses were the same, but this time their testimony was much stronger. They were now able to identify Ashe (D) as one of the robbers and to testify to his features, size, and mannerisms. One of the witnesses claimed to now remember the unusual sound of his voice. This time the jury found him guilty, and he was sentenced to a 35-year prison term.

■ ISSUE

Can a defendant be tried for a related offense after an issue of ultimate fact was determined in a previous trial resulting in an acquittal?

■ DECISION AND RATIONALE

(Stewart, J.) No. The important principle of "collateral estoppel" means that when an issue of ultimate fact has once been determined by a valid and final judgment, that issue cannot again be litigated between the same parties in any future lawsuit. The principle was first developed in civil litigation, but it also applies in the criminal context. To determine whether collateral estoppel applies, we must examine the record of the prior proceeding and determine whether a rational jury could have decided its verdict upon an issue other than that which the defendant seeks to prevent consideration. The only rationally conceivable issue in dispute before the jury in this case was whether Ashe (D) was one of the robbers. Because the jury found Ashe (D) not guilty, it had to have found that he was not one of the robbers. Collateral estoppel then no doubt applies in this case. The only question remaining is whether this rule of law is embodied in the Fifth Amendment guarantee against double jeopardy. We hold that it is. The Double Jeopardy Clause clearly protects a man from being re-tried who has been acquitted. After a jury has determined by its verdict that Ashe (D) was not one of the robbers, the State may not put him before a new jury to litigate that issue again. The fact that the second trial related to a different victim makes no difference. The name of the victim has no bearing on whether Ashe (D) was one of the robbers. The prosecution admits that it refined its presentation in the second trial based on the first trial. This is precisely what the constitution forbids.

■ CONCURRENCE

(Brennan) I agree that the Double Jeopardy Clause incorporates collateral estoppel as a constitutional requirement. However, even aside from the issue of collateral estoppel, the constitution bars the prosecution of Ashe (D) for armed robbery a second time. In my view the Double Jeopardy Clause requires the joinder of all charges that arose from a single criminal act, occurrence, episode or transaction. The state should not be able to refine its case over and over by bringing a separate trial for each victim of a crime.

■ DISSENT

(Burger) Collateral estoppel, a concept of civil litigation, becomes a strange mutant when applied to criminal cases. First, collateral estoppel cannot constitutionally apply to both parties, as it does in civil litigation. Nobody would argue that if the jury had found Ashe (D) guilty, then Ashe (D) would be precluded from forcing that state to prove his guilt in a second trial with relation to a second victim. Second, the Court is forced to psychoanalyze the jury. Today's holding is sheer guesswork as to whether the first jury actually believed that Ashe (D) was not present, and would have believed he was not present had it considered all of the additional evidence that was presented to the second jury.

Analysis:

Collateral estoppel can be a powerful tool to preserve judicial resources and protect the rights to the accused Collateral estoppel only applies to facts that were actually and necessarily decided by the jury in the defendant's favor. In this case, the jury by its verdict had to find that Ashe (D) was not one of the robbers. There was no dispute at trial that a robbery occurred and that items of value were taken. Therefore, the jury could not have acquitted Ashe (D) for these reasons. It could only be because the jury had a reasonable doubt about Ashe (D) being one of the robbers. The basis for the acquittal, however, is not always so clear and collateral estoppel may not be available. When a jury returns a general verdict in favor of the defendant, it may often be impossible to determine what issues the jury necessarily determined.

Schaffer v. United States

(*Clothes Thieves*) v. (*Prosecution*)

362 U.S. 511, 80 S.Ct. 945, 4 L.Ed.2d 921 (1960)

PREJUDICE FROM JOINDER OF DEFENDANTS IS NOT CONCLUSIVELY PRESUMED EVEN THOUGH THE CHARGE THAT ORIGINALLY JUSTIFIED JOINDER IS SUBSEQUENTLY DISMISSED

■ **INSTANT FACTS** The defendants were charged with conspiracy as well as the substantive offense, however the conspiracy count was dismissed at the close of the prosecution's case, and the substantive count alone went to the jury.

■ **BLACK LETTER RULE** Under Fed. R. Crim. P. 14, defendants are not entitled to separate trials unless prejudice from joinder is demonstrated.

■ PROCEDURAL BASIS

Appeal from the jury's conviction of the defendants.

■ FACTS

In Count 1 of the indictment, the two Schaffers (D) and the three Stracuzzas (defendants below, who either pleaded guilty or had the charges against them *nolle prossed* at trial) were charged with transporting stolen ladies' and children's clothing between states. Counts 2 and 3 charged other defendants with the transportation between different states. Count 4 charged Schaffer (D) and all the other defendants with conspiracy to commit the substantive offenses charged in the first three counts. The Schaffers (D) were tried on the indictment simultaneously in a single trial. On Schaffers' (D) motion for acquittal at the close of the prosecution's (P) case, the court dismissed the conspiracy count for failure of proof. The motion was denied as to the substantive counts, however, as the court found that no prejudice would result from the joint trial. Upon submission of the substantive counts to the jury, the Schaffers (D) and all the other defendants were found guilty and thereafter fined and sentenced to prison.

■ ISSUE

Under Fed. R. Crim. P. 14, defendants are not entitled to separate trials unless prejudice from joinder is demonstrated.

■ DECISION AND RATIONALE

(Clark, J.) No. The Schaffers (D) contend that prejudice is implicit in a continuation of the joint trial after dismissal of the conspiracy count. They say that the resulting prejudice could not be cured by any cautionary instructions, and that therefore the trial judge was left with no discretion. They overlook, however, that the joinder was authorized under Rule 8(b) and that subsequent severance was controlled by Rule 14, which provides for separate trials where it appears that a defendant is prejudiced by such joinder for trial. It appears that not only was no prejudice shown, but both the trial court and the Court of Appeals affirmatively found that none was present. We cannot say to the contrary on this record. Nor can we say that when a conspiracy count fails, joinder is error as a matter of law. We do emphasize, however, that in such a situation the trial judge has a continuing duty at all stages of the trial to grant a severance if prejudice does appear. And where, as here, the charge which originally justified joinder turns out to lack the support of sufficient evidence, a trial judge should be particularly sensitive to the possibility of such prejudice. However, the Schaffers (D) here not only failed to show any prejudice that would call Rule 14 into operation, but even failed to request a new trial. The terms of Rule 8(b) having been met and no prejudice under Rule 14 having been shown, there was no misjoinder. Affirmed.

■ DISSENT

(Douglas, J.) Once it becomes apparent during the trial that the defendants have not participated in the "same series" of transactions, it would make a mockery of Rule 8(b) to hold that the allegation alone, known to be false, is enough to continue the joint trial.

Analysis:

The danger in joining defendants in the same trial is that the jury will find one defendant guilty on the merits of the case and then find the other defendant guilty by association. Fed. R. Crim. P. 8(b) allows for the joinder of defendants for trial where they are accused of having participated in the same criminal acts. This case is typical of a joinder of defendants scenario in that it involves a conspiracy among the co-defendants. This should not be surprising, since conspiracy necessarily involves more than one person. It is also arguably easy to prove. The government must only show that the defendants joined in some illegal plot; to be convicted the defendant need not have done anything in furtherance of the plot. There is no need for the defendant to know all of the other co-conspirators (knowledge of one other person is enough). The defendant need not even be aware of the conspiracy's ultimate goal—just that some illegal act was foreseeable. Here, however, the prosecution could not make its burden of proof, and the conspiracy was dismissed. Thus, the charge that arguably justified joinder was gone. There was no longer the same criminal acts, but three separate acts by four separate groups of defendants. However, once the trial had begun, defendants needed to rely on Rule 14 and find some evidence of prejudice in order to sever the charges. The Court did affirm the principle that the trial court has a continuing duty at all stages of trial to grant severance if prejudice appears. But, the Court would not adopt a hard and fast rule that when a conspiracy fails, the charges must automatically be severed.

■ CASE VOCABULARY

NOLLE PROSSED: A formal entry upon the record by the prosecuting attorney by which he declares that he will no further prosecute the case, either as to some of the defendants, or altogether.

Gray v. Maryland

(*Murder Codefendant*) v. (*Prosecution*)
523 U.S. 185, 118 S.Ct. 1151, 140 L.Ed.2d 294 (1998)

REDACTION THAT REPLACES A DEFENDANT'S NAME WITH AN OBVIOUS INDICATION OF DELETION STILL FALLS WITHIN *BRUTON'S* PROTECTIVE RULE

■ **INSTANT FACTS** Gray (D) was convicted of murder after the prosecution used a redacted confession of a codefendant which implicated Gray (D).

■ **BLACK LETTER RULE** Under *Bruton,* certain powerfully incriminating extrajudicial statements of a codefendant—those naming another defendant—considered as a class, are so prejudicial that limiting instructions cannot work.

■ PROCEDURAL BASIS

Appeal from the trial judge's denial of the defendant's motion for a separate trial, and the jury's subsequent conviction of the defendant for murder.

■ FACTS

Bell confessed to the police that he, Gray (D), and Vanlandingham had participated in a beating that had resulted in the death of a man. Bell and Gray (D) were indicted in murder. The trial judge, after denying Gray's (D) motion for a separate trial, permitted the State to introduce a redacted version of Bell's confession. The redacted version of the confession merely contained blanks where Gray's (D) name otherwise appeared. Other witnesses said that six persons (including Bell, Gray (D), and Vanlandingham) participated in the beating. Gray (D) testified and denied his participation; Bell did not testify. The jury was instructed not to use the confession as evidence against Gray (D). Bell and Gray (D) were convicted, and this appeal followed.

■ ISSUE

Is the confession of a co-defendant admissible at a joint trial where it obviously implicates the non-confessing defendant?

■ DECISION AND RATIONALE

(Breyer, J.) No. The issue in this case concerns the application of *Bruton v. United States. Bruton* involved two defendants accused of participating in the same crime and tried jointly before the same jury. One of the defendants had confessed, and his confession named and incriminated the other defendant. The trial judge issued a limiting instruction, telling the jury that it should consider the confession as evidence only against the codefendant who had confessed and not against the defendant named in the confession. *Bruton* held that, despite the limiting instruction, the Constitution forbids the use of such a confession in the joint trial. The case before us differs from *Bruton* in that the prosecution here redacted the codefendant's confession by substituting for the defendant's name in the confession a blank space or the word "deleted." We must decide whether these substitutions make a significant legal difference. We hold that they do. *Bruton,* as interpreted by *Richardson,* holds that certain powerfully incriminating extrajudicial statements of a codefendant—those naming another defendant—considered as a class, are so prejudicial that limiting instructions cannot work. Unless the prosecutor wishes to hold separate trials or to use separate juries or to abandon use of the confession, he must redact the confession to reduce significantly or eliminate the prejudice. Redactions that simply replace a name with an obvious blank space or a word such as "deleted," or a symbol or other similarly obvious indications of alteration, however, leave statements that, considered as a class, so closely resemble Bruton's unredacted statements that, in our view, the law must require the same result. For these reasons, we hold that the confession here at issue, which substituted blanks and the word "delete" for Gray's (D) proper name, falls within the class of statements to which *Bruton*'s protections apply. Reversed.

■ DISSENT

(Scalia, J.) I do not understand the Court to disagree that the redaction itself left unclear to whom the blank referred. That being so, so long as the jury was properly instructed to consider it as to the co-defendant only. This remains, insofar as the Sixth Amendment is concerned, the most reasonable practical accommodation of the interests of the state and the defendant in the criminal justice process.

Analysis:

This case is a progeny of the landmark case of *Bruton v. United States. Bruton* held that where defendants have been joined for trial, the out-of-court confession by one defendant, if it names the non-confessing defendant as a participant in the crime, cannot be used in the joint trial. Where the confessing defendant does not testify, such use of the confession would violate the non-confessing defendant's 6th Amendment right to confront the witnesses against him. Since the other defendant cannot be compelled to take the stand, use of the confession in the same trial is unconstitutional. It has been suggested that a jury instruction, telling the jury to consider the confession as evidence against the confessing defendant but not the non-confessing defendant, should cure the problem. Indeed, jury instructions often do an enormous amount of "work." Normally, juries are presumed to follow jury instructions (for example, when admitting hearsay statements for purposes other than the truth of the matter asserted, the court instructs the jury not to consider whether the statement is true, and limit consideration to the non-hearsay purpose.) However, *Burton* finally recognizes the human limitations of jury instructions. *Burton* does not mean that the case against the non-confessing defendant needs to be dismissed. The prosecutor has several other options to pursue: conduct a separate trial for each defendant, use separate juries for each defendant and exclude the jury whenever inadmissible evidence relative to that defendant will be heard, abandon the confession, or properly redact the confession so that it does not refer to the non-confessing defendant.

■ CASE VOCABULARY

IN CAMERA: A judicial proceeding before the judge in his private chambers or when all spectators are excluded from the courtroom.

REDACTED: Edited.

CHAPTER TWENTY

The Right to Speedy Trial and Other Speedy Disposition

Barker v. Wingo

Instant Facts: The defendant sought to set aside his murder conviction, claiming his right to a speedy trial was violated when the state, in order to first convict the defendant's accomplice, sought and was granted, usually with no objection from the defense, 16 separate continuances over a five year period.

Black Letter Rule: In assessing whether a defendant had been deprived of his right to a speedy trial courts must perform a balancing test that weighs the conduct of the defendant and that of the prosecution.

United States v. Lovasco

Instant Facts: The defendant moved to dismiss his federal indictment for possessing firearms stolen from the United States mails and for dealing in firearms without a license, because the indictment was filed more than 18 months after the offenses allegedly occurred.

Black Letter Rule: A defendant is not deprived of due process simply because the criminal investigation delays his prosecution, even if his defense is prejudiced.

Barker v. Wingo

(*Convicted Murderer*) v. (*Warden*)
407 U.S. 514, 92 S.Ct. 2182 (1972)

SUPREME COURT ADOPTS A BALANCING TEST TO ASSESS WHEN THE ACCUSED HAS BEEN DEPRIVED OF HIS SIXTH AMENDMENT RIGHT TO A SPEEDY TRIAL

■ **INSTANT FACTS** The defendant sought to set aside his murder conviction, claiming his right to a speedy trial was violated when the state, in order to first convict the defendant's accomplice, sought and was granted, usually with no objection from the defense, 16 separate continuances over a five year period.

■ **BLACK LETTER RULE** In assessing whether a defendant had been deprived of his right to a speedy trial courts must perform a balancing test that weighs the conduct of the defendant and that of the prosecution.

■ PROCEDURAL BASIS

Appeal to the United States Supreme Court challenging the decisions of the District Court and the Court of Appeals denying the prisoner habeas corpus relief on the grounds that his failure to raise an objection constituted a waiver of his right.

■ FACTS

Wille Barker (D) and his accomplice, Silas Manning, were indicted by the Commonwealth of Kentucky on September 15, 1958 for murdering an elderly couple early that same year. Barker's (D) trial date was set for October 21. The Commonwealth believed that Barker (D) could only be convicted with Manning's testimony. Logically, the Commonwealth sought to obtain a conviction against Manning and then compel him to testify against Barker (D). Yet obtaining a conviction against Manning proved difficult. It took six trials in a span of four years to finally convict Manning. As a result, Barker's (B) trial was delayed. In the Barker case, the Commonwealth sought and was granted 16 continuances over a five year period. Barker did not object to the first 11 of these motions and failed to do so in two subsequent motions. In total, Barker objected to only 3 of the Commonwealth's motions for continuances. The final trial date was eventually set for October 9, 1963. Barker's (D) motion to dismiss the indictment was denied, and Barker was convicted and given a life sentence.

■ ISSUE

If the defendant fails to assert his right to a speedy trial, is that right deemed waived?

■ DECISION AND RATIONALE

(Powell, J.) No. The defendant's assertion of or failure to assert his right to a speedy trial is only one factor to be considered in any inquiry into the deprivation of that right. The right to a speedy trial is different from any of the rights afforded to those accused of crimes. First, the right benefits both the individual and society. While the right protects individuals from lengthy incarceration and undue anxiety and concern, it also assures society that those who are guilty will not be released on bond for an extended period and that the accused will not be tempted to flea the jurisdiction. A second difference between the right to a speedy trial and those others granted by the Constitution is that the deprivation of the right to a speedy trial often benefits the accused. Delay is a common defense tactic; and thus, deprivation of the right does not *per se* prejudice the accused. A final difference is that the right to a speedy trial is more vague than other rights. It is impossible to precisely determine when the right has been denied. Two approaches are urged upon us as ways of eliminating this uncertainty. The first suggests that a defendant be offered a trial within a specified time period. We must reject this approach because we find no constitutional basis for holding that the speedy trial can be quantified into a specified number of days or months. The second suggestion is that consideration of the right should occur only when the accused has demanded a speedy trial. This approach takes two forms. The first views a defendant's failure to object as one of the factors to be considered in assessing whether the right has been denied. The second is known as the demand-waiver rule and provides that a defendant waives any consideration of his right to a speedy trial for any period prior to which he has not demanded a trial. This was the approach taken below. Yet we must reject this approach because it is inconsistent with this Court's pronouncements holding that inaction cannot be used to presume a waiver of a fundamental right. Therefore, we believe the former view is the better. In determining whether an accused has been deprived of his right to a speedy trial, the court must perform a balancing test on an *ad hoc* basis. Four factors which should be assessed in this balancing test are: Length of delay, the reason for the delay, the defendant's assertion of his right, and prejudice to the defendant. None of these four factors are either a necessary or sufficient condition to the finding of a deprivation of the right to a speedy trial. Rather, they are related factors and must be considered together with such other circumstances as may be relevant The difficulty in performing this balancing test is illustrated by this case. It is clear that the five year delay was extraordinary. Moreover, save for perhaps ten months, much of the delay was too long considering the Commonwealth's objective - to first obtain a conviction against Manning. However, two factors counterbalance these deficiencies. First there seems to have been no prejudice to Barker's (D) defense. Second, and more importantly, Barker (D) did not want a speedy trial. This fact is supported by his failure to object to the Commonwealth's first 11 motions for continuances. We hold therefore, that Barker (D) was not deprived of his due process right to a speedy trial. However, we do not rule that there may never be a situation in which an indictment may be dismissed on speedy trial grounds where the defendant has failed to raise the issue. Extraordinary circumstances may require such a dismissal. Affirmed.

■ CONCURRENCE

(White) A crowded docket and a prosecutor's heavy caseload are insufficient to justify a deprivation of the right to a speedy trial. A defendant who wants a speedy trail should have it. In special circumstances a more pressing public need might justify delay, but in ordinary cases the limitations of public resources do not suffice.

Analysis:

In this well-written and well-reasoned opinion the Court provides lower courts with a test for assessing when the right to a speedy trial has been denied. The court adopts a balancing test, reasoning that a bright-line rule is inappropriate for the right to a speedy trial due to its "vagueness." Is this a good reason for rejecting a bright-line rule? It is arguable that the entire Constitution is vague. Yet there are many stead fast constitutional rules. Regardless, the court sets out four factors which are to be balanced and holds that neither of these factors are determinative. Yet it is evident from the Court's holding that a defendant's failure to assert his right will be the critical factor. Its own application of the balancing test bears this out. The Court notes that such a failure can only be overcome in extraordinary circumstances. The reason that the defendant's failure to object is so critical is that the failure is often the product of a tactical decision by defense counsel. As the court points out, delay often benefits the defendant. The balancing test also suggests that the government could justify a delay even if the defendant asserts his right. The Court leaves unanswered the question of what type of state interest is necessary to justify a deprivation of this right.

■ CASE VOCABULARY

PRO FORMA: Made or carried out merely as a formality.

EX PARTE: Without party present.

United States v. Lovasco

(*Government*) v. (*Firearms Thief*)
431 U.S. 783, 97 S.Ct. 2044 (1977)

ABSENT BAD-FAITH, DUE PROCESS IS NOT VIOLATED WHEN INVESTIGATIVE DELAYS POSTPONE THE FILING OF FORMAL CHARGES

■ **INSTANT FACTS** The defendant moved to dismiss his federal indictment for possessing firearms stolen from the United States mails and for dealing in firearms without a license, because the indictment was filed more than 18 months after the offenses allegedly occurred.

■ **BLACK LETTER RULE** A defendant is not deprived of due process simply because the criminal investigation delays his prosecution, even if his defense is prejudiced.

■ FACTS

On March 6, 1973 Lovasco (D) was indicted for possessing firearms stolen from the United States mails and for dealing in firearms without a license. The indictment was filed over 18 months after the offenses had allegedly occurred. In an effort to prove that this delay was unnecessary, Lovasco (D) presented the District Court with a Postal Inspector's report, prepared one month after the crimes were committed. The report stated that Lovasco (D) had admitted to possessing some of the firearms and that there existed strong evidence linking him to the rest. The United States Attorney stipulated that little additional information was uncovered in the 17 months following the report. To establish prejudice to his case, Lovasco (D) testified that he lost the testimony of two material witnesses due their untimely deaths. Lovasco (D) however, failed to state how the witnesses would have aided his defense. Lovasco (D) sought to suppress the indictment on the grounds of delay in filing it.

■ ISSUE

Is due process violated when the government, after establishing probable cause, decides not to file formal charges because it wishes to further investigate the matter, and the delay prejudices the accused?

■ DECISION AND RATIONALE

(Marshall, J.) No. Our cases have made clear that proof of prejudice is generally a necessary but not sufficient element of a due process claim, and that the inquiry must consider the reasons for the delay as well as the prejudice to the accused. Contrary to the holding of the Court of Appeals, the Due Process Clause does not permit a court to abort criminal prosecutions simply because they disagree with a prosecutor's judgment as to when to seek an indictment. Obviously the Constitution does not require a prosecutor to seek an indictment before obtaining evidence which establishes probable cause. A rule which requires a prosecutor to seek an indictment after establishing probable cause but before obtaining enough evidence to convict would negatively affect both defendants and society. Such a rule would increase the likelihood that unwarranted charges are filed and add to the time during which defendants are accused but untried. From the perspective of law enforcement such a rule might make it difficult to obtain evidence sufficient to convict by causing sources of information to evaporate before being fully exploited. The rule would also clog courts with cases that proved insubstantial. An alternate rule requiring the government to file charges upon obtaining evidence sufficient to prove guilt beyond a reasonable doubt would have many of the same consequences. These consequences include: 1) An impairment on the prosecutor's ability to conduct further investigation; 2) a danger of multiple trials in cases involving multiple defendants since indictments would have to be sought as different times for different individuals; 3) the resolution of doubtful cases in favor of early—and possibly unwarranted—prosecution; and 4) a reduction in the ability of the government to take time and decide not to prosecute. These potential consequences give credence to the view that investigative delay is unlike delay that is sought in order to gain a tactical advantage, because investigative delay is not always one-sided and often benefits the accused. We therefore hold that to prosecute a defendant following investigative delay does not deprive him of due process, even if his defense might have been somewhat prejudiced by the lapse of time. Reversed.

Analysis:

The Court here holds that pre-accusation delays attendant to investigation do not deprive a suspect of due process. This well-reasoned opinion reinforces the idea, established in *United States v. Marion* [Supreme Court holds that the speedy trial provision of the Sixth Amendment attaches only after a formal government accusation], that bad faith is a necessary element of a successful due process claim based on pre-accusation delay. In addition to those problems and consequences that the Court Indicates a different rule might effect, the Court's holding has two logical consequences. First, the rule prevents the absurd arguments that would otherwise have to be forwarded by the parties. The defendant would have to argue that the government's case was strong enough to indict and that the delay prejudiced his strong defense. On the other hand, the government would have to argue that its case was weak. Second, and more importantly, the Court's rule connotes a respect for the separation of powers. The rule keeps courts from deciding how long and to what extent a particular criminal investigation need reach, an area where the Executive Branch, due to limited resources made available by Congress, should enjoy wide latitude.

CHAPTER TWENTY-ONE

Discovery and Related Rights

Williams v. Florida

Instant Facts: The state rules of criminal procedure required Williams (D) to notify the prosecution before trial of any plan to present an alibi defense, along with the identities of witnesses who would testify to the alibi.

Black Letter Rule: Compelling pretrial notice of a defendant's plans to present an alibi defense along with a list of alibi witnesses does not constitute compelled self-incrimination under the Fifth and Fourteenth Amendments.

Taylor v. Illinois

Instant Facts: Taylor appealed his conviction of attempted murder on ground that preclusion sanction that excluded defense witness' testimony was in violation of Sixth Amendment.

Black Letter Rule: The Sixth Amendment does not absolutely bar a court from ordering the preclusion of defense evidence as a sanction for violation of a discovery rule.

United States v. Bagley

Instant Facts: Bagley (D) discovered, years after his conviction, certain impeachment evidence that was not disclosed by the prosecution and he moved to have his sentence vacated.

Black Letter Rule: The standard of materiality to be applied to impeachment evidence under *Brady v. Maryland* is whether it is reasonably probable that the requested, yet undisclosed evidence, would have affected the outcome of the proceedings.

Williams v. Florida

(*Robbery Defendant*) v. (*State*)
399 U.S. 78, 90 S.Ct. 1893 (1970)

REQUIRING A CRIMINAL DEFENDANT TO PROVIDE THE PROSECUTION WITH NOTICE OF AN ALIBI DEFENSE AND THE IDENTITIES OF WITNESSES TO TESTIFY IN SUPPORT OF THE DEFENSE DOES NOT VIOLATE THE DEFENDANT'S FIFTH AMENDMENT RIGHT AGAINST SELF-INCRIMINATION

■ **INSTANT FACTS** The state rules of criminal procedure required Williams (D) to notify the prosecution before trial of any plan to present an alibi defense, along with the identities of witnesses who would testify to the alibi.

■ **BLACK LETTER RULE** Compelling pretrial notice of a defendant's plans to present an alibi defense along with a list of alibi witnesses does not constitute compelled self-incrimination under the Fifth and Fourteenth Amendments.

■ PROCEDURAL BASIS

Certification to the U.S. Supreme Court of a criminal conviction after the trial court denied defendant's motion for a protective order against forced disclosure of plans for an alibi defense.

■ FACTS

Rule 1.200 of the Florida Rules of Criminal Procedure requires a defendant to give notice, upon written demand, in advance of trial of any plans to advance an alibi defense. The rule also requires disclosure of the place where the defendant claims to have been, along with the names and addresses of any alibi witnesses he intends to use. In exchange for the defendant's disclosure of his alibi witnesses, the State (P) is required to notify the defendant of any rebuttal witnesses it intends to use. Both sides have a continuing duty to disclose any additional witnesses as they become available. The sanctions for failure to comply are exclusion of the alibi witnesses for the defendant, and the rebuttal evidence for the State. Williams (D), on trial for robbery, submitted a motion declaring his intent to use an alibi defense. Along with his motion he objected to the disclosure requirements of Rule 1.200 on the ground that the rule compels a defendant to be a witness against himself in violation of his Fifth and Fourteenth Amendment Rights. This motion was denied. Williams (D) then complied with the rule and was subsequently convicted.

■ ISSUE

Does requiring a criminal defendant to notify the prosecution of the plan to advance an alibi, along with the details supporting such a defense, compel the defendant to bear witness against himself?

■ DECISION AND RATIONALE

(White, J.) No. The discovery permitted the prosecution in this case did not deprive Williams (D) of "due process" or a "fair trial." The rules allow the defendant liberal discovery against the State, and the notice-of-alibi rule is hedged with reciprocal duties requiring state disclosure to the defendant. Also, the State (P) has a legitimate interest in protecting itself from hastily constructed eleventh-hour alibi defenses. Because of this there are several states that have such a requirement. Furthermore, such a rule enhances the search for truth by insuring that both the State (P) and the defendant have ample opportunity to investigate facts crucial to the determination of guilt or innocence. Williams (D) contends that he was "compelled to be a witness against himself" in violation of his Fifth and Fourteenth Amendment rights. This is because he was forced to provide the name and address of his alibi witness—information useful to the State (P) in convicting him. Armed with the name and address of the alibi witness, the State (P) was able to depose the witness and use the deposition to impeach the witness to Williams' (D) detriment. Also, requiring Williams (D) to reveal the elements of his defense deprived him of his right to wait until after the State (P) presented its case in order to decide the best way to defend against it. We conclude that the right against self-incrimination is not violated by the Florida rule. The defendant still has the choice of relying on the alibi defense or abandoning it altogether. This is similar to the dilemma a defendant faces when deciding to put on a defense, call his own witness, or testify himself. All may lead to testimony damaging to the defendant. Moreover, Williams (D) concedes that there is no constitutional bar to the court's granting the State (P) a continuance on the ground of surprise as soon as the alibi witness is called. Nor would there be a problem if, during the continuance, the State (P) deposed the witness to find rebuttal evidence. Either way the result is the same. It is simply a difference in timing. If one option is clearly not unconstitutional then the other must not be. Affirmed.

■ CONCURRENCE

(Burger) I see an added benefit to the alibi notice rule in that it will serve important functions by way of disposing of cases without trial in appropriate circumstances. In addition, the prosecutor may be able to determine if the defense was reliable and unimpeachable or contrived and fabricated if advance notice is given.

■ DISSENT

(Black, J.) There is a vast difference between forcing a defendant to reveal his plan of defense before trial and allowing him to wait until the prosecution has presented its case. Before trial the defendant only knows what the State's case might be, and there is no such thing as the strength of the State's case. Therefore, any appraisal of the advantages of pleading alibi will be fraught with guesswork much more so than waiting to decide until the State's case has been presented. The majority's holding opens up the floodgates to allow the State (P) to obtain under threat of sanction complete disclosure by the defendant in advance of trial of all evidence, testimony, and tactics he plans to use. In each case the justification will be that the rule affects only the "timing" of the disclosure, and not the substantive decision itself.

Analysis:

In refuting Williams' (D) claim of Fifth Amendment privilege the Majority relies on the perceived lack of any tangible difference between pretrial discovery of the alibi defense and discovery during trial in conjunction with a continuance to allow the State (P) to prepare for the surprise witness. Justice Black asserts that there is a vast difference between the two in that the decision to present an alibi defense may be ill advised before trial and that forcing such a decision could harm the defendant's substantive rights to due process. Is there a better rationale the Court could have rested its decision on than one of timing? Looking at the issue closely, how does allowing discovery of alibi witnesses before trial present a problem of self-incrimination? The alibi witnesses are individuals in and of themselves. They are not going to testify against themselves, or presumably against the defendant. There isn't any logical argument that testimony elicited from such witnesses with regard to defendant's alibi is self-incriminatory with respect to the defendant. A more accurate Analysis: of Williams' (D) assertion is that by requiring him to provide the alibi witnesses there was a chance the State (P) could glean some information that could be probative in convicting him. Not by any stretch is this "self-incrimination."

■ CASE VOCABULARY

PROBATIVE: Relevant to proving or disproving. Material to the disposition of a case.

Taylor v. Illinois

(*Criminal Defendant*) v. (*State*)
484 U.S. 400, 108 S.Ct. 646, 98 L.Ed.2d 798 (1988)

SUPREME COURT HOLDS THAT COMPULSORY PROCESS CLAUSE OF THE SIXTH AMENDMENT DOES NOT ABSOLUTELY PROHIBIT A WITNESS PRECLUSION SANCTION AGAINST A CRIMINAL DEFENDANT

■ **INSTANT FACTS** Taylor appealed his conviction of attempted murder on ground that preclusion sanction that excluded defense witness' testimony was in violation of Sixth Amendment.

■ **BLACK LETTER RULE** The Sixth Amendment does not absolutely bar a court from ordering the preclusion of defense evidence as a sanction for violation of a discovery rule.

■ PROCEDURAL BASIS

United States Supreme Court granted petition for certiorari following defendant's criminal conviction of attempted murder.

■ FACTS

Taylor (D) was convicted of attempted murder. Well before trial commenced, the prosecutor filed a discovery motion requesting a list of defense witnesses. Taylor's (D) attorney responded by identifying certain witnesses. On the first day of trial, defense counsel was allowed to amend his answer by adding the names of two more witnesses. On the second day of trial, defense counsel sought to amend his answer again to include two more witnesses allegedly because he had just been informed about them, and that they had probably seen the entire incident. In explaining the reason for not disclosing the witnesses earlier, defense counsel told the judge that he obtained the names from the defendant but had been unable to locate one of the witnesses. One of the witnesses, Wormley, appeared in court the following day and counsel was permitted to make an offer of proof in the form of Wormley's testimony outside the presence of the jury. It developed that Wormley had not been a witness to the incident itself, that he had run into Taylor (D) and warned him about the victim being armed, although on cross-examination he testified that he first met Taylor (D) over two years after the incident, and that defense counsel had visited him at his home the week before trial. Wormley's testimony rather dramatically contradicted defense counsel's representation to the court. [The attorney is in trouble now!] Finding that there was a blatant and willful violation of the discovery rules, and that the defense attorneys had been violating the discovery in the last three or four cases blatantly, the judge imposed a sanction for the discovery violation in the form of excluding Wormley's testimony. The court of appeal affirmed Taylor's (D) conviction. Taylor (D) petitioned the Supreme Court for certiorari.

■ ISSUE

Is a criminal defendant's Sixth Amendment right to obtain the testimony of favorable witnesses violated by a discovery sanction order that precludes the testimony of a defense witness?

■ DECISION AND RATIONALE

(Stevens) No. We hold that the Sixth Amendment does not absolutely bar a court from ordering the preclusion of defense evidence as a sanction for violation of a discovery rule. The State (P) contends that the Compulsory Process Clause of the Sixth Amendment does not apply to rulings on the admissibility of evidence and instead merely guarantees that the accused shall have the power to subpoena witnesses. However, the right to offer testimony is grounded in the Sixth Amendment even though it is not expressly described in so many words. The right to compel a witness' presence in court could not protect the integrity of the adversary process if it did not embrace the right to have the witness' testimony heard by the trier of fact. Taylor's (D) claim that the Sixth Amendment creates an absolute bar to the preclusion of testimony of a surprise witness is just as extreme and just as unacceptable as the State's (P) position that the Amendment is simply irrelevant. Discovery minimizes the risk that a judgment will be predicated on incomplete, misleading, or even deliberately fabricated testimony. The State's (P) interest in protecting itself against an eleventh hour defense is merely one component of the broader public interest in a full and truthful disclosure of critical facts. Taylor (D) argues that a less drastic sanction, such as granting a continuance or a mistrial, is always available, and the sanction of preclusion of testimony is so drastic that it should never be imposed. [Taylor (D) should be saying, "It wasn't me who lied to the court, it was my attorney."] It is reasonable to presume that there is something suspect about a defense witness who is not identified until after the eleventh hour has passed. A trial judge may insist on an explanation for a party's failure to comply with a request to identify witnesses in advance of trial. If that explanation reveals that the omission was willful and motivated by a desire to obtain a tactical advantage that would minimize the effectiveness of cross-examination and the ability to adduce rebuttal evidence, it would be entirely consistent with the purposes of the Confrontation Clause simply to exclude the witness' testimony. It would demean the high purpose of the Compulsory Process Clause to construe it as encompassing an absolute right to an automatic continuance or mistrial to allow presumptively perjured testimony to be presented to a jury. We reject Taylor's (D) argument that a preclusion sanction is never appropriate no matter how serious the defendant's discovery violation may be. Since Taylor's (D) counsel had actually interviewed Wormley during the week before the trial began and the further fact that he amended his Answer to Discovery on the first day of trial without identifying Wormley, while he did identify two other witnesses, the inference that he was deliberately seeking a tactical advantage is inescapable. It is plain that the case fits into the category of willful misconduct in which the severest sanction is appropriate. The conduct gives rise to a sufficiently strong inference—that witnesses were being found that really weren't there—to justify the sanction of preclusion. In addition, Taylor (D) has no greater right to disavow his lawyer's decision to conceal Wormley's identify until after the trial had commenced than he has to disavow the decision to refrain from calling witnesses to testify at trial who were identified. Affirmed.

■ DISSENT

(Brennan) The Compulsory Process and Due Process Clauses require courts to conduct a searching substantive inquiry whenever the government seeks to exclude criminal defense evidence. Restrictions on presenting defense evidence are constitutional only if they "accommodate other legitimate interests in the criminal trial process" and are not "arbitrary or disproportionate to the purposes they are designed to serve." The use of the preclusion sanction as a corrective measure has two justifications: (1) it bars the defendant from introducing testimony that has not been tested by discovery, and (2) it screens out witnesses who are inherently suspect because they were not disclosed at trial. Taylor (D) argues that he should not be completely precluded from introducing the testimony. Although persons who are not identified as defense witnesses until trial may not be as trustworthy as other categories of persons, surely any presumption that they are so suspect that the jury can be prevented from even listening to their testimony is at least as arbitrary as a presumption excluding an accomplice's testimony. It is the jury that should determine the credit and weight it wants to attach to such testimony. Although there was ample evidence that the defense attorney willfully violated the discovery rule, there was no evidence that Taylor (D) played any role in that violation. Nor did the trial court make any effort to determine whether Taylor (D) bore any responsibility for the discovery violation. Directly sanctioning the attorneys not only is fairer but more effective in deterring violations than excluding defense evidence. Courts should not be permitted to visit the sins of the lawyer on the innocent client. Although a defendant at times may be bound by tactical errors that his attorney makes, we have not previously suggested that a client can be punished for an attorney's misconduct. The rationales for binding defendants to attorneys' routine tactical errors do not apply to attorney misconduct. Punitive sanctions against attorneys are a deterrent that can prevent them from systemically engaging in misconduct. There is no need to take steps that will inflict the punishment on the defendant. Thus, I cannot agree with the Court's case-by-case balancing approach or with its conclusion in this case that the exclusion was constitutional.

■ DISSENT

(Blackmun) I join Justice Brennan's dissenting opinion as confined in its reach to general reciprocal discovery rules. I do not wish to have it express for me any position as to permissible sanctions for noncompliance with rules designed for specific kinds of evidence.

Analysis:

This case considers the constitutional issues involved when the sanction of preclusion is imposed upon the defense. Taylor (D) argued that the trial court failed to utilize the proper discovery violation sanction, suggesting a continuance or mistrial instead. Rejecting Taylor's (D) assertion that the Sixth Amendment absolutely bars a preclusion sanction, the Court upheld that sanction based upon the particular facts of the case. In so doing, the Court held that the explanation for the discovery violation revealed that the omissions were willful and motivated by a desire to obtain a tactical advantage that would minimize the effectiveness of cross-examination and the ability to adduce rebuttal evidence, and thus, exclusion of the witness' testimony would be entirely consistent with the purposes of the Confrontation Clause. The conduct of Taylor's (D) attorney was willful and blatant and thus the severest sanction was appropriate. However, dissenting Justice Brennan noted that there was no evidence that Taylor (D) played any role in the discovery violation, and the trial court did not make any effort to determine whether Taylor (D) bore any responsibility for the violation. Justice Brennan suggested that a punitive sanction against the attorney should be imposed rather than punishing Taylor (D) by excluding witness testimony.

■ CASE VOCABULARY

COMPULSORY PROCESS CLAUSE: The right given to criminal defendants under the Sixth Amendment to subpoena and obtain witnesses in their favor.

OFFER OF PROOF: Disclosing to the judge outside the presence of the jury the evidence anticipated to be offered in order to urge the court that the evidence should be admissible.

PRECLUSION SANCTION: Punishment for disobeying discovery rules in the form of excluding evidence, such as a witness' testimony.

TRIER OF FACT: Either the judge or a jury who decides the disputed factual matters at trial.

VOIR DIRE: Questioning of prospective jurors by the judge or attorneys to determine if they are qualified and suitable to serve as jurors.

United States v. Bagley

(*Government*) v. (*Convicted Defendant*)

473 U.S. 667, 105 S.Ct. 3375, 87 L.Ed.2d 481 (1985)

SUPREME COURT ESTABLISHES STANDARD FOR WHAT CONSTITUTES "MATERIAL" EVIDENCE THAT MUST BE DISCLOSED BY THE PROSECUTOR TO THE DEFENSE

■ **INSTANT FACTS** Bagley (D) discovered years after his conviction certain impeachment evidence that was not disclosed by the prosecution and he moved to have his sentence vacated.

■ **BLACK LETTER RULE** The standard of materiality applied to impeachment evidence under *Brady v. Maryland* is whether it is reasonably probable that the requested, yet undisclosed evidence would have affected the outcome of the proceedings.

■ PROCEDURAL BASIS

Review by Supreme Court following reversal of the trial court's denial of criminal defendant's motion to vacate sentence stemming from conviction of narcotics violations.

■ FACTS

Bagley (D) was indicted on charges of violating federal narcotics and firearms statutes. Prior to trial, he filed a discovery motion requesting the names and addresses of witnesses that that the Government (P) intended on calling at trial, and also any deals, promises, or inducements made to witnesses in exchange for their testimony. The Government's (P) two principal witnesses were O'Connor and Mitchell, state law-enforcement officers, who assisted the federal Bureau of Alcohol, Tobacco and Firearms (ATF) in conducting an undercover investigation of Bagley (D). The Government's (P) response to the discovery motion did not disclose that any deals, promises, or inducements had been made to O'Connor or Mitchell. It did however disclose in response to a different portion of the discovery request seeking copies of all "Jencks Act material" [gives the defendant a right to inspect the prior statements of prosecution witnesses following their testimony] a series of affidavits that the two witnesses had signed while the undercover investigation was in progress. Each affidavit concluded with the statement, "I made this statement freely and voluntarily without any threats or regards, or promises of reward having been made to me in return for it." Bagley (D), after a non-jury trial, was found guilty on the narcotics charges, but not guilty on the firearms charges. Approximately eight years following his trial, Bagley (D) discovered, through requests for information pursuant to the Freedom of Information Act and the Privacy Act, that O'Connor and Mitchell had signed ATF form contracts, entitled "Contract for Purchase of Information and Payment of Lump Sum Therefor." The contracts provided that they would give information regarding violations committed by Bagley (D), purchase evidence for ATF, act in an undercover capacity for ATF, assist ATF in gathering evidence, and testify against Bagley (D) in federal court. The figure "$300" was handwritten in each form on a line entitled "Sum to Be Paid Vendor." [In other words, if their efforts got him convicted, they got paid!] Because these contracts had not been disclosed to Bagley (D) in response to his pretrial discovery motion, he moved to vacate his sentence on the ground that the Government's (P) failure to disclose the contracts, which Bagley (D) could have used to Impeach O'Connor and Mitchell, violated his right to due process. During the evidentiary hearing, it was disclosed that the printed form contracts were blank when O'Connor and Mitchell signed them and were not signed by an ATF representative until after Bagley's (D) trial. [Sounds as if they intentionally delayed signing the contract until after the trial.] In addition, following the trial, ATF made payments of $300 to both O'Connor and Mitchell. The District Court found beyond a reasonable doubt that had the existence of the agreements been disclosed during trial, the disclosure would have had no effect upon its finding that the Government (P) had proved beyond a reasonable doubt that Bagley (D) was guilty. The court reasoned that most of the two witnesses' testimony pertained to the firearms charges, for which Bagley (D) was acquitted, and their testimony concerning the narcotics charges was relatively very brief. Accordingly, the District Court denied Bagley's (D) motion to vacate his sentence. The Court of Appeals reversed, noting that the Government's (P) failure to provide the requested information requires an automatic reversal. The Government (P) petitioned the Supreme Court for review.

■ ISSUE

Is the standard of *materiality* to be applied in determining whether a conviction should be reversed because the prosecutor failed to disclose requested evidence that could have been used to impeach Government witnesses one of a reasonable probability so that had the evidence been disclosed to the defense, the result of the proceeding would have been different?

■ DECISION AND RATIONALE

(Blackmun) Yes. In *Brady v. Maryland* this Court held that "the suppression by the prosecution of evidence favorable to an accused upon request violates due process where the evidence is material either to guilt or punishment." In the case before us now, we must determine the standard of *materiality* to be applied in determining whether a conviction should be reversed because the prosecutor failed to disclose requested evidence that could have been used to impeach Government witnesses. The holding in *Brady* requires disclosure of evidence that is both favorable to the accused and "material either to guilt or punishment." The prosecutor is not required to deliver his entire file to defense counsel, but only to disclose evidence favorable to the accused that, if suppressed, would deprive the defendant of a fair trial. Both impeachment evidence, as well as exculpatory evidence, falls within the *Brady* rule. The Court of Appeals held that there is a constitutional distinction between impeachment evidence and exculpatory evidence, the former requiring automatic reversal. This Court has rejected such distinction and held that when "the 'reliability of a given witness may well be determinative of guilt or innocence,' nondisclosure of evidence affecting credibility falls within the general rule [of *Brady*]." However, an automatic new trial is not required unless the "false testimony could ... in any reasonable likelihood have affected the judgment of the jury. . . ." *Giglio v. United States.* [Bagley's (D) not out of jail yet.] The constitutional error, if any, in this case was the Government's (P) failure to assist the defense by disclosing information that might have been helpful in conducting the cross-examination. Such suppression amounts to a constitutional violation only if it deprives the defendant of a fair trial. A conviction must be reversed only if the evidence is material in the sense that its suppression undermines confidence in the outcome of the trial. [Not disclosing that the Government paid witnesses who helped convict would seem to undermine the confidence in the outcome!] With respect to the standard of materiality applicable to the non-disclosed evidence at issue in this case, we begin with the three situations involving the discovery, after trial, of information favorable to the accused that had been known to the prosecution but unknown to the defense as discussed in *United States v. Agurs.* The first situation was the prosecutor's knowing use of perjured testimony or, the prosecutor's knowing failure to disclose that testimony used to convict the defendant was false. This is subject to a harmless-error review, which is a materiality standard under which the fact that testimony is perjured is considered material unless failure to disclose it would be harmless beyond a reasonable doubt. Another situation is where the defendant does not make a *Brady* request and the prosecutor fails to disclose certain evidence favorable to the accused. The Court rejected the harmless-error rule, and instead held that the standard of materiality applicable in the absence of a specific *Brady* request is stricter than the harmless-error standard but more lenient to the defense than the newly discovered evidence standard. The third situation identified by the Court in *Agurs* is where the defense makes a specific request and the prosecutor fails to disclose responsive evidence. The Court did not define the standard of materiality applicable in this situation, but suggested it might be more lenient to the defense than in the situation in which the defense makes no request or only a general request. We hold that the test for materiality, which will cover the "no request," "general request," and "specific request" cases of prosecutorial failure to disclose evidence favorable to the accused is as follows: The evidence is material only if there is a reasonable probability that, had the evidence been disclosed to the defense, the result of the proceeding would have been different. A "reasonable probability" is a probability sufficient to undermine confidence in the outcome. In the present case, there is a significant likelihood that the prosecutor's response to Bagley's (D) discovery motion misleadingly induced defense counsel to believe that O'Connor and Mitchell could not be impeached on the basis of bias or interest arising from the inducements offered by the Government (P). The possibility of a reward however gave O'Connor and Mitchell a direct, personal stake in Bagley's (D) conviction. Accordingly, we reverse the judgment of the Court of Appeals and remand the case to that court for a determination whether there is a reasonable probability that, had the inducement offered by the Government (P) to O'Connor and Mitchell been disclosed to the defense, the result of the trial would have been different.

■ CONCURRENCE

(White) I generally agree with the holding of the majority except I see no reason to attempt to elaborate on the relevance to the inquiry of the specificity of the defense's request for disclosure, either generally or with respect to this case. I would hold simply that the proper standard is one of reasonable probability and that the Court of Appeals' failure to apply this standard necessitates reversal. I concur in the judgment.

■ DISSENT

(Marshall) To my mind, the *Brady* decision, the reasoning that underlay it, and the fundamental interest in a fair trial, combine to give the criminal defendant the right to receive from the prosecutor, and the prosecutor the affirmative duty to turn over to the defendant, *all* information known to the government that might reasonably be considered favorable to the defendant's case. If that right is denied, or if that duty is shirked, however, I believe a reviewing court should not automatically reverse but instead should apply the harmless error test the Court has developed for instances of error affecting constitutional rights. To require disclosure of all evidence that might reasonably be considered favorable to the defendant would have the precautionary effect of assuring that no information of potential consequence is mistakenly overlooked.

■ DISSENT

(Stevens) The *Brady* rule unquestionably applied to this case, because the Government (P) failed to disclose favorable evidence that was clearly responsive to Bagley's (D) specific request. His conviction therefore must be set aside if the suppressed evidence was "material"—and it obviously was—and if there is "any reasonable likelihood" that it could have affected the judgment of the trier of fact. Accordingly, although I agree that the judgment of the Court of Appeals should be vacated and that the case should be remanded for further proceedings, I disagree with the Court's statement of the correct standard to be applied.

Analysis:

This case is important not only for its own holding but for its in-depth Analysis: of *Brady v. Maryland.* The prosecution's constitutional duty to disclose evidence to the defense under the Due Process Clause was first established in *Brady,* wherein the Supreme Court held that exculpatory evidence within the prosecutor's possession must be disclosed when that evidence might be material to the outcome of the trial. The evidence in this case was not exculpatory, but rather *impeachment* evidence, which the defense theoretically would have used to discredit the testimony of the two witnesses for the prosecution. The Supreme Court disagreed with the Court of Appeal's ruling that withholding *impeachment* evidence should be characterized as even "more egregious" than the failure to disclose exculpatory evidence, and that automatic reversal was required. Instead, the court fashioned its own "materiality" standard to be applied in all situations where the prosecution fails to disclose evidence to the defense.

■ CASE VOCABULARY

AUTOMATIC REVERSAL: Where the particular error is so egregious that reversal should occur without determining whether the outcome of the matter would have been affected.

HARMLESS-ERROR: Where the court determines that the error did not affect the outcome of the matter, and thus is not a basis for reversal.

MAGISTRATE: A federal officer given powers and functions of a judge.

CHAPTER TWENTY–TWO

Coerced, Induced and Negotiated Guilty Pleas; Professional Responsibility

Bordenkircher v. Hayes

Instant Facts: A man was given the choice of pleading guilty to a felony for a five year prison sentence, or else taking his chances that he would be sent to prison for life because he had two prior felony convictions.

Black Letter Rule: A course of conduct engaged in by a prosecutor which openly presents the defendant with the unpleasant alternatives of foregoing trial or facing charges on which he is plainly subject to prosecution does not violate the Due Process Clause of the Fourteenth Amendment.

Santobello v. New York

Instant Facts: According to a plea agreement, Santobello (D) pleaded guilty in exchange for the prosecutor's (P) promise to make no sentencing recommendations, but a new prosecutor (P) recommended the maximum sentence.

Black Letter Rule: When a plea rests in any significant degree on a promise of the prosecutor (P), such that it is part of the inducement or consideration for the plea, that promise is enforceable.

Newman v. United States

Instant Facts: A prosecutor allowed one co-defendant to plead to lesser offenses after indictment, however the prosecutor refused to give the other co-defendant the same deal.

Black Letter Rule: Even though two persons may have committed what is precisely the same legal offense, the prosecutor is not compelled by law, duty or tradition to treat them the same as to charges.

United States v. Ruiz

Instant Facts: Ruiz (D) declined a plea offer that would have given her a lighter sentence in exchange for a waiver of the right to receive impeaching information about witnesses.

Black Letter Rule: The Constitution does not require disclosure of impeaching information about witness testimony before entry of a guilty plea.

In Re United States

Instant Facts: A federal district judge denied the government's request to dismiss charges against a defendant pursuant to a plea bargain.

Black Letter Rule: A federal judge may not deny a prosecutor's good faith request to dismiss charges pursuant to a plea bargain with a defendant

Bordenkircher v. Hayes

(*Prison Superintendent*) v. (*Three-Time Felon*)

434 U.S. 357, 98 S.Ct. 663, 54 L.Ed.2d 604 (1978)

SUPREME COURT DECLINES TO APPLY THE BAR ON PROSECUTORIAL VINDICTIVENESS IN THE CONTEXT OF PLEA NEGOTIATIONS

■ **INSTANT FACTS** The prosecutor (P) gave Hayes (D) a choice between pleading guilty to forgery for a 5 year prison sentence, and risking trial and a recidivism indictment, which could result in a mandatory life sentence.

■ **BLACK LETTER RULE** As long as a prosecutor (P) has probable cause to support each charge, the choice of which charges to bring rests in his discretion, and his basing that choice on a desire to induce a guilty plea does not violate due process.

■ PROCEDURAL BASIS

Certiorari granted after appellate court reversed denial of habeas challenge to enhanced sentence and indictment procedure.

■ FACTS

Hayes (D), having two prior felony convictions, was indicted for forgery, with a possible sentence of 2 to 10 years. In return for a guilty plea, the prosecutor (P) offered to recommend a 5-year sentence and to refrain from seeking an indictment under the *Kentucky Habitual Criminal Act* [recidivism statute], which would subject Hayes (D) to mandatory life imprisonment. Hayes (D) rejected the plea bargain, and the prosecutor (P) obtained the recidivism indictment. The jury convicted Hayes (D) on both the forgery charge and the recidivism charge, and he therefore received a life sentence. Hayes (D) challenged his sentence and the indictment procedure. The Court of Appeals held that the prosecutor's (P) conduct was a vindictive exercise of his discretion and therefore violated Hayes' (D) due process rights.

■ ISSUE

Does a prosecutor (P) violate due process when he carries out a threat he makes during plea negotiations to bring a more serious charge against an accused if he does not plead guilty to the original charge?

■ DECISION AND RATIONALE

(Stewart) No. Although the prosecutor (P) did not obtain the recidivist indictment until after plea negotiations ended, he made clear that he intended to do so during those negotiations. When Hayes (D) decided to plead not guilty, he knew the true terms of the plea offer. The prosecutor (P) did not bring an additional and more serious charge without notice to Hayes (D). Rather, this situation is the same as if the prosecutor (P) obtained an indictment on both the forgery and recidivism charges at the outset, and then offered to drop the recidivism charge as part of the plea bargain. Nevertheless, concerned about prosecutorial vindictiveness, the Court of Appeals distinguished between concessions to the original indictment and threats to bring additional charges. Further, the Court of Appeals found vindictiveness in the prosecutor's (P) admission that his desire to induce a guilty plea influenced his charging decision. Guilty pleas and plea bargaining are an important part of our criminal justice system, and properly administered, they can benefit all concerned. The Court of Appeals essentially held here that the substance of the plea offer itself violated due process. We disagree. We have addressed unconstitutional prosecutorial vindictiveness in *North Carolina v. Pearce* [vindictiveness against a defendant in new trial after he wins a reversal of his first conviction violates due process] and *Blackledge v. Perry* [vindictiveness likely where a prosecutor reindicts a convict on a more serious charge after the convict invokes an appellate remedy]. However, the due process violation in these cases lay not in the danger of deterring the accused from exercising a legal right, but in unilaterally penalizing him for having exercised his right to attack his conviction. This is very different from the plea bargaining situation we have here. In the give-and-take of plea bargaining, there is no punishment or retaliation as long as the accused remains free to accept or reject the prosecutor's (P) offer. Plea bargaining benefits both prosecutors (P) and defendants, who each have reasons to avoid trial. Defendants are unlikely to condemn themselves falsely. Defense counsel and procedural safeguards make the bargained-for guilty plea presumptively intelligent, and the fact that it results from plea bargaining does not alone make it involuntary. We have accepted as legitimate and even encouraged plea bargaining. Prosecutors (P) attempting to persuade defendants to forego trial, and defendants facing difficult choices between going to trial and risking more severe punishment, are inevitable parts of the plea bargaining system. As long as a prosecutor (P) has probable cause to support each charge, the choice of which charges to pursue rests in his discretion. There are, of course, constitutional limits on a prosecutor's (P) exercise of discretion. Selective enforcement, though permissible, may not be based on an unjustifiable standard such as race, religion, or some other arbitrary classification. The desire to induce a guilty plea is not such an "unjustifiable standard." It is better to allow prosecutors (P) to deal forthrightly with the defense than to force plea bargaining back into the shadows with a rigid constitutional rule. This prosecutor's (P) openly presenting Hayes (D) with the unpleasant alternatives of foregoing trial or facing legitimate charges did not violate due process. Reversed.

■ DISSENT

(Blackmun) As in *Pearce* and *Perry,* bringing more serious charges against a defendant after plea negotiations on the original charges fail creates a "strong inference" of prosecutorial vindictiveness. The Court gives plea bargaining full sway despite vindictiveness. Of course, a contrary holding would only cause prosecutors (P) to bring the more serious charges from the outset. Still, it is better to hold the prosecution (P) to its original charge.

■ DISSENT

(Powell) The question to ask here is whether charging Hayes (D) under the recidivism statute would have been reasonable in the first place. At first, the prosecutor (P) evidently judged that it was not reasonable to subject Hayes (D) to mandatory life imprisonment for forging an $88 check, when his prior convictions made such a sentence seem inappropriate. It may sometimes be reasonable to bring more serious charges, particularly when it would have been reasonable to do so at the outset. In such cases it would be difficult to know the prosecutor's (P) reason for seeking the higher charge. Here, the prosecutor (P) admits he brought the higher charge because Hayes (D) insisted on going to trial. To allow the plea bargaining system to work effectively, prosecutors (P) must have wide discretion. However, a strategy calculated solely to deter the exercise of constitutional rights is not a permissible exercise of this discretion.

Analysis:

Dissenting, Justice Blackmun argues that prosecutorial vindictiveness is prosecutorial vindictiveness, whether it occurs in a trial de novo after reversal of an original conviction, or in the "give-and-take" of plea bargaining. The Court, on the other hand, emphasizes the "mutuality of advantage" in the plea bargaining context, and sees a prosecutor's use of all the legitimate charges at his disposal as simply using all of his bargaining chips, not being vindictive. As the Court noted, if it held such conduct unconstitutional, and forced prosecutors to stick with their original charging decision as the highest charge, then prosecutors would simply bring the most and highest charges they could at the outset, and bargain by offering to drop some, rather than start with the charges they hope ultimately to use, and bargain by threatening to add more. The practical consequence of this would be that prosecutors would have to expend more resources at the outset to obtain indictments on more and higher charges. The defendant would have a better sense of the prosecutor's case, and would not have to trust that he could in fact obtain the indictments he threatens to obtain. However, there would be a significant downside to the defendant as well. As Justice Blackmun points out, the defendant would have to bargain against greater charges, probably face increased bail, and perhaps face a greater risk that the court would not accept a bargained plea. The Court's decision allows the prosecutor more flexibility to pursue the charges and punishment he deems most appropriate in what he perceives to be the most efficient way. The defendant's criminal conduct and the sufficiency of the evidence supporting particular charges always predetermine the prosecutor's "bargaining chips." The defendant will face those bargaining chips one way or the other; the only question is when.

■ CASE VOCABULARY

RECIDIVIST: A repeat offender.

Santobello v. New York

(*Plea-Bargaining Felon*) v. (*State*)
404 U.S. 257, 92 S.Ct. 495, 30 L.Ed.2d 427 (1971)

A PROSECUTOR CANNOT HOLD A DEFENDANT TO A NEGOTIATED PLEA IF THE PROSECUTOR BREAKS THE BARGAIN ON WHICH THE PLEA RESTS

■ **INSTANT FACTS** According to a plea agreement, Santobello (D) pleaded guilty in exchange for the prosecutor's (P) promise to make no sentencing recommendation, but a new prosecutor (P) recommended the maximum sentence.

■ **BLACK LETTER RULE** When a plea rests in any significant degree on a promise of the prosecutor (P), such that it is part of the inducement or consideration for the plea, that promise is enforceable.

■ PROCEDURAL BASIS

Certiorari granted after conviction on challenged guilty plea was affirmed.

■ FACTS

Originally charged with two felony counts, Santobello (D) pleaded guilty to a lesser-included offense in exchange for the prosecutor's (P) promise to make no sentencing recommendation. However, at sentencing a new prosecutor (P) recommended the maximum sentence. Santobello (D) then attempted to withdraw his guilty plea, but was unsuccessful.

■ ISSUE

Are the promises that prosecutors (P) make in plea agreements enforceable?

■ DECISION AND RATIONALE

(Burger) Yes. Plea bargaining is essential to the administration of justice and should be encouraged. Without it, we would need many more judges and court facilities to bring every criminal charge to trial. Plea bargaining also leads to prompt disposition of most criminal cases, which in turn aids rehabilitation. Finally, plea bargaining decreases pre-trial confinement pending trial, and protects the public from additional criminal acts by an accused while on pretrial release. Safeguards are necessary, however. When a plea rests in any significant degree on a promise of the prosecutor (P), such that it is part of the inducement or consideration for the plea, that promise must be fulfilled. We remand to the state courts to determine whether justice would best be served by requiring specific performance of the plea agreement by having a different judge resentence Santobello (D), or by granting Santobello's (D) request to withdraw his guilty plea. Vacated and remanded.

■ CONCURRENCE

(Douglas) I favor a constitutional rule for cases like these. Where a prosecutor (P) does not keep his part of a plea bargain, the sentence must be vacated, and the state court must decide whether to require specific performance of the plea bargain or to allow the defendant to go to trial on the original charges. In making this decision, the state court should give the defendant's preference considerable weight.

■ CONCURRENCE AND DISSENT

(Marshall) Because a prosecutor's (P) breaking a plea bargain undercuts the basis for the defendant's waiver of his right to trial, it justifies the defendant's rescinding his plea. Since that is the remedy Santobello (D) seeks here, I would remand with instructions to vacate the plea and give Santobello (D) the opportunity to replead to the original charges.

Analysis:

Under *Santobello*, the government may not hold a defendant to a negotiated plea when the government itself has broken a promise on which that plea rested. The courts essentially treat the plea agreement as a contract. If the prosecutor breaks his promise, there is a "breach" of the agreement. To remedy this breach, the court might allow the defendant to keep his promise, the plea, and force the government to keep its promises as well. This would be to require "specific performance" of the plea agreement, which is the remedy most courts prefer. Alternatively, since the government broke its promise, the court might relieve the defendant from his obligation to keep his promise by allowing him to withdraw his plea and replead. The *Santobello* rule works both ways in that it will not permit a defendant to enforce a plea agreement when the defendant himself has committed a breach. For example, if a defendant lies to the prosecutor to get him to make concessions in a plea agreement, the plea agreement will not be enforceable. If the concessions allowed the defendant to plead guilty to a lesser included offense, the court can rescind the plea and reinstate the original charges.

■ CASE VOCABULARY

SPECIFIC PERFORMANCE: A remedy which requires parties to fulfill the exact terms of their agreement.

Newman v. United States

(*Thief*) v. (*Federal Government*)
127 U.S. App. D.C. 263, 382 F.2d 479 (1967)

THE CONSTITUTION PERMITS EXERCISES OF PROSECUTORIAL DISCRETION THAT GIVE PEOPLE WHO COMMIT THE SAME OFFENSE DIFFERENT TREATMENT

■ **INSTANT FACTS** Newman (D) and Anderson both committed the same offenses, but the prosecutor (P) offered a plea bargain only to Anderson and not to Newman (D).

■ **BLACK LETTER RULE** Even if two people have committed the same offense, a prosecutor (P) has no duty to treat them alike as to charges.

■ PROCEDURAL BASIS

Appeal from conviction challenging prosecutor's (P) exercise of discretion.

■ FACTS

Newman (D) and Anderson were both indicted for housebreaking and petty larceny. The United States Attorney (US Attorney) (P) agreed to a plea bargain with Anderson that allowed him to plead guilty to lesser included offenses, but he refused to give Newman (D) the same deal. Newman (D) argues that this different treatment denied him due process, "equal standing," and equal protection.

■ ISSUE

Must a prosecutor (P) treat offenders who committed the same offense the same way?

■ DECISION AND RATIONALE

(Burger) No. We must resolve this case based on the constitutional powers of the Executive. The exercise of discretion in charging decisions and plea bargaining is ill-adapted to judicial review. The US Attorney (P), attorney for the Executive, having the duty to faithfully execute the laws, protect United States interests, and prosecute federal offenses, must have broad discretion. It would be impossible for the US Attorney (P) to treat every offense and every offender alike, and requiring him to do so would negate his discretion. A prosecutor's (P) charging decisions can and should take many factors into account, such as the offender's criminal record and his degree of culpability and role in committing a particular offense. No court has jurisdiction to review the prosecutor's (P) decision. While a prosecutor's (P) discretion is subject to misuse or abuse, it is his superiors who must deal with these deviations from duty. A US Attorney (P) is an agent of the Executive, and the President has abundant supervisory and disciplinary powers to deal with misconduct. It is not the judiciary's function to review the exercise of executive discretion. Affirmed.

Analysis:

This case rests on the separation of powers. The exercise of prosecutorial discretion by a US Attorney is an exercise of the executive power by a delegate of the President. Any review by the judicial branch of such discretionary decisions at least runs the risk of usurping that executive function. Prosecutorial discretion is not entirely immune from judicial review. As we have seen in *Bordenkircher v. Hayes* [vindictiveness doctrine does not apply to plea negotiations], selective enforcement based on an unjustifiable standard such as race, religion, or some other arbitrary classification is not constitutionally permissible, nor is prosecutorial vindictiveness aimed at deterring a defendant from exercising a legal right. However, in *Bordenkircher* the court explained that "so long as the prosecutor has probable cause to believe that the accused committed an offense defined by statute, the decision whether or not to prosecute, and what charge to file or bring before a grand jury, generally rests entirely in his discretion." In *Newman,* Judge Burger [later to become Chief Justice Burger] also followed this principle and thus declined to review a prosecutor's plea bargaining decisions.

United States v. Ruiz

(Prosecuting Government) v. *(Drug Possessor)*

536 U.S. 622, 122 S.Ct. 2450, 153 L.Ed.2d 586 (2002)

THE PROSECUTION NEED NOT DISCLOSE IMPEACHMENT INFORMATION BEFORE A DEFENDANT PLEADS GUILTY

■ **INSTANT FACTS** Ruiz (D) declined a plea offer that would have given her a lighter sentence in exchange for a waiver of the right to receive impeaching information about witnesses.

■ **BLACK LETTER RULE** The Constitution does not require disclosure of impeaching information about witness testimony before entry of a guilty plea.

■ PROCEDURAL BASIS

Certiorari to review a decision of the Ninth Circuit Court of Appeals vacating the defendant's sentence.

■ FACTS

Ruiz (D) was offered a "fast track" plea bargain on charges of drug possession. The bargain required Ruiz (D) to waive indictment, trial, and appeal. In return, the U.S. (P) would recommend a downward departure from the sentence that would otherwise have been imposed on Ruiz (D). The agreement also included a statement that the U.S. (P) had turned over any known information regarding the factual innocence of Ruiz (D) and acknowledged the continuing duty of the U.S. (P) to provide such information, but it required Ruiz (D) to waive her right to receive impeachment information regarding any informants or witnesses, as well as the right to receive information supporting any affirmative defense. Ruiz (D) refused to agree to the waiver of the right to receive impeachment information and the plea bargain was withdrawn. Ruiz (D) pleaded guilty without an agreement, and her request for a downward departure in her sentence was denied. The Ninth Circuit vacated her sentence, holding that the obligation to provide impeachment information is the same prior to a plea agreement as it is at trial. The court held that the right to receive this information could not be waived.

■ ISSUE

Do the Fifth and Sixth Amendments require federal prosecutors, before entering into a binding plea agreement with a criminal defendant, to disclose impeachment information relating to any informants or other witnesses?

■ DECISION AND RATIONALE

(Breyer, J.) No. The Constitution does not require disclosure of impeaching information before entry of a guilty plea. Impeachment information relates to the fairness of a trial, not whether a plea was voluntary. "[T]he law ordinarily considers a waiver knowing, intelligent, and sufficiently aware if the defendant fully understands the nature of the right and how it would likely apply *in general* in the circumstances—even though the defendant may not know the *specific detailed* consequences of invoking it." The usefulness of impeachment information is not critical information required to ensure a fair trial because it largely depends upon the defendant's independent knowledge of the prosecution's case. Likewise, a guilty plea may be accepted despite a defendant's misapprehension about various factors, including the penalties, the quality of the prosecution's case, and constitutional flaws in the prosecution. Nor do due process considerations support any right to receive impeachment information. Whether a process is constitutionally required involves a consideration of the nature of the private interest at stake, the value of the additional safeguard, and the adverse impact of the requirement on the interests of the government. As stated, the value of any pre-plea right to impeachment information would depend on the independent knowledge of the defendant about the government's case, and, in any event, even without such a safeguard the government is still required to provide information about the factual innocence of the defendant. At the same time, a constitutional obligation could interfere with the government's interest in securing factually justified plea agreements and disrupt ongoing criminal investigations. Reversed.

■ CONCURRENCE

(Thomas, J.) The majority's focus on the degree of help impeachment information will have at the plea stage is unnecessary because the Constitution ensures only a fair trial. The fairness of trial is not a concern at the plea stage.

Analysis:

Ruiz (D) was arrested in possession of marijuana, so impeachment information may have related more to possible constitutional challenges to her arrest and search than to the accuracy of trial testimony. The line between "factual innocence" information and "impeachment" information may not always be as clear as the Court suggests. For example, suppose the government's case is built on the testimony of witnesses, rather than on physical evidence. Does information that casts doubt on the reliability of those witnesses or their testimony fall on the "impeachment" or "factual innocence" side of the line?

■ CASE VOCABULARY

DOWNWARD DEPARTURE: In the federal sentencing guidelines, a court's imposition of a sentence more lenient than the standard guidelines propose, as when the court concludes that a criminal's history is less serious than it appears.

SENTENCING GUIDELINES: A set of standards for determining the punishment that a convicted criminal should receive, based on the nature of the crime and the offender's criminal history. The federal government and several states have adopted sentencing guidelines in an effort to make judicial sentencing more consistent.

In re United States

(Prosecuting Authority)

345 F.3d 450 (7th Cir. 2003)

A JUDGE MAY NOT REFUSE TO DISMISS CHARGES BASED ON DISAPPROVAL OF PROSECUTORIAL DECISIONS

■ **INSTANT FACTS** A federal district judge denied the government's request to dismiss charges against a defendant pursuant to a plea bargain.

■ **BLACK LETTER RULE** A federal judge may not deny a prosecutor's good faith request to dismiss charges pursuant to a plea bargain with a defendant

■ PROCEDURAL BASIS

Consideration of a petition for mandamus.

■ FACTS

Bitsky, a police officer, was indicted on one count of depriving civil rights under color of state law and two counts of obstruction of justice, stemming from an assault on an arrested person and his attempts to induce a fellow officer to write a false arrest report to cover it up. Bitsky agreed with the Government to plead guilty to one count of obstruction of justice in exchange for dismissal of the other charges. At the sentencing hearing, the Government explained to the judge that the higher-sentence charges were being dropped to secure a felony conviction without the risks of trial, thereby ensuring Bitsky would never work in law enforcement. The court refused to enter the plea agreement because the plea did not reflect the seriousness of the offense charged. Bitsky nonetheless pleaded guilty to one count of obstruction of justice. The Government dismissed the other obstruction count, but pursued the civil rights violation and appointed Bitsky counsel. The Government filed a petition of mandamus to compel the district court to dismiss the civil rights count and rescind the appointment of counsel. The judge contended that the plea agreement was dismissed as an attempt to circumvent his sentencing authority, although his expected sentence would have complied with sentencing guidelines.

■ ISSUE

Absent bad faith, may a federal judge deny a prosecutor's request to dismiss charges pursuant to a plea bargain with a defendant?

■ DECISION AND RATIONALE

(Posner, J.) No. The purpose of mandamus is to "confine officials within the boundaries of their authorized powers." Courts are not authorized to prosecute claims. Although Rule 48(c) of the Federal Rules of Criminal Procedure requires leave of court to dismiss an indictment, that rule is designed to protect the defendant from government harassment by filing charges and dismissing them before adjudication. This threat is not at issue. Here, the judge disagrees with prosecutorial discretion to dismiss more serious charges. Absent bad faith on the part of the Government or the defendant, the judge has no authority to deny the dismissal of charges with the mutual agreement of the parties. The Constitution vests the power to prosecute in the Executive Branch, and the judiciary may not infringe upon that power. Petition granted.

Analysis:

Although the judicial branch is vested with authority to impose sentences, it must do so upon the convictions or pleas on charges brought by the executive branch. By refusing to dismiss the charges against Bitsky, the judge did not lose his sentencing authority, for he was still permitted to impose a sentence on the guilty plea. However, the adoption of uniform sentencing guidelines limits judicial discretion considerably.

■ CASE VOCABULARY

MANDAMUS: A writ issued by a superior court to compel a lower court or a government officer to perform mandatory or purely ministerial duties correctly.

CHAPTER TWENTY–THREE

Trial by Jury

Taylor v. Louisiana

Instant Facts: After denial of his motion to quash the petit jury venire on the grounds that the systematic exclusion of women was unconstitutional, the defendant was tried, convicted and sentenced to death.

Black Letter Rule: It is a violation of the fair-cross-section rule to systematically exclude women from the jury panel from which petit juries are drawn.

Hamer v. United States

Instant Facts: The Government (P) used a "jury book" during voir dire and refused Hamer's (D) attorney's requests both for a jury list prior to trial and for an opportunity to question prospective jurors during voir dire.

Black Letter Rule: The right to a jury trial does not guarantee the right to a jury list in a non-capital case or the right of a personal voir dire by defense counsel (D), and does not forbid the prosecution's (P) use of a "jury book" during voir dire.

Batson v. Kentucky

Instant Facts: After Batson (D), a black man, was indicted, the prosecutor (P) used peremptory challenges to exclude all black veniremen from the jury.

Black Letter Rule: The use of peremptory challenges in a single case to exclude veniremen solely based on race may suffice to establish a prima facie case of purposeful discrimination in violation of the Equal Protection Clause.

Taylor v. Louisiana

(*Convicted Kidnapper*) v. (*State*)
419 U.S. 522, 95 S.Ct. 692 (1975)

THE SYSTEMATIC EXCLUSION OF WOMEN FROM THE JURY POOL VIOLATES THE FAIR-CROSS-SECTION REQUIREMENT OF THE SIXTH AMENDMENT

■ **INSTANT FACTS** After denial of his motion to quash the petit jury venire on the grounds that the systematic exclusion of women was unconstitutional, the defendant was tried, convicted and sentenced to death.

■ **BLACK LETTER RULE** It is a violation of the fair-cross-section rule to systematically exclude women from the jury panel from which petit juries are drawn.

■ PROCEDURAL BASIS

Appeal to the U.S. Supreme Court, challenging the Louisiana Supreme Court decision holding that the State's rules dealing with the service of women on juries was not unconstitutional under federal law.

■ FACTS

Billy Taylor (D) was indicted for aggravated kidnaping. On April 12, 1972, Taylor (D) moved the trial court to quash the petit jury venire drawn for the special criminal term beginning with his trial the following day. Taylor (D) alleged that women were systematically excluded from the venire and that he would therefore be deprived of his federal constitutional right to a jury of a representative segment of the community. [Did he realy believe females would be sympathetic to a kidnapper?] Although 53% of the persons eligible for jury service in the judicial district at issue were female, no more than 10% of the persons on the jury wheel were women. During a one- year period, 12 females were among the 1,800 persons drawn to fill petit jury venires in the district. The discrepancy between females eligible for jury service and those actually included in the venire was the result of the operation of Louisiana law. In the present case, a venire totaling 175 persons was drawn for jury service beginning April 13, 1972. There were no females on the venire. Taylor's motion to quash the jury venire was denied on the same day. He was then tried, convicted and sentenced to death.

■ ISSUE

Is the presence of a fair cross section of the community on venires, panels, or lists from which petit juries are drawn essential to the fulfillment of the Sixth Amendment's guarantee of an impartial jury trial in criminal prosecutions; and is that guarantee violated when women are systematically excluded from such venires, panels, or lists.

■ DECISION AND RATIONALE

(White, J.) Yes and yes. Before addressing the Sixth Amendment issue, we must first reject Louisiana's (P) contention that Taylor (D) lacks standing to object to the exclusion of women from his jury. It is true that Taylor (D) is not a member of the excluded class, but there is no rule that claims of unconstitutional jury pools may be made only by those defendants who are members of the group excluded from jury service. We accept the fair-cross-section requirement as fundamental to the jury trial guaranteed by the Sixth Amendment and are convinced that the requirement has solid foundation.

If jury pools are made up of only special segments of the populace, or if large, distinctive groups are excluded from the polls, the jury is unable to serve its purpose—to guard against government oppression. Consistent with this Court's previous holding that exclusion of women from jury venires violated a statutory fair-cross-section requirement, we hold that the fair-cross-section requirement of the Sixth Amendment is violated by the systematic exclusion of women. Both sexes are not fungible; and a community made up of only one is different from a community composed of both. Moreover, this systematic exclusion cannot be justified on the grounds that women serve a distinctive role in society, a role which would be hindered by compulsory jury service. States are free to grant exemptions in cases of hardship, but may not exclude all women by suggesting that society cannot spare any women from their duties. Reversed.

■ DISSENT

(Rehnquist) Today's decision is not necessary to guard against oppressive or arbitrary law enforcement or miscarriages of justice. The Court concludes that the jury is not an effective vehicle for preventing arbitrary prosecutorial or judicial power if large, distinctive groups are excluded from the jury pool. However, the Court does not satisfactorily explain why the Louisiana system undermines this function of the jury, either in general or in this case.

Analysis:

It is important to note that the Court's unanimous decision here actually delineates two separate but related rules. The Court, for the first time, holds that the fair-cross-section requirement is an essential element of the Sixth Amendment's right to a fair jury trial. Although it had intimated as much in previous cases, and even held that the requirement was an essential element of the Equal Protection Clause of the Fourteenth Amendment, the Court had never been squarely faced with the Sixth Amendment issue. The requirement is simply that juries must be drawn from a source representing a fair cross-section of the community. This requirement extends to all defendants, not just those who are a member of the excluded class. After holding that the fair-cross-section requirement is an essential feature of the Sixth Amendment, the Court addresses the narrower issue and holds that the systematic exclusion of women violates that very requirement. The question left unanswered is what the nature of a class must be so that its exclusion will violate the Sixth Amendment.

■ CASE VOCABULARY

PROPHYLACTIC VEHICLE: A rule designed to prevent some harm, usually a constitutional violation.

VENIRE: The panel from which the jury is selected.

Hamer v. United States

(Drug Dealer) v. *(Federal Government)*
259 F.2d 274 (1958)

THE RIGHT TO A JURY TRIAL PERMITS BUT DOES NOT REQUIRE PRE-TRIAL ACCESS TO INFORMATION ABOUT PROSPECTIVE JURORS

■ **INSTANT FACTS** The Government (P) used a "jury book" during voir dire and refused Hamer's (D) attorney's requests both for a jury list prior to trial and for an opportunity to question prospective jurors during voir dire.

■ **BLACK LETTER RULE** The right to a jury trial does not guarantee the right to a jury list in a non-capital case or the right of a personal voir dire by defense counsel (D), and does not forbid the prosecution's (P) use of a "jury book" during voir dire.

■ PROCEDURAL BASIS

Appeal of conviction after jury trial.

■ FACTS

Hamer (D) was convicted for fraudulently importing narcotics for sale. The Government (P) refused Hamer's (D) request for a list of the names and addresses of prospective jurors prior to trial, and refused her counsel's request for an opportunity to personally question prospective jurors during voir dire. In addition, the prosecutor (P) used a "jury book" during voir dire which described how the prospective jurors acted or voted on previous juries. Hamer (D) claims that the Government's (P) conduct deprived her of her right to a jury trial.

■ ISSUE

Does the denial of a jury list before trial, the denial of a personal voir dire by defense counsel (D), or the prosecutor's (P) use of a "jury book" during voir dire constitute a deprivation of the right to a jury trial?

■ DECISION AND RATIONALE

(Barnes) No. Federal law requires the Government (P) to give defense counsel (D) a jury list before trial in cases involving treason and capital offenses. No court has ever held this statute applicable to non-capital offenses. The fact that Congress imposed this requirement in capital cases, but not in non-capital cases, indicates that it found the requirement unnecessary in non-capital cases. [In other words, if you want to personally voir dire the jury, commit treason or a capital offense!] Further, both case law and the *Federal Rules of Criminal Procedure, rule 24 (a)* [procedure for examining prospective jurors], make clear that there is no constitutional right to a personal voir dire of the jury. While these rules seem sound individually, Hamer (D) argues that the Government's (P) denial of both requests deprived her of her right to an impartial jury and a fair jury trial. However, if there is no violation separately, then there can be none when the two are combined, provided the jury selection as a whole is fair and impartial. In this case the trial court advised defense counsel (D) that if he had any additional voir dire questions, he could request the court to ask them, but defense counsel (D) made no such request. Defense counsel (D) also had nothing to add on challenges for cause. We therefore find the voir dire examination in this case sufficient. Likewise, the use of "jury books" showing how members of the jury acted and voted on previous juries does not constitute a violation of the right to a fair jury trial. Groups of attorneys share information with each other. The fact that this information is about how a juror voted or whether he "held up" a jury does not set it apart. Different attorneys usually have different levels of experience and knowledge about different jurors. The right to a fair jury trial cannot include the right to counsel with equal knowledge and experience. Affirmed.

Analysis:

This case discusses the right of access to information about prospective jurors prior to and during voir dire. The primary function of voir dire is to elicit information for challenges for cause and for peremptory challenges. FRCrP 24(a) lets a court either conduct a voir dire examination itself or allow counsel to do it. Some states follow this rule, some give counsel primary control over the questioning, and some have the judge start the examination and then allow counsel to ask additional questions. Many courts also use detailed questionnaires. Questioning during voir dire probes into jurors' attitudes and practices, including religious beliefs, jobs, hobbies, and experiences with the legal process. The jurors' right to privacy yields to the defendant's right to a fair trial, especially for serious crimes. To aid preparation for voir dire, most states have legislation which gives criminal defendants the right to a list of prospective jurors before trial. Some states give this right in all cases, while others limit it to capital or felony cases. In *Hamer* the court interpreted the federal statute as limiting this right to cases involving treason or capital offenses. In states with no such legislation, courts usually hold that defendants have no right to a jury list, but some give them the list anyway if they request it. When they do know the identity of prospective jurors, counsel may investigate them before trial. The prosecution is generally better able to conduct such an investigation because it usually has better access to criminal and other government records. In addition, it may have access to a "jury book" such as that used in *Hamer,* in which prosecutors pool information on particular jurors' voting habits and behavior in earlier trials. The prosecution may also be able to have the local police or even the FBI obtain background information on prospective jurors. Courts have upheld such investigations on the rationale that they do not result in bias against the defendant, but only eliminate bias against the government. There are limits to this practice, however. Attorneys may not communicate with the prospective jurors, directly or though an investigator, and they may not conduct harassing investigations. The prosecution and defense are usually not entitled to discovery of each other's juror information. In *Hamer,* for example, the court dismissed Hamer's (D) claim that he should have access to the prosecutor's (P) jury book.

■ CASE VOCABULARY

TYRO: A beginner or amateur.

VOIR DIRE: The process of questioning prospective jurors to determine which are unable to serve as fair and impartial jurors.

Batson v. Kentucky

(*Convicted Black Man*) v. (*State*)
476 U.S. 79, 106 S.Ct. 1712, 90 L.Ed.2d 69 (1986)

SUPREME COURT OVERRULES *SWAIN* TO PERMIT EQUAL PROTECTION CLAIMS BASED ON PEREMPTORY CHALLENGES IN A SINGLE CASE

■ **INSTANT FACTS** After Batson (D), a black man, was indicted, the prosecutor (P) used peremptory challenges to exclude all black veniremen from the jury.

■ **BLACK LETTER RULE** The use of peremptory challenges in a single case to exclude veniremen solely based on race may suffice to establish a prima facie case of purposeful discrimination in violation of the Equal Protection Clause.

■ PROCEDURAL BASIS

Certiorari granted after Kentucky Supreme Court affirmed conviction after jury trial and denial of motion to discharge jury.

■ FACTS

Batson (D), a black man, was indicted for burglary and receipt of stolen goods. The prosecutor (P) used his peremptory challenges to strike all four black veniremen, and an all-white jury was selected. Batson (D) moved to discharge the jury, arguing that the prosecutor's (P) removal of all the black veniremen violated his right to a jury drawn from a fair cross section of the community and his right to equal protection of the laws. The trial judge denied Batson's (D) motion, reasoning that the fair cross section requirement applies only to selection of the venire, and not to selection of the jury, and that the parties could use their peremptory challenges to "strike anybody they want to." The jury convicted Batson (D).

■ ISSUE

Can the use of peremptory challenges in a single case to exclude veniremen solely on the basis of race establish a prima facie case of purposeful discrimination in violation of the Equal Protection Clause?

■ DECISION AND RATIONALE

(Powell) Yes. In *Swain v. Alabama* [Equal Protection Clause applies to the systematic use of peremptory challenges to exclude a racial group] we recognized that a State's (P) purposeful exclusion of blacks from jury service on account of race violates the Equal Protection Clause. Batson (D) argues that the prosecutor (P) violated his Sixth Amendment right to an impartial jury drawn from a fair cross section of the community. The State (P) insists that Batson (D) is actually claiming a denial of equal protection, and that we must therefore reconsider *Swain* to find a constitutional violation in this case. We agree that this case turns on equal protection principles and express no opinion on Batson's (D) Sixth Amendment arguments. The State's (P) privilege to strike individual jurors through peremptory challenges is subject to the Equal Protection Clause. A prosecutor (P) may generally use peremptory challenges for any reason related to his view of the case. However, the Equal Protection Clause raises challenges based solely on race or on the assumption that black jurors will be unable to impartially consider the State's (P) case against a black defendant. As here, in *Swain* we considered the application of the Equal Protection Clause to the State's (P) use of peremptory challenges, and sought to accommodate this to the prosecutor's (P) historical privilege to use peremptory challenges free of judicial control. We noted that peremptory challenges have traditionally been viewed as a means of assuring the selection of a qualified and unbiased jury. To preserve the peremptory nature of the prosecutor's (P) challenge, in *Swain* we declined to scrutinize the prosecutor's (P) actions and presumed that he properly exercised the State's (P) challenges. We observed, however, that a prosecutor (P) may not use peremptory challenges to exclude blacks from the jury for reasons wholly unrelated to the outcome of the case or to deny blacks the opportunity to serve on a jury. For example, an inference of purposeful discrimination would arise where a prosecutor (P) always used his peremptory challenges to remove blacks, whatever the circumstances of the case. In *Swain* we held that the defendant did not offer sufficient proof of purposeful discrimination because he did not offer proof of the circumstances of other cases in which prosecutors (P) in his jurisdiction removed black jurors. Lower courts thus reasoned that *Swain* required proof of the repeated exclusion of blacks over a number of cases to establish an equal protection violation. We reject this evidentiary formulation. An equal protection violation does not require a consistent pattern of official racial discrimination, but only a single invidiously discriminatory governmental act. A requirement that several must suffer discrimination before one can object is inconsistent with the promise of equal protection to all. With respect to selection of the venire, a prima facie case of purposeful racial discrimination requires only the facts regarding its selection in a single case. Likewise, a prima facie case of purposeful discrimination in the selection of the petit jury may rest on the prosecutor's (P) use of peremptory challenges in a single case. This prima facie case requires proof that: (1) the defendant is a member of a cognizable racial group; (2) the prosecutor (P) has exercised peremptory challenges to remove members of that race; and (3) the facts and circumstances raise an inference that the prosecutor (P) used peremptory challenges to exclude veniremen from the petit jury based on their race. To establish such a case a defendant may rely on the fact that peremptory challenges permit those who are of a mind to discriminate to do so. The trial court should consider all relevant circumstances, including a pattern of strikes against black jurors and a prosecutor's (P) questions and statements during voir dire and in exercising his challenges. Once a defendant establishes a prima facie case, the burden shifts to the State (P) to give a neutral explanation for challenging black jurors. While this does impose a limitation on the peremptory character of the challenge, the explanation need not rise to the level necessary to justify a challenge for cause. However, a prosecutor (P) may not rebut a prima facie case of discrimination by merely stating that he assumed that the challenged jurors would be biased toward the defendant on account of their race. Just as the Equal Protection Clause prohibits the States (P) from excluding blacks from the venire on the assumption that they are unqualified to serve as jurors, so also it prohibits the States (P) from striking black veniremen on the assumption that they will be biased in a particular case simply because they are black. The State (P) argues that the privilege of unfettered exercise of peremptory challenges is vital to the criminal justice system, and that our holding will eviscerate the fair trial values the peremptory challenge serves. We disagree. The reality is that the challenge may be and has been used to discriminate against black jurors. Protecting citizens from being disqualified from jury service because of their race will strengthen our criminal justice system, not weaken it. Because the trial court rejected Batson's (D) objection to the prosecutor's (P) removal of all black veniremen without requiring the prosecutor (P) to give an explanation, we remand for further proceedings. If the trial court decides that the facts establish a prima facie case of purposeful discrimination and the prosecutor (P) does not provide a neutral explanation for his action, Batson's (D) conviction must be reversed. Reversed and remanded.

■ CONCURRENCE

(Marshall) The evidentiary Analysis: set forth in today's decision provides only limited protection against discrimination. First, because a defendant can only challenge the discriminatory use of peremptory challenges when the discrimination is flagrant enough to establish a prima facie case, prosecutors (P) remain free to discriminate as long as they do so at an "acceptable" level. Second, it is difficult for the trial court to assess the prosecutor's (P) motives, and easy for a prosecutor (P) to assert neutral reasons for striking a juror. For example, if an explanation for striking a juror such as "he never cracked a smile" and therefore "did not possess the sensitivities necessary to realistically look at the issues and decide the facts" will suffice to rebut a prima facie case of discrimination, then today's decision may provide little protection. Finally, unconscious racism may lead prosecutors (P) to assert explanations that would not come to mind if the juror in question were a different race, and may lead trial judges to accept these explanations. Because of the inherent potential of peremptory challenges to permit the exclusion of jurors on racial grounds, the Court should ban the use of peremptory challenges by prosecutors (P) and allow the States (P) to eliminate the defendant's peremptory as well.

■ DISSENT

(Burger) The Court fails to even discuss the rationale of the peremptory challenge. As *Swain* observed, the function of the challenge is not only to eliminate extremes of partiality, but also to assure the parties that the jurors will decide the case based on the evidence. Permitting unexplained peremptories strengthens our jury system by allowing the covert expression of what we cannot say, but what we nonetheless know is usually true, without undercutting our desire for a rational, unbiased society. [Covert discrimination strengthens our jury system?] We concluded in *Swain* that the peremptory challenge is one of the most important rights in our justice system. For close to a century the denial or impairment of this right has been reversible error without a showing of prejudice. The Court relies upon equal protection principles, but, as the Court recognized in *Swain,* parties often use peremptory challenges for reasons such as race, religion, nationality, occupation or affiliations. When using peremptory challenges, counsel necessarily act on limited information or a hunch. We should not, therefore, strike down a challenge because a party bases it on "assumption." Equal protection is simply inapplicable to the peremptory challenges of any particular case. A clause that requires a minimum "rationality" cannot be applicable to "an arbitrary and capricious right." The Court states that it does not require a prosecutor's (P) "neutral explanation" to rise to the level of a challenge for cause. However, it is difficult to distinguish a "clear and reasonably specific" explanation of "legitimate reasons" for exercising a challenge from the type of explanation necessary to support a challenge for cause.

■ DISSENT

(Rehnquist) I disagree with the Court's unprecedented use of the Equal Protection Clause to restrict the historic scope of the peremptory challenge, a necessary part of a jury trial. There is nothing "unequal" about the State (P) using peremptory challenges to strike blacks from the jury in cases involving black defendants as long as it applies this use of peremptories to all races. Because the case-specific use of peremptory challenges does not deny blacks the right to serve as jurors in other cases, it harms neither the excluded jurors nor the community.

Analysis:

In *Batson* the Court overruled the portion of *Swain* that foreclosed an equal protection challenge based on the discriminatory use of peremptories in a single case. In *Swain* the Court held that proof of the systematic exclusion of a particular race through the use of peremptories over a period of time may establish such an equal protection violation. However, it rejected the equal protection claim in that case because it was based on the jury strikes in only that case. Because this was inconsistent with the equal protection standards the Court applied to the selection of the jury venire, where the facts in a single case could suffice, the Court overruled this portion of *Swain* and held that evidence from a single case could suffice with respect to the selection of the petit jury as well. The Court reasoned that the same equal protection principles that apply to the selection of the venire also govern the use of peremptory challenges to strike jurors from the petit jury. In *Swain* the Court explained that the essential nature of the peremptory challenge is that it requires no stated reason and is subject to no inquiry and no judicial control. The Court was therefore unwilling to hold that the Constitution required an examination of the prosecutor's reasons for exercising his challenges in any given case. The Court found a presumption in each case that the prosecutor used peremptory challenges to obtain a fair and impartial jury. This presumption could be overcome if prosecutors consistently exercised their peremptories to excuse blacks from serving as jurors, regardless of the type of case. However, the burden of establishing such a systematic exclusion was "crippling," and few defendants were able to meet it. In *Batson,* the Court rejected *Swain's* evidentiary approach. Instead, the Court held that the Equal Protection Clause forbids challenges based solely on race or on the assumption that jurors of a particular race could not impartially consider the case against a defendant of that race, and that such a claim could rest solely on evidence concerning the challenges in a single case. If a defendant establishes a prima facie case of purposeful discrimination, the prosecutor may rebut it by providing a neutral explanation for his challenges. A "neutral explanation" is one based on something other than the juror's race. The issue then would be whether the prosecutor had a discriminatory intent when making the challenges, not whether the challenges had a racially disproportionate impact. Such an impact may, however, constitute evidence that the explanation was only a pretext for racial discrimination. Explanations are more likely to be acceptable if the prosecutor assessed white jurors on the same basis. Courts have accepted explanations relating to a juror's attitudes about the particular case or about criminal prosecutions. Because prosecutors have had little difficulty coming up with acceptable explanations, some find *Batson* to be a better tool for disguising racial discrimination than for preventing it.

■ CASE VOCABULARY

CHALLENGE FOR CAUSE: A request to dismiss a prospective juror based on a specific reason to believe the person could not be a fair and unbiased juror, such as a relation to a party, counsel, or a witness; personal knowledge of the facts; other facts indicating bias; or incompetency.

PEREMPTORY CHALLENGE: A request to dismiss a prospective juror which generally does not require a stated reason.

CHAPTER TWENTY–FIVE

The Criminal Trial

Illinois v. Allen

Instant Facts: A defendant who was removed from his trial for disrupting the courtroom, appealed his conviction on the grounds that his Sixth Amendment right to be present in the courtroom had been violated.

Black Letter Rule: A trial court may order a defendant removed from the courtroom, if necessary, in order to preserve order in the court.

Griffin v. California

Instant Facts: A defendant appealed his murder conviction claiming that the prosecution and the court's comments on his refusal to testify violated his Fifth Amendment Right against self-incrimination.

Black Letter Rule: The Fifth Amendment's protection against self-incrimination prohibits the prosecution and the court from commenting upon a defendant's decision not to testify at trial.

Darden v. Wainwright

Instant Facts: A prisoner sought Federal Habeas Corpus Relief claiming that a prosecutor's improper comments had violated his Due Process right to a fair trial.

Black Letter Rule: A prosecutor's improper comments will not violate a defendant's right to Due Process unless it is found that the comments rendered the defendant's trial fundamentally unfair.

Illinois v. Allen

(*State*) v. (*Defendant*)
397 U.S. 337, 90 S.Ct. 1057 (1970)

A DEFENDANT'S SIXTH AMENDMENT RIGHT TO BE PRESENT AT TRIAL IS NOT ABSOLUTE

■ **INSTANT FACTS** A defendant who was removed from his trial for disrupting the courtroom, appealed his conviction on the grounds that his Sixth Amendment right to be present in the courtroom had been violated.

■ **BLACK LETTER RULE** A trial court may order a defendant removed from the courtroom, if necessary, in order to preserve order in the court.

■ PROCEDURAL BASIS

Appeal to United States Supreme Court from federal court of appeal's decision to grant defendant's writ of Habeas Corpus.

■ FACTS

Illinois (P) charged Mr. Allen (D) with Armed Robbery. The trial judge allowed Mr. Allen (D) to represent himself however, during voir dire, Mr. Allen (D) became combative and began to argue with the judge in a disrespectful manner. Mr. Allen (D) continuously threatened the judge until the judge finally warned him that he would be removed from the courtroom if he did not restrain himself. Mr. Allen (D) continued to threaten the judge and stated that there would be no trial. Consequently, the judge had Mr. Allen (D) removed from the courtroom. After a recess, the judge brought Mr. Allen (D) back into the courtroom and told him that he could remain for the trial only if he would conduct himself properly. Mr. Allen (D) again argued with the judge and stated that there would be no trial at which point he was again removed from the courtroom. Mr. Allen (D) remained outside of the courtroom for most of the State's case-in-chief, returning only for purposes of identification. He did return to the courtroom for the defense phase of the trial. Mr. Allen (D) was found guilty and sentenced to a term of 10 to 30 years. On appeal, the Supreme Court of Illinois affirmed his conviction and the Federal District Court subsequently refused to issue a writ of Habeas Corpus. The Federal Court of Appeals however, reversed Mr. Allen's (D) conviction on the grounds that the trial court had violated his absolute Sixth Amendment right to be present at his trial. The United States Supreme Court heard the Appeal.

■ ISSUE

Does a defendant have an absolute Sixth Amendment right to be present at trial?

■ DECISION AND RATIONALE

(Black, J.) No. We find no support for the Court of Appeal's conclusion that a defendant's Sixth Amendment right to be present at his trial is "absolute" and that, no matter how unruly or disruptive a defendant's conduct, he cannot be held to have lost the right to be present in the courtroom so long as he insists on it. Writing for this Court many years ago, Justice Cardozo stated that, though courts must indulge in every reasonable presumption against the loss of constitutional rights, a defendant's right to be present at trial is not absolute. If a defendant continues to behave disruptively after being warned by a judge not to do so, the court may order the defendant removed from the courtroom so that the trial may continue in his absence. A defendant who subsequently agrees to conduct himself in a manner consistent with a court proceeding may regain his right to be present in the courtroom. Like Justice Cardozo, we believe that a court may take actions it reasonably deems necessary to maintain courtroom decorum. We believe that there are three constitutionally permissible ways for a court to handle an obstreperous defendant such as Allen (D): (1) bind and gag him, thereby keeping him present; (2) cite him for contempt; (3) take him out of the courtroom until he agrees to conduct himself properly. Admittedly, each of these measures has its shortcomings. Trying a defendant for a crime while he is shackled and gagged might have a significant impact on the jury's view of the defendant and might also insult the dignity and decorum of the courtroom. A citation for contempt may be equally ineffective; a defendant who is facing a significant prison sentence is unlikely to curtail his disruptive behavior simply because he is threatened with contempt of court. Finally, removing a defendant from the courtroom does not perfectly solve the problems posed by unruly behavior because, ideally, a client should be present at his trial. Nevertheless, given the shortcomings of the three remedies we have discussed, it is apparent that in some situations removal is the best and most effective course of action a court can take to preserve order in the courtroom. Under the circumstances, we find that the trial court acted properly when it ordered Mr. Allen (D) removed from the courtroom: Mr. Allen (D) was repeatedly warned that he would be removed from the courtroom if he persisted in his unruly behavior and, after he was removed, the court repeatedly informed him that he would be allowed back into he courtroom if he would conduct himself in an orderly manner. Furthermore, the record demonstrates that Mr. Allen (D) would not have restrained himself had the trial court decided to cite him for contempt. Under the facts of this case, we find that Mr. Allen (D) forfeited his Sixth Amendment right to be present at his trial. The judgment of the Court of Appeals is reversed.

■ CONCURRENCE

(Brennan, J.) I agree that a defendant's Sixth Amendment right to be present at trial is not absolute. I would only like to caution that, to the extent possible, a court should make reasonable efforts to see that a removed defendant is allowed to communicate with his attorney and is kept informed of the proceedings. While it is permissible to remove a defendant from the courtroom, the effects of removal should be mitigated as much as possible.

Analysis:

The most important lesson to take from this case is that a defendant's Sixth Amendment right to be present at trial is not absolute, a court may remove him from the courtroom if necessary. The opinion cautions, however, that removal is not a remedy which should be undertaken lightly. In Mr. Allen's (D) case, the court is careful to note that, before it ordered Mr. Allen (D) removed, the trial court repeatedly admonished him that he would be removed if he did not adjust his behavior. Furthermore, once it did remove him, the trial court repeatedly advised Mr. Allen (D) that he could return to the courtroom if he would behave suitably. The opinion also makes note of the fact that it would not have been practical or effective for the trial court to exercise its contempt powers against Mr. Allen (D), a defendant facing a long prison sentence. Therefore, though the opinion makes clear that a court may remove a defendant from the courtroom, it should not do so unless it finds that less severe measures would be ineffective.

Griffin v. California

(*Defendant*) v. (*State*)
380 U.S. 609, 85 S.Ct. 1229 (1965)

A COMMENT UPON A DEFENDANT'S REFUSAL TO TESTIFY VIOLATES THE DEFENDANT'S FIFTH AMENDMENT RIGHT AGAINST SELF-INCRIMINATION

■ **INSTANT FACTS** A defendant appealed his murder conviction claiming that the prosecution and the court's comments on his refusal to testify violated his Fifth Amendment Right against self-incrimination.

■ **BLACK LETTER RULE** The Fifth Amendment's protection against self-incrimination prohibits the prosecution and the court from commenting upon a defendant's decision not to testify at trial.

■ FACTS

Mr. Griffin (D) was charged with the crime of first degree murder. Mr. Griffin (D) chose not to testify at his trial and at the close of the case, the trial judge instructed the jury that it could hold Mr. Griffin's (P) failure to testify against him if it believed that he had relevant facts within his knowledge. [Although not stated in the edited version of the case, the prosecution also commented on Mr. Griffin's (D) failure to testify.] Mr. Griffin (D) was subsequently convicted and sentenced to death. The California Supreme Court affirmed the conviction and the United States Supreme Court granted a writ of certiorari to consider the single question of whether the prosecution's comment on a defendant's failure to testify violates the Self-Incrimination Clause of the Fifth Amendment as it is applied to the states through the Fourteenth Amendment.

■ ISSUE

Does a comment upon a defendant's decision not to testify at trial violate the defendant's Fifth Amendment right against self-incrimination?

■ DECISION AND RATIONALE

(Douglas, J.) Yes. We hold that, when the prosecution comments upon a defendant's failure to testify on his own behalf, it does violate the defendant's Fifth Amendment right against self-incrimination. Comment on the refusal to testify is a remnant of the inquisitorial system of justice the Fifth Amendment outlaws. When a prosecutor comments upon a defendant's refusal to testify, the prosecutor penalizes the defendant for invoking a constitutional privilege. We are not persuaded by the argument that the jury would be likely to draw negative inferences from the defendant's refusal to testify even if the prosecutor were not allowed to draw attention to it. It is one thing for a jury to infer guilt from a defendant's silence: it is quite another thing for a court to validate the jury's inference of guilt by sanctioning a prosecutor's comments or by giving a formal instruction. Accordingly, we hold that the Fifth Amendment forbids the prosecution from commenting on the accused's silence and forbids instructions by the court that such silence is evidence of guilt. The California Supreme Court is reversed.

■ DISSENT

(Stewart, J.) The majority holds that a comment upon the defendant's decision not to testify violates the defendant's Fifth Amendment right against self-incrimination. In essence, the majority believes that, if the state is allowed to comment upon a defendant's refusal to testify, the defendant will be compelled to testify. I believe that the majority's interpretation stretches the definition of compulsion beyond all reasonable bounds. To say that a comment on a defendant's silence would have an effect upon the defendant's decision to testify or, in fact, compel a defendant to testify is just not reasonable. A jury will draw inferences when a defendant does not testify whether or not it is instructed to do so by the prosecutor or the court. Arguably, allowing comment upon a defendant's refusal to testify favors the defendant because, at least in that instance, he will be allowed to dispel through counsel any negative inferences the jury may have drawn. In sum, a comment upon a defendant's decision not to testify does not violate the defendant's right against self-incrimination because such comment could in no way compel a defendant to testify.

Analysis:

In simple terms, the Court held that the Fifth Amendment right against self-incrimination is really not very meaningful if the prosecution and the court are allowed to comment upon a defendant's failure to testify. Imagine a court telling a defendant, "you have a Fifth Amendment right not to testify in this case but, if you do not testify, we will tell the jury that your refusal may be taken as a sign of your guilt." The majority held that an ultimatum of this sort would effectively deprive a defendant of the right against self-incrimination because it would likely compel a defendant to take the witness stand in his own defense. The dissent, on the other hand, held that such an ultimatum would not have the effect of compelling a defendant's testimony because everyone knows that a jury will draw negative inferences from a defendant's refusal to testify regardless of whether the court or prosecution comments upon the refusal. In the dissent's view, a defendant is better off when a court permits comment on the right not to testify because, in that case, the defendant is afforded the opportunity to dispel any negative inference the jury may have drawn.

Darden v. Wainwright

(*Prisoner*) v. (*Warden*)

477 U.S. 168, 106 S.Ct. 2464 (1986)

IMPROPER COMMENTS BY A PROSECUTOR WILL VIOLATE A DEFENDANT'S RIGHT TO DUE PROCESS ONLY IN THE EVENT THAT THE COMMENTS RENDER A TRIAL FUNDAMENTALLY UNFAIR

■ **INSTANT FACTS** A prisoner sought Federal Habeas Corpus Relief claiming that a prosecutor's improper comments had violated his Due Process right to a fair trial.

■ **BLACK LETTER RULE** A prosecutor's improper comments will not violate a defendant's right to Due Process unless it is found that the comments rendered the defendant's trial fundamentally unfair.

■ PROCEDURAL BASIS

Petitioner filed a Writ of Habeas Corpus to the United States Supreme Court after the Federal District Court of Appeal had denied him relief for the same claim.

■ FACTS

The State of Florida charged Mr. Darden (D) with murder, robbery and assault with intent to kill. It was alleged that, during a particularly brutal robbery, Mr. Darden (D) shot and killed Mr. Turman. At trial, the state presented questionable testimony from eye-witnesses who identified Mr. Darden (D) as the perpetrator of the crime as well as some circumstantial evidence which tied him to the scene. During closing argument, the state attorney prosecuting the case made a number of impermissible arguments in an attempt to persuade the jury of Mr. Darden's (D) guilt. Among other things, the prosecutor expressed personal opinions as to Mr. Darden's (D) guilt; intentionally sought to inflame the passions and prejudices of the jury; and sought to have the jury consider issues beyond the guilt or innocence of the defendant. Subsequently the jury found Mr. Darden (D) guilty of the murder of Mr. Turman and he was sentenced to death. Mr. Darden (D) claimed in his appeal to the Florida Supreme Court and later to the Federal Courts of Appeal that the prosecutor's improper closing arguments so infected the trial with unfairness as to make the resulting conviction a denial of due process. All courts denied Mr. Darden (D) relief and he subsequently appealed to the United States Supreme Court.

■ ISSUE

Do improper arguments by a prosecutor automatically constitute a violation of a defendant's right to Due Process?

■ DECISION AND RATIONALE

(Powell, J.) No. While we agree that the prosecutor's arguments were improper, the issue for this Court to determine is whether the comments rendered the trial fundamentally unfair. As all of the courts below us have noted, it is not enough that the prosecutor's comments were undesirable or that they have been universally condemned, the relevant question is whether the prosecutor's comments so infected the trial with unfairness as to make the resulting conviction a denial of Due Process. Simply put: improper prosecutorial comments do not automatically equal a denial of Due Process which would require a court to reverse a conviction. Viewing the prosecutor's comments as they were made in the context of the trial in this case, we find that the comments did not serve to deprive Mr. Darden (D) of his right to a fair trial and that his Due Process rights were therefore not violated. The prosecutor's comments did not manipulate or misstate the evidence nor did the prosecutor implicate other rights of the accused such as the right to remain silent. We also note that much of the objectionable content in the prosecutor's summation was invited by arguments put forth by the defense. While the idea of "invited response" does not excuse improper comments, it may nevertheless diminish the harmful effects of the comments. Finally, we note that the prosecution offered substantial proof of Mr. Darden's (D) guilt. The fact that the state offered overwhelming eyewitness and circumstantial evidence of the defendant's guilt diminishes the chance that the jury found him guilty on the basis of the prosecutor's improper argument. For these reasons, we agree with the lower court's conclusion that, while the prosecutor's comments were improper, they did not render the trial fundamentally unfair. The prosecutor's comments did not violate Mr. Darden's (D) constitutional right to Due Process. Affirmed.

■ DISSENT

(Blackmun, J.) Although it is true that the Constitution guarantees only a fair trial, not a perfect one, the Constitution also requires a heightened degree of reliability when a defendant is being tried for a capital crime. In this case, I find that the prosecutor's comments were so pervasive and outrageous that they rendered the trial unfair. Unlike the majority, I believe that there is a good possibility that the jury took the prosecution's improper statements into consideration when it found Mr. Darden (D) guilty. Contrary to the majority's conclusion, the evidence the prosecution presented against Mr. Darden (D) was anything but overwhelming. If we are to put a man to death on the basis of questionable eyewitness identifications and other, equally questionable, circumstantial evidence, we should at least be sure that the trial itself was conducted in a fair manner. Because I believe that Mr. Darden (D) did not have a fair trial, I would reverse his conviction as a violation of Due Process.

Analysis:

This case makes clear that the determination of whether a prosecutor's improper arguments violate a defendant's right to Due Process depends not only on the nature of the comments themselves, but also upon the context in which the comments were made. The Court in this case was careful to note that, while the prosecutor's comments were improper and even offensive, the comments did not misstate or manipulate the evidence, nor did they implicate any of the defendant's constitutional rights. Presumably then, the court would have been more likely to find that the state had violated Mr. Darden's (D) right to Due Process had the prosecutor made reference to facts not in evidence or if the prosecutor had attempted to shift the burden of proof to Darden. The Court would likely have been even more likely to find that the prosecutor's comments served to deny Mr. Darden his right to a fair trial had it not concluded that the evidence against him was overwhelming. Though the dissent pointed out that the majority's characterization of the evidence as overwhelming was questionable at best, the point is that the strength of the state's case is an important factor in the Due Process equation. In essence, the stronger the case the state is able to put forth, the less likely an appeals court will be to find that improper prosecutorial comments constitute a violation of Due Process. Though a prosecutor should never intentionally make an improper argument, a prosecutor could nevertheless conclude from this opinion that, improper arguments or not, it is unlikely that a verdict will be overturned on Due Process grounds so long as the state presents strong evidence of a defendant's guilt.

■ CASE VOCABULARY

HABEAS CORPUS: A mechanism by which a defendant can complain to a court of superior jurisdiction that the state has detained or convicted him of a crime in violation of the Constitution.

CHAPTER TWENTY–SIX

Reprosecution and the Ban Against Double Jeopardy

Illinois v. Somerville

Instant Facts: A mistrial was granted over Somerville's (D) objection based on a defective indictment. Somerville (D) was subsequently re-tried and convicted for theft.

Black Letter Rule: A declaration of mistrial over defendant's objection does not preclude a second trial where there is a "manifest necessity" for the mistrial or it is otherwise required by the "ends of public justice."

Oregon v. Kennedy

Instant Facts: The defendant's motion to dismiss due to double jeopardy was granted after the prosecutor provoked the defendant into moving for a mistrial during his first trial.

Black Letter Rule: The circumstances under which a defendant who has successfully moved for a mistrial may invoke the bar of double jeopardy in a second effort to try him are limited to those cases in which the conduct giving rise to the successful motion for a mistrial was intended to provoke the defendant into moving for mistrial.

United States v. Scott

Instant Facts: An indictment against a drug-dealing cop was dismissed on the grounds of prejudice, and the Government was prohibited from appealing the dismissal based on the Double Jeopardy Clause.

Black Letter Rule: Where the defendant himself seeks to have the trial terminated without any submission to either judge or jury as to his guilt or innocence, an appeal by the Government from his successful effort to do so is not barred by the Double Jeopardy Clause.

Lockhart v. Nelson

Instant Facts: A reviewing court set aside the defendant's conviction because certain evidence was erroneously admitted against him, and further held that the Double Jeopardy Clause forbade the state to retry him.

Black Letter Rule: In a case where the evidence offered by the State and admitted by the trial court whether erroneously or not would have been sufficient to sustain a guilty verdict, the Double Jeopardy Clause does not preclude retrial.

Heath v. Alabama

Instant Facts: The defendant was tried and convicted in an Alabama Court for murdering his wife after he had already been convicted and sentenced in a Georgia court for the same crime.

Black Letter Rule: The dual sovereignty doctrine compels the conclusion that successive prosecutions by two States for the same conduct are not barred by the Double Jeopardy Clause.

Illinois v. Somerville

(*State*) v. (*Convicted*)
410 U.S. 458, 93 S.Ct. 1066 (1973)

A MISTRIAL GRANTED OVER DEFENDANT'S OBJECTION DOES NOT PRECLUDE A SECOND TRIAL IF THERE WAS A MANIFEST NECESSITY FOR THE MISTRIAL

■ **INSTANT FACTS** A mistrial was granted over Somerville's (D) objection based on a defective indictment. Somerville (D) was subsequently retried and convicted for theft.

■ **BLACK LETTER RULE** A declaration of mistrial over defendant's objection does not preclude a second trial where there is a "manifest necessity" for the mistrial or it is otherwise required by the "ends of public justice."

■ PROCEDURAL BASIS

Writ of habeas corpus after conviction in a second trial.

■ FACTS

Somerville (D) was indicted for theft. After the jury was sworn, but before any evidence was presented, the court granted the State's motion for a mistrial over the objection of Somerville (D). The mistrial was granted because the indictment was fatally defective for failure to allege the requisite intent. After a new trial and conviction, Somerville (D) sought a writ of habeas corpus alleging that the new trial violated his rights under the Double Jeopardy Clause.

■ ISSUE

Does a mistrial granted over the defendant's objection, because of a defective indictment, prevent the State from subsequently trying the defendant under a valid indictment?

■ DECISION AND RATIONALE

(Rehnquist, J.) No, not if the "manifest necessity" requirement was met. Here, we hold that it was met since the trial court reasonably concluded that the "ends of public justice" would be defeated by allowing the trial to continue. The case of *United States v. Perez* established the "manifest necessity" standard. The court there found that a trial judge has the authority to grant a mistrial whenever there is a manifest necessity for the act or the ends of public justice would otherwise be defeated. There is no mechanical formula to be followed in making this determination. Rather, the trial court may exercise its broad discretion based on the facts of each case. Some situations where a trial judge properly exercises her discretion to declare a mistrial are when an impartial verdict cannot be reached or if an error would make reversal on appeal a certainty. In the instant case, the trial court declared a mistrial because there was an incurable defect in the indictment. Illinois law holds that even after conviction, a defendant may be released if there was a defective indictment because such an indictment deprives the trial court of jurisdiction. Therefore, the trial court had to grant the mistrial to avoid an impartial verdict or a verdict that would certainly be reversed on appeal. Here, the delay to Somerville (D) was minimal, and a mistrial was the only way under Illinois law that the defect in the indictment could be cured. We cannot say that the decision was not required by "manifest necessity" or the "ends of public justice." Of course, the decision to abort a trial after jeopardy has attached should not be taken lightly. The defendant has an interest in being tried by the first jury impaneled. But here where the declaration of mistrial implements a reasonable state policy, and a verdict would have likely been upset, the defendant's interest in proceeding to a verdict is outweighed by the legitimate demand for public justice. Somerville's (D) conviction is sustained.

■ DISSENT

(White, J.) Even when the prosecutorial misconduct consists of a mistake, the defendant's interest in having the trial completed by the first jury prevails. In this case, the reason for the mistrial was the State's error. The conviction should be reversed.

■ DISSENT

(Marshall, J.) The court's balancing approach used here underemphasizes the defendant's interest in continuing with the trial. Continuation, in this case, was a viable alternative to a mistrial. Reversed.

Analysis:

This case is generally considered a retreat from the more strict treatment given to mistrials granted without the defendant's consent in earlier cases. The Court seems to be backing away from the defendant's right to be tried by the first jury impaneled. "Manifest necessity" most clearly exists where there is a hung jury or when a juror or the judge dies. When the defendant or his counsel causes the mistrial by making prejudicial remarks to the jury, double jeopardy does not prevent retrial. This makes sense because the defendant could purposely cause a mistrial and not be retried if he thought he was going to lose. Imagine defense attorneys around the country inventing creative ways to cause a mistrial.

■ CASE VOCABULARY

WRIT OF HABEAS CORPUS: A writ to test the legality of imprisonment rather than the guilt or innocence of the petitioner. It is a right guaranteed by the U.S.Const. Art. I, § 9, and also by state constitutions.

Oregon v. Kennedy

(*Government*) v. (*Oriental Rug Thief*)

456 U.S. 667, 102 S.Ct. 2083, 72 L.Ed.2d 416 (1982)

EVEN WHERE THE DEFENDANT MOVES FOR A MISTRIAL, THERE IS A NARROW EXCEPTION TO THE RULE THAT THE DOUBLE JEOPARDY CLAUSE IS NO BAR TO RETRIAL

■ **INSTANT FACTS** The defendant's motion to dismiss due to double jeopardy was granted after the prosecutor provoked the defendant into moving for a mistrial during his first trial.

■ **BLACK LETTER RULE** The circumstances under which a defendant who has successfully moved for a mistrial may invoke the bar of double jeopardy in a second effort to try him are limited to those cases in which the conduct giving rise to the successful motion for a mistrial was intended to provoke the defendant into moving for mistrial.

■ PROCEDURAL BASIS

Appeal from the Court of Appeals' reversal of the trial court's judgment against the defendant.

■ FACTS

Kennedy (D) was charged with the theft of an oriental rug. During his first trial, the State (P) called an expert witness on the subject to testify as to the value and the identity of the rug in question. On cross-examination, Kennedy's (D) attorney attempted to establish bias on the part of the expert witness by asking him whether he had filed a criminal complaint against Kennedy (D). The witness eventually responded that he had, but that no action had been taken on his complaint. On redirect examination, the prosecutor sought to elicit the reasons why the witness had filed the complaint, but the trial court sustained a series of objections to this line of inquiry. The prosecutor then asked the witness if he had ever done business with Kennedy (D). When the witness responded in the negative, the prosecutor asked him if it was because Kennedy (D) was a crook. The trial court then granted Kennedy's (D) motion for a mistrial. When the State (P) later sought to retry Kennedy (D), he moved to dismiss the charges because of double jeopardy. The trial court held that double jeopardy principles did not bar retrial, and Kennedy (D) was then tried and convicted. Kennedy (D) then appealed to the Court of Appeals, which sustained his double jeopardy claim.

■ ISSUE

May a defendant who has successfully moved for a mistrial invoke the bar of double jeopardy in a second effort to try him when the conduct which gave rise to the motion was intended to provoke the defendant into moving for mistrial?

■ DECISION AND RATIONALE

(Rehnquist, J.) Yes. Even where the defendant moves for a mistrial, there is a narrow exception to the rule that the Double Jeopardy Clause is no bar to retrial. The circumstances under which Kennedy's (D) first trial was terminated require us to delineate the bounds of that exception more fully than we have in previous cases. The precise phrasing of the circumstances which *will* allow a defendant to interpose the defense of double jeopardy to a second prosecution where the first has terminated on his own motion for a mistrial have been stated with less than crystal clarity in our cases which deal with this area of the law. The language in prior cases would seem to broaden the test from one of *intent* to provoke a motion for a mistrial to a more generalized standard of "bad faith conduct" or "harassment" on the part of the judge or prosecutor. It was upon this language that the Court of Appeals apparently relied in concluding that the prosecutor's colloquy with the expert witness in this case amount to "overreaching." Prosecutorial conduct that might be viewed as harassment or overreaching, even if sufficient to justify a mistrial on the defendant's motion, does not bar retrial absent intent on the part of the prosecutor to subvert the protections afforded by the Double Jeopardy Clause. A defendant's motion for a mistrial constitutes a deliberate election on his part to forgo his valued right to have his guilt or innocence determined before the first trier of fact. Where prosecutorial error even of a degree sufficient to warrant a mistrial has occurred, the important consideration, for purposes of the Double Jeopardy Clause, is that the defendant retain primary control over the course to be followed in the event of such an error. Only where the governmental conduct in question is intended to "goad" the defendant into moving for a mistrial may a defendant raise the bar of double jeopardy to a second trial after having succeeded in aborting the first on his own motion. We do not by this opinion lay down a flat rule that where a defendant in a criminal trial successfully moves for a mistrial, he may not thereafter invoke the bar of double jeopardy against a second trial. But we do hold that the circumstances under which such a defendant may invoke the bar of double jeopardy in a second effort to try him are limited to those cases in which the conduct giving rise to the successful motion for a mistrial was intended to provoke the defendant into moving for a mistrial. Since the trial court found, and the Court of Appeals accepted, that the prosecutorial conduct culminating in the termination of the first trial in this case was not so intended by the prosecutor, that is the end of the matter for purposes of the Double Jeopardy Clause of the Fifth Amendment of the United States Constitution.

■ CONCURRENCE

(Brennan, J.) I concur in the judgment and join in the opinion of Justice Stevens. However, it should be noted that nothing in the holding of the Court today prevents the state courts, on remand, from concluding that Kennedy's (D) retrial would violate the provision of the State Constitution that prohibits double jeopardy.

■ CONCURRENCE

(Powell, J.) I join the Court's opinion that the *intention* of a prosecutor determines whether his conduct, viewed by the defendant and the court as justifying a mistrial, bars a retrial of the defendant under the Double Jeopardy Clause. Because "subjective" intent often may be unknowable, I emphasize that a court—in considering a double jeopardy motion—should rely primarily upon the objective facts and circumstances of the particular case.

■ CONCURRENCE

(Stevens, J.) Today the Court once again recognizes that the exception properly encompasses the situation in which the prosecutor commits prejudicial error with the intent to provoke a mistrial. But the Court reaches out to limit the exception to that one situation, rejecting the previous recognition that prosecutorial overreaching or harassment is also within the exception. Even if I agreed that the balance of competing interests tipped in favor of a bar to reprosecution only in the situation in which the prosecutor intended to provoke a mistrial, I would not subscribe to a standard that conditioned such a bar on the determination that the prosecutor harbored such intent when he committed prejudicial error. It is almost inconceivable that a defendant could prove that the prosecutor's deliberate misconduct was motivated by an intent to provoke a mistrial instead of an intent simply to prejudice the defendant. The defendant must shoulder a strong burden to establish a bar to reprosecution when he has consented to the mistrial, but the Court's subjective intent standard would eviscerate the exception.

Analysis:

Kennedy's holding does a good job of balancing both sides' interests. Remember, one policy reason for extending the "double jeopardy" rule to some trials ending in mistrial is to prevent the prosecution from misconduct forcing a mistrial, solely to avoid a final acquittal and allow later reprosecution.

However, similarly, the defense should also be stopped from forcing a mistrial solely to prevent retrial. Here, the court reconciles both interests. Under its holding, if the defendant moves for mistrial, then (generally) retrial is allowed. But if the defendant's motion for mistrial is effectively necessitated by the prosecutor's own conduct, then that's equivalent to the prosecution forcing a retrial to gain tactical advantage, and should bar reprosecution, for policy reasons.

■ CASE VOCABULARY

DOUBLE JEOPARDY: Constitutional guarantee which protects against a second prosecution for the same offense after acquittal or conviction, and against multiple punishments for the same offense.

MISTRIAL: A device used to halt trial proceedings when error is so prejudicial and fundamental that the expenditure of further time and expense would be wasteful if not futile.

REDIRECT EXAMINATION: An examination of a witness by the direct examiner subsequent to the cross-examination of the witness.

SUA SPONTE: Of its own will or motion, without prompting or suggesting.

United States v. Scott

(*Government*) v. (*Drug Dealing Cop*)

437 U.S. 82, 98 S.Ct. 2187, 57 L.Ed.2d 65 (1978)

NO INTEREST PROTECTED BY THE DOUBLE JEOPARDY CLAUSE IS INVADED WHEN THE GOVERNMENT IS ALLOWED TO APPEAL AND SEEK REVERSAL OF A DISMISSAL OF THE INDICTMENT

■ **INSTANT FACTS** An indictment against a drug-dealing cop was dismissed on the grounds of prejudice, and the Government was prohibited from appealing the dismissal based on the Double Jeopardy Clause.

■ **BLACK LETTER RULE** Where the defendant himself seeks to have the trial terminated without any submission to either judge or jury as to his guilt or innocence, an appeal by the Government from his successful effort to do so is not barred by the Double Jeopardy Clause.

■ PROCEDURAL BASIS

Appeal from the Court of Appeals' affirmance of the trial court's grant of the defendant's motion to dismiss two counts of the indictment against him.

■ FACTS

Scott (D), a member of the police force, was charged with distribution of various narcotics. Both before his trial, and twice during the trial, Scott (D) moved to dismiss the two counts of the indictment on the ground that his defense had been prejudiced by preindictment delay. At the close of all the evidence, the court granted Scott's (D) motion. The Government (P) sought to appeal the dismissals of the counts, however the Court of Appeals, relying on the Court's opinion in *United States v. Jenkins,* concluded that any further prosecution of Scott (D) was barred by the Double Jeopardy Clause, and therefore dismissed the appeal. The Government sought review to this Court, and certiorari was granted.

■ ISSUE

Does the Double Jeopardy Clause prohibit a Governmental appeal from an order granting the defendant's motions to terminate a trial before the verdict?

■ DECISION AND RATIONALE

(Rehnquist, J.) No. In *Jenkins,* we held that whether or not a dismissal of an indictment after jeopardy had attached amounted to an acquittal on the merits, the Government (P) had no right to appeal, because further proceedings of some sort, devoted to the resolution of factual issues going to the elements of the offense charged, would have been required upon reversal and remand. If *Jenkins* is a correct statement of the law, the judgment of the Court of Appeals relying on that decision, as it was bound to do, would in all likelihood have to be affirmed. Yet, our vastly increased exposure to the various facets of the Double Jeopardy Clause has now convinced us that *Jenkins* was wrongly decided. It placed an unwarrantedly great emphasis on the defendant's right to have his guilt decided by the first jury empaneled to try him so as to include those cases where the defendant himself seeks to terminate the trial before verdict on grounds unrelated to factual guilt or innocence. We have therefore decided to overrule *Jenkins,* and thus to reverse the judgment of the Court of Appeals in this case. We turn now to the relationship between the Double Jeopardy Clause and reprosecution of a defendant who has successfully obtained not a mistrial, but a termination of the trial in his favor before any determination of factual guilt or innocence. Unlike the typical mistrial, the granting of a motion such as this obviously contemplates that the proceedings will terminate then and there in favor of the defendant. The prosecution, if it wishes to reinstate the proceedings in the face of such a ruling, ordinarily must seek reversal of the decision of the trial court. *Jenkins* held that, regardless of the character of the mistrial termination, appeal was barred if further proceedings of some sort, devoted to the resolution of factual issues going to the elements of the offense charged, would have been required upon reversal and remand. However, in *Lee v. United States,* the Government was permitted to institute a second prosecution after a midtrial dismissal of an indictment. The Court found the circumstances presented by that case functionally indistinguishable from a declaration of a mistrial. Thus, *Lee* demonstrated that, at least in some cases, the dismissal of an indictment may be treated on the same basis as the declaration of a mistrial. Our growing experience with Government appeals convinces us that we must reexamine the rationale of *Jenkins* in light of *Lee* and other recent expositions of the Double Jeopardy Clause. It is quite true that the Government with all its resources and power should not be allowed to make repeated attempts to convict an individual for an alleged offense. This truth is expressed in the three common-law pleas of autrefois acquit, autrefois convict, and pardon, which lie at the core of the area protected by the Double Jeopardy Clause. But that situation is obviously a far cry from the present case, where the Government (P) was quite willing to continue with its production of evidence to show the defendant guilty before the jury first empaneled to try him, but the defendant elected to seek termination of the trial on grounds unrelated to guilt or innocence. This is scarcely a picture of an all-powerful state relentlessly pursuing a defendant who had either been found not guilty or who had at least insisted on having the issue of guilt submitted to the first trier of fact. It is instead a picture of a defendant who chooses to avoid conviction and imprisonment, not because of his assertion that the Government (P) has failed to make out a case against him, but because of a legal claim that the Government's (P) case against him must fail even though it might satisfy the trier of fact that he was guilty beyond a reasonable doubt. The dismissal of an indictment for preindictment delay represents a legal judgment that a defendant, although criminally culpable, may not be punished because of a supposed constitutional violation. It is obvious from what we have said that we believe we pressed too far in *Jenkins,* the concept of the defendant's valued right to have his trial contemplated by a particular tribunal. We now conclude that where the defendant himself seeks to have the trial terminated without any submission to either judge or jury as to his guilt or innocence, an appeal by the Government (P) from his successful effort to do so is not barred by the Double Jeopardy Clause.

■ DISSENT

(Brennan, J.) The whole premise for today's retreat from *Jenkins* is the Court's new theory that a criminal defendant who seeks to avoid conviction on a ground "unrelated to factual innocence" somehow stands on a different constitutional footing than a defendant whose participation in his criminal trial creates a situation in which a judgment of acquittal has to be entered. This premise is simply untenable. The reasons that bar a retrial following an acquittal are equally applicable to a final judgment entered on a ground "unrelated to factual innocence." The heavy personal strain of the second trial is the same in either case. So too is the risk that, though innocent, the defendant may be found guilty at a second trial. If the appeal is allowed in either situation, the Government (P) will, following any reversal, not only obtain the benefit of the favorable appellate ruling but also be permitted to shore up any other weak points of its case and obtain all the other advantages at the second trial that the Double Jeopardy Clause was designed to forbid.

Analysis:

Previously in the 1900s, the Court held the prosecution could never appeal criminal cases, absent explicit statutory authority. Thus, Congress was forced to enact the Criminal Appeals Act of 1097, which permitted appeal from a dismissal of the indictment, or similar grounds. At the time the Fifth Amendment's double jeopardy rule was enacted, the issue of appeals from dismissed indictments and other "technical" dismissals arose rarely, because most trials proceeded to a final verdict. But the policy underlying the double jeopardy rule is not just to preserve *final* judgements' finality, but also simply to avoid multiple, inconclusive prosecutions. But it is felt that, when the defendant himself manages to have a case dismissed for reasons unrelated to his innocence, before the jury he impaneled is allowed to decide, then he has not been "deprived" of any right to submit his case to his regularly-impaneled jury. In other words, the government's interest in having the case decided on the merits is stronger.

■ CASE VOCABULARY

AUTREFOIS ACQUIT: The name of a plea to a criminal action, stating that the defendant has been once already indicted and tried for the same alleged offense and has been acquitted.

AUTREFOIS CONVICT: A plea in a criminal action to an indictment that the defendant has been formerly convicted of the same crime.

PARDON: An executive action that mitigates or sets aside punishment for a crime.

VEL NON: "Or not."

Lockhart v. Nelson

(*Prosecution*) v. (*Habitual Criminal*)

488 U.S. 33, 109 S.Ct. 285, 102 L.Ed.2d 265 (1988)

THE DOUBLE JEOPARDY CLAUSE DOES NOT BAR THE RETRIAL OF A DEFENDANT WHO HAS SUCCEEDED IN GETTING HIS CONVICTION SET ASIDE FOR ERROR IN THE PROCEEDINGS BELOW

■ **INSTANT FACTS** A reviewing court set aside the defendant's conviction because certain evidence was erroneously admitted against him, and further held that the Double Jeopardy Clause forbade the state to retry him.

■ **BLACK LETTER RULE** In a case where the evidence offered by the State and admitted by the trial court—whether erroneously or not—would have been sufficient to sustain a guilty verdict, the Double Jeopardy Clause does not preclude retrial.

■ PROCEDURAL BASIS

Appeal from the Court of Appeals' affirmance of the District Court's judgment in favor of the defendant.

■ FACTS

Nelson (D) pleaded guilty to burglary. He was sentenced under the State's habitual criminal statute, which provides that a defendant who has previously been convicted of four or more felonies may be sentenced to an enhanced term of imprisonment of between 20 and 40 years. To have a convicted defendant's sentence enhanced under the statute, the State must prove beyond a reasonable doubt, at a separate sentencing hearing, that the defendant has the requisite number of prior felony convictions. The defendant is entitled to challenge the State's evidence of his prior convictions and to rebut it with evidence of his own. At Nelson's (D) sentencing hearing, the State (P) introduced, without objection from the defense, certified copies of four prior felony convictions. Unbeknownst to the prosecutor, one of these convictions had been pardoned by the Governor several years after its entry. Defense counsel made no objection to the admission of the pardoned conviction, because he too was unaware of the Governor's action. On cross-examination, Nelson (D) indicated his belief that the conviction in question had been pardoned. Under questioning from the court, it was decided that the conviction had been commuted rather than pardoned, and the matter was not pursued any further. Nelson (D) was given an enhanced sentence, which was upheld on both direct and collateral review, despite Nelson's (D) protestations that one of the convictions relied upon by the State had been pardoned. Several years later, Nelson (D) sought a writ of habeas corpus in District Court, contending once again that the enhanced sentence was invalid because one of the prior convictions had been pardoned. When an investigation undertaken by the State at the Court's request revealed that the conviction had in fact been pardoned, the District Court declared the enhanced sentence to be invalid. The State announced its intention to resentence Nelson (D) as a habitual offender, using another prior conviction not offered or admitted at the initial sentencing hearing, and Nelson (D) interposed a claim of double jeopardy. The District Court decided that the Double Jeopardy Clause prevented the State from attempting to resentence Nelson (D) as a habitual offender on the burglary charge, and the Court of Appeals affirmed. The Court of Appeals reasoned that the pardoned conviction was not admissible under state law, and that without it, the state failed to provide sufficient evidence to sustain the enhanced sentence. This Court granted certiorari to review this interpretation of the Double Jeopardy Clause.

■ ISSUE

Does the Double Jeopardy Clause preclude retrial in a case where the evidence offered by the State and admitted by the trial court—whether erroneously or not—would have been sufficient to sustain a guilty verdict?

■ DECISION AND RATIONALE

(Rehnquist, C.J.) No. It has long been settled that the Double Jeopardy Clause's general prohibition against successive prosecutions does not prevent the government from retrying a defendant who succeeds in getting his first conviction set aside, through direct appeal or collateral attack, because of some error in the proceedings leading to conviction. This rule, which is a well established part of our constitutional jurisprudence, is necessary in order to ensure the sound administration of justice. In *Burks v. United States,* we recognized an exception to the general rule that the Double Jeopardy Clause does not bar the retrial of a defendant who has succeeded in getting his conviction set aside for error in the proceedings below. *Burks* held that when a defendant's conviction is reversed by an appellate court on the sole ground that the evidence was insufficient to sustain the jury's verdict, the Double Jeopardy Clause bars a retrial on the same charge. *Burks* was careful to point out that a reversal based solely on evidentiary insufficiency has fundamentally different implications, for double jeopardy purposes, that a reversal based on such ordinary "trial errors" as the incorrect receipt or rejection of evidence. While the former is in effect a finding that the government has failed to prove its case against the defendant, the latter implies nothing with respect to the guilt or innocence of the defendant, but is simply a determination that he has been convicted through a judicial *process* which is defective in some fundamental respect. It appears to us beyond dispute that this is a situation described in *Burks* as reversal for "trial error"—the trial court erred in admitting a particular piece of evidence, and without it there was insufficient evidence to support a judgment of conviction. But clearly *with* that evidence, there was enough to support the sentence: the court and the jury had before them certified copies of four prior felony convictions, and that is sufficient to support a verdict of enhancement under the statute. The fact that one of the convictions had been later pardoned by the Governor vitiated its legal effect, but it did not deprive the certified copy of that conviction of its probative value under the statute. Permitting retrial in this instance is not the sort of governmental oppression at which the Double Jeopardy Clause is aimed; rather, it serves the interest of the defendant by affording him an opportunity to obtain a fair readjudication of his guilt free from error. Had Nelson (D) offered evidence at the sentencing hearing to prove that the conviction had become a nullity by reason of the pardon, the trial judge would presumably have allowed the prosecutor an opportunity to offer evidence of another prior conviction to support the habitual offender charge. Our holding today thus merely recreates the situation that would have been obtained if the trial court had excluded the evidence of the conviction because of the showing of a pardon. The judgment of the Court of Appeals is accordingly reversed.

■ DISSENT

(Marshall, J.) The majority errs in treating this as a case of mere trial error, and in reaching the unsettled issue of whether, after a trial error reversal based on the improper admission of evidence, a reviewing court should evaluate the sufficiency of the evidence by including, or excluding, the tainted evidence.

Analysis:

The decision here is based on a balancing of interests; the accused's right to a fair trial, versus society's interest in punishing the guilty. The Court decided, properly, that too many guilty criminals would walk free if every reversible error automatically created a non-appealable acquittal. *Burks*, cited in this opinion, shows that when a court considers the issue of whether retrial should be permitted, it should consider *all* the evidence admitted by the trial court. Similarly, the reviewing court should use the same level of proof as the trial court used.

■ CASE VOCABULARY

COLLATERAL ATTACK: An attack made by or in an action or proceeding that has an independent purpose other than impeaching or overturning a judgment.

COMMUTATION: The change of a punishment to one which is less severe.

RATIO DECIDENDI: The ground or reason of decision.

SENTENCE ENHANCEMENT: A statutory provision which allows for an increased penalty to a defendant based upon the fact that he has been previously convicted of a crime.

Heath v. Alabama

(*Wife Murderer*) v. (*Government*)

474 U.S. 82, 106 S.Ct. 433, 88 L.Ed.2d 387 (1985)

WHEN THE SAME ACT VIOLATES THE LAWS OF TWO SOVEREIGNS, A PERSON HAS COMMITTED TWO OFFENSES, FOR EACH OF WHICH HE MAY BE PUNISHED

■ **INSTANT FACTS** The defendant was tried and convicted in an Alabama Court for murdering his wife after he had already been convicted and sentenced in a Georgia court for the same crime.

■ **BLACK LETTER RULE** The dual sovereignty doctrine compels the conclusion that successive prosecutions by two States for the same conduct are not barred by the Double Jeopardy Clause.

■ PROCEDURAL BASIS

Appeal from the Alabama Court's conviction of the defendant after a Georgia Court had convicted the defendant for the same offense.

■ FACTS

Heath (D) hired two men to kill his wife. He met the men in Georgia, and led them back to his home in Alabama. Heath then gave the men the keys to his car and house, and left the premises in his girlfriend's truck. The two men then kidnapped Mrs. Heath from her home. The Heath car, with Mrs. Heath's body inside, was later found on the side of a road in Georgia. The cause of death was a gunshot wound in the head. The estimated time of death and the distance from the Heath residence to the spot where Mrs. Heath's body was found are consistent with the theory that the murder took place in Georgia, and Heath (D) does not contend otherwise. Georgia and Alabama authorities pursued dual investigations in which they cooperated to some extent. Georgia indicted Heath (D) for the offense of malice murder. Heath (D) pleaded guilty to the Georgia murder charge in exchange for a sentence of life imprisonment, which he understood could involve his serving as few as seven years in prison. Three months after Heath's (D) guilty plea in the Georgia Court, Alabama returned an indictment against Heath (D) for the capital offense of murder during a kidnapping. Before trial on this indictment, Heath (D) entered pleas of autrefois convict and former jeopardy under the Alabama and United States Constitutions, arguing that his conviction and sentence in Georgia barred his prosecution in Alabama for the same conduct. After a hearing, the trial court rejected Heath's (D) double jeopardy claims. Heath (D) was subsequently found guilty of the murder and sentenced to death. Heath (D) sought a writ of certiorari from this Court, which was granted.

■ ISSUE

Does the dual sovereignty doctrine permit successive prosecutions under the laws of different States for the same conduct?

■ DECISION AND RATIONALE

(O'Connor, J.) Yes. Successive prosecutions are barred by the Fifth Amendment only if the two offenses for which the defendant is prosecuted are the "same" for double jeopardy purposes. Alabama (P) does not contravene Heath's (D) contention that the offenses "murder during a kidnapping" and "malice murder" may be considered greater and lesser offenses and, thus, the "same" offense absent operation of the dual sovereignty principle. We, therefore, assume arguendo that, had these offenses arisen under the laws of one State, the second conviction would have been barred by the Double Jeopardy Clause. The sole question upon which we granted certiorari is whether the dual sovereignty doctrine permits successive prosecutions under the laws of different States which otherwise would be held to subject the defendant for the same offense to be put twice in jeopardy. Although we have not previously so held, we believe the answer to this query inescapable. The dual sovereignty doctrine, as originally articulated and consistently applied by this Court, compels the conclusion that successive prosecutions by two States for the same conduct are not barred by the Double Jeopardy Clause. The dual sovereignty doctrine is founded on the common law conception of crime as an offense against the sovereignty of the government. When a defendant in a single act violates the "peace and dignity" of two sovereigns by breaking the laws of each, he has committed two distinct offenses. Consequently, when the same act transgresses the laws of two sovereigns, it cannot truly be said that the offender has been twice punished for the same offense; but only that by one act he has committed two offenses, for each of which he is justly punishable. It is axiomatic that in America, the powers of sovereignty are divided between the government of the Union, and those of the States. They are each sovereign, with respect to the objects committed to the other. Foremost among the prerogatives of sovereignty is the power to create and enforce a criminal code. To deny a State its power to enforce its criminal laws because another State has won the race to the courthouse would be a shocking and untoward deprivation of the historic right and obligation of the States to maintain peace and order within their confines. Such a deprivation of a State's sovereign powers cannot be justified by the assertion that under an "interest Analysis:" the State's legitimate penal interest will be satisfied through a prosecution conducted by another State. A State's interest in vindicating its sovereign authority through enforcement of its laws by definition can never be satisfied by another State's enforcement of its own laws. Just as the Federal Government has the right to decide that a state prosecution has not vindicated a violation of the "peace and dignity" of the Federal Government, a State must be entitled to decide that a prosecution by another State has not satisfied its legitimate sovereign interest. In recognition of this fact, the Court consistently has endorsed the principle that a single act constitutes an "offense" against each sovereign whose laws are violated by that act. We have always understood the words of the Double Jeopardy Clause to reflect this fundamental principle, and we see no reason why we should reconsider that understanding today. Affirmed.

■ DISSENT

(Marshall, J.) Where two States seek to prosecute the same defendant for the same crime in two separate proceedings, the justifications found in the federal-state context for an exemption from double jeopardy constraints simply do not hold. Although the two States may have opted for different policies within their assigned territorial jurisdictions, the sovereign concerns with whose vindication each State has been charged are identical. Thus, in contrast to the federal-state context, barring the second prosecution would still permit one government to act upon the broad range of sovereign concerns that would have been reserved to the States by the Constitution. The compelling need in the federal-state context to subordinate double jeopardy concerns is thus considerably diminished in cases involving successive prosecutions by different States. Moreover, from the defendant's perspective, the burden of successive prosecutions cannot be justified as the quid pro quo of dual citizenship. Whether viewed as a violation of the Double Jeopardy Clause or simply as an affront to the due process guarantee of fundamental fairness, Alabama's prosecution of Heath (D) cannot survive constitutional scrutiny. I therefore must dissent.

Analysis:

In applying the "dual sovereignty" doctrine, the question is whether the two prosecuting jurisdictions can be termed separate "sovereigns," meaning they derive their authority from distinct sources. States are deemed separate from the federal government, since they have their own traditionally-recognized power to punish crimes within their borders, which is recognized by the Tenth Amendment. Similarly, states are separate from each other. Really, the only case where sovereigns are *not* deemed separate is the case of a state and one of its cities or municipalities. That's because such lesser governments are deemed mere creations, or instrumentalities, of the state.

■ CASE VOCABULARY

ARGUENDO: In the course of the argument.

DUAL SOVEREIGNTY DOCTRINE: When a defendant in a single act violates the "peace and dignity" of two sovereigns by breaking the laws of each, he has committed two distinct offenses, for which he may be punished.

DUE PROCESS CLAIMS: Claims of the violation of procedural and substantive rights of citizens against government actions that threaten the denial of life, liberty, or property.

MALICE MURDER: That condition of the mind which prompts one to take the life of another without just cause, legal justification, or provocation.

QUID PRO QUO: The giving of something for something else; mutual consideration.

CHAPTER TWENTY–SEVEN

Sentencing

Williams v. New York

Instant Facts: A jury found a man guilty of murder and recommended life imprisonment, but the trial judge disregarded the jury's recommendation and sentenced the man to death.

Black Letter Rule: A trial judge in his discretion is entitled to consider a broad range of factors when deciding upon a sentence, even though the information has been obtained outside the courtroom and from persons the defendant has not had the opportunity to cross-examine.

United States v. Booker

Instant Facts: After additional evidence was found at the defendants' sentencing hearings, one was sentenced to enhanced penalties under the Sentencing Guidelines, while the other was not.

Black Letter Rule: The Sixth Amendment applies to the imposition of criminal sentencing under the Federal Sentencing Guidelines.

Williams v. New York

(*Murderer*) v. (*State*)

337 U.S. 241, 69 S.Ct. 1079 (1949)

A JUDGE MAY CONSIDER OUT-OF-COURT INFORMATION AND UNRELATED CRIMINAL CONDUCT WHEN IMPOSING A SENTENCE WITHOUT VIOLATING DUE PROCESS

■ **INSTANT FACTS** A jury found a man guilty of murder and recommended life imprisonment, but the trial judge disregarded the jury's recommendation and sentenced the man to death.

■ **BLACK LETTER RULE** A trial judge in his discretion is entitled to consider a broad range of factors when deciding upon a sentence, even though the information has been obtained outside the courtroom and from persons the defendant has not had the opportunity to cross-examine.

■ PROCEDURAL BASIS

Appeal to United States Supreme Court of death sentence imposed by trial court and affirmed by New York Court of Appeals.

■ FACTS

Williams (D) was tried and convicted of first degree murder. The jury recommended a sentence of life imprisonment. Williams' (D) lawyers [all three of them] appealed to the judge to accept the jury's recommendation and Williams (D) himself proclaimed his innocence. [Surprise, surprise.] The trial judge considered the jury's recommendation, but sentenced Williams (D) to death. In imposing the sentence, the judge considered information revealed by the presentence report along with factors such as non-convicted criminal activity and Williams' (D) moral indecency. He openly expressed his belief in Williams' (D) guilt and referred to thirty other burglaries in the same vicinity for which Williams (D) was believed to be responsible. Williams' (D) attorneys did not challenge any of the judge's statements or ask for an opportunity to refute or discredit the allegations.

■ ISSUE

May a judge properly consider out-of-court information that would have been inadmissible against a defendant at trial for purposes of sentencing without violating due process?

■ DECISION AND RATIONALE

(Black, J.) Yes. A judge may properly consider a broad range of factors that may not have been admissible against the defendant at trial when he is deciding upon a sentence. There is no constitutional infirmity associated with such a practice. There is a distinct difference between the guilt-determining phase of a trial and the sentencing phase. Until a verdict has been reached, the defendant is presumed innocent and the strict evidentiary rules of trial have been fashioned to ensure that only relevant evidence is admitted. After a guilty verdict is returned, however, that presumption is no longer applicable. Historically, judges have been able to consider a wide variety of factors, consisting of both admissible and inadmissible evidence, to assist them in issuing appropriate sentences. The sentencing judge must possess the fullest information possible concerning the defendant's life and characteristics to impose a sentence that is appropriately individualized. It would be unconscionable to deny judges the opportunity to obtain all pertinent information necessary to impose an adequate sentence by restricting them to information given in open court and subject to cross-examination. Affirmed.

■ DISSENT

(Murphy, J.) Due process requires that a person be afforded a fair hearing throughout every phase of a trial. As sentencing is a phase like any other in a trial, the procedures required by due process should be required. In a capital case, such as this one, where the judge relied upon a sentencing report that would have been inadmissible at trial and the defendant was not given an opportunity to refute the report, I am convinced that due process was lacking.

Analysis:

Although a 1949 case, *Williams* is still good law. The Supreme Court has cited it regularly with approval when faced with a due process challenge to discretionary sentencing. Williams' (D) counsel were essentially arguing that the rules of evidence that apply to the pre-verdict portion of the trial should apply also to sentencing. If the Court had accepted their argument, it would mean that highly relevant and dependable evidence that would be helpful in determining an appropriate sentence would be unavailable to the judge. That is so because the rules of evidence were created so that only evidence relevant to the *specific offense charged* is admissible at trial. The defendant's past conduct, lifestyle, and criminal history are rarely relevant to whether he committed the offense charged. (There are exceptions, of course, when past conduct and criminal history are relevant. There are also instances where highly relevant evidence is still inadmissible due to extreme prejudice or lack of dependability.) The Court rejected the invitation to apply the same due process requirements to both the guilt determining and the sentencing phases of trial, reasoning that the two phases have distinctly different goals. The pre-verdict phase has the all-important goal of determining the defendant's innocence or guilt. Because our system presumes innocence, it is necessary to have the highly rigid structure of the evidence rules to protect a defendant and ensure the fairest possible trial. But after a guilty verdict is returned, it is more important for the judge to have at his disposal *all* relevant evidence so that he may impose a sentence that is in tune with the gravity of the offense, the attendant circumstances and the characteristics of the individual defendant.

United States v. Booker

(*Prosecuting Authority*) v. (*Convicted Drug Dealer*)
___ U.S. ___, 125 S.Ct. 738, 160 L.Ed.2d 621 (2005)

SENTENCING MUST BE BASED ON FACTS DETERMINED BY A JURY BEYOND A REASONABLE DOUBT

■ **INSTANT FACTS** After additional evidence was found at the defendants' sentencing hearings, one was sentenced to enhanced penalties under the Sentencing Guidelines, while the other was not.

■ **BLACK LETTER RULE** The Sixth Amendment applies to the imposition of criminal sentencing under the Federal Sentencing Guidelines.

■ PROCEDURAL BASIS

Certiorari to review the defendants' sentences.

■ FACTS

Booker (D) was convicted of possession of at least fifty grams of crack cocaine with intent to distribute under 21 U.S.C. § 841(a)(1). The offense carries a minimum ten-year prison sentence, with a maximum sentence of life. Based on Booker's (D) criminal history and the quantity of drugs involved, the Sentencing Guidelines required the judge to establish a base sentence between 210 and 262 months in prison. At a post-trial sentencing hearing, the judge concluded by a preponderance of the evidence that Booker (D) possessed an additional 566 grams of crack beyond that found by the jury and that he was also guilty of obstructing justice. Those offenses required a base sentence between 360 months and life in prison. Booker (D) was sentenced to thirty years in prison rather than the twenty-one years and ten months that could have been imposed under the jury's verdict. The Seventh Circuit Court of Appeals determined on appeal that the application of the Sentencing Guidelines violated the Sixth Amendment and remanded for resentencing or a new sentencing hearing before the jury.

In a consolidated case, Fanfan (D) was convicted of conspiracy to distribute and to possess with intent to distribute at least 500 grams of cocaine in violation of 21 U.S.C. §§ 846, 841(a)(1), and 841(b). Based on the Sentencing Guidelines, Fanfan's (D) sentence was a maximum of seventy-eight months. At the sentencing hearing, the judge determined by a preponderance of the evidence that Fanfan (D) possessed more cocaine than found by the jury, enhancing the possible sentence to fifteen or sixteen years rather than five or six years under the jury's verdict. A few days after the Court's decision in *Blakely v. Washington*, the judge sentenced Fanfan (D) by applying the Sentencing Guidelines to the jury's verdict without consideration of the additional evidence.

Issue I: Does the Sixth Amendment apply to the Federal Sentencing Guidelines?

■ DECISION AND RATIONALE

(Stevens, J.) Yes. Under *Apprendi v. New Jersey*, 530 U.S. 466 (2000), "any fact that increases the penalty for a crime beyond the prescribed statutory maximum must be submitted to a jury, and proved beyond a reasonable doubt." Likewise, in *Blakely v. Washington*, 542 U.S. 296 (2004), the Court established that any sentencing scheme that predicated an enhanced sentence on a judge's findings of "aggravating facts" by a preponderance of the evidence violated the Sixth Amendment because the defendant is entitled to trial by jury. The Sentencing Guidelines prescribe a mandatory range of sentences to be imposed in a given case and deprive the court of meaningful discretion to depart from their requirements. Because the Guidelines require, rather than recommend, a specified course of judicial action, they have the force of laws and the Sixth Amendment applies. While the Guidelines permit some limited discretion to depart from the required sentencing range, this departure is limited to rare cases, and these situations are too limited to bring the application of the Guidelines out from under the Sixth Amendment. Indeed, in Booker's (D) case, the judge would have been reversed if he had imposed a lesser sentence than the Guidelines required on the jury's verdict. The judge, however, enhanced the penalty upon evidence found by a preponderance of the evidence and not determined by the jury. Because the defendant's sentence must be authorized by the jury's sentence, the enhanced penalty violates the Sixth Amendment.

Although the Sentencing Guidelines were promulgated by the Sentencing Commission, rather than by legislative action as in *Blakely*, the infringement on the defendant's Sixth Amendment rights are the same. It matters not whether the source of the infringement is legislative, so long as the authority requires the court to determine facts by a preponderance of the evidence in violation of the Sixth Amendment. Similarly, the Guidelines' insistence on a jury determination of the fact supporting the sentence does not offend the separation of powers doctrine. The Commission has performed no adjudicatory function, and it is perfectly within the legislative purview to delegate non-adjudicatory tasks to independent agencies.

While jury factfinding may impair swift, efficient sentencing, the threats to the defendant's Sixth Amendment rights are too great to empower factfinding authority to the court. *Apprendi* is reaffirmed, and all facts supporting the defendant's sentence must be determined by a jury beyond a reasonable doubt.

■ DISSENT IN PART

(Breyer, J.) Facts relevant to a crime are not the same as facts relevant to sentencing, and the Constitution affords no right to a jury trial over sentencing facts. Legislatures have traditionally and constitutionally been vested the power to specify criminal sentences. Yet, the Guidelines are administrative rules, not legislative statutes. There is less justification for imposing constitutional restraints on rules than there is on statutes.

Issue II: Does severance of the unconstitutional mandatory sentencing provisions from the Sentencing Act best serve the legislative intent?

■ DECISION AND RATIONALE

(Breyer, J.) Yes. Because the Sixth Amendment applies to the Sentencing Guidelines, those provisions requiring the sentencing judge to impose a sentence under the Guidelines are unconstitutional. To determine the remedy for the constitutional violation, the Court must review the legislative intent of the Act in light of the Court's holding.

By striking the mandatory provisions, Congress's design for the Act is altered, for no longer may judicial factfinding support the court's sentencing function. Leaving the mandatory provisions but inserting the Court's constitutional requirements of jury review into the Act would, however, grossly strain congressional intent.

First, the new requirement would involve a reinterpretation of the term "the court" to mean "the court working together with the jury." But the design of the statute does not provide for the jury's involvement at the sentencing phase, placing the revised statute "plainly contrary to the intent of Congress." Second, the new requirement would destroy Congress's goal of consistency in federal sentencing. Judges often consider information not presented to the jury, such as presentence reports, to determine the appropriate sentence. Denial of such crucial information would weaken the tie between the sentence imposed and the real conduct of the defendant, resulting in disparate sentences among similar offenders. Third, a requirement that the jury determine the aggravating circumstances involved in a crime would unduly complicate criminal proceedings. No longer would jurors be required to determine only whether a crime was committed, but also how and by what degree of egregious conduct. Fourth, the new requirements would affect sentencing on a plea bargain because the statute would apply equally to convictions at trial and to guilty pleas. Judges, however, would be prohibited from considering presentence reports and other evidence of aggravating circumstances to impose an appropriate penalty, for such information has not been presented to the jury and established beyond a reasonable doubt. Under such a system, prosecutors, not judges, would determine the severity of a sentence by choosing which information to include in the plea, regardless of the defendant's actual conduct. Finally, the revised system would make it easier to adjust a sentence downward than it would upward. Congress could not have intended such an effect.

Because Congress could not have intended the Act as it would result with the insertion of the jury requirement, severance is necessary to leave the Act constitutional. To save the Act, the Court must retain those portions that are constitutionally valid, capable of functioning independently and consistent with Congress' basic objectives. Accordingly, the provisions requiring sentencing courts to impose a sentence within the applicable Guidelines range and setting forth standards of review on appeal must be stricken. By striking these two provisions, sentencing courts may still impose sentences within a suggested range and must also consider the seriousness of the offense. Likewise, defendants retain their appeal rights to determine whether the sentence is unreasonable. Although this course undermines Congress's goal of establishing consistency of sentencing for similar offenses, it is the best alternative to constitutionally serve those objectives. Should Congress desire a different course, it is free to legislatively revise the statute under terms meeting the Court's constitutional demands.

Because Booker's (D) sentence was vacated as beyond the reach of the Sentencing Guidelines, it is affirmed and remanded for resentencing. Similarly, because Fanfan's sentence was properly imposed under the jury's findings, there was no Sixth Amendment violation. However, the matter is remanded for resentencing so that the Government may benefit from the Court's holding.

■ DISSENT IN PART

(Stevens, J.) Nothing in the mandatory provisions stricken by the Court is facially unconstitutional. In fact, the vast majority of criminal cases are disposed of on plea bargains and a large portion of those that go to trial involve no sentence enhancements at all. The statutes themselves do not violate the Sixth Amendment, but rather judicial administration of them *may* be unconstitutional in given situations. While Congress has the authority to repeal the statutes, the Court has undertaken legislative action beyond the scope of its constitutional authority. Instead, the Court should merely demand the insertion of language complying with its Sixth Amendment mandate and leave the statutes to exist. The sentencing court would be free to consider information contained in a presentence report or the prosecution could ensure that the necessary facts for an enhanced sentence are presented and proven to a jury. While such a requirement may make prosecution complex, it would do so only in a small number of criminal cases. The result from the Court's decision will be a return to sentencing as it existed before the Sentencing Act was enacted. Judges are afforded unbridled discretion in setting a sentence without any consistent guidelines to regulate disparity. The vague concept of reasonableness on appellate review does not save this defect.

■ DISSENT IN PART

(Scalia, J.) The majority's decision repeatedly acknowledges that Congress would rather have a sentencing scheme without mandatory provisions than a return to the pre-Guidelines scheme of judicial inconsistency, yet it encourages discretionary sentencing.

Analysis

The impact of *Booker* on defendants remains uncertain. As long as judges are free to consider the Guidelines, it is reasonable to assume that many defendants will continue to receive the sentences prescribed, for the reasonableness standard on appellate review will undoubtedly be met. Other defendants, however, may receive higher or lower sentences based on the mercy of the court or aggravating circumstances established by the jury.

■ CASE VOCABULARY

SENTENCE: The judgment that a court formally pronounces after finding a criminal defendant guilty; the punishment imposed on a criminal wrongdoer.

SIXTH AMENDMENT: The constitutional amendment, ratified with the Bill of Rights of 1791, guaranteeing in criminal cases the right to a speedy and public trial by jury, the right to be informed of the nature of the accusation, the right to confront witnesses, the right to counsel, and the right to compulsory process for obtaining favorable witnesses.

CHAPTER TWENTY–EIGHT

Appeals

North Carolina v. Pearce

Instant Facts: Defendants successfully attacked their convictions but were subsequently re-convicted and given harsher sentences.

Black Letter Rule: After having successfully attacked his original conviction, a defendant may be given a harsher sentence on re-conviction if there is no judicial vindictiveness involved.

Texas v. McCullough

Instant Facts: The defendant received a 50 year prison sentence on retrial from the same judge who presided over his first trial, where he was convicted of murder and sentenced to 20 years in prison by the jury.

Black Letter Rule: It is not a violation of the Due Process Clause when the defendant in a state court receives a greater sentence on retrial, where the earlier sentence was imposed by the jury, the trial judge granted the defendant's motion for a new trial, the defendant requested that in the second trial the judge fix the sentence, and the judge entered findings of fact justifying the longer sentence.

Chapman v. California

Instant Facts: The defendants were convicted of murder after the prosecutor and the trial judge commented to the jury about their failure to testify, and advised it that it could infer guilt based on that failure.

Black Letter Rule: Before a federal constitutional error can be held harmless, the court must be able to declare a belief that it was harmless beyond a reasonable doubt.

Neder v. United States

Instant Facts: When a tax cheat's trial judge erroneously instructed the jury not to consider the element of his fraud's "materiality," he appealed, claiming the deprivation of his "jury trial" right requires automatic reversal.

Black Letter Rule: Erroneous jury instructions which keep jurors from deciding one necessary element of the crime constitute "harmless error," which does not require reversal on appeal.

North Carolina v. Pearce

(*State*) v. (*Convicted Criminal*)

395 U.S. 711, 89 S.Ct. 2072 (1969)

AFTER SUCCESSFULLY ATTACKING A CONVICTION, A DEFENDANT MAY BE RE-CONVICTED AND GIVEN A HARSHER SENTENCE ABSENT JUDICIAL VINDICTIVENESS

■ **INSTANT FACTS** Defendants successfully attacked their convictions but were subsequently re-convicted and given harsher sentences.

■ **BLACK LETTER RULE** After having successfully attacked his original conviction, a defendant may be given a harsher sentence on re-conviction if there is no judicial vindictiveness involved.

■ PROCEDURAL BASIS

Writ of certiorari granted after defendants were retried, convicted, and given harsher sentences.

■ FACTS

This case involves two cases which were combined on appeal. In the first one, Pearce (D) was convicted in North Carolina of assault with intent to commit rape. He was sentenced to a term of 12 to 15 years. Several years later he succeeded in having his conviction reversed. He was retried, convicted and sentenced to an eight-year term, which, when added to the time he had already spent in prison, amounted to a longer total sentence than originally imposed. In the second case, Rice (D) pled guilty to four charges of burglary and was sentenced to 10 years. Two and one-half years later the judgments were set aside on the ground that Rice (D) had been deprived his right to counsel. He was retried on three of the charges and sentenced to prison for 25 years.

■ ISSUE

May a more severe punishment constitutionally be imposed after a defendant is re-convicted for the same offense after having successfully reversed a prior conviction?

■ DECISION AND RATIONALE

(Stewart, J.) Yes, if vindictiveness against the defendant for successfully attacking his first conviction plays no part in the new sentence. The Double Jeopardy Clause imposes no restrictions upon the length of a sentence imposed upon reconviction. Since *United States v. Ball,* it has been clear that there is no limitation upon the power to retry a defendant who has succeeded in getting his first conviction reversed. A corollary to the power to retry a defendant is the power to impose whatever sentence on reconviction that may be legally authorized. The rational for this rule is that the original conviction has been nullified at the defendant's request and the slate wiped clean. Therefore, we hold that the neither the Double Jeopardy Clause nor the Equal Protection Clause forbid a more severe sentence upon reconviction. However, the Due Process Clause of the Fourteenth Amendment must also be considered. It would be a flagrant violation of this clause for a state to follow the practice of imposing bigger sentences upon every re-convicted defendant for the explicit purpose of punishing the defendant for having had his first conviction set aside. The very threat of such a policy would chill the exercise of basic constitutional rights. To assure that vindictiveness plays no part in the imposition of a more severe sentence after a new trial, we conclude that the reasons for the more severe sentence must affirmatively appear in the court's order. Those reasons must be based on identifiable conduct of the defendant after the original sentencing. In the cases of both Pearce (D) and Rice (D), the respective states have failed to offer any evidence to justify the increased sentences. Therefore, we must reverse the convictions of both Pearce (D) and Rice (D).

Analysis:

This case establishes a presumption of vindictiveness whenever a defendant is given a harsher sentence after having been re-convicted after a successful reversal of a first conviction. This presumption can be rebutted if the trial court explicitly identifies specific conduct by the defendant which justifies the harsher sentence. Despite these protections, might the possibility of receiving a harsher sentence still prevent some defendants from exercising their constitutional right to appeal? If a defendant was wrongly convicted the first time, is that defendant likely to trust the system to be free of vindictiveness? Note that this case was decided on due process rather than double jeopardy grounds. The Due Process Clause allows a more flexible approach which led to later rulings which narrowed the rule in this case.

Texas v. McCullough

(*Government*) v. (*Retried Murderer*)

475 U.S. 134, 106 S.Ct. 976, 89 L.Ed.2d 104 (1986)

TRIAL JUDGES MUST BE ACCORDED BROAD DISCRETION IN SENTENCING

■ **INSTANT FACTS** The defendant received a 50 year prison sentence on retrial from the same judge who presided over his first trial, where he was convicted of murder and sentenced to 20 years in prison by the jury.

■ **BLACK LETTER RULE** It is not a violation of the Due Process Clause when the defendant in a state court receives a greater sentence on retrial, where the earlier sentence was imposed by the jury, the trial judge granted the defendant's motion for a new trial, the defendant requested that in the second trial the judge fix the sentence, and the judge entered findings of fact justifying the longer sentence.

■ PROCEDURAL BASIS

Appeal from the Court of Appeals' reversal of the trial judge's sentence for the defendant.

■ FACTS

McCullough (D) was tried before a jury and convicted of murder. The jury imposed a 20-year sentence. Judge Harney, the trial judge, then granted McCullough's (D) motion for a new trial on the basis of prosecutorial misconduct. Three months later, McCullough (D) was retried before a jury, with Judge Harney again presiding. At this trial, the State (P) presented testimony from two witnesses who had not testified at the first trial that McCullough (D) rather than his two accomplices had slashed the victim's throat. McCullough (D) was again found guilty by the jury. This time, however, he elected to have his sentence fixed by the trial judge. Judge Harney sentenced him to 50 years in prison and, upon his motion, made findings of fact as to why the sentence was longer than that fixed by the jury in the first trial. The judge found that in fixing the sentence she relied on new evidence about the murder that was not presented in the first trial and hence never made known to the sentencing jury. In addition, Judge Harney explained that she would have imposed more than twenty years had she fixed the first sentence. On appeal, the Court of Appeals reversed and resentenced McCullough (D) to 20 years' imprisonment. That court held that a longer sentence upon retrial could be imposed only if it was based upon conduct of the defendant occurring after the original trial.

■ ISSUE

Is it a violation of the Due Process Clause when the defendant in a state court receives a greater sentence on retrial where the earlier sentence was imposed by the jury, the trial judge granted the defendant's motion for a new trial, the defendant requested that in the second trial the judge fix the sentence, and the judge entered findings of fact justifying the longer sentence?

■ DECISION AND RATIONALE

(Burger, C.J.) No. In *North Carolina v. Pearce*, the Court placed a limitation on the power of a sentencing authority to increase a sentence after reconviction following a new trial. It held that the Due Process Clause of the Fourteenth Amendment prevented increased sentences when that increase was motivated by vindictiveness on the part of the sentencing judge. Beyond doubt, vindictiveness of a sentencing judge is the evil the Court sought to prevent rather than simply enlarged sentences after a new trial. The *Pearce* requirements thus do not apply in every case where a convicted defendant receives a higher sentence on retrial. Accordingly, in each case, we look to the need, under the circumstances, to guard against vindictiveness in the resentencing process. The presumption of *Pearce* does not apply in situations where the possibility of vindictiveness is speculative, particularly since the presumption may often operate in the absence of any proof of an improper motive and thus block a legitimate response to criminal conduct. McCullough (D) was entitled by law to choose to be sentenced by either a judge or a jury. Faced with that choice, on retrial McCullough (D) chose to be sentenced by Judge Harney. There can hardly be more emphatic affirmation of his appraisal of Judge Harney's fairness than this choice. Because there was no realistic motive for vindictive sentencing, the *Pearce* presumption was inappropriate. We recognize that when different sentencers are involved it may often be that the second sentencer will impose a punishment more severe than that received from the first. But it no more follows that such a sentence is a vindictive penalty for seeking a new trial than that the first sentencer imposed a lenient penalty. Here, the second sentencer provides an on-the-record, wholly logical, nonvindictive reason for the sentence. We read *Pearce* to require no more, particularly since trial judges must be accorded broad discretion in sentencing. Even if the *Pearce* presumption were to apply here, we hold that the findings of the trial judge overcome that presumption. Nothing in *Pearce* is to be read as precluding a rebuttal of intimations of vindictiveness. As we have explained, *Pearce* permits a sentencing authority to justify an increased sentence by affirmatively identifying relevant conduct or events that occurred subsequent to the original sentencing proceedings. This language, however, was never intended to describe exhaustively all of the possible circumstances in which a sentence increase could be justified. Restricting justifications for a sentence increase to *only* events that occurred subsequent to the original sentencing proceedings could in some circumstances lead to absurd results. In sum, the Court in *Pearce* applied a presumption of vindictiveness, which may be overcome only by objective information justifying the increased sentence. Nothing in the Constitution requires a judge to ignore such objective information justifying the increased sentence. It is clear that the careful explanation by the trial judge for the sentence imposed here fits well within our prior holdings. In setting aside the second sentence, the Court of Appeals recognized that the new information bore legitimately on the appropriate sentence to impose, but concluded, reluctantly, that *Pearce* precluded reliance on this information. It is appropriate that we clarify the scope and thrust of *Pearce*, and we do so here. The case is remanded to the Court of Appeals for further proceedings not inconsistent with this opinion.

■ CONCURRENCE

(Brennan, J.) I believe that the possibility that an increased sentence upon retrial resulted from judicial vindictiveness is sufficiently remote that the presumption established in *Pearce* should not apply. I emphasize, however, that were I able to find that vindictiveness should be presumed here, I would agree with Justice Marshall that "the reasons offered by Judge Harney [were] far from adequate to rebut any presumption of vindictiveness." The Court's dictum to the contrary, serves in my view only to distort the holding of *Pearce.*

■ DISSENT

(Marshall, J.) I find the reasons offered by Judge Harney far from adequate to rebut any presumption of vindictiveness. Moreover, I believe that by holding those reasons sufficient, the Court effectively eviscerates the effort made in *Pearce* to ensure both that vindictiveness against a defendant for having successfully attacked his first conviction play no part in the sentence he receives after a new trial, and that the defendant be freed of apprehension of such a retaliatory motivation on the part of the sentencing judge. The presumption of vindictiveness established in *Pearce* was made rebuttable. But the Court was quite clear that the conduct or event used to justify an increased sentence must have taken place after the original sentencing proceeding. By finding the reasons given by Judge Harney adequate to rebut a presumption of vindictiveness, the majority not only disregards the clear rule in *Pearce*, it announces a new regime in which the "chill" that plagued defendants in the days before *Pearce* will once again be felt by those deciding whether to contest their convictions.

Analysis:

The facts of this case provide no basis for a presumption of vindictiveness. In contrast to *Pearce*, McCullough's (D) second trial came about because the trial judge herself concluded that the prosecutor's misconduct required it. Granting McCullough's (D) motion for a new trial hardly suggests any vindictiveness on the part of the judge towards him. Unlike a judge who has been reversed, the trial judge here had no motivation to engage in self-vindication. In granting McCullough's (D) new trial motion. Judge Harney went on record as agreeing that his "claims" had merit. Presuming vindictiveness on this basis alone would be tantamount to presuming that a judge will be vindictive towards a defendant merely because he seeks an acquittal. In this case, the trial judge stated candidly her belief that the 20-year sentence McCullough (D) received initially was unduly lenient in light of significant evidence not before the sentencing jury in the first trial. On this record, that appraisal cannot be faulted. In any event, nothing in the Constitution prohibits a state from permitting such discretion to play a role in sentencing.

■ CASE VOCABULARY

AMICUS CURIAE: A person with a strong interest in or views on the subject matter of an action, but who is not a party to the action, who submits a brief to the Court to suggest a rationale consistent with his own beliefs.

CERTIORARI: A writ issued so that a superior court may review the proceedings of a lower court to determine whether there have been any irregularities.

DICTUM: An opinion of a judge which does not embody the resolution or determination of the Court, and which lack the force of an adjudication.

RECIDIVISM: The repeated criminal acts by one who makes crime a trade.

Chapman v. California

(Murderer) v. *(Government)*
386 U.S. 18, 87 S.Ct. 824, 17 L.Ed.2d 705 (1967)

AN ERROR IN ADMITTING PLAINLY RELEVANT EVIDENCE WHICH POSSIBLY INFLUENCED THE JURY ADVERSELY TO A LITIGANT CANNOT BE CONCEIVED OF AS HARMLESS

■ INSTANT FACTS The defendants were convicted of murder after the prosecutor and the trial judge commented to the jury about their failure to testify, and advised it that it could infer guilt based on that failure.

■ BLACK LETTER RULE Before a federal constitutional error can be held harmless, the court must be able to declare a belief that it was harmless beyond a reasonable doubt.

■ PROCEDURAL BASIS

Appeal from the Appellate Court's affirmance of the trial court's conviction of the defendant.

■ FACTS

Chapman (D) and another man were convicted of the robbery, kidnapping, and murder of a bartender, with one defendant sentenced to life imprisonment and the other to death. At the time of the trial, California law allowed the prosecutor to comment on a defendant's failure to take the stand. Neither defendant chose to testify, and the prosecutor took full advantage of his right to comment upon their failure to testify, filling his argument to the jury with numerous references to their silence and inferences of their guilt resulting from it. As allowed by California law, the trial judge also instructed the jury that it could draw adverse inferences from the defendants' failure to testify. Shortly after the trial, the Supreme Court decided *Griffin v. California*, holding unconstitutional both prosecutorial comment and adverse judicial instructions on a defendant's failure to testify. The California Supreme Court recognized that the comments and instructions upon the defendants' silence had violated the rule announced in *Griffin*, but held that the constitutional error had been harmless, and affirmed under a state harmless-error provision that prohibited appellate reversal unless the error complained of has resulted in a miscarriage of justice.

■ ISSUE

Are improper prosecutorial comment and adverse judicial instructions on a defendant's failure to testify considered harmless error, thus prohibiting appellate reversal?

■ DECISION AND RATIONALE

(Black, J.) No. Whether a conviction for crime should stand when a State has failed to accord federal constitutionally guaranteed rights is as much of a federal question as what particular federal constitutional provisions themselves mean, what they guarantee, and whether they have been denied. With faithfulness to the constitutional union of the States, we cannot leave to the States the formulation of the authoritative laws, rules, and remedies designed to protect people form infractions by the States of federally guaranteed rights. We have no hesitation in saying that the right of these petitioners not to be punished for exercising their Fifth and Fourteenth Amendment right to be silent—expressly created by the Federal Constitution itself—is a federal right which, in the absence of appropriate congressional action, it is our responsibility to protect by fashioning the necessary rule. An error in admitting plainly relevant evidence which possibly influenced the jury adversely to a litigant cannot be conceived of as harmless. Certainly error, constitutional error, in illegally admitting highly prejudicial evidence or comments, casts on someone other than the person prejudiced by it a burden to show that it was harmless. It is for that reason that the original common-law harmless-error rule put the burden on the beneficiary of the error either to prove that there was no injury or to suffer a reversal of his erroneously obtained judgment. We hold, therefore, that before a federal constitutional error can be held harmless, the court must be able to declare a belief that it was harmless beyond a reasonable doubt. While appellate courts do not ordinarily have the original task of applying such a test, it is a familiar standard to all courts, and we believe its adoption will provide a more workable standard. Applying the foregoing standard, we have no doubt that the error in these cases was not harmless to the defendants. The state prosecutor's argument and the trial judge's instruction to the jury continuously and repeatedly impressed the jury that from the failure of the defendants to testify, to all intents and purposes, the inferences from the facts in evidence had to be drawn in favor of the State—in short, that by their silence the defendants had served as irrefutable witnesses against themselves. And though the case in which this occurred presented a reasonably strong circumstantial web of evidence against the defendants, it was also a case in which, absent the constitutionally forbidden comments, honest, fair-minded jurors might very well have brought in not-guilty verdicts. Under these circumstances, it is completely impossible for us to say that the State has demonstrated, beyond a reasonable doubt, that the prosecutor's comments and the trial judge's instruction did not contribute to the defendants' convictions. Such repetition of a denial of constitutional rights, designed and calculated to make the defendants' version of the evidence worthless, can no more be considered harmless than the introduction against a defendant of a coerced confession. The defendants are entitled to a trial free from the pressure of unconstitutional inferences. Reversed.

Analysis:

All 50 States have harmless-error statutes or rules, and the United States long ago through Congress established for its courts the rule that judgments will not be reversed for errors or defects which do not affect the substantial rights of the parties. None of these rules on its face distinguishes between federal constitutional errors and errors of state law or federal statutes and rules. All of these rules, state or federal, serve a very useful purpose insofar that they block setting aside convictions for small errors or defects that have little, if any, likelihood of having changed the result of the trial. Thus, there may be some constitutional errors which in the setting of a particular case are so unimportant and insignificant that they may, consistent with the Federal Constitution, be deemed harmless, not requiring the automatic reversal of the conviction. In this case, however, it cannot be said that the prosecutor's comments; and the trial judge's instructions, were unimportant and insignificant. Juries put a great deal of stock in what the judge says, thus his comments cannot be deemed harmless.

Neder v. United States

(*Tax Evader*) v. (*Federal Prosecution*)
527 U.S. 1, 119 S.Ct. 1827, 144 L.Ed.2d 35 (1999)

EVEN MOST CONSTITUTIONAL ERRORS ARE NOT APPEALABLE IF "HARMLESS"

■ **INSTANT FACTS** When a tax cheat's trial judge erroneously instructed the jury not to consider the element of his fraud's "materiality," he appealed, claiming the deprivation of his "jury trial" right requires automatic reversal.

■ **BLACK LETTER RULE** Erroneous jury instructions which keep jurors from deciding one necessary element of the crime constitute "harmless error," which does not require reversal on appeal.

■ PROCEDURAL BASIS

In federal prosecution for filing fraudulent tax returns (and other federal frauds), post-conviction appeal based on improper jury instructions, seeking reversal.

■ FACTS

Real estate swindler Neder (D) was charged federally with various frauds, including filing false tax returns which omitted $5M in income. (Apparently, the prosecution (P) claimed Neder (D) fraudulently borrowed money without intending to repay it, and thus should have declared the (theft) proceeds as "income.") Neder (D) defended, claiming he properly omitted the proceeds from income, because he intended to repay it, and because his accountant and lawyer advised him they were not "income." [Who is his accountant? Arthur Andersen?] At trial, the district court instructed the jury that it "need not consider" the charged element of "materiality" (i.e., whether the misstatement was "material"), because that was "not a question for the jury" (over Neder's (D) objection). Neder (D) was convicted, sentenced to 12 years, and ordered to restitute $25M. Neder (D) appealed, claiming the trial judge's jury instruction constituted reversible error. The Eleventh Circuit affirmed. It found the judge's instruction was wrong; materiality *is* an element for the jury. But it concluded it was "harmless error," because Neder's (D) understating his income *by five million dollars* (!) was so blatant that "materiality was not in dispute," so the instruction did not sway the verdict. Neder (D) appeals.

■ ISSUE

Does an erroneous jury instruction, forcing the jury not to consider *one* element of a criminal charge, constitute constitutional error requiring automatic reversal?

■ DECISION AND RATIONALE

(Rehnquist) No. Erroneous jury instructions which keep jurors from deciding one necessary element of the crime constitute "harmless error," which does not require reversal on appeal. Direct appeals from convictions in federal courts are governed by *Fed. R. Crim. P. Rule 52(a)*, which applies the "harmless error" principle—"any error, defect, irregularity or variance which does not affect substantial rights shall be disregarded." But our caselaw recognizes that *some* fundamental, *constitutional* errors are so basic they defy "harmless error" standards, and require automatic reversal, even if they didn't change the trial's outcome. Even for constitutional error, there is a strong presumption of harmlessness, as long as the defendant (i) had counsel, and (ii) was tried by an impartial adjudicator. The few constitutional errors which we found "structural" (and thus necessitating automatic reversal) generally contain "a defect affecting the framework within which the trial proceeds, rather than simply an error in the trial process itself"; such errors "infect the entire trial process" and "necessarily render a trial fundamentally unfair," depriving defendants of "basic [procedural] protections." Such "structural" errors include: denial of counsel, biased judge, racial discrimination in selecting jurors, denial of self-representation, denial of public trial, defective reasonable-doubt instruction, etc. But erroneous jury instructions which omit an element of the offense may be disregarded if they caused "harmless error," since they don't *necessarily* render the entire trial fundamentally unfair. This error is analogous to instructing the jury erroneously on a single element of the offense, or incorrectly applying a conclusive presumption; both are reviewable under "harmless error" standards. This holding is (somewhat) consistent with our prior caselaw [yes, it always is, isn't it?], including the cases Neder (D) cites. *Sullivan v. Louisiana* [failure to instruct jury to find all elements beyond "reasonable doubt" requires automatic reversal, because it vitiates *all* the jury's findings] is distinguishable; there, *all* the findings were in doubt, while here, only the finding of "materiality" is in question. This is consistent with our later cases *Pope* [in prosecution for obscenity, mistaken instruction to evaluate materials' offensiveness by "community standard" rather than "reasonable person" standard is harmless], *Carella* [in theft trial for failing to return rented car, erroneous instruction to presume intent to steal was harmless], and *Roy* [in murder conviction, incorrect instruction failing to state that abettor liability required intent to assist crime was harmless]. Those cases apply automatic reversal basically when the jury tends to find either a "complete verdict" on every element charged, or the "functional equivalent" of an omitted element. However, we instead adopt a categorical rule: some classes of errors should be deemed "structural" and subject to automatic reversal, while others should be evaluated under "harmless error" standards. Holding otherwise would entangle federal appellate courts in voluminous, fact-specific appeals using vague standards. For *constitutional* error, "harmless error" means "the error . . . did not contribute to the verdict obtained," "beyond a reasonable doubt." If an omitted element is supported by uncontroverted evidence, then its omission would not have swayed the verdict, beyond reasonable doubt. Here, the error was harmless, since Neder's (D) misstatements' "materiality" would have been found by any fact-finder. "Materiality" means "a natural tendency to influence . . . the decision of the decisionmaking body." Courts hold that, in prosecutions for failure to report income, *any* such failure is "material." Under this standard, no jury could find Neder's (D) failure to report over $5M was immaterial. Further, Neder (D) presented no proof of immateriality, thus basically conceding materiality. Thus, Neder's (D) guilty verdict would not have been different under a proper jury instruction, and the error was thus harmless and irreversible. Conviction affirmed.

■ DISSENT

(Scalia) The constitutional right to jury trial includes the defendant's right to have *every* element of his charge determined by jury. Deprivations of this right are never "harmless." The Constitution doesn't trust judges to determine criminal guilt, which is what the majority's standard effectively requires appellate courts to do. Also, there is no sound principle for holding that, while error which vitiates all the jury's findings is reversible, an error which takes *just one* element away from the jury is harmless; if a jury had found even that single element lacking, it would have to acquit. This holding also opens the possibility that several more elements can be taken away from the jury, without triggering reversible error. Further, the whole point of "structural" error Analysis: is that it *automatically* reverses a conviction, even if the defendant would have been convicted anyway on other grounds. Finally, the majority opinion encourages appellate judges to deny reversal based on their *own* opinion that the record suggests overwhelming guilt; this decision is not theirs to make, and is not equivalent to merely affirming the jury's decision.

Analysis:

Neder is presented as the most recent available application of *Chapman* [most constitutional errors don't require automatic reversal if the appellate court finds the error "harmless," beyond reasonable doubt]. As the rationale shows, courts deem certain, specified errors to be so unconstitutional that they require automatic reversal, even if the defendant would have been convicted anyway. But these few types are fixed, and the Court here signals its reluctance to expand them, or replace its bright-line categories with a discretionary, case-by-case standard. The reason is that requiring automatic reversal for (inevitable) technical, inconsequential errors will let guilty crooks like Neder (D) walk free.

■ CASE VOCABULARY

CAVIL: An objection which is frivolous.

EXTANT: Still standing [precedent].

"HARMLESS ERROR" ANALYSIS: Standard whereby actual trial errors don't require the appellate court to reverse the judgment, if the error was "harmless" (usually because the outcome would have been the same).

MATERIALITY: In fraud, the requirement that the fraudulent misrepresentation have been "material" (sufficient to induce the defendant).

VITIATE: To invalidate.

CHAPTER TWENTY–NINE

Post–Conviction Review: Federal Habeas Corpus

Stone v. Powell

Instant Facts: A state prisoner is seeking habeas corpus relief, claiming that evidence obtained by an unconstitutional search or seizure was introduced at his trial.

Black Letter Rule: Where the State has provided an opportunity for full and fair litigation of a Fourth Amendment claim, the Constitution does not require that a state prisoner be granted federal habeas corpus relief on the ground that evidence obtained in an unconstitutional search or seizure was introduced at his trial.

Wainwright v. Sykes

Instant Facts: Sykes (D) filed a writ of habeas corpus claiming that his confession had been obtained without his understanding the Miranda warnings even though his counsel had neither moved to suppress the confession nor objected to the evidence when introduced at trial.

Black Letter Rule: A habeas corpus petitioner can be excused from a procedural default made in the state courts only by showing good cause for the procedural default and that the violation of his federal rights actually prejudiced his case.

Teague v. Lane

Instant Facts: A black man claims the fair cross section requirement of the Sixth Amendment was violated when he was convicted by an all-white jury after the prosecution used all his peremptory challenges to exclude blacks from the jury.

Black Letter Rule: Unless cases on collateral review fall within an exception to the general rule, new constitutional rules of criminal procedure will not be applicable to those cases which have become final before the new rules are announced.

(Terry) Williams v. Taylor

Instant Facts: After a federal court refused to rule that a condemned killer's counsel was ineffective for failing to present extensive mitigating evidence, the killer appealed, contending this decision clearly violated Supreme Court precedent.

Black Letter Rule: Federal habeas courts should review state courts' legal and factual decisions independently, without deference.

Stone v. Powell

(*Prisoner*) v. (*Government*)

428 U.S. 465, 96 S.Ct. 3037, 49 L.Ed.2d 1067 (1976)

HABEAS CORPUS REVIEW MAY NOT BE AVAILABLE TO EFFECTUATE CLAIMED FOURTH AMENDMENT VIOLATIONS

■ **INSTANT FACTS** A state prisoner is seeking habeas corpus relief, claiming that evidence obtained by an unconstitutional search or seizure was introduced at his trial.

■ **BLACK LETTER RULE** Where the State has provided an opportunity for full and fair litigation of a Fourth Amendment claim, the Constitution does not require that a state prisoner be granted federal habeas corpus relief on the ground that evidence obtained in an unconstitutional search or seizure was introduced at his trial.

■ PROCEDURAL BASIS

Petition for habeas corpus relief.

■ FACTS

A state prisoner is seeking habeas corpus relief, claiming that evidence obtained by an unconstitutional search or seizure was introduced at his trial.

■ ISSUE

Should a federal court consider, in ruling on a petition for habeas corpus relief filed by a state prisoner, a claim that evidence obtained by an unconstitutional search or seizure was introduced at his trial, when he has previously been afforded an opportunity for full and fair litigation of his claim in the state courts?

■ DECISION AND RATIONALE

(Powell, J.) No. Prior to our decision in *Kaufman v. United States*, a substantial majority of the federal courts of appeals had concluded that collateral review of search-and-seizure claims was inappropriate on motions filed by federal prisoners under *28 USC § 2255*, the modern postconviction procedure available to federal prisoners in lieu of habeas corpus. *Kaufman* rejected this position and held that search and seizure claims are cognizable in Section 2255 proceedings. The discussion in *Kaufman* of the scope of federal habeas corpus rests on the view that the effectuation of the Fourth Amendment requires the granting of habeas corpus relief when a prisoner has been convicted in state court on the basis of evidence obtained in an illegal search or seizure since those Amendments were held in *Mapp v. Ohio*, to require exclusion of such evidence at trial and reversal of conviction upon direct review. Until this case we have not had occasion fully to consider the validity of this view. Upon examination, we conclude, in light of the nature and purpose of the Fourth Amendment exclusionary rule, that this view is unjustified. Evidence obtained by police officers in violation of the Fourth Amendment is excluded at trial in the hope that the frequency of future violations will decrease. Despite the absence of supportive empirical evidence, we have assumed that the immediate effect of exclusion will be to discourage law enforcement officials from violating the Fourth Amendment by removing the incentive to disregard it. More importantly, over the long term, this demonstration that our society attaches serious consequences to violation of constitutional rights is thought to encourage those who formulate law enforcement policies, and the officers who implement them, to incorporate Fourth Amendment ideals into their value system. We adhere to the view that these considerations support the implementation of the exclusionary rule at trial and its enforcement on direct appeal of state court convictions. But the additional contribution, if any, of the consideration of search-and-seizure claims of state prisoners on collateral review is small in relation to the costs. In sum, we conclude that where the State has provided an opportunity for full and fair litigation of a Fourth Amendment claim, the Constitution does not require that a state prisoner be granted federal habeas corpus relief on the ground that evidence obtained in an unconstitutional search or seizure was introduced at his trial. In this context, the contribution of the exclusionary rule, if any, to the effectuation of the Fourth Amendment is minimal and the substantial societal costs of application of the rule persist with special force.

■ DISSENT

(Brennan, J.) The real ground of today's decision—a ground that is particularly troubling in light of its portent for habeas jurisdiction generally—is the Court's novel reinterpretation of the habeas statutes; this would read the statutes as requiring the District Courts routinely to deny habeas relief to prisoners in custody in violation of the Constitution or laws of the United States as a matter of judicial discretion—a "discretion" judicially manufactured today contrary to the express statutory language.

■ DISSENT

(White, J.) [In a separate dissent, Justice White offered a hypothetical as an illustration of what he perceived to be the flaw in the majority's opinion.] Unless the Court's reservation, in its present opinion, of those situations where the defendant has not had a full and fair hearing in the state courts is intended to encompass all those circumstances under which a state criminal judgment may be reexamined under section 2254, one defendant's petition could be dismissed and he would spend his life in prison, while another defendant would be a free man. This cannot be the result Congress intended.

Analysis:

Remember, the "exclusionary rule" is a judicial doctrine which says that evidence obtained improperly, in violation of the Fourth Amendment guarantee against unreasonable search, must be excluded. This rule's purpose is to give the Fourth Amendment teeth, and deter police from collecting evidence improperly. But later cases established that the rule was not intended as a *personal* right against unreasonable search, or violations of privacy. Thus, courts don't apply the exclusionary rule to all persons in all proceedings; instead, they perform an interest-balancing test. Here, the Court finds that Fourth Amendment claims in habeas corpus proceedings are insufficiently important to deserve the exclusionary rule.

■ CASE VOCABULARY

CERTIORARI: A means of appellate review whereby a court of superior authority reviews the proceeding below to determine whether there were any irregularities.

EXCLUSIONARY RULE: Where evidence has been obtained in violation of the search and seizure protections guaranteed by the Constitution, the illegally obtained evidence cannot be used at the trial of the defendant.

HABEAS CORPUS RELIEF: A petition from a prisoner which challenges a state conviction on constitutional grounds.

Wainwright v. Sykes

(*Government*) v. (*Convicted Murderer*)

433 U.S. 72, 97 S.Ct. 2497 (1977)

THE "CAUSE-AND-PREJUDICE" TEST FOR HABEAS CORPUS REVIEW IS APPLICABLE TO TRIAL ERRORS

■ **INSTANT FACTS** Sykes (D) filed a writ of habeas corpus claiming that his confession had been obtained without his understanding the Miranda warnings even though his counsel had neither moved to suppress the confession nor objected to the evidence when introduced at trial.

■ **BLACK LETTER RULE** A habeas corpus petitioner can be excused from a procedural default made in the state courts only by showing good cause for the procedural default and that the violation of his federal rights actually prejudiced his case.

■ PROCEDURAL BASIS

Writ of habeas corpus after a conviction for third-degree murder.

■ FACTS

Sykes (D) was convicted of third-degree murder at trial. He testified at his trial that he told his wife to summon the police on the night of the murder because he had just shot Willie Gilbert. The police arrived to find Gilbert dead from a shotgun wound. Sykes (D) approached the police and told them that he had shot Gilbert, and Sykes' (D) wife told the police the same thing. Sykes (D) was immediately arrested and taken into custody. He was Mirandized, declined to speak to counsel and indicated a willingness to talk to the investigators. He then made a statement, which was later entered into evidence at trial via the testimony of the two officers who heard it. His counsel did not object to the statement being admitted, nor did his counsel move to have the statement suppressed prior to the trial. Sykes (D) appealed his conviction but, again, his counsel did not challenge the admissibility of the inculpatory statement. [Time for new counsel?] He then sought habeas relief in state court but was unsuccessful. He was successful in federal court, however, and the Court of Appeals held that Florida's contemporary objection rule did not bar review by way of habeas corpus.

■ ISSUE

Should a habeas petitioner who defaulted under state procedure be barred from federal habeas review absent a showing of cause and prejudice?

■ DECISION AND RATIONALE

(Rehnquist, J.) Yes. In the case of a procedural default made in the state court, a habeas petitioner should be barred from federal habeas review unless he can show cause and prejudice. That is, the petitioner is required to show good cause for the procedural defect and that the alleged violation of federal law has actually prejudiced his case. Florida's contemporaneous objection rule, like many other states,' provides a procedural method of preserving issues for appellate review. It deserves greater respect than the prior "deliberate bypass" rule would accord it. The contemporaneous objection rule serves the important function of ensuring that the record is made when the recollections of the witnesses are freshest and the judge is best able to observe the demeanor of the parties and witnesses before him. Also, the retention of the "deliberate bypass" rule encourages sandbagging by defense lawyers. Defense lawyers may deliberately decide to take their chances in state court, knowing that even if a conviction is obtained, they can always raise the federal rights violations in a federal habeas proceeding at a later time. Finally, the "deliberate bypass" rule demeans the proper role of the trial court. The trial should be considered a decisive and portentous event rather than a tryout that will ultimately only be determined by a federal habeas corpus hearing. The "cause and prejudice" rule will make the trial the "main event" rather than a dry run. We believe that the "cause and prejudice" rule will not prevent a petitioner from seeking federal habeas relief when its denial would be a miscarriage of justice. The rule will, however, bar those defendants who, without good cause and to no actual prejudice, failed to follow proper state procedures for preserving a claim.

■ DISSENT

(Brennan, J.) The "deliberate bypass" rule has the laudable effect of disallowing federal habeas review for intentional procedural defaults, but not for inadvertent ones. It adequately protects against what the majority terms "sandbagging" and should be retained. On the other hand, the adoption of the "cause and prejudice" rule has the unhappy effect of penalizing the habeas petitioner for the incompetence or carelessness of his attorney. When such fundamental rights are involved, we should not deny the criminal defendant the chance to receive habeas review simply because his counsel negligently or carelessly did not follow proper procedures. It is especially inappropriate to penalize the habeas petitioner who was indigent and who had no real choice in selecting his defense counsel.

Analysis:

Wainwright overturned the prior rule, exemplified by *Fay*. *Fay*'s "deliberate bypass" rules generally excused failure to object, unless they were deliberate, tactical attempts to avoid raising the federal claims in the state court. This "deliberate bypass" rule was highly protective of petitioners, perhaps at the expense of ignoring states' procedural requirements. *Wainwright*'s new "cause and prejudice" standard is much harsher for petitioners, and is predicated on the Court's belief that this is necessary to respect state procedures. Eventually, the Court overruled *Fay* explicitly, applying the "cause and prejudice" standard to all cases of procedural default.

■ CASE VOCABULARY

CONTEMPORANEOUS OBJECTION RULE: A rule of procedure that requires that a timely objection be made in order to preserve an issue for appellate review.

HABEAS CORPUS: An independent, collateral proceeding to determine whether the prisoner is being unlawfully retained; that is, whether the prisoner has been denied his due process rights and should therefore be set free.

Teague v. Lane

(*Convicted Felon*) v. (*Government*)

489 U.S. 288, 109 S.Ct. 1060, 103 L.Ed.2d 334 (1989)

THE COSTS IMPOSED UPON THE STATES BY RETROACTIVE APPLICATION OF NEW RULES OF CONSTITUTIONAL LAW ON HABEAS CORPUS GENERALLY FAR OUTWEIGH THE BENEFITS OF THIS APPLICATION

■ **INSTANT FACTS** A black man claims the fair cross section requirement of the Sixth Amendment was violated when he was convicted by an all-white jury after the prosecution used all his peremptory challenges to exclude blacks from the jury.

■ **BLACK LETTER RULE** Unless cases on collateral review fall within an exception to the general rule, new constitutional rules of criminal procedure will not be applicable to those cases which have become final before the new rules are announced.

■ PROCEDURAL BASIS

Appeal from the Court of Appeals' rejection of the defendant's petition for a writ of habeas corpus.

■ FACTS

Teague (D), a black man, was convicted by an all-white jury of three counts of attempted murder, two counts of armed robbery, and one count of aggravated battery. During jury selection for the trial, the prosecutor used all 10 of his peremptory challenges to exclude blacks. When Teague's (D) counsel moved for a mistrial, arguing that Teague (D) was entitled to a jury of his peers, the prosecutor defended the challenges by stating that he was trying to achieve a balance of men and women on the jury. The trial court denied the motion. On appeal, Teague (D) argued that the prosecutor's use of peremptory challenges denied him the right to be tried by a jury that was representative of the community. This claim was rejected, the State Supreme Court denied leave to appeal, and this Court denied certiorari. Teague (D) then filed a petition for a writ of habeas corpus, repeating his fair cross section claim, and also that, under *Swain v. Alabama*, a prosecutor could be questioned about his use of peremptory challenges once he volunteered an explanation. While the case was before the Court of Appeals, this Court decided *Batson v. Kentucky*, which overruled a portion of *Swain*. After *Batson* was decided, the Court of Appeals held that Teague (D) could not benefit from the rule in that case because *Allen v. Hardy* had held that *Batson* would not be applied retroactively to cases on collateral review. The Court of Appeals also held that Teague's (D) *Swain* claim was procedurally barred and in any event meritless. The Court of Appeals rejected Teague's (D) fair cross section claim, holding that the fair cross section requirement was limited to the jury venire.

■ ISSUE

Should the Sixth Amendment's fair cross section requirement be extended to the petit jury?

■ DECISION AND RATIONALE

(O'Connor, J.) Resolution left for another day. Teague's (D) first contention is that he should receive the benefit of our decision in *Batson* even though his conviction became final before *Batson* was decided. We find that *Allen v. Hardy* is dispositive, and that Teague (D) cannot benefit from the rule announced in *Batson.* Teague's (D) second contention is that he has established a violation of the Equal Protection Clause under *Swain.* However, we agree with the Court of Appeals that the *Swain* claim is procedurally barred since it had not been properly raised before the state courts and Teague (D) made no showing of "cause and prejudice." Teague's (D) third and final contention is that the Sixth Amendment's fair cross section requirement applies to the petit jury. However, *Taylor v. Louisiana* expressly stated that the fair cross section requirement does not apply to the petit jury. Teague (D) nevertheless contends that the ratio decidendi of *Taylor* cannot be limited to the jury venire, and he urges adoption of a new rule. Because we hold that the rule urged by Teague (D) should not be applied retroactively to cases on collateral review, however, we decline to address Teague's (D) contention. In the past, we have, without discussion, often applied a new constitutional rule of criminal procedure to the defendant in the case announcing the new rule, and have confronted the question of retroactivity later when a different defendant sought the benefit of that rule. In several cases, however, we have addressed the retroactivity question in the very case announcing the new rule. These two lines do not have a unifying theme, and we think it is time to clarify how the question of retroactivity should be resolved for cases on collateral review. In our view, the question whether a decision announcing a new rule should be given prospective or retroactive effect should be faced at the time of that decision. Retroactivity is properly treated as a threshold question, for, once a new rule is applied to the defendant in the case announcing the rule, even-handed justice requires that it be applied retroactively to all who are similarly situated. Thus, before deciding whether the fair cross section requirement should be extended to the petit jury, we should ask whether such a rule would be applied retroactively to the case at issue. In *Mackey v. United States*, Justice Harlan argued that new rules should always be applied retroactively to cases on direct review, but that generally they should not be applied retroactively to criminal cases on collateral review. Justice Harlan believed that new rules generally should not be applied retroactively to cases on collateral review. He argued that retroactivity for cases on collateral review could be responsibly determined only by focusing, in the first instance, on the nature, function, and scope of the adjudicatory process in which such cases arise. Justice Harlan identified only two exceptions to his general rule of nonretroactivity for cases on collateral review. First, a new rule should be applied retroactively if it places certain kinds of primary, private individual conduct beyond the power of the criminal law-making authority to proscribe. Second, a new rule should be applied retroactively if it requires the observance of those procedures that are implicit in the concept of ordered liberty. We find this view persuasive and we now adopt Justice Harlan's view of retroactivity for cases on collateral review. Unless they fall within an exception to the general rule, new constitutional rules of criminal procedure will not be applicable to those cases which have become final before the new rules are announced. Were we to recognize the new rule urged by Teague (D) in this case, we would have to give him the benefit of that rule even though it would not be applied retroactively to others similarly situated. Such an inequitable result would be an unavoidable consequence of the necessity that constitutional adjudications not stand as mere dictum. If there were no other way to avoid rendering advisory opinions, we might well agree that the inequitable treatment described above is an insignificant cost for adherence to sound principles of decisionmaking. But there is a more principled way of dealing with the problem. We can simply refuse to announce a new rule in a given case unless the rule would be applied retroactively to the defendant in the case and to all others similarly situated. We think this approach is a sound one. Not only does it eliminate any problems of rendering advisory opinions, it also avoids the inequity resulting from the uneven application of new rules to similarly situated defendants. We therefore hold that, implicit in the retroactivity approach we adopt today, is the principle that habeas corpus cannot be used as a vehicle to create new constitutional rules of criminal procedure unless those rules would be applied retroactively to all defendants on collateral review through one of the two exceptions we have articulated. Because a decision extending the fair cross section requirement to the petit jury would not be applied retroactively to cases on collateral review under the approach we adopt today, we do not address Teague's (D) claim.

■ CONCURRENCE

(Stevens, J.) As a matter of first impression, I would conclude that a guilty verdict delivered by a jury whose impartiality might have been eroded by racial prejudice is fundamentally unfair. Constraining that conclusion is the Court's holding in *Allen v. Hardy*—an opinion I did not join—that *Batson v.*

Kentucky cannot be applied retroactively to permit collateral review of convictions that became final before it was decided. If there is no fundamental unfairness in denying retroactive relief to a petitioner denied his Fourteenth Amendment right to a fairly chosen jury, as the Court held in *Allen*, there cannot be fundamental unfairness in denying Teague (D) relief for the violation of his Sixth Amendment right to an impartial jury. I therefore agree that the judgment of the Court of Appeals must be affirmed.

■ DISSENT

(Brennan, J.) From the plurality's exposition of its new rule, one might infer that its novel fabrication will work no great change in the availability of federal collateral review of state convictions. Nothing could be further from the truth. Few decisions on appeal or collateral review are "dictated" by what came before. Most such cases involve a question of law that is at least debatable, permitting a rational judge to resolve the case in more than one way. Virtually no case that prompts a dissent on the relevant legal point, for example, could be said to be "dictated" by prior decisions. By the plurality's test, therefore, a great many cases could only be heard on habeas if the rule urged by Teague (D) fell within one of the two exceptions the plurality has sketched. Those exceptions, however, are narrow. The plurality's approach today can thus be expected to contract substantially the Great Writ's sweep.

Analysis:

Admittedly, sometimes it's hard to decide whether a case is actually announcing a "new" rule [Not just for you and me, but also for Justices.] So, the Court doesn't even try to define what constitutes a "new" rule. But generally, a case is new if it imposes new obligations on the government. Here, it's clear that the new rule—the fair cross-section requirement—was a new obligation on prosecutors. But the Court is unsympathetic, since it recognizes that applying rules retroactively on collateral review immediately encourages many state convicts to appeal their convictions, thus effectively forcing states to expend resources to re-litigate trials which were proper under then-current law.

■ CASE VOCABULARY

DICTA: Opinions of a judge which do not embody the resolution or determination of the specific case before the court.

JURY VENIRE: The group of citizens from whom a jury is chosen in a given case.

PEREMPTORY CHALLENGE: The right to eliminate a juror without assigning, or being required to assign, a reason for the elimination.

PETIT JURY: The ordinary jury for the trial of a civil or criminal action.

RATIO DECIDENDI: The ground or reason of a decision.

RES JUDICATA: Rule that a final judgment rendered by a court is conclusive as to the rights of the parties and which constitutes an absolute bar to a subsequent action involving the same claim, demand or cause of action.

SIXTH AMENDMENT FAIR CROSS SECTION REQUIREMENT: Requirement that the jury venire be representative of the community.

(Terry) Williams v. Taylor

(*Convict*) v. (*State*)

529 U.S. 362, 120 S.Ct. 1495, 146 L.Ed.2d 389 (2000)

HABEAS COURTS OWE LOWER COURTS NO DEFERENCE

■ **INSTANT FACTS** After a federal court refused to rule that a condemned killer's counsel was ineffective for failing to present extensive mitigating evidence, the killer appealed, contending this decision clearly violated Supreme Court precedent.

■ **BLACK LETTER RULE** Federal habeas courts should review state courts' legal and factual decisions independently, without deference.

■ PROCEDURAL BASIS

In state prosecution for capital murder, appeal from federal appellate court's affirmation of death sentence on writ of habeas corpus.

■ FACTS

Williams (D) was convicted of robbery and capital murder in Virginia (P). At sentencing, Virginia (P) offered evidence that Williams (D) had prior convictions, and was later implicated in 2 car thefts, 2 violent robberies, and arson. Virginia's (P) expert psychiatrist testified there was a "high probability" Williams (D) would pose continued serious threats to society. Williams' (D) counsel presented a weak argument, basically consisting of statements by Williams' (D) mother and neighbors that he was a "nice" boy. Williams' (D) counsel basically conceded the jury was unlikely to spare Williams (D), saying, "I will admit to that it is very difficult to ask you to show mercy to a man who has not shown much mercy himself. I doubt .... that he thought much about mercy when [he killed or assaulted his victims]. Admittedly it is very difficult to ... ask that you give this man mercy when he has shown so little ... himself. But I ask that you would." Williams' (D) counsel failed to introduce evidence that Williams (D) was abused and borderline retarded, behaved well in jail, and had character witnesses and jailers who would testify he was not dangerous. Williams (D) was sentenced to death. On appeal, the Virginia Supreme Court affirmed. Williams (D) sought state collateral relief. The state trial judge held an evidentiary hearing, which found Williams' (D) counsel was ineffective. But Virginia (P) appealed, and the Virginia Supreme Court affirmed the sentence, holding that there was no "prejudice" unless there was outcome determination, and finding no reasonable probability the omitted evidence would have changed the sentence. Williams (D) sought a writ of habeas corpus. At trial, the federal trial judge found Williams' (D) counsel failed to investigate adequately and raise mitigating factors, creating a "reasonable probability" the outcome might be different. Also, the federal judge found the Virginia Supreme Court misconstrued the law, by misinterpreting the Supreme Court decision *Lockhart* as modifying *Strickland*'s definition of "prejudice." Thus, the federal trial judge reversed. On appeal, the Court of Appeals reinstated the conviction. Williams (D) appeals, claiming (i) his constitutional right to effective counsel, under *Strickland*, was violated, and (ii) the Virginia Supreme Court's refusal to set aside his sentence was contrary to Supreme Court caselaw, and thus required reversal under *28 U.S.C. § 2254(d).*

■ ISSUE

If a state court sentences a convict after his counsel fails to present mitigating factors, must a federal habeas court set aside the conviction?

■ DECISION AND RATIONALE, PART II

(O'Connor) Yes. First, we find federal courts reviewing habeas petitions should decide the issue de novo. II. Under the Constitution's Art. III, interpreting federal law is the jurisdiction of federal courts. This is not changed by *AEDPA.* On habeas appeal, reversal is mandatory if the state court's decision "was contrary to, or involved an unreasonable application of, clearly established Federal law, as determined by the Supreme Court." *28 U.S.C. § 2254(d)(1).* "Clearly established law" means this Court must have broken sufficient legal ground to establish an asked-for constitutional principle, and announced its decision before petitioner's state conviction became final. (This principle is consistent with *Teague* [petitioner cannot demand new rule, adopted after conviction, be made retroactive].) The statutory phrase "... contrary to, or ... unreasonable application of [federal law]" has an unclear meaning. We hold it to mean that federal courts must conduct an independent review of whether the state court's decision violates the Constitution.

■ DECISION AND RATIONALE, PARTS I, III, IV, V

(Stevens) Next, we find Williams' (D) constitutional right to effective counsel was violated. This result is dictated by our decision in *Strickland*, which qualifies as "clearly established Federal law, as determined by the Supreme Court." Since the Virginia Supreme Court refused to apply *Strickland*, its decision violated Federal law unreasonably. Next, the Virginia Supreme Court's holding—that *Strickland* was supplanted by *Lockhart*—was erroneous. First, the Virginia court's decision was based on the view that a likely-different outcome was insufficient to establish counsel's ineffectiveness, which is mistaken. Second, the court failed to consider the total available mitigating evidence, by refusing to consider additional evidence developed in post-conviction proceedings. Reversed and remanded.

■ CONCURRENCE

(O'Connor) The majority opinion would be correct under the federal habeas statute effective before *AEDPA.* II.A. But the result is different under *AEDPA,* which applies to Williams' (D) appeal. The majority's interpretation—that *AEDPA* doesn't change prior law—is incorrect. The proper interpretation is that the reviewing federal court may reverse the state court's decision only if it (A) contradicts Supreme Court caselaw, or (B) applies the correct law unreasonably to the facts, or (C) unreasonably extends Supreme Court caselaw to situations where it's inapplicable, or fails to apply it to similar situations. This interpretation is dictated by the plain language. [In fact, the reasoning here is so convoluted and inconclusive that there's no point in reprinting it.] II.B. This standard requires deference to state courts' decisions which are incorrect, but reasonable. III. Here, I find the Virginia Supreme Court's review of Williams' (D) "ineffective assistance" claim was unreasonable, under any standard.

■ DISSENT

(Rehnquist) I agree the proper standard of review is O'Connor's. But here, I find the Virginia Supreme Court's decision was reasonable, because the evidence suggests Williams (D) remains a danger to society.

Analysis:

Procedural note: In the majority opinion, Parts III-V were written by Stevens, but Part II is by O'Connor, who also concurred. *Williams* is included mainly to illustrate the proper standard for federal courts reviewing state courts' decisions on habeas—the federal court essentially owes *no* deference on either legal holdings or factual findings, but instead should examine both de novo. Each side buttresses its argument with vague, inconclusive arguments about what the text's language "clearly" says, but neither side's reading is obviously better.

■ CASE VOCABULARY

COLLATERAL RELIEF: Here, an appeal to a different court, usually while the case is pending in another court.

DE NOVO: ("New") Standard whereby appellate courts scrutinize lower courts' decisions independently, without any deference to their holdings / findings.

OUTCOME DETERMINATION: Standard of "prejudice" whereby an error is deemed prejudicial if, but for that error, the trial's outcome would have been different.